Creating
UNDERSTANDING

Creating
UNDERSTANDING

A HANDBOOK FOR
CHRISTIAN
COMMUNICATION
ACROSS
CULTURAL
LANDSCAPES

Donald K. Smith

ZondervanPublishingHouse
Grand Rapids, Michigan

A Division of HarperCollinsPublishers

Creating Understanding
Copyright © 1992 by Donald K. Smith

Requests for information should be addressed to:
Zondervan Publishing House
Academic and Professional Books
Grand Rapids, Michigan 49530

Library of Congress Cataloging-in-Publication Data

Smith, Donald K., 1929–
    Creating understanding : a handbook for Christian communication across cultural landscapes / Donald K. Smith.
      p.   cm.
    Includes bibliographical references and index.
    ISBN 0–310–53121–7
    1. Communication—Religious aspects—Christianity. 2. Intercultural communication. 3. Interpersonal communication. I. Title.
BV4319.S65   1991
261.5'2—dc20   91-35954
                                         CIP

All Scripture quotations, unless otherwise noted, are taken from THE HOLY BIBLE: NEW INTERNATIONAL VERSION (North American Edition), copyright © 1973, 1978, 1984 by the International Bible Society. Used by permission of Zondervan Bible Publishers.

Edited by Ruth Goring Stewart
Interior design by Rachel Hostetter
Cover design by Rachel Hostetter

Printed in the United States of America

98 99 00 01 02 03 /QK/ 10 9 8 7 6 5 4

CONTENTS

*Communication is a process for
creating understanding
in which two or more parties are involved.*

Introduction

Communication is crucial

This is a book about proclamation.

The Message we have received is for giving, not for keeping. This means that Christian workers must give primary attention to the business of communication. How does it happen? What makes it so difficult at times? How do we surmount differences that separate people? Where can we turn for help?

Theology deals with the content, anthropology emphasizes cultural aspects of proclamation, sociology highlights community in building the body of Christ, and psychology shows us individual need and response. These important viewpoints are incorporated in a communications approach, along with major contributions from the disciplines of management, education, history, social research, and communication arts.

The content must be known and experienced, of course, or the proclamation will have no substance or credibility. If we know what we are to proclaim, then, how do we do it? More fundamental than method and technique is the question of how understanding is achieved. When we know that, we can use methods that are appropriate to each occasion.

Seeing our task essentially as communication gives us a framework for constructing effective ministry. Communication stresses process, the process of creating understanding. It is dynamic, focusing on interchange rather than structured method.

Interchange between people always deals with differences, whether they are called personal differences or cultural differences. The variation between people may be small, or it may be so great that even talking together poses real difficulty. This is the central problem in communication: how to achieve understanding across differences, no matter what causes them.

When the differences are relatively small, they are seen as interpersonal problems. When the differences are large and marked by distinctions in language, clothing, skin color, and other such variables, they are considered intercultural problems. Still, the underlying dynamics are very similar. And once the basic dynamics for creating understanding are recognized, they can be used in every situation.

7

Very Important →

Thus, *Creating Understanding* is built on three foundational positions:

1. All communication is cross-cultural to some degree.

2. Culture is the way we organize our experiences to develop a worldview, values, beliefs, a social framework, and behavior patterns.

3. Communication is the human part of proclamation and discipling. The Spirit of God works inwardly to produce response and transformation.

Insights concerning human communication are scattered throughout books, journal articles, research reports, and textbooks. There are hundreds of committed men and women in ministry who need this information. Their frequent inability to reach deep needs of their people frustrates, and even breaks, the will to serve. If they could gain access to what has been learned by others, many could change their pattern of service.

This book makes available many significant points of what has been learned about human communication, presented as propositions. These propositions provide a way to approach persistent, much-discussed problems such as the effectiveness of foreign missionaries; the contextualization of method and message; the penetration of resistant cultures; relationships among co-workers, minister and congregation, and local people and foreigners; church and mission relationships; and the effective use of the media.

These basic propositions have to do with a *process*—communication—and must be used, expanded, and applied in the process of ministry before they can fulfill their potential value to Christian workers. When the principles they provide are used, long-standing difficulties can be resolved and new opportunities grasped. These propositions can change your ministry, and I hope they will.

As you take part in the communication process using the propositions given, you will find that many talked-about issues are not simply a matter of opinion. Rather, they are questions of what is functional or dysfunctional, productive or counterproductive.

It is my prayer that you will find these propositions useful in resolving many of those questions in your ministry.

Donald K. Smith
Portland, Oregon

It is increasingly seen that everyone lives in a multi-cultural world. There are "macro-cultures" that guide behavior for a society as a whole, and there are "micro-cultures"—variations on the standard used throughout a society. A macro-culture may well encompass hundreds of micro-cultures, each involving differing relationships and roles to be learned by the individual. Each different set of expectations represents a different culture to be learned.
—Ward Goodenough, "Multiculturalism as the Normal Human Experience"

Acknowledgments

Creating Understanding has developed over twenty years of intercultural ministry, teaching, and field research. The concepts began to crystallize during graduate studies at the University of Oregon, but were largely articulated through interaction with church leaders and missionaries in Africa, Asia, and Europe. I am grateful for the *many* friends from various cultures who have opened new perspectives and deepened my understanding.

Over and over, it was my wife, Faye, who has sharpened my thinking and expression as we have ministered together in many different nations and settings. Our children, D. Vance Smith and Mrs. Julisa Rowe, not only have been illustrations, but also have demonstrated how the propositions work in their own lives and ministry.

And without friends to help me in producing this material, there would still be no book. Mrs. Elizabeth Hagler has furnished a good number of the illustrative cartoons; Ernest Sit helped greatly in preparing teaching diagrams in the text, as did Marty Bogan of Pepper Graphix. Skilled friends are a gift of the Lord.

These propositions provided the foundation for course development at the Institute for International Christian Communication (IICC), first in Zimbabwe, then in Kenya. Subsequently, Daystar University College (Nairobi, Kenya) grew on that foundation.

Each of the propositions could well be expanded (perhaps "completed" is a better word) to provide the basis for twenty-three different courses. Do not expect, therefore, that everything is said that could be said on any given subject.

Bringing the manuscript to this point of completion has been possible through a sabbatical leave granted by Western Seminary, Portland, Oregon. I am grateful, and I hope my fellow-messengers will be as well.

Permissions

I am grateful for permission from publishers and creators to use extensive quotations or graphic materials from the following sources. Where sources are expressed in shortened form in the text, the complete data are given in the general bibliography.

Proposition 1:

Eugene Nida, "The Word Is Winning," *Decision* (December 1987). Copyright © 1987 Billy Graham Evangelistic Association.

Robert Hirschfield, "Rebuilding the City," *The Other Side* (December 1987). Copyright © 1987 *The Other Side* 300 W. Apsley, Philadelphia, PA 19144.

"Motley's Crew," comic strip, copyright © 1987 Tribune Media Syndicate.

Proposition 2:

Jan Myrdal, *Report from a Chinese Village* (New York: Pantheon, 1965).

Vincent Guerry, *Life with the Baoulé*, trans. Nora Hodges (Washington, D.C.: Three Continents, 1975).

Richard Mason, *The World of Suzie Wong* (London: Collins, 1957).

Proposition 3:

Joseph T. Bayly, *Psalms of My Life* (Wheaton, Ill.: Tyndale House, 1969).

Kenneth Ericksen, *The Power of Communication* (St. Louis: Concordia, 1986).

Elizabeth Hagler, cartoon, "Have you ever been on a boat?"

David Augsburger, "Writing Is Translating," *Festival Quarterly* (Summer 1975), Main Street, Intercourse, PA 17534.

Proposition 4:

Craig Massey, "Communication Is Not the Key to Marriage," *Moody Monthly* 89, no. 3 (November 1988).

"Peanuts," comic strip, copyright © 1989 United Feature Syndicate.

Dan Sellard, "Teaching Listening," Eugene (Oreg.) *Register-Guard*, 1 June 1980.

"Andy Capp," comic strip, copyright © 1986 Daily Mirror Newspapers, Ltd.

David Augsburger, *Caring Enough to Hear* (Ventura, Calif.: Regal, 1982).

Proposition 5:

Alpha E. Anderson, *Pelendo* (Minneapolis: Free Church Publications, 1967).

"Hagar," comic strip, copyright © 1987 King Features Syndicate.

"Andy Capp," comic strip, copyright © Daily Mirror Newspapers, Ltd.

Proposition 7:

Frank Kerwin, "The Right Answer," *Guideposts* (June 1988).

James L. Johnson, "The Shadow That Hangs over the Communicator," *Spectrum* (n.d.), Wheaton College Graduate School.

Jack W. Hayford, "Character Before Communication," *Religious Broadcasting* (February 1985).

Russell Stendal, *Rescue the Captors* (Burnsville, Minn.: Ransom, 1984).

Proposition 8:
Cartoon, talking to a brick wall, copyright © 1983 Rob Portlock.

H. S. Vigeveno, *The Listener* (Glendale, Calif.: Regal, 1981).

"Cathy," comic strip, copyright © 1988 Universal Press Syndicate.

Cartoon, witnessing aids, copyright © Rob Portlock.

J. H. Bavinck, *An Introduction to the Science of Missions*, part 2, trans. David Hugh Freeman (Philadelphia: Presbyterian and Reformed, 1960).

Proposition 9:
Alan Paton, *Cry, the Beloved Country* (New York: Scribner, 1948). Reprinted with permission of Charles Scribner's Sons, an imprint of Macmillan Publishing Company. Copyright © 1948 Alan Paton; renewed © 1976 Alan Paton.

James F. Engel, "Whom Do We Serve—the Sheep or the Shepherd?" *Spectrum* (Winter 1977–1978), Wheaton College Graduate School.

Proposition 10:
Douglas D. Priest, Sr., Daystar University College, Box 44400, Nairobi, Kenya.

Propositions 11 and 12:
Timothy Botts, "God Is for Me!" in *Doorposts* (Wheaton, Ill.: Tyndale House, 1986).

"Better of Worse," comic strip, copyright © 1988 Universal Press Syndicate.

Elizabeth Hagler, cartoon, "Time's up."

Boyd Gibbons, "The Intimate Sense of Smell," *National Geographic* 170, no. 3 (September 1986).

Proposition 13:
"Letter to the Editor," *World Christian* 2, no. 1 (January–February 1983).

Oswald C. J. Hoffmann, "The Electronic Church: An Extension, Not a Substitute," *Religious Broadcasting*, November 1983.

Jerry Mander, *Four Arguments for the Elimination of Television* (New York: Morrow, 1978).

Proposition 14:
Arbind K. Sinha, *Mass Media and Rural Development* (New Delhi: Concept Publishing, 1985).

Wilbur Schramm, *Mass Media and National Development: The Role of Information in the Developing Countries* (Stanford, Calif.: Stanford University Press and the United Nations Educational, Scientific and Cultural Organization, 1964).

Viggo Sogaard, *Everything You Need to Know for a Cassette Ministry* (Minneapolis: Bethany House, 1975).

Proposition 15:

Cartoon by Bill Schorr, copyright © *Kansas City Star.*

Neville D. Jayaweera, "Christian Communication in the Third World," *Occasional Essays* (December 1978), Latin American Evangelical Center for Pastoral Studies, CELEP.

Cartoon by William Hoest, copyright © 1975 Saturday Review and William Hoest.

Cartoon by Mouton-Chambers, copyright © 1983 Mary Chambers.

Proposition 16:

"Peanuts," comic strip, copyright © 1960 United Feature Syndicate.

Ray Giles, in *Impact* 31, no. 2 (N.d.), Christian Missionary Fellowship.

Carol B. Stack, *All Our Kin: Strategies for Survival in a Black Community* (New York: Harper & Row, 1974).

Proposition 17:

Ada Lum, "What Does It Take to Be a Missionary?" *His* 37 (November 1976).

Sandra Banasik, "A Living Language," *Wherever* (Spring 1982).

Elizabeth Hagler, cartoon, "I wonder who's supposed to close?"

Proposition 18:

Camara Laye, *A Dream of Africa* (London: Collins, 1968).

Cartoon, copyright © 1987 *Leadership*. Concept: David McAllister, art: Rob Suggs.

"Peanuts," comic strip, copyright © United Feature Syndicate.

Eric Newby, ed., *A Book of Traveller's Tales* (New York: Viking Penguin, 1985).

Proposition 19:

"The Family Circus," comic strip, copyright © Cowles Syndicate.

"Hi and Lois," comic strip, copyright © 1987 King Features Syndicate.

Ruth Tucker, *Sacred Stories* (Grand Rapids: Zondervan, 1989).

Proposition 20:

Ralph G. Otte, "Are We Worshiping or Watching?" *Eternity* 22, no. 9 (April 1971).

Cartoon, "Admit it, Madge," copyright © Post/Dispatch Features.

Elizabeth Hagler, cartoon, "It's amazing how much guilt. . . ."

David Seamands, *The Healing of Memories* (Wheaton, Ill.: Victor, 1985).

James Melvin, *A Testament of Hope: The Essential Writings of Martin Luther King, Jr.* (San Francisco: Harper & Row, 1986). Quotations copyright © 1963 by Martin Luther King, Jr. Used by permission of Joan Daves.

Proposition 21:

"Dauntless Eagles," *Impact* (September 1978), Singapore.

Cartoon, "Before you make any snap decisions. . . ," copyright © 1988 Ed Koehler. Used by permission of InterVarsity Press, P.O. Box 1400, Downers Grove, IL 60515.

Isobel Kuhn, *In the Arena* (Robesonia, Pa.: OMF Books, 1960).

Samir Khalaf, "The Americanization of George," *Christian Science Monitor,* 22 September 1987.

Cartoon, "We're in debt. . . ," copyright © 1983 Eric and Vicki Johnson.

Vincent Guerry, *Life with the Baoulé,* trans. Nora Hodges (Washington, D.C.: Three Continents, 1975).

Proposition 22:

Cartoon, "Church of the Air, " copyright © 1984 *Leadership* (Fall 1984). Concept: Dave McCasland. Artist: Larry Thomas.

Elizabeth Hagler, cartoon, "She was right. It works!"

Karl-Johan Lundstrom, *The Lotuho and the Verona Fathers: A Case Study of Communication in Development* (Doctoral diss., Uppsala University, Sweden, 1990).

Robert Cramer, "Many Groups, One World," *Media Development* 28, no. 2 (1981).

John Bowers, unpublished paper on Anno Domini, Jacksonville, FL 32223. At Western Seminary, Portland, Oregon.

Proposition 23:

Elizabeth Hagler, cartoon, flat tire, and cartoon, "OK, now do it again. . . ."

Robert Cramer, "Many Groups, One World," *Media Development* 28, no. 2 (1981).

Cartoon, "Feel free to let me know, . . ." copyright © 1979 Rob Portlock.

Elizabeth Hagler, cartoon, "Any questions?"

About the Bibliographies

The purpose of this book is essentially pragmatic rather than theoretical. It seeks to introduce the Christian communicator to basic perspectives. The area covered by each proposition deserves much more study. Given that reality, the bibliography with each proposition (or set of propositions) indicates material for additional reading, though obviously no chapter bibliography in this book is complete for any subject. The suggested further readings will permit the basic course material to be expanded into a comprehensive study at graduate and seminary level.

Even though this is certainly not a research document, the general bibliography at the end of the text lists many of the sources from which the propositions have been derived. It is difficult to be comprehensive, since literally hundreds of books, readings, and journal articles have been consulted in the more than twenty years during which these propositions have been developed. Bibliographies cannot adequately document the research and writings from which the propositions are derived. My sincere apologies to any scholar whose work I may have used without acknowledgment.

Editor's note: The attributions for quotations and citations in the text are expressed in shortened form whenever the complete source data are given in the general bibliography.

➤ How can these propositions be used?

➤ Is there a way these can make a difference in my ministry?

➤ Why can't you just tell me how I should act and what I should say? Give me a formula!

KNOWING WHERE YOU ARE GOING

It is easier to travel in unfamiliar places if a map is available. The map is limited in detail and is usually only two-dimensional. Its symbols only suggest reality. But these shortcomings are actually a help in understanding the overall picture. Only on a map can most people ever see the full course of a great river or the pathways through mountain barriers. The map allows one to grasp relationships between continents and seas, winds and rainfall, that could be only poorly perceived in the real world.

In a similar way, the propositions offered in this book provide a map of human communication. Much is left for each person to find as he or she follows the map and experiences his or her own unique involvement in different situations and different cultures.

When problems arise, it is always useful to review the situation. Where did misunderstanding begin? What is the root cause of this conflict? How can I shape the message, and the timing of its presentation, so it will be more readily understood and accepted? Is there a way to prevent resistance to or rejection of the message or the messenger? Having a way to look at intercultural communication systematically, to review what is happening, can help to answer such important questions.

The basic propositions, assembled here in one place, provide a map for reexamining the effort that went wrong and for planning an approach that will go right. When you need such help, review the statements one by one, remembering the major applications of each. Compare what is indicated in the proposition with what happened, or what you are planning.

When you find discrepancies, you have a creative opportunity to alter your methods and form a plan uniquely suited to your situation. It is of much greater value to review these propositions carefully and develop your own strategy than to spend hard effort mastering and imitating someone else's program. What works in one place seldom will work as effectively in another place.

Simply following the traditional way of doing things may be merely a familiar way to failure. "Brave Christian communicators are courageously trying to break out of the old patterns, seeking really to communicate to their specific audience," Phill Butler wrote to me.

Why call them *brave*? Shouldn't they be called creative, imaginative, or spiritually sensitive? No. *Brave* is the right word. If you have tried something new in your determination to communicate, you will agree.

"In such efforts," continues Butler, "you can count on an aggressive adversary. Satan will attack with incredible vengeance from without and from within. Our only hope for survival is in total honesty, in-depth professional preparation, a genuine biblical basis for what we are doing, and spending time on our knees.

"No format is a panacea. . . . I only plead that we know exactly where we are going . . . why we are going there and that we have a willingness to stick to the path we chart once we are underway," he concludes.

Let's take an overall view, then, of how communication works when people of different cultures meet.

We need to establish a basic understanding of how communication works before we can consider how cultural differences affect communication. The first four propositions will give that foundation.

▼ FUNDAMENTALS

Four propositions give the essential foundation.

Proposition 1. Communication is involvement.

Proposition 2. Communication is a process.

Proposition 3. Meaning is internal and individual.

Proposition 4. Communication is what is heard, not only what is said. *How do I influence what is heard?*

"Freezing" something as fascinating and complex as communication can be misleading. It creates an illusion of order, making the relationships reasonably obvious. But live communication is pulsating, erratic, warm, dynamic—and often disorderly. Nevertheless, here is a "frozen" view of intercultural communication. The human tempest is stilled so that we can begin to grasp what is actually happening. *7 Techniques of:*

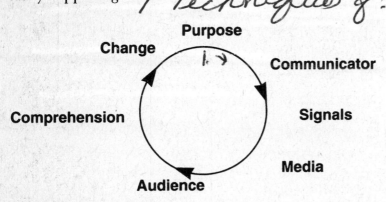

The real world of communication is not only much more complex, but also dynamic. A fuller understanding of communication comes through *understanding relationships;* it is the purpose of this diagram to give a beginning point in understanding those relationships, a kind of framework within which important propositions about intercultural communication can be learned.

▼ PURPOSE: Having Something to Say

The purpose for a particular communication is often not overtly recognized, though usually it can be identified with a little thought. What is to be achieved, the content to be shared, the needs to be met, and the tensions to be resolved are stimuli that prompt communication between individuals and groups.

> Proposition 5. Clarification of goals increases the possibility of effective communication.

> Proposition 6. Mastery of content is the necessary foundation for effective communication.

▼ COMMUNICATOR: Who Says It

The purpose is really inseparable from the communicator; the diagram misleads at this point. Nothing happens without a communicator. Who conveys the message, as well as who hears it and the interaction between the messenger, message, and audience deeply influences the communication process. This triangle of tensions between audience, communicator, and purpose creates the energy that drives the entire process.

Proposition 7. The communicator's personality and experiences modify the form of a message.

Proposition 8. The communicator's image of the audience and understanding of the context are primary factors in shaping the form of the message.

Proposition 9. A communicator almost always communicates with multiple audiences.

Proposition 10. Communication increases commitment.

▼ SIGNALS: How It Is Said

Signals are the raw materials of communication, to be refined into billions of differing patterns, each capable of conveying ideas. These signals are an integral part of being alive, essential to expressing and shaping culture. Mutually understood signals are the fabric of culture, indistinguishable from culture itself. It is by the use of signals that the essential bond is built between audience and communicator. Because culture and signals are inseparable, effective intercultural communication begins with learning how signals are used in different cultures.

Proposition 11. All human communication occurs through the use of twelve signal systems.

Proposition 12. Usage of the signal systems is a function of culture; thus they are used differently in different cultures.

▼ MEDIA: So That More Can Hear

Signals can be extended beyond face-to-face relationships and even beyond the limits of time and space. These extensions, the media, inevitably change the nature of the message and its perception by the audience. New dimensions are added to the communication experience by the media—along with new problems.

Proposition 13. Mass media extend the range of a message but inevitably distort the message.

Proposition 14. Communication effectiveness normally decreases with increasing size of the audience.

Proposition 15. The effectiveness of a medium is largely determined by factors other than the medium itself.

▼ AUDIENCE: Receiving the Signals

Audiences actively participate in the communication process, selecting, interpreting, and interacting within the social networks involved in communication. Because the audience is active, the message originator should select and shape the signals according to the audience's context, experience, preferences, and understandings.

> Proposition 16. Messages are mediated.

> Proposition 17. Cultural patterns of a society fundamentally influence the form of communication.

> Proposition 18. Existing beliefs and value systems are a major factor in building communication.

▼ COMPREHENSION: Did They Understand What They Heard?

It is individuals who perceive the message, even though their perception is filtered through group processes and the cultural framework. Comprehension is individual; thus, message perception ultimately depends on personal psychological patterns.

> Proposition 19. The interpretation of messages is related to experiences and needs.

> Proposition 20. All communication has simultaneously rational and emotional dimensions.

▼ CHANGE AND FEEDBACK: Has Anything Happened?

Though individual perception is the very foundation of communication, attitudes and actions largely depend on group response. Change therefore requires the use of channels reaching both the group and the individual. The message originator monitors signals from participants in the communication process, adjusting form and content so the message will be more clearly perceived by both the group and the individual.

> Proposition 21. People react to communications as members of social groups.

> Proposition 22. A decision to change results from the combined effects of public or mass media and interpersonal networks.

> Proposition 23. Perceived and actual feedback shapes the message.

▼ THE HUMAN ROLE IN GOD'S COMMUNICATIONS

Pavlov rang a bell; a dog salivated.

The pastor rings the church bells; a person feels spirituality.

Is, then, the only difference between a dog's hunger and a person's spirit-hunger the kind of stimulus and response involved? There are Christian communicators who apparently believe so.

Polish in production and successful marketing are commonly confused with good communication. They are thought to be synonymous; they may not even be related.

Reaction to this thinly concealed secularism in Christian ministry usually comes from "the brethren." But the solutions offered are often just "easier," not better or more spiritual. Shoddiness is no more spiritual than slickness. Withdrawal by assuming a superspiritual stance solves nothing. Fruits resulting from that aloofness are like diamonds—valuable principally because of their rarity.

Statements that appear deeply spiritual may actually be evasions of personal responsibility in ministry, "I simply preach God's Word, adding nothing of my own." Or the common excuse for unwillingness to plan, "I respond to the Spirit's leading; detailed planning gets in the way." And there is the unanswerable self-justification, "People will always reject the truth; I should not be surprised if that happens in my ministry."

The difficulty in answering those statements is that they are correct, in certain places at certain times. But when they are used as blanket explanations, they explain little. They conceal the real problem.

The real problem is also not identified or helped by the hackneyed diagnosis "failure to communicate." The failure is in not knowing what happens in communication and what its true purpose is.

Understanding is the purpose of communicating. Communication tries to build a commonness of understanding without manipulating a person into artificial agreement. Agreement may not result; genuine understanding may lead to total and perhaps violent rejection. What the message recipient does with the new understanding is his or her decision and responsibility.

It is the communicator's obligation to create understanding of a message, nothing more and nothing less. Too frequently we are satisfied with some behavioral response as proof that "God is at work." We aim for the

"If 'they' can do it, why can't we do it for a better purpose?"

Commonly, such superficial remarks show that the distinctive dimension of Christian communication is not understood.

"If it sells soap, why can't the same methods sell spiritual cleansing?"

Methods are learned and skills developed. Praise from secular producers is heralded as proof that quality has been achieved. If such praise is not forthcoming, then we set up a system of "Christian" awards. Anyone who questions motive and expense receives a ready answer: "The best is not too good for the King of Kings." No, indeed. But is this the best? Is this Christian communication—or merely communication done by Christians?

wrong thing and consequently use the wrong methods—methods appropriate for that wrong goal but not suited to the goal of achieving understanding of God's message.

After the message is understood, what happens? In some, rejection. In others, an eager welcome. In this latter group, a reaching out to know more and to obey more follows initial understanding. What brings this acceptance in some but not others?

We don't really know. But we do know that somehow the Holy Spirit does it. "The Holy Spirit . . . shall guide you into all truth" (John 16:13). "And no one can know God's thoughts except God's own Spirit. And God has actually given us His Spirit . . . to tell us about the wonderful free gifts of grace and blessing that God has given us. . . . But the man who isn't a Christian can't understand and can't accept these thoughts from God, which the Holy Spirit teaches us. They sound foolish to him, because only those who have the Holy Spirit within them can understand what the Holy Spirit means. Others just can't take it in" (1 Cor. 2:11–14 LB).

The Holy Spirit brings a response that we can never produce by artful communication skills. We may stimulate the reality by manipulative use of stimulus-and-response in religion, but the reality of beginning a new life in Jesus Christ, of being born again, is a result only of the Holy Spirit's transmuting mental understanding into spirit life.

The best we can do is strive to give understanding. We can give the message so that there will be clarity in hearing. When we have helped someone comprehend the message, the Holy Spirit makes the mysterious inner link. The person's spirit, taught by the Holy Spirit, responds to the wooing of God.

Communication, then, is not throwing the message at people's eyes and ears. Throwing it with style and finesse is still just throwing it. Bombardment of a fort does not guarantee access to the fort, unless you intend to demolish the fort totally and crush its occupants. Neither does bombardment of a mind guarantee access to that mind, unless you shatter the individual's understanding and will by methods akin to brainwashing.

The legitimate purpose of communication is to gain access to the mind through the gate of understanding. Efforts to communicate should concentrate on what is needed to give understanding. Style and technique are secondary. These skills may be useful, or they may be a distraction. The thing that counts is ensuring understanding by the way the message is shaped, the context in which it is given, and the relevance of its content.

No Christian communicator dare attempt to reach within the will and manipulate it to respond to God. That spiritual response is within the domain only of God's Spirit. Our role in the decisive weighing of alternatives is prayer, and even there we are helped by the Spirit to pray as we should.

Whenever we attempt to substitute communication techniques for prayers of intercession, we will succeed only in forming a soft, spongy Christian community that is dependent on a created environment instead of God himself. Those techniques may be expensive, polished TV specials or tasteful sanctuaries that create meditative moods. Or they may be carefully cultivated voices that soothe and melt resistance.

Such techniques can be legitimate; there is no special sanctity inherent in poor technique or the lack of any attempt at polish. The error is *substitution* of technique for intercession, dependence upon skill rather than dependence upon God to do the work inside the heart.

Our responsibility, then, is to create understanding. Our thinking, planning, and presentations must be directed to that goal. In all your learning, learn the ways of *understanding*.

> Give me *understanding*, and I will keep your law and obey it with all my heart (Ps. 119:34).
>
> Give me *understanding* to learn your commands (Ps. 119:73).
>
> Give me *understanding* that I may live (Ps. 119:144).
>
> I will give you shepherds after my own heart, who will lead you with knowledge and *understanding* (Jer. 3:15).

SUMMARY

Our proper role, as custodians of God's Word and communicators of his truth, is to give understanding of our topic, the issues involved, and the consequences of differing responses. Attempts to manipulate those responses go beyond the sphere of human responsibility and may even intrude upon the working of the Holy Spirit. The response of people to communicated truth is the work of God's Spirit, not human techniques.

➤ I just don't have the time to get involved with people in my church. I must study so that I can preach the Word more effectively on Sunday.

➤ The problems of my church take so much time! I am learning communications so that I can reach more people. If I learn how to use the media, maybe it will help.

I NVOLVE ME, SO I CAN UNDERSTAND

PROPOSITION 1: Communication is involvement. *Spending time with*

Those whom we don't know always seem different, sometimes even frightening. But as we become acquainted, we are astonished to learn how similar our needs and fears really are. Strangers become friends through steadily increasing involvement. A traveler points out, "The inscrutability of the East is, I believe, a myth. . . . The ordinary inhabitant is incomprehensible merely to people who never trouble to have anything much to do with him" (Dame Freya Stark, *The Journey's Echo*, 26).

Those we have been trained to dislike or even hate are changed in our eyes to "good people" when we share in the same activities. Every four years at the Olympic Games, athletes enjoy getting to know competitors from nations that normally are considered "enemies." An Arab entertainer in a Middle Eastern restaurant selected a Jewish student to assist. With laughing enjoyment, they finished the act together. Both of them were involved in the small success, though their peoples have ruthlessly warred against each other countless times over the centuries.

A young Christian in Sudan was asked what he would do if he found an enemy tribesman alongside the path,

Evangelism takes place only when there is communication. Communication takes place only when there is involvement.

23

Preaching, tracts, and TV specials are not necessarily communication. They are at times useful for communication. They can be tools of communication, but are not, by themselves, communication.

sick and helpless. "I would kill him," he responded instantly.

"What would you do if you found this man?" the questioner asked, gesturing toward one of his workmates from the same enemy tribe.

"Well, I'd help him, of course."

"But why would you kill the one man, and not this man?"

"They are different."

The only difference was that he was involved with one man and not the other.

The key to understanding each case is involvement, sharing something in common. Having that "commonness" is the basis of communication. Involvement is inseparable from communication, as the root of the word itself shows.

The root word: *Communis*
From that root come many related words:
- Common
- Commune
- Community
- Communism
- Communion
- Communication

Having in common—sharing the same things. *Community* means sharing the same geographical space or the same interests. With *commune*, we go beyond simple sharing to a commitment to one another in broad areas of living—economics, social activities, and perhaps worship. In *communion*, we share understandings at the deepest levels of human experience. And in the communion service there is sharing between God and humanity, remembering the basis of such impossible sharing in Christ's broken body and shed blood. The communion service also celebrates the sharing of persons within the body of Christ.

All these are occasions of *communication*, a constantly broadening involvement that finds and builds more and more commonness, more areas of sharing. Sharing, in popular Christian usage, unfortunately has little of real communication in it. It is too often simply *telling* somebody else your information, without the listening that would make it truly sharing. It is telling without involvement, and thus not genuine communication. True sharing is the best of communication. It is people moving together into widening areas of common joys, problems,

When we ask the Lord's blessing upon our drinking from the cup of wine at the Lord's Table, this means, doesn't it, that all who drink it are *sharing together* the blessing of Christ's blood? And when we break off pieces of the bread from the loaf to eat there together, this shows that we are *sharing together* in the benefits of His body.
—1 Corinthians 10:16 LB

COMMUNICATION MEANS TRYING TO ESTABLISH "COMMONNESS" WITH SOMEONE.

find area of common ground

and answers. This true sharing ripens into communion, about persons, about God, and together with God.

At least one culture recognizes in its language the inseparability of involvement and communication. In Malagasy (Madagascar), the same word is used for communication and involvement—*fifandraisanat*. Too frequently, we use a different pair of words as if they were interchangeable—*communication* and *technology*. Technology may in practice be a substitute for involvement.

Can we reach more people more quickly by using mass media rather than the time-consuming approach of involvement? Can we, in other words, communicate the Gospel by saturating the world via satellites, printing presses, or any other technology? Our imaginations are awed and excited by the capabilities of new tools. Surely we should be using these to evangelize! But there is more to consider than the power and marvels of new technology.

Technology may lead merely to transmission, which should not be confused with communication. Transmission occurs without involvement. It is a spreading out of words and symbols that does not take into account the responses of the audience. Once the message is transmitted, responsibility appears to have been discharged: "Well, I told them and they didn't listen." And thereby everything is seemingly explained. The spiritual parallel is,

Communication is co-response. To communicate with you is to respond to you and to recognize your response to me. Being in each other's presence is communicating. . . .

Communication is co-response-ability. To communicate effectively is to honor the mutuality of our relationship and to respect our equal privilege to respond to each other.

—David Augsburger, "Communication Is Co-response"

Words. Words. Words. The ceaseless flow of words is substituted for reality. Divine revelation has been reversed—the Word become flesh has been changed into the flesh become words. Empty words, when people long for a tangible demonstration of God's love. Words.

There are serious problems when we treat the Gospel as primarily words.

1. Concern and compassion for others are made less important.

2. A code of behavior has replaced the explosive power of new birth and a new life in Christ. If I do the right things (and don't do the wrong things), that makes me a Christian, doesn't it?

3. Words define *spiritual* as quiet, placid, possessed of a set of rosy-tinted spectacles that enables the Christian to smile sweetly at everything—even fraud and exploitation.

4. Words let us be satisfied with knowledge, instead of God himself. With our traditions, our forms, our definitions, we can explain, interpret, and commend Christian experience without ever having to experience it ourselves.

Syncretism—the mixing of true and false religion—is inevitable when words become more important than reality.

"I simply preach the Word. If they don't listen, I can't help it."

Tools transmit; people get involved. Sophisticated technical tools may be useful in evangelism, but they may also keep us from effective evangelism. Their very power causes users to overlook involvement as the essential condition for communication. Transmitting the right content does not, by itself, create communication. Neville Jayaweera, a Sri Lankan Christian leader, issues this warning:

> We may invest millions more in Christian communication, straddle the globe with yet more powerful transmitters and still more sophisticated printing apparatus, train whole armies of professional communicators—we may do all these things and more, and yet not reap the harvest. I believe that those who are in Christian communication must face up to more fundamental and deeper going issues than those related to "professional" questions.
>
> —"Christian Communication in the Third World"

What are those "deeper going" issues? They differ from people to people. It is certain, however, that those issues will be understood and utilized for credible proclamation of the Gospel only as communicators become involved deeply with their audience. Only by involvement will Christians effectively make Christ known.

It is not involvement in programs that matters, but involvement with people. Programs are no substitute for personal involvement. Literature, radio, dial-a-prayer, welfare efforts, relief projects—all may be useful, even necessary, at certain times. But frequently they absorb so much effort in administration, production, and financing that there is no time left for individual involvement. It does not have to be that way, but programs frequently shield Christians from direct contact with people.

The Gospel is transmitted, and that is thought to be the desired end result. But communication may not even have begun. It cannot begin until time is planned for people. Involvement with people is almost always more costly than involvement with a program. The preferred medium for the message of Christ is always people, not electronic and mechanical exhibitions. Why do some speakers create boredom when they speak? Despite the pastor's careful study, sometimes a congregation remains indifferent to the teaching of God's Word. *Are* the people simply indifferent? Oscar Wilde writes of familiar attitudes in one of his fairy tales, *The Devoted Friend*. "'How well you talk,' said the Miller's wife, 'really I feel quite drowsy. It is just like being in church.'" It even seems that people expect to be tranquilized with good words, but words that do not touch their wills.

There are many reasons for audience boredom, of course, such as inadequate preparation, a dull delivery, or the speaker's looking at the ceiling instead of the audience. But the thread common to almost all ineffective preachers is failure to be involved with the audience.

A Chinese preacher in Singapore struggled with this common problem. "People say I must have content in what I preach, so I studied. But the more I studied, the more I felt removed from real human struggles." He has found that striking up conversations with people at shopping centers, talking with them about their feeling toward life, their aspirations and frustrations, helps him to keep in touch with the reality of his people's emotions. "This way," he said, "whenever I stand behind the pulpit and preach the Gospel, I know what I'm talking about."

▼ KNOW YOUR AUDIENCE

It is important to know the audience. But that by itself also suggests an overly simple view of communication: Study the audience, learn their needs, interests, and ways of expressing their concerns; then rephrase the message to capitalize on their susceptibilities—after all, the message is so important that they must be made to listen. But this is still transmission. It is still the would-be communicator standing apart from the listeners instead of with them, involved in their lives.

Transmission is employed most profitably by advertisers. Research and experience show advertisers vulnerable spots in the market. They seek to identify areas of common interest. For example, product H is toothpaste; how can there be any common ground between a young man and the toothpaste? The young man wants a personality that wins acceptance for him with young women, so the task becomes quite simple: Persuade the young man that product H is also concerned about acceptance and that it can help win acceptance for him. The fact that toothpaste may prevent tooth decay is not very significant for the young man. So don't sell him prevention; instead, sell social acceptance. "Use product H and you will be admired by the girls!" is the message implicit in an image of a handsome young man with a pretty young woman smiling at him. The formula for successful transmission is

It's been said that the greatest sin in the church today is not thievery or adultery. The thief injures himself and another person; the adulterer defiles his own body. Rather, the greatest sin in the church today is that of boring a congregation. That boredom gives God a bad reputation!
—*Jews for Jesus Newsletter* 6 (1981)

Rev. Wood went seeking a new member of his congregation. He found the new member in the railroad yards where the man worked.

"Can't shake hands with you, reverend," said the man apologetically. "They're too grimy."

Rev. Wood reached down to the ground and rubbed his hands in coal dust. Then offering a blackened hand, the minister replied, "How about it now?"

Such an action demonstrated respect and readiness to be involved with every part of the man's life.
—Gerald R. Mulliken

straightforward: Find areas of common interest and exploit them to achieve your real objective.

Similar approaches are sometimes used in Christian ministry. For example, a young minister who was not the athletic type began telling sports stories to teenagers, trying to use the special jargon of his youth group. The strategy did not succeed. One youth with whom he was particularly striving to communicate called him a fake. The pastor was hurt, and the young people spun off into other activities that seemed more interesting than church.

It was not wrong for the minister to want to talk about the young people's interests and to use their language, but when that approach did not grow out of genuine involvement it was indeed a fake. If the pastor had been involved enough to care genuinely about who won the local school games, he would have communicated regardless of vocabulary or stories.

The advertiser and the youth worker used essentially the same method: finding or building an area of commonality, then exploiting it to bring the desired action. The concerns of the audience are manipulated to achieve the sender's goal.

Too frequently, church outreach efforts offer solutions to life's problems, social acceptance, or friendship in order to stimulate interest. Those things are honorable by-products of reconciliation with God through Christ. But if they are used primarily to promote the church's self-interests (for example, rapid church growth is a good professional credit for the church and its pastor), that is dishonorable manipulation.

Cynically, a person asks, "How many stars do you get in your crown for converting me?" That person feels used despite smooth words promising that God loves and wants the best for him or her. The high-priority goal is to win another person for Christ; it just happens to be person A, who is nearby when conscience compels the Christian to "witness" to someone. Transmission is the result, not communication.

Suppose that the people of an isolated region in a developing nation are discovered to have no Gospel witness. There is no question that a Christian witness should be established, but how?

A missionary arrives. Soon he builds his house, then develops support facilities—a generator, an airstrip, and a workshop to build furniture and to maintain his equipment. A small church is built where he meets weekly with

> In Mexico City there is a church of more than 10,000 members. Everybody in that church has a job to do. They try to have at least one family living in every square block within almost a mile of that church. They're to know everybody in that square block, and if a new family moves in, they are to visit within the first hour to see if the new family needs food, furniture, a job or something else. You can imagine what a dynamic influence that church has.
> —Eugene Nida, "The Word Is Winning"

the workers he has employed in his building projects. But no one else comes, except curious children and occasionally some of the workmen's wives. The missionary ponders and prays, but he sees only indifference.

The issue is not spiritual failure, though some of the good man's supporters might think so. It is not laziness. His preaching is not merely a misguided attempt at spiritual colonialism. People do need Jesus Christ.

The failure is at the very core of communication. He has been busy building and establishing a base, but he has failed to become involved with the people themselves. He "visits" them, but he is not involved *with* them. This missionary is transmitting, but he is not communicating. The normal response is exactly what he has received—indifference.

It is not only in pioneering situations that lack of involvement results in indifference. Often Christians are busy with church programs, pastors study diligently to give good sermons, and campaigns and door-to-door visitations are planned. But no one has time to go fishing with non-Christian neighbors, to be active in the school Parent Teachers' Association, or to be just friendly.

Who can argue the value of being in a Bible study group? "It really is shocking," commented a longtime Christian, "when I think of the many hours I spent in such groups and how little I remember." Bible study took on new excitement for this man, however, when, as he explains it, "I was first introduced to Bible study that made me dig out the meaning of the text. I was forced to get involved since the method itself relied on participation and involvement of the group."

It may be called reciprocity, dialogue, or co-response, but whatever the name, the basis of effective communication is mutual involvement of sender and receiver. It must be the special concern of the initiator of communication to ensure the involvement of the participants.

The initiator must also be aware of dangers in involvement. When involvement is motivated by the desire for self-success rather than achieving the best for the respondent, two serious problems can arise: possessiveness and creating dependence.

A feeling of possessiveness—"my work," "my people"—can lead to deep involvement to ensure success. But inevitably others become dependent on such a hard worker for approval, guidance, and even material things.

I have talked with many, many people about why they became Christians, and seldom does just reading the Bible win someone to Christ. There are exceptions, but predominantly we are the "epistles read" by all people. The attractiveness of this new kind of life, made possible by the power of the Holy Spirit, draws people to Jesus Christ.
—Eugene Nida, "The Word Is Winning"

His preaching is deep, they say. . . .
Does that mean abstract?
Full of finely drawn theological statements, distinguishing between the unimportant and the less important, comparing the obscure with the unknown.
Does that mean otherworldly?
Out of touch with the bruises and discouragements in my heart, offering prepackaged answers to my unique misery, ignoring my confusion in zeal to exhort me, giving empty answers to full problems.
God, give me a Christian who can laugh, who can cry for one who hurts, who can take small pieces of the Infinite and make me understand and want all of it, who holds my arm so that I can begin to walk—even with my crippled trust.

The work has become crippled—person-centered with little room for God's Spirit.

Proper involvement is reciprocal, preventing these problems from developing. True communication is involvement, two-way help. Learning becomes mutual instruction, as the teacher learns from the student's special skills and insights. A problem arises that one member of the communicating pair cannot solve, but the other can. Encouragement or warning, as appropriate, is given *and received* by both parties in a relationship where there is genuine communication.

▼ BECOME INVOLVED

Where do you begin to be involved? A new community or a totally new culture is bewildering and fatiguing. Becoming involved may be necessary, but the immediate problems are obtaining food, arranging for transport needs, and learning what problems to avoid. In such new situations, you are particularly sensitive. That heightened sensitivity can lead to stress and frustration, or it can be channeled to bond you with the new situation and people.

Bonding is a term used for the deep relationship established between newborn infants and mothers or fathers in the first few hours after birth. If the delivery is a normal one, the baby is especially sensitive and alert in these first hours. This is the time when bonding is divinely arranged to occur.

"There are some important parallels between the infant's entrance into his new culture and the entrance into a new, foreign culture by an adult," write Elizabeth and Thomas Brewster. The new experiences are exciting and perhaps overwhelming. It is at this time that the adult "is ready to bond—to become a belonger with those to whom he is called to be good news. The timing is critical. . . . The new missionary's first couple of weeks in his new country are of critical importance if he is to establish a sense of belonging with the local people" (E. Thomas Brewster and Elizabeth S. Brewster, "Bonding and the Missionary Task," 453–54).

Even in one's land of birth, entering a new community is very much like entering a new culture. If needed help does not come from local people, a sense of belonging in the new place will develop slowly, if ever. When the newcomer is dependent on other outsiders, the Brewsters write, "it is then predictable that he will carry out his ministry by the 'foray' method—he will live isolated from the local people . . . and then make a few forays out into the community each week." Deep involvement seldom follows, and communication remains inadequate.

But if the newcomer accepts a position of dependence on the local people, especially during the first two weeks or so, he or she will quickly become bonded to the new people and new situation. On that basis, involvement grows, and the basis of a fruitful ministry is laid.

Even with bonding as the beginning, involvement must continue to develop. It does not happen all at once. There are at least four overlapping phases: developing use of a common language, sharing experiences, participating in a common culture, and understanding people's basic assumptions about life.

Learn the Language

Working with any group other than your own always means learning a language. Perhaps it is only a variation of your mother tongue, but the language must be learned. It is deceptive to assume that English is always "plain English." Teenagers may use the same words as adults, but their meaning content may be quite different. Sharp differences in language may exist between the inner city and the suburbs or among regions of the country. The language of a seminary is certainly not the language of a coastal fishing village.

In some mission settings it seems unnecessary to learn another language, because English is the lingua franca. Everyone seems to use it with ease. But is that the language of the home? Is it used by close friends in personal conversation? Even where the formal role of teaching or preaching can be satisfactorily carried out in English, fruitful involvement requires learning the language of the "hearth and heart." Involvement with any new community means learning the language of that community. Language, in fact, is best learned as a part of the total cultural learning experience by what is called the "direct method," or "social learning." This is the way an infant learns to speak: listening, imitating, and participating in the life of its family and community.

Share Experiences

Learning a language socially will naturally pull a person into the second level of involvement, the sharing of experiences. Language gains its meaning from experi-

> He (Adoniram Judson) built a schoolhouse . . . like any other Rangoon schoolhouse. Judson took his position every morning cross-legged. . . .
>
> Thirty-three years before he had made a tremendous sacrifice: he had forfeited the English language. He made his choice when he determined to *think* Burmese. Since then he had not spoken in a public meeting in his own tongue. Before an audience he could not put more than three sentences together in English. This yellow-skinned, weary missionary was more truly Burmese than American.
> —Faith C. Bailey, *Adoniram Judson: Missionary to Burma*

ences. Without them, language learning is a sterile study of codes and rules. As experiences are shared, commonality increases. In other words, do things with people; don't just talk "at" them.

Readiness to share in whatever situations arise opens ears—and hearts—without special gimmicks. On the night a missionary friend arrived at a church in western Kenya, the brother of the pastor died in a hospital some distance away. "We naturally volunteered to use our car to bring the body to his own home. There was no other way available," the missionary said. He assisted in the funeral that followed, although, he said, "I was initially unaware of the intensity of emotion and the great significance of being at home and having the family return home at the death of the father.

"In the five days that followed, expressions of gratitude were profuse," the man said, "with invitations to speak to the mourners during evenings, when the feeling is most intense. Letters since then have assured me, 'The people remember what you said' and 'We are waiting for you to return.'" But his preaching was not what was actually remembered. It was his readiness to share in the people's life experiences that opened the way for a continuing ministry.

A great strength of church camping programs is the sharing of experiences by the whole group. In a church construction program, more valuable than the new building is the common effort involved. A weekend retreat gives opportunity for several kinds of common experiences: conversation, group Bible study, prayer—and even the difficulties that come from bad weather!

Related discussions under propositions 9, 20, and 25 show more fully the necessity of shared experiences in communication.

Participate in the Culture

The next level of involvement in building communication follows naturally—participating in the culture of the people to whom you minister. Learning the cultural patterns of a new group is like learning the streets when you move to a new city. Following the streets is the way you move within the city to take part in the city's activities. Similarly, the cultural patterns provide the routes by which you become part of people's lives.

Learning these patterns is not a matter of satisfying curiosity, but the way to relate smoothly to the group. For

Like a proud father introducing his children, Clarence Williams shows me the new, two-story, red and brown brick houses. They stand near the church which Williams pastors in the Brownsville section of Brooklyn, New York, a poor black and Hispanic neighborhood.

"Because of these houses, Brownsville is on the upswing," declares Williams. "Nehemiah went back to Jerusalem to rebuild the walls of the city. We wanted to rebuild Brownsville, and we wanted it to have a biblical base."

Williams cofounded a coalition of churches—the East Brooklyn Churches—which devised the Nehemiah Plan that makes it possible for low wage earners to buy their own home. Five hundred houses had been built by the end of 1987, with a goal of 5,000 in the multi-denominational plan.

The East Brooklyn Churches organize house meetings to discuss neighborhood problems. "A lot of what we do or don't do as an organization stems from what is said at the house meetings," Williams notes.

—Robert Hirschfield, "Rebuilding the City"

effectiveness, you must deliberately learn the living patterns of those with whom you want to be involved for Christ's sake.

Learning the exact way to participate comfortably and correctly in a new culture takes practice—and the willingness to make some mistakes.

Daily routines differ. For example, luncheon meetings are a fixture of life for American business and professional people but a rarity among their colleagues in southern Italy. There shops and offices close at midday, and everyone goes home for the main meal of the day and a good nap. A luncheon meeting would be a very unwelcome break in the rhythm of life. Evening meals may be at 5:30 P.M in the Pacific Northwest of the United States, while in England dinner for special guests may not be before 9:00 P.M

The nature of important events differs from community to community. High school sports may be the center of community interest, or it may be the price of the corn, wheat, or mint oil produced by a farming community. In a coastal town, the year may revolve around the fishing season and the influx of visitors.

Ways to become part of these patterns vary as much as people do. We lived several years in a small African city where we found it difficult to meet our neighbors. Finally, in frustration, I asked a man who seemed to know everybody, "How do you get to know people here?"

"It's really quite easy," he explained. "When you pick up your children from birthday parties [a distinctive feature of family life in that city], go early and start talking to all the other fathers who are waiting for their children." Being efficiency-oriented, I had worked to the last possible moment before picking up my children . . . and

No missionary or other foreigner adopted Chinese dress, since this would involve social ostracism. But it was access to the people (Hudson Taylor) desired. In European clothing, attention was continually distracted from his message by his appearance, which to his hearers was as undignified as it was comical. And after all, surely it mattered more to be suitably attired from the Chinese point of view—when it was the Chinese he wanted to win.
  —Howard Taylor and Mary G. Taylor, *Hudson Taylor's Spiritual Secret*

MOTLEYS CREW

missed a key way to share in the cultural patterns of my community.

The Christian worker who fails to become involved in the living patterns of a people will not have much chance to become involved in their dying patterns, to help them in dealing with eternity and knowing God.

Understand Beliefs

The most difficult level of involvement to achieve is understanding the fundamental ideas people have about the world, life, God, and their relationship to it all. What are the fundamental ideas that lie unspoken behind daily conversations?

Rains came later than usual to a farming area in Zimbabwe, so one white farmowner gave instructions to irrigate, then left to take care of other business. When he returned a week later, no irrigation had been done, and the crops were nearly dead. The workers had refused to turn on the pumps that would have taken water from the large pools remaining in the riverbed. "Yes," the African workers explained to the owner, "we did understand what you told us to do—to put water on the crops so they would not die. But if we had done that by drawing water from the river pools, greater disaster would have come to the whole farm than just losing the crops. We didn't want that to happen to you!"

The owner's first reaction was frustration at their apparent carelessness in letting the crops die unnecessarily. He scolded them for deliberate neglect of their work. Had they been drinking so much at a beer party they did not, or could not, lay out the pipes and start the pumps? Were they just lazy? No, he knew the workmen were not lazy, nor had they been drinking beer when they should have been working. The owner was wise and did not become angry but tried to understand why his instructions were not followed.

The Africans of that area, he eventually learned, never took water from the pools remaining in the bed of the river at the end of the dry season. Only when a particular fruit ripened and fell from the tree was it considered safe to begin drawing water. Anyone doing so before that time would bring disaster to himself and his extended family, because he had offended certain spirits.

His workmen, the owner realized, were intending to protect him—even when his crops died as a result. They made certain assumptions about the nature of the world

Discipleship is the primary way to stimulate spiritual growth. Usually a structured meeting time is determined and goals are set. The key to growth, however, is the quality of relationship that is built. It is important to meet in one another's home, bake cookies together, shop together, take walks, eat meals with one another's family, even spend a weekend or more together. Through building such relationships, understanding, accountability, challenge, and encouragement are communicated. A willingness to be transparent and vulnerable develops, and this is essential to achieving the purposes of discipleship. Discipleship means involvement.

and relationships within the world that were different from his beliefs. The workmen "knew" that disaster would come if the real nature of the world was violated by irrigating at that time. They did not want him to suffer as a result of that disaster, so, with his best interests in mind, they did not follow instructions.

Europeans holding a scientific orientation to the world cannot accept such a "superstitious" reason for allowing the crops to die. Some have carefully explained the reasonable nature of the prohibition on taking water from the river pools. But those scientific reasons satisfy only those who approach the world with a scientific mindset. The essential difference is one of basic belief systems, the assumptions made about the nature of the world.

People of the West—Europeans and North Americans—assume that the earth is a machine to be understood and controlled or a commodity to be used and consumed. Talk of spirit forces or apparently nonsensical relationships is frustrating evidence of ignorance and superstition.

Many of the African peoples assume that the world is a living thing. Primary attention must be given to maintain harmony and balance within the world, and with the world. Upset of this balance is caused by evil witchcraft and by violating the spirit forces with which the world is impregnated.

Another result of these different assumptions is apparent in the area of human relationships. For the traditional African, maintaining balance and harmony in relationships within his family and tribe is extremely important. Possession of material goods is far less important than maintaining proper interaction with other people. For the Westerner, on the other hand, the worth of people tends to be measured by the quantity of their possessions—land, money, goods. A result is the drive for success that means long hours of work and readiness to push aside co-workers, friends, and even family in order to make greater profits.

The Lotuho people of southern Sudan for some time rejected the use of oxen to pull plows, even though using them would have increased their production of food. With oxen, the large work parties during which fields were prepared for sowing would no longer be needed, and those work parties were crucial in maintaining relationships within the society. Better to have less food, they said, than to jeopardize harmony within the village.

Once I spent all day—a rather exhausting day—in the study of orchids with a young man for whom orchids was an obsession. To have a word with him about Christ and the Church, I had to invest hours creating within myself a sincere interest in what was of major concern to him. Then he was ready to listen with an open heart to my message.
—Benjamin P. Browne, *Interlit, 2*

All peoples organize their experience and living patterns around such unwritten assumptions about the nature of things. All activities must be in harmony with those assumptions, or there will be deep uneasiness and dissatisfaction in the individual and the community. A new message that seems to be at odds with these presuppositions will be ignored or openly rejected. Rejection of the change or idea usually includes rejection of the messenger, somewhat like the custom in the ancient world of slaying the messenger who brings the king news of a defeat.

How can these basic values be learned, to avoid unnecessary rejection? This task is particularly difficult, since these values are unwritten and seldom can be directly stated by those holding them. One reasonably direct way is to note the causes of arguments and learn what lies behind apparently irrational outbursts of anger. People seldom become upset about things that are trivial to them. To others an offense may seem unimportant, but the anger or argument indicates that something of value has been violated. Discovering what that is will frequently provide access to fundamental beliefs.

The Christian worker who desires effectiveness in ministry must understand the nature of spiritual warfare and also the exact nature of the battleground. One learns this by thorough participation in the life of one's people, remembering that involvement does not merely prepare the way for communication: Involvement *is* communication.

▼ INVOLVEMENT WITH HOW MANY?

Is it possible to be involved with everyone we want to reach for Christ? Can we be involved with everyone in our church, mission, or community? The sheer number of people seems to make true involvement an impossibility.

No pastor, no missionary, no Christian can be involved with everyone. Management studies show that ten to twelve people is probably the maximum with whom anyone can have close involvement. It is significant that Christ had twelve disciples with whom he was closely involved. Others were near, but not so intimately involved as the Twelve. The Twelve acted in Christ's place to be involved with many others, as in the feeding of the five thousand and in handling the multitudes who wanted to see, hear, and even touch Christ. In this he modeled for us a way to handle involvement in our lives: Be intimately

I've been involved with short-term missions to an American Indian tribe for several years. We stay for three or four days, meeting their veterinary needs. I have learned that this is one of the most evangelized tribes in North America. Yet there are very few results.

There has been a lack of real involvement for many years. What is needed is a greater commitment to involvement from someone who is committed to stay among the people. Communicating Christ takes daily involvement in the lives of the people.
—Tom Sager, UIM International

involved with a few, who are in turn involved with others in a widening circle of effective ministry.

Discipline is required if one is to be meaningfully involved with only a few. It is more satisfying to report large attendance at our meetings, with hundreds listening to our preaching. Large numbers look good in the traditional prayer letter or in reports to the church board. But too often many people are "won" and tallied as converts, but then are not found in Christian fellowship. A message was transmitted and apparently received, with little or no true communication.

Communication is involvement. One must have the discipline to ensure that those seeking Christ become involved with someone who will communicate Christ over and over again—at the coffee shop, in home visits, and in the fields and factories where life is lived. And one needs discipline to focus on the few, resisting the attraction of being "indispensable" to dozens or hundreds of followers.

In country after country, those Christians who have made the greatest impact have been those who concentrated on a few seekers or converts at a time. Carey Francis was a great schoolteacher and principal in Kenya, developing the finest young men's high school in the country. His students, "Francis's men," became the leaders of independent Kenya. Many kept a clear confession of Christ even when they held the highest posts in the nation. Francis made his impact in a few lives at a time.

Great preachers such as Bakht Singh in India, Dwight L. Moody in America, and John Wesley in England have given a greater proportion of their time to close involvement with a few than to mass meetings more visible to the public. Each of these men extended that principle of involvement by the founding of Christian training programs that developed into colleges, seminaries, Bible schools, and universities.

When God wanted to speak to human beings, he did not send a tract or preach a sermon. He came in person. His life was completely involved with people, sharing their language, experience, and culture and seeing to the very core of their values and false assumptions. The incarnational model of communication that Jesus gave us needs to be carefully studied and understood; it is our pattern for effective completion of our task.

▼ A BIBLICAL PERSPECTIVE ON INVOLVEMENT

In the beginning was the Word, and the Word was with God, and the Word was God. He was with God in the beginning.

Through him all things were made; without him nothing was made that has been made. In him was life, and that life was the light of men. The light shines in the darkness, but the darkness has not understood it. . . .

He was in the world, and though the world was made through him, the world did not recognize him. He came to that which was his own, but his own did not receive him. Yet to all who received him, to those who believed in his name, he gave the right to become children of God—children born not of natural descent, nor of human decision or a husband's will, but born of God.

The Word became flesh and made his dwelling among us.

—John 1:1–5, 10–14

He is Life, but we are certain only of dying.

He is the Light, but in darkness we do not understand it. How can darkness comprehend that which is opposite, totally different?

He is the Creator, but the created do not even recognize him. How can we understand, or even recognize, One with power beyond our comprehension?

He became flesh, and flesh we are. Flesh we understand.

To be understood, God himself came in the flesh of a baby. He ate, he slept, he played, and he obeyed his parents here on earth. He watched and learned what the days of persons are like.

He celebrated wedding joy and wept at the burden of disease, dismay, deceit, and death that humanity carried.

He, the holy God, saw evil and evil persons. He faced temptation and knew triumph over the worst—which was the best that Satan had to offer.

He had friends who loved him and yet denied and betrayed him. He felt the sting of injustice, false accusations, and mockery, and he died under the rule of an oppressor.

He was completely involved with humankind. That is how we understand. His life is the Word, a Word spoken in the language of humanity, a Word that we can comprehend.

> Since the children have flesh and blood, he too shared in their humanity so that by his death he might destroy him who holds the power of death—that is, the devil—and free those who all their lives were held in slavery by their fear of death. . . . Because he himself suffered when he was tempted, he is able to help those who are being tempted.
>
> —Hebrews 2:14–15, 18

Jesus, the Christ, totally involved himself with human beings and thus communicated with humanity. In no other way could we comprehend. And it is because of his total involvement with humankind that he intercedes for us today. "We do not have a high priest who is unable to sympathize with our weaknesses, but we have one who has been tempted in every way, just as we are—yet without sin" (Heb. 4:15).

The foundation for our involvement in ministry is the life, death, and continuing life of Jesus Christ. No bridges we seek to cross through involvement will span a gap as wide as the one Jesus crossed when he became flesh.

Paul was sent as an ambassador of this King, Jesus, and so sought clearly and honestly to represent that King in the world. His method was the same as that of the King—involvement so that everyone could understand.

> Though I am free and belong to no man, I make myself a slave to everyone, to win as many as possible. To the Jews I became like a Jew, to win the Jews. To those under the law I became like one under the law (though I myself am not under the law), so as to win those under the law. To those not having the law I became like one not having the law, . . . so as to win those not having the law. To the weak I became weak, to win the weak. I have become all things to all men so that by all possible means I might save some.
>
> —1 Corinthians 9:19–22

Paul's description of his "ministry method" is the clearest possible statement of involvement for ministry. There is no better pattern for the ambassadors of Christ to follow.

SUMMARY

Communication is a relationship. We do not get involved in order to communicate. We communicate by being involved. Involvement is the foundation of all communication. Cultural differences only emphasize its importance.

CREATING UNDERSTANDING

To separate an act of "communication" from a continuing involvement between equal participants is to reduce communication to a babble of symbols with uncertain meanings. Without constantly increasing commonness in interests and experience, there cannot be an increase in understanding.

Sending and receiving messages can be coldly impersonal, a separate thing from real communication. Effective communication that leads to deep comprehension and response occurs only through involvement in each other's life and interests. Without involvement, the most skilled use of media and techniques may be only an imitation of communication.

The critical thing is to establish commonness; for that, there must be a willingness to be "with" one another. Mutual understanding comes with interaction. Reciprocity, co-response, co-orientation, dialogue, bonding—all these ideas point to involvement in communication.

> For want of a nail, a horse could not be shod; for want of a horse, a message could not be sent; for want of a message, a battle was lost; for want of victory, a kingdom was lost.

> Building for tomorrow seems too distant. This demands a solution now.

A LINK IN A LONG CHAIN

PROPOSITION 2: Communication is a process.

The desire of farm laborers and small landowners in Hengshan, China, was to improve their food supply and ease their very harsh living conditions. They had lost virtually everything but life during war and raids of robber bands. Now the farmers were seeking to develop a cooperative despite centuries of tradition that had led them to work only their own land and be primarily concerned only for one's own family. The following story related by Jan Myrdal reveals the slow process of decision-making and change.

As the villager Ching Chung-ying reports it, the beginning of change involved observation, discussions, and many meetings. It was a process of communication, not of issuing a single directive or even a series of directives.

On the other side of the valley the Old Secretary and some others were building up their farmers' cooperative. We watched them. Their working together there seemed to bring them luck. More people meant more strength and more manpower. They did the ploughing better than we and they manured more thoroughly. They had nice harvests. We discussed whether we shouldn't form our own labour group for mutual help.

Some of us were for this. I thought it would be good. Mau Keyeh and Ma Juei-ching also worked for the proposal. Others were against the idea. Fu Hai-tsao, for example. Their family had more manpower. They said, "We can manage our fields ourselves. We don't really like the idea of others looking after our land." Then I went over and talked to them, "If the others on the other side of the valley can do their job properly, why shouldn't we be able to do so?" I said. Three weeks later, Fu Hai-tsao came to me and said that he had thought it over and that he would join. We held many meetings. We kept on at it evening after evening. There was great discussion.

—Jan Myrdal, *Report from a Chinese Village*, 129–34

There were no quick decisions with immediate action. But step by step the farmers made small decisions, discussed, watched others. Their increasing prosperity was convincing to themselves, increasing their confidence and helping them move on to more difficult actions.

Fourteen years from the beginning of the process, they obtained electricity and set up an electric pump for their vegetable gardens. Things were going well. "We work. I am not a party member. I have never been interested in politics. Before, we . . . owned nothing. Now I should need several oxcarts to move all my things. If one works hard, one can live really well."

The communication process continues, an integral part of development. This report shows just one series of incidents in a long chain of communication similar to that which stretches through every life.

The process of communication through words, gestures, actions, gifts, and exchanges is the thread that binds a group of people together, making them a society. Single words or conversations are not fully understood unless they are seen as part of this intricately woven social fabric. Isolated communicative acts are less important for understanding than is the total process of which they are a part.

Vincent Guerry lived with the Baoulé people of Côte d'Ivoire for many years, learning their emphasis on group solidarity and communal existence. Here is an example of the communication process that brings individuals into a commonness of life.

It is worse never to ask for anything than not to give anything. In fact, it is as bad as not to talk to somebody. A Baoulé will ask for something as easily as he will say good morning or good evening, without really caring very much for the thing he requests. It is quite customary, for instance, when one sees someone leaving for the market or the city, to say to him, "bring me a nice present from there, won't you?" It is obvious that the traveller cannot satisfy everybody but—who knows?—he just might bring something anyway. There's no harm in asking, and it is another way of expressing the wish to remain united: the farewell expression in Baoulé is *é te o nou*—we stay together.

When I first came to the village, I coldly refused these requests, thereby hurting the feelings of both children and grown-ups who considered my attitude almost insulting. In due course, I got to understand the meaning of these requests; from then on, I promised to buy everything I was asked, and had the pleasure of watching those broad smiles of happiness. So I return empty-handed. But nobody asks me for the promised scarf, or bread, or candy; nobody is disappointed, as I was not really expected to come back laden with presents. The requests were made primarily to confirm our ties of friendship, to strengthen the expression of desire for my speedy return.

The real meaning of requests is the acceptance of being united, tied together by self-made bonds. The very unity of the village has been woven in the course of time by these exchanges of gifts and services: people tied to one another as closely as the woven threads of cloth.

—Vincent Guerry, *Life with the Baoulé*, 77–78

Both this account and that of the Chinese farmers illustrate the long thread of communication. An action brings a reaction, then further discussion and action, and another reaction. On and on it goes, until the beginning reason for communicating is at least partly achieved.

Communication is never cut and dried, contained in a moment of time. It has no specific beginning and continues to develop and change over days and years. This process has a major part in the formation of the individual—remembering, building on the past, moving toward understanding of surrounding people and the world that envelops one.

When two people receive the same message from the same communicator, they frequently have different understandings of the message. For example, a man may hear that friends have just had a new baby. His first thought is, "How will he support this child? He's already having a difficult time." But the man's wife may well respond, "Wonderful! How much did the baby weigh? What is her name?" The same message is thought of in different ways because of different responsibilities, different experiences, and different values. If communication stops there, misunderstanding is inevitable.

Our discussion of proposition 1 showed that communication involves building commonness. Building com-

When I played the role of the blind, deaf, and dumb lady Helen Keller in *The Miracle Worker*, this proposition was especially clear. I studied Helen Keller's life and visited another deaf-blind-dumb girl.

When Annie Sullivan came to teach Helen, there was no instant comprehension. It took months of constant work, teaching letters that were meaningless to Helen, constant association with the objects that were spelled out to Helen by touch. As Annie said to Helen's mother: "It's how I watch you talk to any baby. Gibberish, grown-up gibberish. . . . Do they understand one word of it to start? Somehow they begin to."

"But after a child hears how many words, Miss Annie, a million?"

"I guess no mother's ever minded enough to count."

And sure enough, the breakthrough happened, because of the process that had occurred.

—Julisa Smith

monness is a process, often a long process, especially when there are multiple differences. Crossing cultural boundaries involves much more than differences in language or clothing or lifestyle. And so development of commonness requires much more time and effort than even crossing the hurdle of differences between men and women. Building within existing experiences and associations requires extended interaction.

The history of a people is as important in communication as the immediate visible needs of those people. Likewise, their desires for the future affect what they understand today and how they will respond. Communication is rooted in yesterday, flowers today, and bears fruit tomorrow. To think that only the present moment matters is to fail to use all opportunities for building understanding. It is to run the risk of shallow understanding and superficial responses.

Dealing with an immediate problem in isolation from the past and the future seldom brings a good solution. At least the highlights of the whole chain of communication must be learned before there can be good answers.

Hundreds of thousands of international students studying in the United States, England, or any country other than their own have to make difficult adjustments. To master academic studies, students usually must first master the culture of which the university is a part. Often that culture is very different from the home culture; learning to function in it demands different habits, different relationships, and often different goals. As students succeed in adjusting, they become less and less comfortable with their home culture. The very process of succeeding in immediate study goals undermines the students' long-term goal of being of greater value to their own people. In other words, immediate success brings long-term failure. Often the most adaptable of the international students simply stay in the host culture; they never return home, except for visits.

Why? How can this "brain drain" be stopped? Nations greatly needing the help of these gifted students often lose their most promising sons and daughters to countries having the great universities and training institutions.

Simply recognizing that communication is a process extending into both the past and the future would help. The help that is given to the students needs to take account of their background, the ultimate purpose for their training and where it will be used, as well as immediate adjustment. Remembering that communication is an unending process will help teachers and counselors give appropriate and adequate help.

When the whole process of communication is overlooked, the students are helped only to adjust to the host culture, earn a degree, and develop skills. Intent on helping students succeed now, counselors and faculty members often overlook past experiences and future use of the training. Attention must be given to relating past experiences and future use in the home culture to the new world of ideas gained from the host culture. Without that, internationals are left highly trained yet unequipped to fulfill their life goals—because the *process* of communication is not understood.

The continuing nature of communication must be recognized so that past, present, and future all influence the nature of teaching, discipling, and ministry.

Frequently churches seek to witness to their community through an evangelistic campaign. Within the church, a long process of preparation—planning, prayer, publicity—leads up to the campaign. Much prayer is focused on attracting non-Christians to the event. Appealing films, famous guest speakers such as sports stars or national leaders, and excellent music are used to entice people to come. *Within* the church the event is part of a process of communication, but it is seen as having a one-time impact on the non-Christians for whom it is intended. "If we can just get them to hear" seems to be the motto.

They may hear, but do they understand? Understanding is not achieved on a "one-shot" basis. It results from a process that extends over time. To evaluate the evangelistic campaign on the basis of how many professed to receive Christ or how many attended is to overlook the whole working of God through the *process* of communication. National events, natural catastrophes, social trends such as major migrations and change in lifestyles—many things are as much part of the response as the campaign itself. The great surge of church membership and acceptance of the Christian message in Africa between 1960 and 1980 was probably a result of great social and political changes as much as a fruit of excellent evangelistic work. Openness to the Gospel and positive response to the mes-

Falah is a Middle Eastern friend of ours who had seen her husband convert to Christianity. This was inconceivable to her as a faithful Muslim; she could not understand that an Arab could be anything but a Muslim.

Four years later, Falah still had little understanding of the Gospel. We began to share meals with her and her husband weekly, to watch their children, to shop together, and to have Bible studies. We shared the Gospel, yet it was clear that little of what we said made sense to her. Over the following year, we repeatedly shared small pieces of the whole truth whenever it was appropriate. When she lacked funds for a medical need, we would pray with her and ask Jesus to supply the need. When her children were very unruly, we read to her how God expected her to discipline her children.

Over a long period of many small opportunities, the light was beginning to dawn. Misconceptions fell one by one. She came to Christ, and the process called discipleship began.

—Paul Steven

A changed situation changes the understanding of a message. Many factors affecting communication do not appear to be part of the message itself.

sage in Argentina during the last part of the 1980s was doubtless part of the process of visible change beginning with Argentina's defeat in the Falkland Islands War and changes in national government.

None of these different factors explain the events. They show us the finger of God stirring within a people and provide evidence that salvation is a *process* instead of an isolated, instantaneous result of a particular communication effort.

The first Gospel messengers to the Ndebele people of Zimbabwe were there for thirty years before there was outward acceptance of Christ by anyone. Today there is a large and growing church among those same people. William Carey labored most of a lifetime in India, yet left only a few converts. The church has never become powerful among the Bengali people with whom he worked, even two hundred years later. Raymond Lull sought to show the love of Christ to Muslims in North Africa, dying a martyr's death with no apparent converts. Were these, and countless others like them, not part of God's process of communication with humankind?

Communication has sometimes been defined as a simple point-to-point giving and receiving of a message. In this common view, communication is envisioned as a straight line. Between the messenger and the receiver there are hindrances—noise that may confuse the message or cultural barriers. But if the strength of the message is increased, then the signal gets through to the receiver. This simple view is so inadequate that it is misleading.

It is much better to compare communication to a circle in which not only sender and receiver are involved, but also the past and the future, the cultural setting, and the message itself. Each time communication goes "around the circle," understanding is brought closer. Circle after circle, the process continues. If it could be diagramed, it would look something like an ascending helix—a rising spiral.

Committee work is frequently considered tedious and time-consuming. "Why must we discuss, discuss, discuss? If we did our work before the meeting begins, the committee could listen and then approve. It would save a lot of time." True, it does appear to save time. But if full agreement has not been reached, winning the vote may only delay sharp disagreement and serious division.

46

It is a widespread custom in Africa to delay a formal decision until all points of view are expressed and lengthy discussion has followed. When a decision is taken, there is strong support for it. Genuine consensus has been achieved, and time is actually saved. This consensus approach to decision making recognizes the process that is involved far more than the "time-efficient" approach common in Western societies.

A clear expression of communication as process comes from the novel *The World of Suzie Wong*. The storyteller is a young artist who has realized why he wants to paint rather than use photography to interpret life to others. From the perspective of communication, he shows how every act is part of a larger whole.

> I had taken photographs by the score. But amongst all these photographs, not more than a dozen had caught the look, the gesture, the moment at which I had aimed; and these indeed had been the most disappointing of them all, for nothing that I had expected was to be found in them. They had turned out empty, flat, devoid of meaning. But why, why? Since they were true records of moments that had moved me, why weren't they moving in themselves?
>
> And then I began to understand. A moment could never be complete in itself, since it belonged to a context of movement and mood, and only in this context had meaning; and moreover part of this context was the observer himself, interpreting the moment in the light of his own mind—his own personality and knowledge. Thus when I had seen the Burmese woman by the Irawaddy it was not her actual expression that had moved me, but what this had suggested to me when filtered through my own vision: when fused with my own experience. . . . And on another person standing at my side, the moment would have made a different impression. Indeed on a dozen people, it would have made a dozen different impressions.
>
> —Richard Mason, *The World of Suzie Wong*, 16–17

Enter the flowing river of communication, and it changes—perhaps only slightly. Greater change can be caused as it is understood that the flow comes from somewhere outside one person's experience and flows onward beyond that experience. Having learned the course of the river, one can enter its currents with greater effect.

An example of process is seen in Acts as the church defines its policy regarding Gentile Christians. In chapter 11, after the conversion of Cornelius, Peter meets with the apostles and brothers to discuss the situation. The conclusion was, "When they heard this, they had no further objections and praised God saying, 'So then, God has granted even the Gentiles repentance unto life'" (Acts 11:18).

This is only the beginning, however. In chapter 15 we read of the Jerusalem Council, which was called about nine years later to further define the Gentile position in the church. The communication seen here is deeply rooted in Judaic laws of separation and cleanliness. The strength of Peter's statement in Acts 10:13 and the wide criticism he received in 11:2–3 show that this new acceptance of Gentiles violated Jewish core beliefs. Therefore, it required a long process of communication and adjustment.

—Diane Walker

▼ A BIBLICAL PERSPECTIVE
ON COMMUNICATION AS PROCESS

Frequently, the way God deals with humanity is illuminated in Scripture through the use of word-pictures from agriculture. Agriculture itself is a process, always extending over time.

Humanity's initial rebellion came through a step-by-step wavering from full obedience. When the process led to disaster, Adam and Eve tried to excuse the disobedience. Continuing downward in sin, people became hardened and schemed to find ways to shut God out of their lives; consider Cain, the Tower of Babel, and even those especially chosen for God's purposes, the children of Abraham. All ignored the faithfulness of God and the messengers of God.

How would God build communication with those who were hard in their rejection of him? By "plowing their hearts," "breaking up the fallow ground." God began by breaking up the hearts where his seed of truth was to be sown. The sojourn in Egypt and the Babylonian exile doubtless appeared to be tragedies of defeat, captivity, and slavery. But without plowed—broken—hearts God's Word would not have found place to grow and bear fruit among humankind.

Then God gave the seed of the Gospel, telling us to plant the seed in all people. And he warns that all hearts are not equally prepared or receptive. It cannot be predicted in advance which are most likely to yield the greatest harvest. Some respond to the truth eagerly and quickly, but just as quickly wilt and die. Others remain hard, giving no chance for the seed to germinate, while still others allow the seed to be choked out so that it cannot grow. Only a few respond with richly prepared hearts.

Even with those few, there is need to water and weed and to give the seed time to grow into plants, to flower, and to become ripe, ready for harvest.

God's work is not completed instantly. Growth and increase are his work alone, yet they are clearly processes requiring time. Every step leading to the harvest is part of a long and continuing process by which generation after generation learns of him, responds, and then tells the next generation.

SUMMARY

A particular conversation, sermon, song, or drama never stands by itself. There is no solitary act of communication. Communication is rooted in a person's experiences and hopes for the future and reflects present felt needs. Those needs shift and change as situations change. The past and future are part of any given conversation or media message. Each of the comments at the head of this chapter illustrates the process nature of communication, showing that its beginning and end are timeless.

Communication cannot be treated as an isolated act, but is a process for which there is no clear beginning or ending. Effective communication requires awareness of the past, present, and future dimensions for all involved in communicating.

There is not a single word or message that "does it all." Instead, the effective communicator will seek to link his or her message into the lifelong chain of communication in a way that will ensure understanding.

3

➤ Just tell me what you mean!

➤ *Which* meaning do you give in teaching or preaching—your meaning, what the text says, what it seems to say today? How can you be sure you have given true biblical meaning?

YOU KNOW WHAT I MEAN!

PROPOSITION 3: Meaning is internal and individual.

As Joseph Bayly develops "A Psalm at Children's Hospital," the reader is able to share something of Bayly's emotional feeling and response to unexpected crisis:

I find it hard Lord
agonizing hard
to stand here
looking through the glass
at this my infant son.
What suffering
is in this world
to go through pain of birth
and then through
pain of the knife
within the day.
What suffering is in the world
this never ending
pain parade
from birth
to death.
He moves
a bit
not much
how could an infant
stuffed with tubes
cut sewed and bandaged
move more than that?
Some day he'll shout

50

and run a race
roll down a grassy hill
ice skate
on frosty night like this.
He'll sing
and laugh
I know he will Lord.
But if not
if You should take him home
to Your home
help me then remember
how Your Son suffered
and You stood by
watching
agonizing watching
waiting
to bring all suffering to an end
forever
on a day
yet to be.
Look Lord
he sleeps.
I must go now.
Thank You for staying
nearer than oxygen
than dripping plasma
to my son.
Please be that near
to mother
sister brothers
and to me.

—*Psalms of My Life*, 21–22

Bayly lost three sons before they were adults; sadly, the hospital was a familiar place to him. What he gained from these losses is shared in his later book *The View from a Hearse*.

With this further information about the author, one's emotive response to "A Psalm at Children's Hospital" is heightened. More information brings us closer to the experience of the author. Undoubtedly, anyone who has shared some part of Bayly's grief will respond with even greater understanding. Shared experience has given rise to similar mental models, so similar meaning is more easily developed.

▼ HOW IS MEANING DEVELOPED?

We talk, make motions, draw pictures, touch others, and use food and objects to send signals to others. We know that these signals are received by the five senses: hearing, sight, touch, taste, and smell. Somehow meaning

Justice Oliver Wendell Holmes said that a word is not crystal, transparent and unchanged. He claimed that it is skin of a living thought and may vary greatly in color and content according to the circumstances and the time in which it is used.

Rather than inquiring, "What is *the* meaning of the word?" I should ask, "What does this word mean to *you?*" Without a clear understanding of what you have in mind, I can't be sure our dialog is on target.

—Kenneth Ericksen, *The Power of Communication*

51

is developed from this jumble of signals. When the meaning developed is similar to the meaning intended, we have achieved at least a measure of communication. But many times there seems to be "no communication," despite our best efforts. The meaning developed is not at all the meaning intended.

Part of the problem lies with the differing ways we use signals. Another part lies with interpretation of those signals. The same signals will be interpreted in different ways because we have differing experiences and differing needs and often are in differing environments. In addition, though we think we are talking about the same thing, we may even be referring to different things. A diagram that simplifies the process may clarify how meaning develops internally:

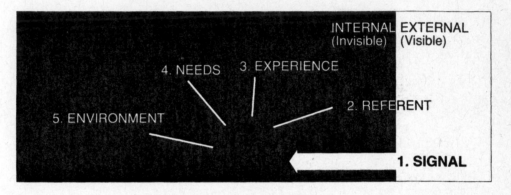

We begin a view of the process with the **signal** (1), which may be a word, a body motion, or anything else capable of conveying information. That signal refers to an object or idea, the **referent** (2)—for example, a table or the idea of happiness. Sometimes the referent will be visible, seen by everyone involved in the communication. At other times the referent may be seen by only one of the parties communicating; others involved in the actions of communicating may imagine a quite different referent for the received signal. Or the referent may be an idea that is held in a communicator's mind; the same idea may well have a different shape in another communicator's mind, even though the two communicators are using the same signal.

Experience (3) is drawn upon to interpret the signal: what that signal referred to in the past, and the good or bad associated with the signal in the communicator's memory. The present **needs** (4) also affect perception of the signal. A person who is hungry will have a different response to a description of a feast from a person who is sick with digestive problems. The man and woman who are to be married in a month will listen more closely to advice on how to have a happy home than will a young boy who is not even interested in girls.

The total **environment** (5) in which communication is happening also shapes interpretation of the signal. An Eskimo living in northern Canada and a woman of south India protecting her baby against a draft in her home will have different interpretations of the idea of "cold." The context within which the signal is used has a large influence on the meaning that will be given to it. This is, of course, a basic principle of literary interpretation and correct understanding of the Bible.

All these factors influencing meaning are present in both communicator and audience. But the content of each of the factors is different—sometimes very different— between the two parties in communication. The result is different meanings given to the same signal.

This can be compared to the blanks in a completion puzzle; everyone has the same blank lines, but the words put into those blanks may be very different:

> The _____ house is all right for him, even though the _____ is old and may leak. The _____ needs repair, but there is _____ furniture for the family.

What words did you put in the blanks? The words I *intended* and would call correct are (1) *teacher's*, (2) *roof,* (3) *plumbing*, and (4) *fine*. In this very simple example, how many words did we agree on? The differences between us are due to different experiences, needs, and environments—and probably each of us had in mind a quite different house or situation.

Each of us combined these four major factors to develop an internal picture or mental model as we attempted to fill in the blank spaces above.

▼ WHAT IS A MENTAL MODEL?

The mental model is like an interpreter, taking unknown signals and "translating" them, giving the signals significance for the receiver. Significance is given to the signals so that they agree, "make sense," with the model that seems most appropriate at the moment. It may be similar to the sender's model or very different. If differ-

> Meaning is a picture which is painted in the receiver's mind as a result of information which is communicated by a sender. No matter how good the message, it is up to the receiver to interpret the information and apply his experiences to that information in order to paint the picture.
> —Tom Sager, UIM International

The need to understand how the reciever thinks
seek clearity

53

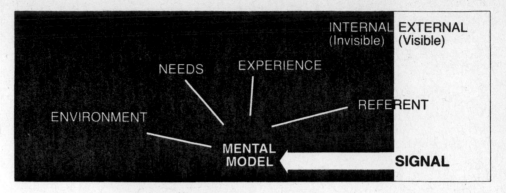

ent, the signals sent are given a quite different meaning from the one intended.

A Canadian friend's experience in Tokyo illustrates how an incorrect mental model leads to incorrect interpretation. Unable to find an address, my friend went to a Japanese policeman and asked, in excellent Japanese, how to find the place. The policeman replied in Japanese, "I do not speak English." This happened twice. Then my friend responded, "If you will listen carefully you will hear that I am speaking Japanese." Without repeating the request for directions, the Canadian waited. Suddenly a smile came to the Japanese policeman's face: "Oh! Yes, I can tell you how to get there." And he gave full directions.

The policeman saw a white man—his face, size, and style of clothes—and remembered his experiences with visitors who could not speak Japanese. His mental model left him unprepared to hear anything but English and prompted his automatic reply that he could not speak English. With more information, a different model was called up; the policeman "heard" the request and was able to answer without the words being repeated.

What picture is formed when one hears the word *post*? More than forty possible meanings are given in *Webster's International Dictionary*. Post may be part of a fence, letters in a post office, a place where a soldier is stationed, or the act of sending someone on an assignment. Which meaning would be correct? Several different mental models of *post* could be used to interpret a simple request, "Please give me the post." Which one is intended? You could be sure only if the sender gave you enough information to help you choose a model similar to the one the sender used. The context (environment) might help, as well as experience—if both knew the context and had had similar experiences. An Englishman asking whether the

When my youngest daughter was two years old, we crossed a busy street to bring her home from the neighbor's. As we waited for the traffic to pass, I said to her, "God is right here with us and he's taking care of us."

When we had safely arrived at our doorstep, she turned to me and asked, "Are you God?"

A little surprised, I answered, "Why no, I'm not God." She then remarked, "Well, I'm not God either."

I knew immediately that she did not understand the concept of the invisible God. She was trying to make my comment about God fit into her limited experience.
—Gail Burns

post has come probably will not be understood by a listening American. But another Englishman has little trouble understanding that the question is (as translated into American usage), "Has the mail been delivered yet?"

A conscious thought arises from the mental model, leading to an outward response, conveyed by a signal of some type. It is only through these outward signals that we are able to determine how close the meaning is to what we originally intended to develop in our audience:

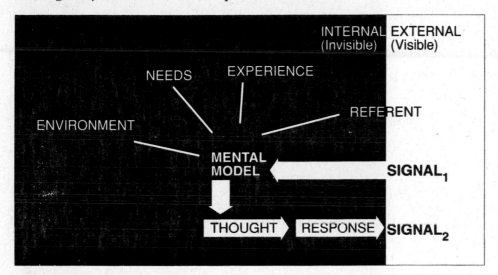

True meaning lies in the object or experience itself, the referent in this diagram. The difficulty begins when I try to share that meaning with another person. The best we can achieve is a close approximation of the original. Human communication does not work like a copy machine.

Trying to capture meaning is a bit like trying to put smoke into a bottle. A suggestion of the smell and color may be caught, but even then it soon changes. When the bottle is opened, it seems empty.

Meaning exists in people's minds. When it is recorded, it seems a different thing, because I interpret the record according to my experience, needs, and environment. The meaning I develop internally will be as different from the original intended meaning as my experience, needs, and environment are different from those of the originator of the meaning.

When we attempt to ascertain meaning, we are not dealing with a substance that can be transmitted in some way, or a code that simply needs to be decoded to guarantee full understanding. We are seeking to rebuild the true

Draw a picture

"I don't see much sense in that," said Rabbit.

"No," said Pooh humbly, "there isn't. But there was going to be when I began it. It's just that something happened to it on the way."
—A. A. Milne, "The House at Pooh Corner," 264

when using objects in illustration explain, to transfer an accurate understanding

(original) meaning while working amid constantly changing factors, beyond the direct grasp of communicators.

As many mental models can exist as there are individuals.

Nevertheless, we can develop meanings that are approximately the same between two individuals. To do so requires careful learning of (1) the original context and (2) the receiver's context, and it also requires (3) concentration on transferring sufficient information.

▼ WHAT IS INFORMATION?

Information, as the term is used in communication, is roughly equivalent to *facts.* The concept of information was developed originally as a way to measure how well telephones functioned. It is used extensively in computer science, where it has been fundamental in the design of the electronics on which the computer depends.

Information is measured in BITs: **B**inary **I**nformation uni**T**s. A BIT is the smallest possible choice made. No matter how long or complicated, every decision or choice is made up of a series of BITs. In its simplest form, a BIT is the choice between two things—for example, 1 or 2. Making a series of such choices builds a "decision tree" that eventually leads to a particular course of action.

Computers are built on this basis. The machine can only respond to a 1 or a 2, an "on" or "off" choice. A se-

56

ries of such simple choices leads to a particular outcome. These choices are made very rapidly, following a predetermined program in which the machine (by previously entered instructions) follows a course something like this: 1 or 2; if 2, then at the next step it must be 1; and then at the next step a choice again is made, 1 or 2. If it is 1, then 1 must again follow—and so forth. Each choice is a BIT. (The diagram on the side helps to illustrate how a particular outcome results from a series of simple decisions.)

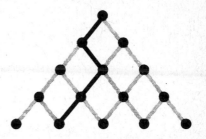

The user is aware only of the result of the series of BITs, when after a very small lapse of time an action is initiated by the machine or a message appears on the screen. Every process can be broken down into such a series of BITs. Thus, a BIT is the basic unit for measuring quantity of information. BIT by BIT, *information* is transferable.

It is from BITs of information that meaning is developed within the receiver's mind. Each "fact" is actually composed of dozens or hundreds of BITs. When sufficient facts (BITs) are received, a meaning is developed that approximates closely the intended meaning.

People living in different cultures, however, have fewer similar or shared experiences than do those living in the same culture. Therefore the development of similar meaning becomes more difficult. Difficulty in intercultural communication is further increased by differing interpretations (because of different mental models) of those experiences that are similar. The challenge of intercultural communication is to overcome these two major barriers to understanding—different experiences and different interpretations of similar experiences.

George Bernard Shaw once described England and America as "two countries separated by the same language." When an American visits England, he believes he shares the language, values, and culture of the British Isles. After only a few hours, however, he realizes to his disappointment that the words he uses convey a whole different set of meanings to the British from the ones he intends. He misunderstands the simplest things: He orders "biscuits" and is surprised when the waitress brings cookies (he has no idea what "scones" are); he looks for an elevator and is told there is no "lift" in the building; his use of some words common to everyday American speech shock his hosts, who consider those words crude. The meaning assigned to gestures as well as words is different in York from what it is in New York.

The same words may be used,
BUT
    Different experiences
  + Different environments
  + Different needs
  = MISCOMMUNICATION

A clear example of culturally rooted differences in understanding the same words in the same language was given in *Spectrum,* a journal of Christian communication:

> I'm writing, Ransford is translating, and the radio programs are taking shape in Jamaican thought forms—Caribbean English.
>
> I write, "So you're angry with your wife and resenting her," and Ransford transforms it to "so you're vexed at your spouse and you're malicing her." Malicing? Vexed? That's the only way to say it here if the meaning is to come through.
>
> As I write, I fancy we speak the same language in Jamaica and in the States. We don't. So we must translate. Knowing this, every word I choose is a temporary attempt at meaning. Each word is the best bet I have at the moment, but it is destined to be changed. If the meaning is the important thing, then I dare not love the words. If the content is to be communicated, then the words will need to be expendable.
>
> What we want to say is clear.
>
> How it must be said is open to question.
>
> The meanings in Ransford and the meanings in me are meeting as we hear each other deeply. (Meanings are in persons, not in the words.) Can we get them through to the listening audience of Radio Jamaica?
>
> As I am writing now, I rethink my experience, rephrase my expressions, and translate my vision of life into words that may either mate with your experience, or match your expressions. If either happens, then my meanings may meet your meanings and for the moment, we commune.
>
> But my meanings and your meanings may never meet, and we will not communicate. Or we will think that we are communicating but miss each other's meanings. And you will not hear the meanings in me, though you catch every word. And I will mistake the meanings in you, though I can repeat you word for word.
>
> We are co-authors, co-laborers, co-communicators. It's a mutual process, this communication thing—inevitably two-way, mutual—involving us both in continuous translation and retranslation.
>
> —David Augsburger, "Writing Is Translating," 4

Dialect differences can be troubling whether they are in words, in body motions, or in other signs used between people. But dialect differences are one of the lesser problems to overcome in intercultural communication.

Great difficulties result from differing mental models held by members of different cultures. Further problems result from differing ways information is shared. Some cultures rely almost entirely on face-to-face communication; others use semiformal gatherings for discussion

What Mexicans call "plátano" is called "banana" in Guatemala and the United States. Plátano in Guatemala is a kind of banana, but it is harder, bigger, and much more expensive than the common banana. Usually it is necessary to cook them to eat them, and then they are very delicious.

The first time I heard a Mexican say, "I ate two plátanos already," I thought, "How could this man eat two plátanos by himself?"

Now, when I listen to Mexican friends talking about plátanos, I understand that they are talking about what I know as bananas.

—Hector Rodríguez

and decision on group affairs. Still other societies depend on more formal media such as newspapers, letters, and broadcasts to share information. In some groups information may be packaged in stories that appear to be entertainment, while other groups carefully separate "fact" from "fiction."

These intercultural differences magnify difficulties that are present in all communication. We can seldom be sure that the words or actions we use will create the same understanding in others that they form in us. That is the very heart of the challenge in achieving effective communication.

Concentration on three key tasks can give great help in developing communication effectiveness:

1. *Understand the models* held in people's minds. Different groups as well as different individuals will have different mental models. The "general" model of a people must be learned first and then, through dialogue, the specific model of the individual with whom we are communicating.

2. *Understand how information is transferred* in the specific culture and situations where we seek to minister.

3. *Transfer sufficient information* so the recipient can reconstruct a meaning closely approximating that which is intended.

The following fictional incident is set in Hawaii of the 1840s, when the islands were still a difficult mission field. Thorn, the mission director, is visiting from mission headquarters in Boston. Abner has pioneered Christian ministry in one of the islands at great cost—death threats from American whalers, severe illnesses, nonacceptance from the Hawaiians, loss of his own health. Now Thorn is trying to urge Abner into more modern missionary methods.

The two men hold very different mental models in several areas as a result of different needs, environments, and experiences. On the surface, however, they appear to be talking about the same thing.

> Thorn . . . thought, He is accusing me of intemperate judgment on the grounds that I know nothing of local conditions. Yet every error begins with a special condition. But he was not at ease in delivering rebukes, and he turned to happier topics, saying, "I wish you could have witnessed the phenomenal changes in our Boston churches these past few years. Our leaders have brought to the fore God's love rather than John Calvin's bitter rectitude. We live in a new world of the spirit, and although it

A friend from Singapore was attending college in Canada. Soon after writing an important exam, he saw his professor across a crowded room. Intending to ask, "Did I pass?" The student raised one eyebrow.

The teacher saw the signal and correctly understood the meaning intended. He in turn answered with a signal: forefinger and thumb together forming a circle. The meaning intended was "Right on target," or "OK, you passed."

The student reached into his memory and assigned a totally different meaning to the signal—zero, goose egg, failure!

A deeply disappointed student only learned the correct meaning at a private meeting several days later.

is not easy for us older men to accommodate ourselves to change, there is no greater exaltation than to submit to the will of God." The minister stopped, for Abner was looking at him strangely, and Thorn thought: he is a difficult, custom-ridden man and cannot understand these changes.

But Abner was thinking: Jerusha instituted these changes in Lahaina seven years ago. Without the aid of theologians or Harvard professors she found God's love. Why is this man so arrogant?

And Thorn, noticing Abner's aloofness, thought: He was excitable and opinionated even when I interviewed him at Yale. He's no better now.

Out loud, he said, "Brother Abner, when Keoki betrayed the church, why didn't you recruit better prospects? Have you no candidates?"

Abner's head felt out of balance, and he jogged himself. "The most important thing was to protect the church from another such debacle."

Thorn said, "I have brought with me two fine young Hawaiians from Honolulu. I'm going to ordain them in your church, and I would be particularly happy if you could nominate some young men of Lahaina."

"The Hawaiians here, Reverend Thorn—well, there's this man Pupali, who had four daughters, and his youngest Iliki—" Then his mind cleared and he thought: He would not understand about Iliki. . . .

To Micah [his son] he added, "When you return a minister I shall turn my church over to you." Thorn, overhearing these words, thought: He will forever regard it as his church, not God's and surely not the Hawaiians'. If the score were tallied, I suspect he has done more harm than good.

Abner thought: Brother Thorn moves about the world dispensing advice and thinks that by being in Lahaina for a few days he can detect where we have gone astray. Has he ever faced cannon, or a rioting mob of whalers? He will never know.

—James Michener, *Farm of Bitterness*, 216–17. Originally from *Hawaii*

Clearly, Abner and Thorn hold different mental models that make understanding virtually impossible. What should be done so that Thorn and Abner can create understanding between them?

Gaining access to the hidden mental models may be difficult and to some degree uncertain. Nevertheless, the attempt is crucial to effective ministry. The greatest lack in Christian communication is not the low wattage of a radio station or the lack of color on a printed page. It is the

lack of knowing other people's patterns of thought—their mental models.

▼ WHAT IS THE BIBLICAL VIEW OF MEANING?

Does proposition 3 suggest that there is no absolute meaning? No. There is absolute meaning, but it does not lie in human communication, which we are considering.

God is Absolute Meaning, pure and complete. He described himself as "I am who I am," appealing to nothing else or anyone else to explain himself. Jesus could say "I am the truth" because he is God; the total meaning of truth lies in him.

Similarly, Jesus showed us absolute meaning by breaking the great "I am who I am" into parts that we could more easily comprehend: "I am the Way . . . the Life . . . the Light . . . the Door." With each statement, he gave us a piece of absolute meaning. Then, at the close of the record of God's revealing himself to humankind, Jesus summed up by including all in himself: "I am the First and the Last." This echoes the great "I am" statement of the Old Testament, and its New Testament equivalent, "I am the Alpha and the Omega, . . . who is, and was, and who is to come, the Almighty." This is the infinite God showing finite humanity that he is the Absolute.

In him lies true meaning. For finite human beings, the difficulty lies in seeking to comprehend and express that infinity within the teacup of our experience. We can communicate only a tiny part, and we can comprehend only a tiny part. Seldom, if ever, will the parts seem to be in total agreement, simply because we cannot see the whole.

How then, can we be sure that we comprehend and communicate any part of the Absolute? It is often claimed that every religion and philosophy has a part of the truth. Agreement between these different religious philosophies should not be expected, goes the argument, so we ought to consider every bit of information as valid. It may simply lie outside our finite boundaries of understanding.

That would be correct if God had left it all to human beings to perceive and understand him. If he had remained no more visible to us than "I am who I am," every struggling grasp for fragments of information would be welcome. But God took the initiative in communication and revealed all of himself that humankind could comprehend at that point. The supreme revealing of Absolute Meaning was in Jesus Christ—God poured into the finite teacup. "Christ Jesus: Who being in very nature God . . . made himself nothing, . . . being made in human likeness" (Phil. 2:6–7).

The record of God's self-revealing is in the Bible, "the Word of God." That Word is our certainty, the standard of what is true and what is wrong. Records of the human quest to know God are not in the same category as this record of God's showing himself to humanity. Humans may have elsewhere learned part of the truth about the Absolute, but we can only know whether that part is correct by comparing it to what God himself has told us.

All claims of information about the Infinite are not of equal value, precisely because they may be nothing more than finite humans' attempt to understand something beyond their comprehension. Only that information which demonstrably comes from the Infinite, the Absolute, himself can be reliable.

But our discussion in this book is of human communication, between people. It is there our difficulties lie in sharing the knowledge God has given us in his Word. The beginning problem is our ability to comprehend. Can we ever apprehend true meaning? Yes. Our understanding will be incomplete, of course, because it is a matter of the finite grasping infinity, of the teacup holding oceans.

But understanding will grow, because the Holy Spirit is present as the Teacher. He reveals the Infinite to us, working within us, enlarging our ability to understand so that we can grasp the true nature of humanity, the world, and God. Without him as Teacher, no accurate meaning in matters of the Divine is possible.

> "No eye has seen, no ear has heard, no mind has conceived what God has prepared for those who love him"—*but God has revealed it to us by his Spirit.* The Spirit searches all things, even the deep things of God. For who among men knows the thoughts of a man except the man's spirit within him? In the same way no one knows the thoughts of God except the Spirit of God. . . . This is what we speak, not in words taught us by human wisdom but in words taught by the Spirit. . . . The man without the Spirit does not accept the things that come from the Spirit of God, for they are foolishness to him, and he cannot understand them.
>
> —1 Corinthians 2:9–14

Again, the difficulties we are addressing in this book are those that develop when we try to pass on what we understand. Always we must be alert to the danger of substituting our still-growing perception for absolute truth itself. Always we must test what we seek to communicate of God's truth against his own revelation of that truth in Scripture. And we must always be aware of the meanings and possible meanings attached by listeners to the information we share.

An awareness of the difficulties of human communication brings us to deep thankfulness for the teaching ministry of the Holy Spirit, and to dependence on him in all efforts at communicating God's Good News.

SUMMARY

*Meaning is always personal and unique to each individual. Similar meanings are held by different people, but precise meanings are personal. There is no way to transfer meaning directly from teacher to student, from employer to employee, or from preacher to congregation. Meaning is developed indirectly. The person sending a message can only give information—BITs, **B**inary **I**nformation uni**T**s. The receiver of a message assembles the BIT of that message into* a meaning, using a mental model that seems related to the new message. That mental model, which has been formed from earlier experiences, acts something like an interpreter, giving a sense (meaning) to signals that are otherwise just noises and images.

If the mental models are similar in sender and receiver, and if an adequate amount of information has been given, the meaning developed in the receiver's mind will be close to the meaning in the sender's mind.

Thus emphasis must be on the transfer of the right kind of, and enough, information from the sender to the receiver. When that is achieved, they will share similar meanings—and they have successfully communicated. Understanding is being created between the participants.

4

➤ There is no such thing as an uninteresting subject; there are only uninterested people. (G. K. Chesterton)

DID I HEAR RIGHT?

PROPOSITION 4: Communication is what is heard, not only what is said.

• George was an Indian Christian who moved from his home in the south of India, where he had many Christian friends and relatives. He went to a northern Indian city with perhaps five or ten Christians among a half-million people. Month after month he tried to interest his newly chosen neighbors in Jesus Christ. George told of Christ's atoning death, of the new life all who believed in him could receive. But there was no response.

So George decided that he should present the gospel as simply as possible. He would select just one point, then stress that until it was understood. Only then would he move on to another point of teaching. His beginning point would be the new birth.

He invited some of his new friends for a Bible study. Being interested in religion, they came gladly, and George taught from John 3, "You must be born again." He taught, that is, until he was interrupted by a loud objection from a Hindu friend: "That's exactly the trouble! You Christians teach us what we already know. We know we must be born again, and we don't want that. We want to be freed from being born again, and again, and again. You are only telling us what we already know and fear."

George was teaching of a new life that was eternal. His friend heard condemnation—that he was doomed to live on earth over and over again, reincarnated in different forms.

• I was walking on the quiet streets of a university town with a friend who did not understand the simplicity of trusting Christ, despite his fine career as a professor. As we passed a church that displayed the familiar sign "Jesus Saves," he looked at it and remarked, "Oh, that reminds me. I must open a savings account at the bank."

The message given by the sign was not at all the message "heard" by at least one person in the intended audience.

• A concerned Christian woman regularly spent Saturday afternoons in a shopping mall giving well-chosen tracts to passersby. She courteously gave one to a young man with the words, "Do you know the way of salvation?" He stopped, thought a moment, then replied, "No, I don't. I'm new here, too. I don't know the streets yet."

These three incidents illustrate a central problem in communication: What is heard is not necessarily what was said. Gross misunderstandings not only are possible, but indeed happen regularly, even within one culture, one community, or one family. Between cultures, such misunderstandings are the central problem.

How can I teach the truth so that it will be understood by the hearers? Missionary work becomes so inefficient when this question is ignored that it is almost pointless. If we can never be sure that the truth is heard, how can cross-cultural mission ever be accomplished?

Roland Allen lists "understandable teaching" as the first rule in founding churches following the apostle Paul's methods. "All teaching to be permanent must be intelligible and so capable of being grasped and understood that those who have once received it can retain it, use it, and hand it on" (*The Compulsion of the Spirit*, 10). Allen suggests that how well something is understood can be seen quite readily. "The test of all teaching is practice. Nothing should be taught which cannot be so grasped and used."

If a missionary sees no evidence of spontaneous witnessing and church growth, it may well be that the message has not been understood. If what is said cannot be shared with others and used daily in living the Christian life, communication is not complete.

What can be done to ensure that intended meaning is the same as received meaning? We are often perplexed at confusion over meanings that seem perfectly obvious to

One day, after finishing a glass of water, I asked my four-year-old son if he would "throw my empty glass in the kitchen sink." He eagerly grasped the glass, carefully so as not to drop it, and set off on his task. I completely forgot what he was doing until the sound of breaking glass pierced the silence. Tommy had thrown the glass into the sink, where it shattered into pieces.

I know what I meant, but he heard something completely different. I intended for him to place the glass in the sink, but used an idiom to say so. He heard me actually say to throw the glass. My words did not carry the meaning intended.

—Tom Sager

us. "How then," we ask, "can I make myself clear? I may *say* the right things, but is the right thing *heard?*"

Proposition 4 shifts the focus of communication from the speaker to the speaker *and* listener. There is a joint responsibility for effective communication; the listener and speaker share in the process of developing understanding. The speaker should never simply blame the hearer if the message is not understood. Nor should the hearer blame the speaker. Both must enter into the process of communication remembering the different things that can affect meaning. Development of meaning is a mutual effort.

Communication is a transaction in which there is simultaneous giving and receiving. The message is modified even as it is being communicated.

When one has a need, one goes into the marketplace to buy a product, hire a worker, or enter into an agreement; in other words, one meets the need through a transaction. Similarly, communication is used to meet a need. The need may be for information, understanding of a problem, or social acceptance. A question is asked; it is answered by someone who wishes to be helpful, to gain prestige by being knowledgeable, or perhaps to build a friendship. The original questioner's need for information is satisfied, and the answer also gives the status of "friendly" or "helpful" to the one who answered. A transaction has taken place; both parties have gained at least part of what they wanted.

Other transactions probably will follow; when needs are met in communicating with particular people or groups, understanding and friendship steadily develops. The circle of communication develops into a steadily rising spiral, or helix, as F. X. V. Dance has described it.

Let's expand the communication model given in the last chapter to show the transactional nature of communication. We will start the model with the sending of a signal. The signal is chosen according to the initiator's need, shaped by the environment, psychological needs, experience, and the referent in the initiator's mind.

In this model that signal is perceived by the responder and interpreted according to the responder's idea of the referent, environment, experience, and needs. These factors, plus the context in which the signal is placed, are essential clues needed to get behind the visible—the veil of flesh—and into someone's mind, as it were. A meaning is assigned to the signal, and a signal is

A village health worker in East Africa stressed the importance of community hygiene. To emphasize why latrines and garbage must be covered, he used a large plastic model of a fly. He explained how flies transmit disease and warned the people not to let them crawl on food and around their children's faces.

After his presentation, he wisely asked for feedback from the people, to be sure they understood what he had intended. One elder responded, "Oh yes, I well understand how your fly would be very bad and could bring sickness. But our flies are good. They are very small."
—Diane Walker

then sent in response to the first signal from the sender. The transaction proceeds until meanings are developed, meanings that are at least thought to be shared.

Information can be shared externally only through signals, as diagramed below.

This process continues, with increased and different information being sent between the participants, until the transaction is complete—that is, until the immediate needs of both the sender and the receiver are satisfied or the process is interrupted by some outside event.

The message is not a gift-wrapped package handed to a recipient. It is fully developed only during the transaction. The core content usually remains, but the way in which it is communicated changes. Content considered nonessential may be modified as the transaction develops between participants.

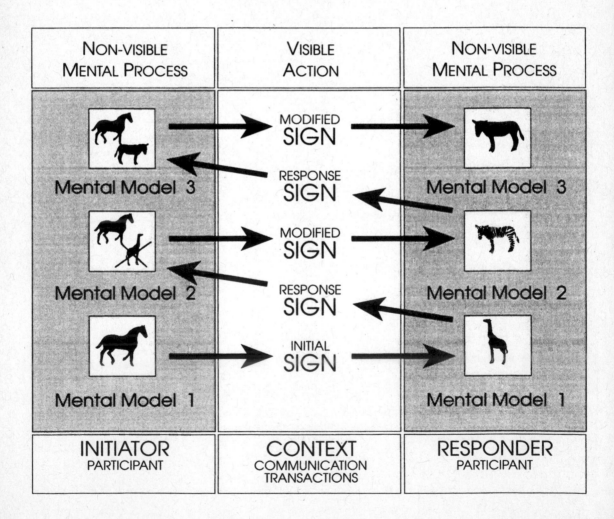

This may be seen more readily when one thinks of how the same sermon or lecture seems different when given to different audiences. Even though the same notes are used, it comes across differently. Some audiences, speakers comment, seem indifferent or sleepy. Other groups are so responsive that the speaker develops extra confidence and enthusiasm. Actors and musicians speak of some audiences as "dead," others as so "alive" that maximum artistry is virtually pulled out of the performers. In explaining why some performances are better than others, the performer credits the audience. Some churches seem regularly to have excellent preaching and become known for the quality of their Bible teaching; is it the preachers or a listening, responsive congregation that makes the difference?

It is probably a combination of both.

Communication can be compared to shopping in a store. As you walk down rows of shelves filled with flour, sugar, soap, bread, crackers, and canned goods, each item demands your attention. Some are wrapped in brightly printed paper; others are in boxes made to look big and necessary for your home. The delicious smells of bread stimulate your hunger. Skill, artistry, and knowledge of the intended buyer are used to gain attention and start a transaction. How does the shopper choose? You choose those that meet a need you have. You look at the shelves and read the labels; another way to say it is that you "listen." Until you "listen," no selection can be made; the transaction cannot be completed.

A similar thing happens when worshiping in church, when turning on the television, or when meeting a friend. Even when the message is well presented, the production is superb, or your friend is excited to tell you some news, no communication happens until you decide to listen. Listening is an essential part of communication.

Articulate preachers or teachers are often called "good communicators." But are they? Not necessarily. They may be good transmitters, able to handle part of the communication transaction but not the equally important listening and responding part. If preachers never listen, how will they know what to say and how to say it?

Talking, speaking, writing, or any other way by which signals are sent is only *a part of communication*. Incomplete communication attempts are common in every culture, even in the close relationship of marriage, as seen in the following example.

The signs used are clues available for communicators to use in "getting inside" someone else's mind. The most significant parts of communication can only be inferred and consequently are only partially and often inaccurately understood. Perceiving the mental models is the core challenge in any communication transaction, especially so in cross-cultural involvement.

The key points for improving cross-cultural communication can be quickly stated: (1) understand the mental models held in communicators' minds, (2) learn the significance of all signs used, and (3) learn about the contexts of communication.

Carrying out these three things is far more difficult than listing them. Nevertheless, these are the broad areas of attack in reducing the problems of communication between members of differing cultures.

Preachers may be great at talking . . . but how well are they communicating?

After a few preliminary remarks, Paul threw up his hands. "I've had it! I can't go on this way any longer. She never listens to me!"

Lois countered, "He thinks I never listen to him! Well, I'll tell you something; he never, never listens to me!" [A description of the resulting argument follows.]

From the beginning, they had engaged in verbal warfare. They were excellent communicators—articulate, analytical, and precise—but poor conversationalists.

Lois knew what she wanted from Paul and told him so, but he never heard the message. Paul knew what he wanted from Lois and told her so, but she never heard the message, either.

If communication were the key to marriage, this couple should have had all the answers. But communication is not the key to marriage. By definition, communication is basically one-sided. It is the act of sending a message . . . and expecting obedience.

—Craig Massey, "Communication
Is Not the Key to Marriage," 61

Massey's article not only shows the importance of listening, but also exemplifies a common confusion of *communication* with *transmission*. Transmission is only one side of the picture. It is only a small "blip" in the total process by which understanding is created.

Actually, there seems to have been no communication between Paul and Lois. They were not "excellent" communicators, but only caricatures of communicators. Each only wanted the other to listen, yet without listening there could never be a completed circle of understanding. Speaking and listening are like a nut and bolt; neither is much good for holding a machine together without the other.

When attempted communication never goes beyond sending signals, misunderstanding will usually be the result.

Because communication consists of what is *heard* as well as what is *said*, considerable attention should be given

PEANUTS

to the simple act of listening. There are thousands of study courses on how to speak, how to write, how to produce radio or television programs, how to preach, how to use art, and other ways to transmit information. But rarely does any kind of school teach how to listen, and listening is *half* of the communication process. For example, in 1980 it was reported that there was only one full-time teacher of listening in American educational institutions (at Lane Community College in Eugene, Oregon).

That teacher explains how she came to teach listening even though her training was in theater and broadcast arts:

> We talk a lot and we're taught to talk. We're taught to read and to write. And yet we spend more of our communication day in "listening" than in talking, reading or writing. Forty-five percent . . . is spent in listening, or at least trying to listen. Research shows us that if we listen to a 10-minute talk, immediately following, we will retain about 50 percent of it. Within 24 hours, the rate of retention goes down to less than 25 percent.
>
> The reason for this is that we are never taught the skills of listening. When we talk, we talk about 125 words a minute, and the average person's brain operates at about 800 words a minute. So the brain processes the words coming in as if they are coming in slow motion. So the brain gets bored and wanders off.
>
> We don't take the time to listen through another person. We are a nation of interrupters. . . . We form what we want to say while we're pretending to listen to the other person.
>
> It's popular now to learn how to listen. But it's not new; it goes back to biblical times. Christ talked about listening to learn.

> —Dan Sellard, "Teaching
> Listening"

If Lois and Paul, introduced above, had learned to listen, their marriage would certainly have been different. The listening teacher reminisces, "I had one student who said, 'I know that this isn't a goal of this class but I want you to know this class saved my marriage.'"

The student added, "We learned about the techniques of listening to boring material and boring people. I said to myself, 'Who could be more boring than my wife? All right, I'm going to listen to her. . . .' The strangest thing happened—she actually was interesting."

Once it was obvious that he was listening, the student's wife began to relate things that she had never told

For Christian communicators, some simple ways to learn whether understanding is being developed can help the communication transaction, especially when cultural differences are involved.

1. Allow several minutes at the beginning of a teaching time for group members to summarize what they already know about the subject.

2. Encourage questions about the topic before the formal teaching begins. What do the students wish to know? What is the importance to them of what you wish to teach? Never dismiss a question as trivial or pointless; what is spoken may give clues to what lies unspoken in the mind.

3. Sharing news and interesting experiences among group members develops a sense of involvement. It also gives the teacher-missionary-pastor a better idea of how much is understood and applied, making it easier to shape the message specifically for that group.

4. Allow time for questions after a message or teaching, perhaps during a fellowship time following the more formal session.

5. Do not teach truth without creating an opportunity for response, for acting on what is taught. Even the most relevant, contextualized message is not fully "heard" until the listener completes the communication transaction by acting out a response.

6. Continue the communication process by conversing with listeners *about the topic* after the meeting—perhaps the next day, the next week, or even during the next month.

him before. "All of a sudden," the student marveled, "we were like newlyweds."

Medical science has shown the importance God places on listening. Doctors report that hearing is usually the last sense to be lost in a coma and at death. The Designer of humankind made us for listening, not merely talking. A common jest carries an important message: "God wants us to listen twice as much as we talk. He gave us two ears and only one mouth." How can we improve listening, the receiving part of a transaction?

The most important thing is simply to pay attention. Instead of half-listening while your mind is pursuing other thoughts, focus on the words, trying to identify the purpose of the message and discerning the context from which the message comes.

Hold your immediate reactions until you are reasonably sure that you have understood these basic parts of the message. If you are in a conference, make brief notes that summarize the content, its background, and your first reactions. Better to put those reactions quietly on paper than speak prematurely; quick responses may only show your shallow grasp of what is happening.

Listen. Listen patiently, and attempt to experience what the other person is transmitting. Gladys Hunt writes, "No basic communication occurs until we listen so sympathetically and acceptingly that we hear more than words, we feel the 'why' behind the verbal communication. . . . We need to hear the other person out, encouraging him to tell it like he sees and feels it is. When we are threatened by uncomfortable ideas, we must not interrupt to argue, but continue listening until he is finished. . . . Only then will adequate perception begin" (*Listen to Me!* 5–6).

Attempting to experience, even partially, what others experience is emotionally demanding. We are forced

ANDY CAPP

to draw on our own experiences to find parallels, and sometimes those personal memories are painful; sometimes, however, they are uplifting and joyful. Either way, seeking to experience what others experience requires that we draw on both our knowledge and our store of emotion. There is a price in every transaction; a communication transaction carries mental and emotional costs.

Mohandas K. Gandhi, known by hundreds of millions as "Mahatma"—the Great Soul—was born in India and lived there until as a young man he went to Great Britain to study law. He then spent twenty years in South Africa, struggling against the government's racist policies. During those years, he visited India and was never out of touch with Indian people. But when he finally returned to live in his homeland, a leader of the Indian efforts for independence commanded him to spend the first year in India "with his ears open but his mouth shut." Gandhi had come to help India toward independence; he was already famous for his victories in South Africa. Further, he was Indian. Even so, his first important task was to *listen* (see Louis Fischer, *The Life of Mahatma Gandhi*).

> Experiencing the other side is the heart of dialogue.
> —Martin Buber

How to listen and hear has been well summarized in David Augsburger's "Ten Commandments for Hearing."

1. I will first understand, then judge. I will suspend judgment, postpone evaluation, defer closure until the other feels heard.

2. I will not fill in the gaps with my ideas. I will listen to you, not to my improvements, my embellishments or my supporting data.

3. I will not assume that the intent in you and the impact on me are one and the same. I will not infer that you said what I heard, think as I thought, meant what I felt.

4. I will attend to your words, your feelings, your meanings. I will not ramble off, race ahead, or drop off asleep.

5. I will listen to your whole message, even if I would rather not hear it, see it, consider it.

6. I will avoid wishful hearing. I will neither use my ears to hear what the heart wants to hear, nor the mind to filter what the head will heed.

7. I will test both your meanings and my meanings until they meet. The content of your words is yours. I want to discover it. The word is the package, the meaning is the contents.

8. I will listen to your full statement without using your time to polish my response or prepare my arguments.

73

9. I will not be afraid to listen, to learn, to change, to grow. The listener is not inferior, the speaker superior; each enriches the other.

10. I will respect your right to be equally heard; I will claim my right to be equally heard.

—David Augsburger, *Caring Enough to Hear*

Even when we determine to listen well, some messages are easier to listen to than others. Some preachers keep our attention; others seem to be speaking of things that are completely unreal. Our attention wanders to something that is more personal and immediate. There are teachers who might as well be speaking to an empty room, for they have no real listeners. Political leaders, family members, even our chosen friends—all of us often suffer from inability to get people to listen and understand.

▼ HELPING PEOPLE LISTEN TO YOU

There are ways to give messages that help people listen. Remembering some basics in giving a message will help the transaction with intended receivers.

1. Be aware of their world. Listening is helped when the speaker is aware of the needs, viewpoints, and experiences of those with whom he or she is communicating. This awareness is a matter both of avoiding unnecessary antagonisms and of building on existing knowledge to increase and enrich understanding. A principle that is considered basic to sound pedagogy is "Proceed from the known to the unknown." To do that, you must know your audience.

2. Use words and signals accurately. The way you use words and other signals matters. By common agreement, words have general meanings within a society. That society may be as small as a family or group of friends, or it may be as large as all speakers of a language. Through usage, members have come to understand, for example, that *water* refers to a particular liquid, that *anger* refers to a cluster of attitudes and actions, and that *beautiful* is something pleasing to the senses. Even though the precise meaning varies with each person within a society, there is broad overlap in understandings of the meaning of any given word. These broad meanings must be known if the right word is to be chosen for building a particular meaning in another person.

Several of the propositions in this book deal directly with effective presentation: 5, 7, 9, 12, 14, 20, and 23. Several others indirectly give a framework within which more effective presentations can be made.

3. Use the right word. Seldom will just any word do; the right word must be chosen to stimulate the right thought. "You can't think well if you can't use the language well," explain teachers of rhetoric. Neither can you help others to think well if you cannot speak precisely—that is, use words that accurately create the meaning you intend.

Sloppy speech or writing, full of "You know . . . you know . . ." or "I mean—OK?" creates only sloppy understanding. With one exception. It often gives a clear understanding that the mind behind the words is empty of well-formed opinions but full of half-shaped thoughts and vague impressions. Seldom is that the understanding that a communicator desires to give.

4. The context is part of communication. The effective communicator pays attention to the context in which communication is happening. A simple example is the statement "It is cold in this room." Is this being said in a living room where family members are talking together? Or inside a food storage plant where the temperature is deliberately kept at near freezing level? Perhaps it is said in an air-conditioned room when the outside temperature is over 100 degrees Fahrenheit. The context must be known before the sentence can be correctly understood.

Words and conversations appropriate at a sporting event are not the same ones suitable for a meeting between teachers and the parents of the children they teach. When inappropriate words are used, misunderstanding is the result. Context not only helps to interpret words or signals already given, but also guides in the selection of words and signals to be used. Scholarly language is necessary in a seminary paper discussing theological issues. But in the context of a Saturday-morning men's Bible study breakfast, the same language would probably stop communication.

Written communication must be carefully interpreted—another kind of listening. We lean heavily on words and grammar in understanding the intended meaning of Scripture, for example, as well as the literary context. Attention must also be given to the cultural context to avoid forcing a meaning that comes from our own experience.

Let us assume that these and other important points are all remembered and used. The communication transaction proceeds well. Speaking is done with the listener in mind. Listening is done with careful attention to the

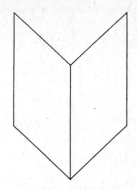

Are you looking at the back of a book—or at an open book with blank pages? Look again, carefully. What are you seeing?

What you "see" depends largely on what you expect to see. And that depends on what you are told, on your previous experiences, and your present needs.

Words are often so powerful that they prepare people to hear or see something that is not really there, or something that is quite different from what they think they are hearing or seeing.

Because the words *used* and *secondhand* carry the idea of "not as good," an advertisement contains a phrase that helps the audience *hear* that "this is good quality." The listening is changed through the use of different word-signals.

When I gained enough language proficiency to begin verbally communicating the Gospel, I would often speak of Christ in the same manner as I might in my own culture. I would very casually steer the conversation to spiritual things and in a low-key manner begin to outline the plan of salvation.

However, over a period of time I realized I was not being "heard." I had overlooked important cultural practices in discussing religious matters. My mild-mannered way of speaking of religious matters and my readiness to make concessions in a discussion signaled to my listeners that I really did not believe strongly in the things I was saying. Anything which is true about God, they felt, must be forcefully and dogmatically stated.

—Paul Steven

speaker. Understanding is increased. Does that mean that agreement has been gained? No. *Increasing understanding may increase disagreement.* Successful communication is not the same thing as agreement. Communication may be considered successful in some situations when disagreement is sharp and clear. Communication that brings acceptance of every idea without clear-eyed assessment of each is not successful: Genuine understanding has not been gained.

Creating understanding, changing attitudes, and developing relationships require the full transaction of communication—listening to hear correctly, speaking to the communication partner's world of experience. Speaking, or any kind of transmission, must be done with the listener in mind. And listening must give careful attention to the speaker's purpose and experience. The saying and the hearing are equally important. Communication is what is heard, not only what is said.

▼ BIBLICAL PERSPECTIVES ON HEARING

"He doesn't *listen* to me! Before he knows what my problem really is, he has a Bible verse!" The young Christian man was frustrated. "But he hasn't listened, so how does he know what to tell me."

The young man is still deeply troubled by traumatic experiences in his childhood. He wants help but is not getting much, despite the zeal of a Christian brother who leads him in Bible studies. Prepackaged answers are abundant; they seem biblically correct. But they are not helping.

Many keen Christians are so quick to tell the Good News that they forget that listening is *at least* half of proclamation. Proclamation begins by listening to God, to know him and to understand his message. Ezekiel's stunning vision of God's presence overwhelmed his senses: "When I saw it, I fell facedown, and I heard the voice of one speaking. . . . And he said to me, 'Son of man, listen carefully and take to heart all the words I speak to you'" (Ezek. 1:28; 3:10).

Ezekiel's prophetic speaking began with listening. "At the end of seven days the word of the LORD came to me: 'Son of man, I have made you a watchman for the house of Israel; so hear the word I speak and give them warning from me'" (Ezek. 2:16–17). His ministry to Israel rested on his ability to listen.

Repeatedly throughout the Old Testament, God's people are commanded to hear, to hear the word of the Lord. To this day, the Jewish people are reminded in their synagogues, "Hear, O Israel. . . ." To each of the seven churches in Revelation, the same command is solemnly repeated: "He who has an ear, let him hear what the Spirit says to the churches" (Rev. 2:7, 11, 17, 29; 3:6, 13, 22). The Christian's ability to live in obedience to God rests on listening to God.

The Christian's life with God is strengthened by talking *with* people to share the message received from God's Word. How do we know whether we are sharing effectively? How do we know whether the message is being understood, or whether we need to use different words and ways to make it more understandable? Only by listening, to learn what is being heard. Idols are scornfully described in Scripture as having ears, but unable to hear— unable to listen (Pss. 115:6; 135:17). Unfortunately, Christian speakers, would-be communicators, sometimes behave like idols.

If there is no listening, what is the point of speaking? Our gatherings would soon become nothing but noise— everyone speaking at once, and no new ideas gained because we would be listening only to ourselves. We come perilously close to such anarchy at times. Eager to speak our own words, we fail to listen carefully to others.

When someone was consecrated for the Aaronic priesthood, an atoning sacrifice was offered to cover his sin. Blood from the sacrifice was applied specifically to the ear, the thumb, and the great toe. Thus a special cleansing was applied to the organs of listening in those singled out for ministry, but interestingly, the organ of speech did not receive such cleansing (Exod. 29, particularly verse 30).

When differences of accent, language, and culture make listening difficult, we too often hide behind "simple proclamation"— that is, just telling the facts of the gospel. This mind-set leads to quick mission trips during which "gospel teams" sing, pass out tracts, do a rapid survey, hold evangelistic mass meetings, or perform some other specialty.

God has been listened to, and the message to be proclaimed is understood. But the people are treated as blank paper on which the message is to be inscribed. There is seldom any listening to learn what is already be-

77

lieved and what is being understood from the new proclamation.

The paper is not blank. The new message is placed on top of messages already heard and believed. Even so, sometimes it is understood. At other times, the new message is hopelessly confused with the old, so that there can be no comprehension of Jesus Christ. We must sanctify our ears—*listen*—to learn how to proclaim the message of Christ clearly and to discern how that message is being heard.

When we listen, we know when it is necessary to express the same truth in different ways. God himself is concerned about his audience; in his Word, different words are used for salvation for different audiences: the new birth, redemption, deliverance, atonement, ransom, reconciliation. The different words express various aspects of the same truth so that it can be more clearly understood by different hearers. The truth of salvation is not changed; only the expression in different cultural settings is changed.

Over the history of God's self-revelation, the words and illustrations of truth change from nomadic to agricultural to urban and cosmopolitan. They change as the context within which God is showing his ways changes. Abraham, living a nomadic lifestyle, is succeeded by his descendants living in agricultural Egypt. A landless tribe becomes a conquering people who settle in towns, then a sophisticated nation of farmers, traders, and skilled craftsmen. Then they become a conquered people, and God's truth is expressed through the dominant Greek and Roman cultures. There are many changes in audience, and with each change there is a change in the words, examples, and ways of telling truth. The prophets of God spoke so that their audiences could hear—and understand.

Effective communication requires listening, not simply fine speaking and excellent content. Influential speakers give primary attention to what the listeners are hearing from their words. They follow the example of Paul in shaping the Good News to the specific audience. Note Paul's emphases in Damascus (Acts 9) and Pisidian Antioch (Acts 13) compared with those in Lystra (Acts 14); or compare his approach in Thessalonica, Berea, and Athens (Acts 17) with that used in Jerusalem (Acts 22). When he was arrested and held at Caesarea, Paul spoke to two governors and a king (Acts 24–26). In each of his three defenses, there was a different emphasis, though the centrality of Jesus and his Way remained. Paul did not change content, but he did distinctly change the emphasis according to the specific person he was addressing.

Preachers less sure of their message focus on techniques rather than on the audience. Paul knew Scripture thoroughly; he knew by experience the power of the Holy Spirit and the living Jesus Christ. Consequently, he was so confident of the message that he could give careful attention to the audience, building bridges of understanding. When rejection of the message came, it was not because of failure to understand. It was usually because the hearers understood too well the consequences of believing; change of lifestyle or loss of advantage and position.

Stressing the obligation of the speaker does not excuse the listeners from responsibility for adequate response. In Galatia, the problem was not in the preacher or the message given, but in the hearers. Paul himself was the preacher, in the power and authority of the risen Christ. The message was only of Christ, telling of the salvation he brings. Yet the Galatians distorted the message so greatly that Paul said they were turning away from God and following "a different way to heaven which really doesn't go to heaven at all" (Gal. 1:6–7 LB).

Heavy responsibility indeed rests on messengers to speak so that their message is comprehensible and relevant to the hearers. But responsibility for the final impact of the message rests equally with the hearers. The most effective messenger cannot force anyone to hear, to remember, or to act on the message. For the message to have effect, the willingness of the hearer is equal in importance to the relevance of the messenger's proclamation.

> Hear my words, you wise men;
> listen to me, you men of learning.
> For the ear tests words
> as the tongue tastes food.
> Let us discern for ourselves what is right;
> let us learn together what is good. . . .
> If they obey and serve him,
> they will spend the rest of their days in prosperity
> and their years in contentment.
> But if they do not listen,
> they will perish by the sword
> and die without knowledge.
> —Job 34:1–4; 36:11–12

SUMMARY

One of the most familiar statements in any argument is "What I said was . . ." along with the reply, "Well, this is what I heard. . . ." Rarely do the two sound like the same thing.

Only together can male and female form life, and only when speaking and hearing are seen as equal parts of communication can understanding be formed. Good communication requires the ability to hear as well as the ability to speak.

Communication is a transaction during which understandings are shared and developed. The exchange involved in this transaction is listening and speaking; one party listens, another speaks, and then a response reverses the flow. Through this reciprocity, understanding, but not necessarily agreement, is developed.

Good speaking is a matter not simply of pleasant words, but instead, of words and symbols chosen so that the hearer will develop the intended meaning. Senders must be aware that many filters always exist between themselves and their hearers—experience, culture, mood, personal needs, physical environment. Even with the best of intentions and the greatest of care, the message heard will seldom be the same as the message spoken.

▼ BIBLIOGRAPHY: PROPOSITIONS 1–4, THE FUNDAMENTALS

COMMUNICATION THEORY

The distinctions traditionally made between interpersonal, small-group, mass, and intercultural (or cross-cultural) communication are increasingly blurred. Contemporary writings are stressing the common process of communication in various settings, even while identifying variations. The readings in *Handbook of Communication Science* will especially make this clear.

Aldrich, Joseph C. *Life-Style Evangelism*. Portland, Oreg.: Multnomah, 1981.

Barnlund, Dean. "A Transactional Model of Communication." In *Foundation of Communication Theory*. Edited by Kenneth Soreno and C. David Mortenson. New York: Harper & Row, 1970.

Brewster, E. Thomas, and Elizabeth S. Brewster. "Bonding and the Missionary Task." In *Perspectives on the World Christian Movement*. Edited by Ralph Winter and Steve Hawthorne. Pasadena, Calif.: William Carey Library, 1981.

Chaffee, Steven H., and Charles R. Berger. "What Communication Scientists Do." In *Handbook of Communication Science*. Edited by Charles R. Berger and Steven H. Chaffee. Newbury Park, Calif.: Sage, 1987.

Delia, Jesse G. "Communication Research: A History." In *Handbook of Communication Science*. Edited by Charles R. Berger and Steven H. Chaffee. Newbury Park, Calif.: Sage, 1987.

Kincaid, D. Lawrence, ed. *Communication Theory: Eastern and Western Perspectives*. San Diego: Academic Press, 1987.

Littlejohn, Stephen W. *Theories of Human Communication*. 3d ed. Belmont, Calif.: Wadsworth, 1989.

Loewen, Jacob A. "Self-Exposure: Bridge to Fellowship." In *Culture and Human Values: Christian Intervention in Anthropological Perspective*. Edited by William A. Smalley. South Pasadena, Calif.: William Carey Library, 1975.

Wenburg, John R., and William W. Wilmot. *The Personal Communication Process*. New York: John Wiley & Sons, 1973.

LISTENING AND UNDERSTANDING

A few fine books on listening, how to do it, and its values are suggested here. Many good libraries contain workbooks and course outlines designed to help one to improve listening skills or to teach others to do so.

Augsburger, David. *Caring Enough to Hear*. Ventura, Calif.: Regal, 1982.

Barbara, Dominick A. *How to Make People Listen to You*. Springfield, Ill.: Charles C. Thomas, 1971.

Tournier, Paul. *A Listening Ear*. Minneapolis: Augsburg, 1987.

Weaver, Carl H. *Human Listening*. Indianapolis: Bobbs-Merrill, 1972.

SPEAKING AND WRITING FOR UNDERSTANDING

Many useful books have been written on the skills of speaking, writing, and other kinds of transmission. Some helpful material on communicating for easier understanding is included in Weaver (above). A brief list of books on improving written communication is given here.

Bernstein, Theodore. *Watch Your Language!* New York: Great Neck, 1958.

Horton, Susan R. *Thinking Is Writing*. Baltimore: Johns Hopkins University Press, 1982.

Nichols, Sue. *Words on Target: For Better Christian Communication*. Richmond, Va.: John Knox, 1970.

Wilson, Ron. *Multimedia Handbook for the Church*. Elgin, Ill.: David C. Cook, 1975.

➤ I really don't know where I'm going. But I'm trying hard.

➤ God will guide me; there's no need for setting objectives.

➤ He who has no target is sure to hit it.

KNOWING WHAT YOU ARE DOING

PROPOSITION 5: Clarification of goals increases the possibility of effective communication.

Walking through a forest on a dark, rainy night is awkward, difficult, and at times even dangerous. Bushes cling to your coat; treacherous tree roots can make you stumble. Every step is taken carefully, because your eyes can provide very little warning of boulders, holes, or tree branches. It is with great relief that you break out of the forest into a clearing where you can at least see faintly.

Such a dark, gloomy walk is no worse than plunging into communication without a sense of where you are going. You attain direction by knowing what you are trying to achieve. Without that direction there are thickets of confusion, and you stumble over every obstacle. Soon the only thing you really want is to break into a clearing—away from the demands of trying to communicate through differences.

Direction in ministry comes from goals, from knowing what it is you are trying to accomplish. The Ubangi evangelist Pelendo demonstrated the effectiveness that comes from knowing clearly what is to be done. One incident in his ministry illustrates how he recognized a need, then prayed and challenged his people with the clear goal of bringing them into a full relationship with God in Jesus Christ.

Scanning his audience he was not pleased with what he saw. The group was made up mainly of school boys. There were a few women in attendance and two men. That was all. He spoke briefly to the group, saying nothing of the thought going through his mind. . . .

Pelendo would talk to God about the situation here at Kelo village.

"God of heaven, God of Abraham, Isaac and Jacob, hear me," he prayed. "Has not your Word been preached many times in this village? Men have come to listen, but they have not believed. If they had believed they would surely have been there to hear your Word this morning.

"O God, how long are we to sit here and preach surrounded by all these fetishes and altars in this village? How can people really believe in the power of your Word when they are still slaves in the chains of Satan? Show me, oh God, how to reach these village elders with the gospel that will make them free from this bondage."

In his prayer, Pelendo clearly stated his goal: that the people would be free to believe and follow Christ. He knew what was necessary and prayed with that specific objective in mind.

The old preacher sat a long time with bowed head, praying. . . . When he stood to his feet he knew what he was going to do. He would go to the house where Wangbia, the missionary, was staying and tell him about it. . . .

"Let's not beat any drums or gather the people together to preach to them" [explained Pelendo to the missionary]. "This evening we'll just call the old men together and talk to them about their magical practices. If it is really God who has sent us, He'll help us get rid of these things of Satan. . . ."

This was a part of the spiritual battle and only by God's help would they know how to proceed.

Pelendo asked the village chief to call the elders together so they could talk together about what they believed, and what Pelendo believed. The elders came, listened and spoke carefully. When Pelendo began to speak, they listened intently.

"Can anyone tell me the reason for that vine? Did your ancestors plant such things by their houses?"

It took some time before an old man replied, "Our ancestors never planted anything like that, but we found out from the Ngbaka people that such a vine was strong magic against witches. . . ."

"And that," asked Pelendo, pointing his tongue in the direction of a row of stunted cacti.

"No," came the reply again, "our ancestors didn't have that either. We found out about that from the Furu tribe. Our ancestors had only two things that they used. . . . We really don't know the meaning of all the plants and sticks and fetishes we have around our houses today."

"And yet you keep these things in your village and trust in them? . . . You obeyed Satan and he has made you his slaves. You are slaves of fear. If you are to be free you will have to tear all these things down and remove all the magic and fetishes hidden in your houses. Only then will you be able to really believe in God."

—Alpha E. Anderson, *Pelendo*, 136–39

The elders were afraid to touch the objects. "If we did that, then everyone in the village would surely die," worried the leading elder. But Pelendo waited and allowed time for discussion. For two days the elders debated; then they made the decision to tear down all the objects. Pelendo would gather them and burn them.

Everything was heaped together and burned. "Soon the whole heap had been reduced to ashes, and no harm had come to a single soul! . . . It was true, then, what Pelendo had been saying all along. . . . Now they stood ready to become free men in Christ Jesus. Many believed in Pelendo's God that day."

News spread quickly into every village for miles around. People came from other villages asking him "to come and help them get rid of their magic."

Pelendo had a clear goal—to see the villagers throughout his area following Jesus.

There were specific objectives that needed to be reached along the way, such as removal of trust in magic. He understood those steps, prayed, and worked toward them. The results were an outstanding response to the gospel and many villages turning to Christ.

▼ GOALS CLARIFY OUR WORK

It is not too difficult to state broad goals: "to preach Christ," "to evangelize and build the church." But how can you know what you should be doing daily or even weekly? How do you leave aside urgent but peripheral tasks? How can you know which are, in fact, peripheral—those urgent and interesting tasks that so often lead nowhere?

VAGUE GOALS lead to
VAGUE METHODS and
VAGUE SUCCESS

When we fail to set goals for communication, we run the risk of simply responding to vague desires, of reacting to immediate pressures. We can easily confuse these aimless promptings with guidance: "I *feel* the Spirit is guiding

We knew our church had to be "different." We wanted to be attractive to unbelievers without compromising the Gospel. So we asked God for a specific mission that would be uniquely ours for this moment in time, for this community.

We decided that our unique mission is to train parents to equip their children with the good news of Jesus Christ. This simple statement (1) focuses the church on a specific need in the community, (2) utilizes the strength of our congregation, and (3) guides all major programming.

—Linden Kirby

me to do this. . . ." Failing to set goals makes it very difficult to sort out personal desires from divine guidance. Goals are essential. They are as a rudder to a ship or as a path to a person walking through the bush.

In the absence of clearly stated goals and objectives, there is no way to know which things can and even should be left undone. Neither is there a way to know when one has fulfilled the reason for doing a particular thing.

▼ OBJECTIVES SHOW US HOW TO REACH OUR GOALS

All Christian workers begin with very high ideals, but we need objectives to help bring daily tasks into harmony with those ideals and then to achieve them. Intercultural workers especially can become so baffled by culture stress that each day is a struggle. Objectives can lift us out of confused uncertainty by helping us see what to do *next*, not just in the long term.

Goals tell us where we need to go; objectives show the steps to be completed on the way to the goal. The goal of a Bible school in Zimbabwe, for example, was to stimulate revival in the churches of its denomination. That statement gave a very general sense of direction. What specific things needed to be done to prepare the way for revival? Objectives were developed that represented steps toward revival.

One objective stated that the school would maintain regular communication with all its graduates. Yet even this more specific objective had to be broken down into smaller components:

1. Every three months an inspirational and informative letter would be sent to all graduates.

2. Personal letters would be written to each graduate at least twice yearly by staff members.

3. A personal visit by the staff to each graduate would be made at least once each year. Return visits, with graduates as guests in staff members' homes, were to be encouraged.

4. An annual three-day ministry-life conference would be held for graduates only. Matters such as how to do visitation, beginning and leading home Bible studies, church administration, music in the life of the church, and church financial records would receive major emphasis in the conferences.

Goals are sometimes called objectives, and vice versa. Which is correct?

In the field of education, goals are the larger direction-setting statements and objectives the steps needed to accomplish a goal. The usage in business is just the reverse.

Either usage is right, but one pattern should be used consistently in an organization to avoid confusion. In *Creating Understanding*, the educational usage is followed.

Setting specific goals helps avoid, or overcome, an often hidden problem—*goal discrepancy*.

Two groups of people may appear to agree on goals, if they are stated in a broad, general way. "Our goal as a church is to know Christ." Who would disagree with that? But the pastor and the people may have quite different ideas of how that broad goal can be reached. If they never become more definite, each works with the idea that his or her understanding of the goal is accepted by everyone.

But the pastor and the people grow further and further apart. Each is pursuing a different idea of the common goal. Sooner or later, there will be disagreement and division, and everyone is hurt in the argument over who is right.

Well-defined goals in the beginning may prevent ending in strife.

It is easier to hammer out clearly stated, specific goals than it is to attempt to heal wounded relationships.

5. Each graduate would receive a personal invitation each year to be an honored guest at the Bible school graduation celebration.

▼ HOW TO DEVELOP ADEQUATE GOALS

Developing adequate goals entails no mystery. There is a straightforward process to follow as a group lays out the way into its future. Perhaps the most difficult part is simply allowing enough time to pray and think together.

1. State your ultimate intention.

Sometimes this is referred to as the "mission" or overall purpose of the organization. Perhaps it will be very broad: "Our task is to evangelize in world-class urban centers," or "We seek to develop high-quality leadership for the churches of Asia."

You may find it useful to eliminate alternatives—in writing—as a way of narrowing down to that particular thing that is your central concern. Try to answer questions like these:

- What is our overall goal in Christian ministry?
- Is our purpose to combat social ills directly? Or do we expect that those ills will be cared for if churches are started?
- Are we trying to evangelize a particular group or perhaps to strengthen others who are directly evangelizing?

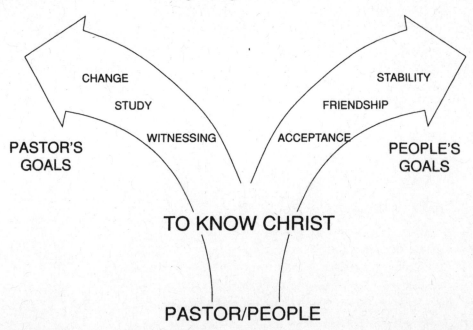

- Do we, or should we, have working relationships with other groups? How do we relate to each such group?

While these questions are geared to groups, the same approach should be followed by individuals seeking to clarify their goals.

2. Break down your "mission statement"— ultimate intention—into the steps necessary to accomplish this large goal.

It may be impossible to move a boulder the size of a house, no matter how great the need to move it. But if the boulder is broken up, it can quite easily be moved—one small piece at a time. Break up the large goal into progressively smaller and smaller steps that can be more easily accomplished.

The example of the Zimbabwean Bible school shows how this can be done. Stimulating revival is a very broad goal, almost too broad to grasp. But under that purpose, many smaller steps were suggested that could lead to revival, such as maintaining contact with graduates. Each of these tasks, in turn, was seen to have still smaller and more specific steps. Reducing the huge to simply large and then to manageable steps gave direction to Bible school activities.

3. Write down in phrases and short sentences the performances that, if achieved, would make you feel the goal is being reached.

The Bible school goal, for example, was to stimulate revival among the churches of its denomination. What specific evidence would show that the goal was being reached? A list produced by small-group brainstorming might look like this:

- Graduates asking for help in planning preaching series
- An increasing number of men attending church services
- More professions of faith in Christ
- Less beer drinking and alcoholism
- Groups going from congregations to witness and start new house churches
- Christians confessing sin and making restitution
- An increasing number of men and women enrolling in Bible school

I once belonged to a committee that had long meetings with little decision making. There was a lot of opinion sharing, but not much problem resolution and creative problem solving. We did not have a clear purpose or goals as a group.

In time, one member emerged as the leader. Through directed questions (and prayer, I'm sure!) he helped the group identify why we existed. He then helped us decide how to structure ourselves to accomplish our purpose.

Once we developed into a purpose-directed group with well-identified goals, our communication was much more efficient and constructive plans were made.

—Mark Elefritz

The list would probably be much longer, and it would be added to over a period of time. At this stage, accept all contributions, making no decisions about what is valuable or what is irrelevant.

4. Sort the notes made in the third step. Delete duplications and remove items that the group agrees do not relate to the goal. Some "performances" may be good in themselves but may not lead toward the goal. At this point the good is separated from the best to provide clearer guidance for what should be done in a ministry.

Items that are abstract and do not clearly state what is to be accomplished should be rewritten or taken off the list. It is fairly simple to state good intentions in a vague way—"to encourage the graduates of our Bible school" or "to hear improved preaching in the churches." There is certainly nothing wrong with those desires, but how can it be known when they are fulfilled? They are abstract intentions, not performance standards that help indicate when the goal is being reached.

5. Write a complete statement of each performance that can be used as a marker of progress. What is to be done? What is to be accomplished? How much, and to what specific standard? Beware: Don't just list things to do; state the results expected.

Test each statement with a question, "If someone did this, would I be willing to say he or she has achieved the objective?" When you can answer yes, you have adequate standards to measure progress toward the goal.

▼ HOW TO DEVELOP GOOD OBJECTIVES

As you develop objectives that will carry you to the larger goal, keep in mind five qualities of good objectives.

1. Objectives must be *relevant* to the larger goal. It is nice if the schoolchildren have new choir uniforms, but will that help them to sound better? A new pulpit would be attractive in the church, but will it straighten out the confused theology of a preacher?

2. Progress, or lack of it, must be *measurable*. It is easy to say, "I feel sure we're making progress, even though we don't see much change yet." But such statements are often made to avoid the pain of failure to achieve.

Before progress can be measured, it is necessary to agree on criteria by which progress can be determined. Criteria may be expressed in numbers of people attending a service, scores received on a test of knowledge, or numbers of new students enrolling in a correspondence

---

Objectives state *what* is to be accomplished. Activities are what you do to reach an objective. It is common to confuse the two, leading to much busyness but little progress.

This list was intended to be a set of objectives:

1. Recruit, train, and supervise persons to call on prospective church members.

a. Train in the basic knowhow of an effective call.

b. Coordinate the overall visitation program.

c. Supervise this ministry.

2. Prepare candidates for meeting with the membership committee.

a. Have a personal interview with each candidate regarding his or her salvation and Christian experience.

b. Instruct candidates to be prepared to share a personal testimony with the membership committee.

But these are all activities. They do not answer the basic questions of *why* they are to be done and *what* is to be achieved. The result is activity with no visible purpose.

course. Anything that is related to the objectives and is observable by people other than those responsible for the program can be used as a criterion.

Criteria must be established when the objectives are established, or the objectives may well be meaningless. Without criteria, an objective is not measurable.

3. Objectives must require a *significant effort*. They should not require only a trivial gain to be successful. "To increase our membership" is a trivial objective, because only one additional member would be enough to achieve the objective. One additional person in a congregation of one hundred or one thousand would still be more. In the light of a goal of "evangelizing the nation," an objective satisfied by such a small gain is virtually meaningless.

4. A time period must be stated for reaching each objective. In other words, it must be *time-limited*.

"We will begin five churches among this unreached group of people" is a worthy objective on the way to the goal of evangelizing a nation. But when it is stated that way, one can always rationalize failure by saying, "Conditions were unfavorable this year, but in five years. . . ." A time limit forces thorough evaluation to see why the objectives were not met. Sidestepping the consequences of failing to meet objectives robs us of the opportunity to make changes in response to failure.

5. Objectives must be *manageable* given the resources that will likely be available.

It is faith to attempt a task larger than visible resources when there is the confidence that God has guided the attempt. But there must be readiness to begin by accomplishing small parts of the task. Faithfulness in little is the prelude to God's responding to larger faith. Stating a grand goal may not be faith; it may simply be dreaming. Real faith functions one step by one step by one step—within the available resources. As one step is taken, God supplies more resources when his desires are being followed.

Measurable goals are difficult to set. How do you measure friendliness, acceptance, or personal devotion? These things cannot be measured directly, but only indirectly through *behavioral equivalents*. In other words, measure what can be seen or heard that results from the invisible behavior that is your goal. These visible behaviors are indicators, or "equivalents," for purposes of measurement.

"When I came to this congregation, I soon learned that the people were scattered all over the hills. I prayed that God would give me a car so I could pastor my people . . . and he gave me a new pair of shoes."

A few pairs of shoes later, God also gave that African pastor a car.

▼ FAILING TO REACH OBJECTIVES

What can be done when objectives are not being reached and the goal seems no closer?

The goal or mission has been discussed and agreed upon; it is important, worth spending our time and money to reach. Objectives have been clearly stated and meet the requirements of good objectives: They are relevant, measurable, significant, time-limited, and manageable. But they have not been fulfilled. What should we do next?

First, there is some reason for encouragement. It can be a healthy sign indeed to recognize that objectives have not been reached. If we do not have objectives, we do not know when we are failing. Activities by themselves become habit, or even worse, they become almost sacred things that no one dares challenge. It is not the activities that matter, but reaching the goal. Objectives provide not only an understanding of the steps that are necessary, but also an opportunity to change programs and activities when they are unproductive.

Seldom will anyone or any group decide on a goal, develop statements of objectives, and then follow an unchanged plan toward that goal. There will be many adjustments, modifications of objectives, and changes of activities along the way.

When objectives are not reached, we need to ask and answer three questions, one at a time:

- Has activity been conducted as agreed when plans were made for fulfilling the objectives?
- If activities have been undertaken as agreed, what alternative actions are possible?
- If no alternative actions are possible, are the objectives agreed upon even possible?

Do not at this stage consider changing the objective. The first thing to do is to review activities: What has been done? How were those things done? Can they be modified and improved? Careful examination may show that some activities thought to be very good are not merely unproductive but actually counterproductive. Even experience with poor methods may show the way to better procedures.

Time must be allowed for change to become visible. Impatience leads to expecting quick results in Christian ministry. But fundamental shifts in commitments require *time*—hence the value of carefully setting time limits for objectives. Changing activities too quickly, before enough time has been given to allow results to appear, defeats the use of objectives.

When action has been as agreed, appropriate modifications have been tried, and there is still failure to reach objectives, we should seek alternative ways of doing things. Without shifting objectives, can we find better ways to follow? Can new methods be learned, or is it necessary to shift personnel so that new approaches can be

Goal setting seems to increase the possibility of failure! I did not feel too poorly when I failed. After all, I was "faithful." Now I understand that failure may mean that I was not faithful in the activity that was to bring me to my goal. Bringing goals into the picture makes me more aware of being accountable to God.
— Scott Clark

used? Examine the alternatives and consider the financial and personnel cost of each. Then try the best apparent alternative.

There may come a time when there are no alternatives for reaching unfulfilled objectives. This would be the time to consider changing the objectives, not the goal. Perhaps the objectives are unrealistic, given the available resources and the lack of indications that those resources will increase. Insufficient time may have been allowed, or it may not be possible to know with certainty what is happening in the work—in other words, the objectives are not measurable. At this point, and not before, alter the objectives so that there is a stronger possibility of reaching the goal.

Like a rocket, we reach our target by a series of approximations. The rocket is initially launched upward, but then its direction is modified so that it heads more toward a target. Later, the direction is modified again and again. As it approaches the target, the modifications become smaller and less frequent.

The very last thing to consider is changing the goal or mission of the group. The purpose should be guarded with care, even when it is restated and clarified. To lose a clear goal is really to lose the reason for the organization's existence. It is sad when groups have lost sight of their true goal, yet continue to assume that their existence is synonymous with Christian ministry.

▼ OBJECTIVES AS A GUIDE TO CONTENT

A blank piece of paper lay in front of the pastor. Several crumpled sheets had already been tossed into the wastebasket. Still he fretted, "What can I preach about tomorrow?" Devotional studies, commentaries, and books on Christian living were scattered on the desk in front of him. He did not lack ideas, in fact, he had too many. How could he narrow his message to a single topic? What would be "right" for his congregation?

Where *should* the pastor begin in planning his sermon? Not by scanning the work of other preachers and writers. Not by looking for something of current interest in the newspaper or in magazines. Not even by simply selecting a powerful passage from Scripture at random. He should begin by identifying his purpose for preaching or teaching. His overall goal is to help members of his congregation know God in their lives. How is this particular sermon to help them? What is the objective?

Knowledge of particular needs in the local church will lead to specific preaching and teaching topics to meet those needs. This, of course, assumes that the preacher already has a thorough grasp of the Bible's message. Without such a foundation, it is a small step to becoming simply a people-pleaser. The question is not whether to teach

HAGAR

the Bible or to interest the people. Both are necessary. The question is what to give from Scripture's vast resources at a particular time to a particular group of people. Objectives guide selection of content and also determine style, timing of delivery, and the kind of follow-up needed.

Purpose is central, not only for a pastor, but in any communication. In more formal situations—preaching, teaching, seminars, worship services—the purpose must be specifically identified. If it is assumed or not clearly stated, unfocused and ineffective communication can be expected as a result.

A diagram may make the central role of objectives clear.

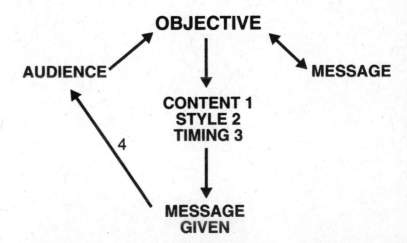

Objectives alone do not determine the message. Often the message itself influences the objective. Thus the double-ended arrow indicates interaction between message and objective. It is from the biblical message of forgiveness, for example, that the purpose is developed to teach "Forgive one another, as Christ forgave you."

The objective is at least partly determined by audience needs. Their readiness to listen, their felt needs and previous understanding, and their attitude toward the speaker (among other factors) influence selection of the specific content, timing, and style of the presentation.

Even in informal situations there is always a purpose in communication, even if it is not consciously recognized. Making the purpose explicit can help resolve difficulties in communication. What do I expect my children to do when I tell them this? What is the expected result of this appointment? Why is this committee meeting?

Understanding someone else's reason for communicating can lead to better responses. What is it that X desires in this conversation? Is there a need to be met? Can I summarize the content being given, to help perceive the purpose? Behind the spoken or written words lie purposes that are seldom explicitly stated.

In many cultures it would be improper to state directly the need or the purpose behind actions. The words spoken may appear to have little relationship to a situation. The objective is stated indirectly, perhaps in a story or a proverb. It is the responsibility of the listener to note the context, determine the referents, and interpret the story. The reply should come in the same indirect manner. The fact that objectives are camouflaged does not mean that there are none.

> Several years ago my wife and I established life goals, and then objectives for the major areas of our lives—physical, financial, family, etc. Having these goals has made it much easier to understand each other. It has enhanced our private relationship and our relationship to others, and it allows us to evaluate our activities in the light of major goals. The little, daily decisions are influenced as well as the way we interact with each other.
> —George Bradley

▼ WHY WE DO NOT REACH OBJECTIVES

MBO—management by objectives—became popular in Christian ministry during the 1980s along with enthusiastic calls for efficiency and sharp thinking. This approach provided a sense of direction in the vast landscape of need in which we minister. Overwhelmed by the magnitude of the task, uncertain of how to go about the work,

and unsure of when enough had been done or even when a part of the task was finished, many Christian workers found that developing a set of objectives gave something tangible for guidance. Just having the objectives helped remove the helpless feeling that can arise in the face of what seems to be the total unpredictability of Christian ministry.

Then evaluation began so we could see where we were in relation to our objectives. Sometimes they were reached, more often not. It was puzzling to see that they were reached in some areas and not in others, even though the same effort was apparently put forth in all areas. Success seemed unrelated to plans.

What might be happening? There are six possibilities.

1. The tyranny of the urgent: Daily tasks are performed without any reference to the objectives we are supposed to be achieving. Even weekly or monthly assessments of activities against plans and objectives are lacking.

2. The objectives that were originally chosen were inappropriate. Such objectives typically ignored or minimized the felt and real needs of the group with which we have been working, concentrating only on the needs perceived by outsiders. The receptivity of the audience to the changes proposed may well have been overlooked. As a result, the work was started in a place that was wrong socially, geographically, and intellectually and has proceeded on a wrong set of assumptions.

3. An inadequate strategy has been laid out for reaching the objectives—or perhaps there is no strategy at all. The context of ministry may have been ignored and the true need and opportunity misunderstood. The result is inadequate preparation for the work required to reach the objectives.

4. The resources required are either totally lacking or nearly so. Inadequate action has been planned to obtain the needed resources.

5. The objectives represent wishes rather than real possibilities of what might happen if the work is done correctly.

6. Even though Christian ministry is primarily a spiritual work, the spiritual dimension is ignored in practice. There is failure to develop fellowship, prayer, and holiness of life as a group. An individual emphasis on these things may be present, but group objectives in ministry

cannot be achieved unless these basic elements are developed as a group.

▼ DO GOALS QUENCH THE SPIRIT?

Is it spiritual to have definite goals? If we bind ourselves to goals, will we begin trusting in our own understanding and hindering the free movement of the Spirit of God?

Think of it this way: God can show us what he desires in advance as well as he can show us at the last moment. Timing is not the issue, but conscious dependence on him, whether for setting goals and objectives or for carrying out the work to achieve them.

Goals are spiritual; indeed, they are part of the nature of God and should therefore be a part of our work as children of God. God works according to purpose, or he would not be God—only random chance. God is a God of order. A major difference between the materialistic and the spiritual views of the world is that one assumes chance and the other purpose. Our responsibility is to work in harmony with God's purpose.

Consider faith itself. Faith implies a goal, or it would not be faith. "Now faith is being sure of what we hope for and certain of what we do not see" (Heb. 11:1). When we pray in faith, we expect to receive what we ask. Prayer itself indicates that there is a goal; without one, we would hardly pray.

In Scripture there is a recurrent theme of God's purpose, God's planning. "In him we were also chosen, having been predestined according to the plan of him who works out everything in conformity with the purpose of his will" (Eph. 1:11). It is a cornerstone of our confidence in God to "know that in all things God works for the good of those who love him, who have been called according to his purpose" (Rom. 8:28).

It is indeed wrong—and will prove futile—to work out a set of goals mechanically with no effort to follow the clear principles of Scripture. It is foolish to set goals without seeking to know God's will through prayer and sensitivity to his guidance.

But if we can be conscious of God's guidance, then why bother to set goals at all? Perhaps we should leave it to him and cease being concerned with the consequences of our actions.

We cannot escape goal setting. It is a part of every activity, whether or not the goals are explicitly stated. We

Much of what is called Christian communication ignores the difference in goals between selling a product and changing a life commitment. Consequently, the techniques of advertising are imitated, with excellent production and manipulative techniques. The "Christian communicator" carefully packages and presents the Story, unconsciously emphasizing the production. Excellent production is always desirable, but totally different techniques may be needed, given the Christian's distinctive goals. We must carefully examine what we are trying to achieve beyond the production itself. Otherwise, the production may prevent us from achieving the true spiritual goal.

don't simply go to town and then decide when we are there whether we will buy a shirt, mail a package, or perhaps try to visit with the mayor. We go to town with purpose in mind, even though it may not be well thought out.

Even our most aimless wanderings seek to satisfy some desire. We may be only partly aware of what the desire is, until we suddenly have a flush of recognition: "Ah, that's it! That's what I've wanted." When we fail to set goals for more important activities, we run the risk of simply responding to vague desires, reacting to immediate pressures.

Knowing ourselves as poorly as we do, we can easily confuse these aimless promptings of desire with guidance—"I feel the Spirit is guiding me to do this . . . or that." But that feeling may arise from emotional pressures. The setting of goals, conscious of God's advance guidance, does not quench the Spirit. Actually, failing to set goals is more likely to quench his Spirit. Without fixed purpose it is difficult to sort out immediate pressures from the fulfillment of God's long-term purpose through our life.

SUMMARY

People who do not know where they are going will almost certainly reach a destination, but they won't know when they do.

Without goals and objectives there is no clear way to develop a sense of direction or fix priorities. How can we know what we should be doing? Which tasks must be left undone because they are peripheral? Goals reduce uncertainty and help toward efficient use of time for ministry. It is especially important that goals be clear when we are working in an intercultural situation in which familiar guidelines are absent.

Goals give broad direction, but should be reduced to a series of objectives. Objectives are the steps that lead toward accomplishment of a goal. They are relevant to the goal, measurable, time-limited, and manageable with expected resources, and they require a significant effort to achieve.

Objectives provide a standard against which to evaluate work and consider desirable changes so that the overall goal will be reached. Without goals and objectives, intercultural workers can become so baffled by culture stress that nothing is achieved. Objectives help translate high ideals into necessary daily tasks.

▼ BIBLIOGRAPHY

Mager, Robert F. *Preparing Instructional Objectives*. Palo Alto, Calif.: Fearon, 1962.

Morris, Lynn Lyons, and Carol Taylor Fitz-Gibbons. *How to Deal with Goals and Objectives*. Beverly Hills, Calif.: Sage, 1978.

➤ He doesn't know what he's talking about!

➤ "How well you talk," said the Miller's wife, "really I feel quite drowsy. It is just like being in church." (Oscar Wilde, *The Devoted Friend*)

TELL ME WHAT YOU KNOW!

PROPOSITION 6: Mastery of content is the necessary foundation for effective communication.

How devastating it is when a speaker or writer is dismissed with a scornful "He doesn't know what he's talking about!" A message may be beautifully stated, but if there is weak knowledge of the subject, or even error, listeners quickly sense the lack. Fine-sounding words are no substitute for knowledge of the subject. Sincerity is not all that is necessary.

A pastor admitted his lack: "There have been times when I have been uncertain of my material. I knew what I was saying was true, but I couldn't clearly tell people why it was true or how to apply it to themselves. I knew how the subject had affected me and where to find related verses in the Bible. But I still didn't have a clear enough understanding to communicate it to others. The people might have appreciated my sincerity, but they didn't benefit very much from what I said.

"When I did master the content," he went on, "I was able to cut the wording to the essential points. I was able to put the message across in terms the people understood, for now I myself knew it so well that I was able to relate the message to their lives." He knew the material well enough to be free to understand the audience.

▼ KNOW THE CONTENT

Before teaching, one must master what is to be taught. The principle is the same in any form of communication. Good intentions are no substitute for mastery of content. There is, in fact, no substitute for thorough learning—internalization—of the material to be communicated. There are at least three reasons that effective communication can be developed only on the basis of familiarity with the subject.

1. The ability to adapt vocabulary and illustrations rests on knowing the content. If the subject is known only superficially, then changing words, illustrative stories, or the order of presentation is risky. As one changes a presentation to make it more interesting, necessary parts may be left out or introduced in a confusing sequence. How much can be changed and what can be changed can be decided only on the basis of the content itself. Thorough mastery of the material is essential so that the key elements are known and can be retained, even when the form is different. Knowledge of what is basic and what is peripheral is required before any adaptation can be done safely.

2. Content must be known so well that it can be communicated in a different sequence if necessary, without perplexity at what needs to come next. Memorization of content does not ensure understanding. In fact, memorization usually requires that material be learned in a particular order. If a listener responds with a new question, or changes the order of the questions, it may not be possible to recall the right answer. Mastery of content means much more than simple memorization. Beginning there, it adds understanding of the material.

3. We must have "learning readiness." There are times when we are ready to learn something new. We may feel an urgent need to understand how children develop—our first child has just been born. In years past the developmental psychology of children sounded like a subject much too complex to master, but now that we have responsibility for our own children, we are eager to learn. Learning does not seem difficult, because it is related to a major felt need and a specific personal situation. That is learning readiness.

▼ USE LEARNING READINESS

It is a wise parent who answers children's questions with carefully chosen words and help. Asking a question

A denomination is given time on government radio; they would say that content is primary. They are careful that no one who is unsound doctrinally speaks on the program. However, churches rotate in their speaking responsibility with no regard for who can clearly teach God's Word. There is little thought about what the message should be; often it is put together in a last-minute scramble. Simply putting a Bible message on the radio is thought to ensure effectiveness. The medium is treated with greater importance than the message content.

—Mikel Neumann

is evidence that the child is ready to learn. That learning readiness is a marvelous opportunity. It will not wait; attention will have passed on to one or two dozen other things by tomorrow. *Now* is the time an answer will be grasped. But that answer must be within the child's experience and language capabilities. That often demands reshaping the answer, simplifying, making comparisons with something within the child's experience. To give such an answer requires understanding of the subject. Perhaps that is why parents sometimes ignore children's questions—or use silly fairy tales to give answers to serious questions.

Points of learning readiness occur in every life. We are ready to learn about different subjects at different times. We will learn about even the most difficult matters, *if* someone is there to give us answers within our experience and language ability, someone who knows the subject well enough to adapt the message to suit our readiness.

Evangelism is best accomplished through the window of learning readiness. More than eighty percent of those who learn of God through accepting Jesus Christ as their Lord begin that pilgrimage through friends. The most effective evangelism happens in informal conversation with someone who is alert to recognize readiness to listen and who is able to express the content of the Christian message clearly.

▼ WHAT ARE THE ESSENTIALS?

What is the essence of the Gospel? What can be said in different words to meet the needs of different people? The problems surrounding contextualization of the Christian message so that it is "at home" in many different cultures can be resolved only when the biblical content is thoroughly known. While the audience obviously must be known if the communicator is to reshape a presentation suitably, the presentation may not be faithful to the original revelation unless that revelation is equally well known.

What are the essentials we must communicate to others in order to fulfill our responsibility as witnesses? Paul knew the message superbly well, having been trained in the most rigorous school of Judaism and having learned to know Christ during years in the desert and time spent with fellow believers. He knew what he must communicate. Precisely what did Paul mean, then, by "the whole will of God"? What had he taught so that he could say, "I am innocent of the blood of all men" (Acts 20:26–27)?

The larger passage in which these phrases appear (Acts 20:17–35) shows a steady confidence that is rare when a pastor or missionary moves to work in a new location. Paul recognized limitations in the continuation of the ministry at Ephesus. He knew that the church would not be all that he desired and that danger and division would come. Yet he was still sure that he should leave. On what grounds could he be so confident that he should leave a young church?

Part of the answer is in the content he taught to the Ephesians. He knew when he had completed his teaching task, because he knew what he had aimed to teach. He was totally confident that the Holy Spirit would continue teaching, enlightening, and convicting on the basis of the facts already shared.

Content is particularly critical in Christian communication. Divine revelation demands assent and commitment to truth, as distinct from an emotional reaction to created moods. In Christian communication, it is the content that is intended to mold action. Response based on manipulating emotion will last only as long as the right emotions are stirred.

▼ CONTENT OR STYLE?

Is the way the message is said as important as what is said? Some communication theorists argue that the medium carrying the message, the context in which it is given, and the style are more powerful than the content itself.

Marshall McLuhan has helped us see more clearly that message and media are both important. McLuhan contends that the media stir emotions and cause a response without any reference to content. "Societies have always been shaped more by the nature of the media than by the content of the communication." The media's primary effect, he contends, is to "massage" their audience rather than inform it. In other words, they manipulate emotions and attitudes rather than informing as a basis for rational decisions (*The Medium Is the Message*, 7).

The Muslim attitude to the Qur'an illustrates how the medium itself can be considered more important than the meaning and content it carries:

> The Qur'an cannot be translated. The Book is here rendered almost literally and every effort has been made to choose befitting language. But the result is not the Glorious Qur'an, that inimitable symphony, the very sounds of which move men to tears and ecstasy. It is only an attempt to present the meaning of the Qur'an in English. It can never take the place of the Qur'an in Arabic, nor is it meant to do so.
>
> —Muhammad Marmaduke Pickthall, Translator's Foreword, in *The Glorious Qur'an*, xv

The sound of the language and the beauty of the Qur'an's Arabic poetry are valued very highly by the Muslim. The content is not ignored, of course; instead, the medium (the Arabic language in this case) enhances its significance.

McLuhan argues that the nature of communication (oral or written) even determines the nature of a society's development. In Africa the tradition of oral communication has emphasized personal relationships. For this reason, African cultures tend to have less concern with material prosperity and technical skills than do Western cultures; Germany, for example, has a tradition of written communication, which places less emphasis on interpersonal relationships. Point-by-point, linear thinking is usually predominant in a writing society. Such a society also tends to stress cause-and-effect relationships and to be technical and scientific in orientation.

While McLuhan's position seems extreme, it provides a valuable corrective to the common error of thinking only about content. Christians consider it all-important to "give the Word." Isaiah 55:11 is often misused to say that *how* we communicate is not important, only *what* we say: "So is my word that goes out from my mouth: It shall not return to me empty." Closer to the true picture of communication, however, is Proverbs 25:11: "A word aptly spoken is like apples of gold in settings of silver." The medium—the context of the message—is like the silver setting for a lovely golden sculpture.

Is the medium ever the message in Christian communication? Consider a cathedral; is it a message? Is the architecture not intended to draw a person's attention to God? Compare a Gothic cathedral with a small, red-carpeted sanctuary in which there is no altar. A pulpit, organ, and piano are at the front. Only a wooden cross adorns the white wall. It is warm, quiet, and peaceful. Such a

I have spoken when I knew the message was true, but could not clearly tell why or apply it in life. I knew the principle and where to find verses in Scripture, but I did not have clear enough understanding myself to know how to communicate it to the young people in the group I was leading. They might have appreciated my sincerity, but they did not benefit personally.

building is as much a message as the magnificent five-hundred-year-old stone cathedral.

The medium is important—but is it *more* important than content? Without content, communication is simply an exercise in manipulating people. But the medium (including context and style) is correctly considered a part of the message. It is much more than a neutral vehicle for the content.

CONTENT + MEDIUM = MESSAGE RECEIVED

Content is crucial, but it cannot be considered the totality of the message. It is never possible to give content without any effect from the media used. In Philippians 3:17 Paul says, in essence, "Copy me." He recognized that his behavior was a medium; he was confident that it correlated well with the message content he was delivering.

Correctness of content is fundamental, but the channel by which it is presented (the medium) is also significant. What we have to say must be communicated effectively, but it is of the highest importance that we know well what we are trying to communicate. With impressive technologies, clever techniques, lights and cameras, endless buttons and switches, and our great ideas for using all of it, have we mastered what we are trying to say?

SUMMARY

You cannot tell someone what you do not know yourself. It is of little value to learn technique if you have not learned thoroughly what it is you want to communicate.

In every communication situation, the adequate communicator will know the material thoroughly so that he or she can change the order or style of presentation, to use unexpected opportunities and questions that develop audience interest. An advantage of live communication over recordings is the ability to adapt to the responses of one's audience—If one has thorough knowledge of the content to be communicated.

The adaptability of a "live" medium points out that the way content is carried has an effect on the total message received. Content is critical, but the nature of the medium modifies the total impact. The message received is the content plus the medium used.

7

➤ What you are speaks so loudly, I cannot hear what you say.

The Messenger and the Message

PROPOSITION 7: The communicator's personality and experiences modify the form of a message.

What shape is water? Obviously, its shape depends entirely on the container holding the water, or whether it is falling as rain or snow or flowing in a stream.

Water takes almost any shape, without changing what it is. It remains colorless, tasteless, and liquid at temperatures between 0 and 100 degrees Celsius.

Impurities may be introduced whether it is running free in a mountain brook, falling as acid rain, or carrying waste from towns and factories that are located along the river. The impurities may be life-threatening, so that the water cannot be used for drinking or cooking, yet the water may seem safe. Normal "impurities" make the ocean so different from a freshwater lake that it has very different forms of plant and animal life.

Water, were it free of impurities, would be the same everywhere. Yet we have many names for its various forms—lake, river, mud puddle, ocean, bay, swamp, ice, snow, fog, pool, brook, cloud. Each of the many names refers to a different experience of the same substance.

A message that we try to give to others is very much like water. The message content is fixed. We are not trying to say new things, but simply to make the existing message understandable to someone else. We have mastered

104

the content we intend to deliver. We understandably assume that the content will remain the same, regardless of our personality, character, or social involvements. But all these things are like the different places where water is held or the different ways in which it is carried from one place to another. The communicator is the container, and the container inevitably shapes the message.

It does indeed matter what the communicator *is*. That person colors the message, determines the choice of illustration and of vocabulary. The communicator stresses some things and ignores others, speaks with conviction or boredom, uses humor or pours facts on the listeners, all according to what kind of person he or she is. One communicator brings a sense of the holy to the audience, another flippancy and indifference, even though the apparent subject matter is the same. The same story told by different storytellers is a different experience. The personalities of the storytellers make the difference.

To understand the message, we often need to understand the messenger. What shapes the messenger? What are the factors to consider in knowing more about the messenger? There are hundreds of differences between individuals, but it is useful to identify three clusters of these differences. Because the three are equally important in shaping the individual "container," a triangle surrounding the message is a helpful way to visualize the three clusters.

The **physical** experiences of the communicator are shaped by geography and climate, lifestyle and work, and the amount and kind of wealth available in the society. There is a vast range of possible physical experiences. Consider the lifestyle of a family living on the African savannah. The semi-arid climate, shallow soils, and lack of industry mean that there is no real alternative to a livestock-oriented way of life. The roads are poor, and there is no train or passenger airline except to link the capital city with the capitals of other countries. Money is scarce and not really very important; it cannot buy essentials anyway if one is in a year of drought.

Contrast those experiences with those of someone living in a green and fertile European valley where rainfall is evenly distributed throughout the year. Small industries are scattered across the valley, and travel is rapid and easy, even to neighboring nations. Money is fairly plentiful. Almost anything desired, from basic food needs to entertainment, can be purchased in local stores.

Thousands and tens of thousands of such differing sets of physical experiences shape virtually an infinite variety of communicators. Even within one kind of physical setting, the occupational variations are overwhelming—grocery clerk, medical doctor, schoolteacher, carpenter, airplane mechanic, salesperson, government worker. Each individual's distinctive way of life makes that person a special kind of container that inevitably shapes any message in a unique way.

The great English preacher Charles Spurgeon selected illustrations from the physical world that he knew to clarify spiritual truth. For example, "It is ordained of old, that the cross of trouble should be engraven on every vessel of mercy, as the royal mark whereby the King's vessels of honor are distinguished" (*Morning by Morning*, 52). Spurgeon lived in the United Kingdom, where the royal family has a special mark to indicate its ownership of an item. From this experience, he could draw a beautifully clear parallel for the Christian life—clear for the English, that is.

Spurgeon's knowledge of prisons and historic dungeons in England was used in illustrating the value of knowing Scripture. "There may be a promise in the Word which would exactly fit your case, but you may not know of it, and therefore you miss its comfort. You are like prisoners in a dungeon, and there may be one key in the bunch which would unlock the door, and you might be free; but if you will not look for it, you may remain a prisoner still, though liberty is so near at hand" (*Morning by Morning*, 52).

Someone with experience of a different nation and way of life would doubtless make different comparisons even when the same truth is being taught. When material is translated from one language to another, it becomes apparent that many comparisons are inappropriate, given the physical experiences of people in the receiving language and culture. A team skilled in two different languages compared original phrases written for an American audience with the translated phrases (see chart on next page). These examples (back-translated into English) show how differences in physical referents caused miscommunication.

The first communicator quite correctly mentioned physical things with which he was familiar. But those experiences were not even present, or had a very different significance, in the receiving culture. To communicate the

It's the same words, but they don't sound the way they do when Grandpa prays.

106

Original	Translation
Power Pills	Strengthening medicine (as in an aphrodisiac)
Moral detergents	Medicine to clean out morals (moral laxative)
Spiritual roller coaster	Coastal ship tossed by the waves
Cheese and crackers (a cheap, simple food)	Cheese and biscuits (an exotic food of the rich and of foreigners)

same meaning, changes had to be made in the message for the second society. Because of differences in experience, the original could not accurately communicate the meaning intended.

Our Lord used illustrations of vines, fishermen, farmers sowing and harvesting crops, and wells and water. Paul wrote about athletic races, soldiers, and farmers. Jeremiah spoke of clay and potters, David of shepherds and sheep. The sights, sounds, and struggles of the physical world in which each lived and taught shaped the form of his message.

Beyond the physical differences there are **psychological** differences. This person is highly intelligent, that one is average; this woman is emotionally secure and cares much for others' needs, that girl feels rejected by her mother and lacks confidence in her ability to do well in a new job. And the distinctions between individuals multiply. Each difference makes its mark on how the message is carried and passed on to others. The confident, aggressive salesperson will pass on information differently from a timid, self-doubting teenager.

The academic is trained to express ideas in a carefully precise way, a way that may be incomprehensible to nonacademics. George Orwell has illustrated this mental difference by a paragraph written in the "Academish" language:

> Objective consideration of contemporary phenomena compels the conclusion that success or failure in competitive activities exhibits no tendency to be commensurate

with innate capacity, but that a considerable amount of the unpredictable must invariably be taken into account.

—"Politics and the English Language"

What is Orwell saying, in language that is comprehensible to people with different mental preparation? Ecclesiastes 9:11 offers a clear, even poetic statement of the same message:

I have seen something else under the sun:
The race is not to the swift
or the battle to the strong,
nor does food come to the wise
or wealth to the brilliant
or favor to the learned;
but time and chance happen to them all.

Another Bible version expresses the same passage differently for easy comprehension by the average American of the late twentieth century:

Again I looked throughout the earth and saw that the swiftest person does not always win the race, nor the strongest man the battle, and that wise men are often poor, and skillful men are not necessarily famous; but it is all by chance, by happening to be at the right place at the right time (LB).

Each version has the same content, but each translator's language expresses a different mental world.

A graphic illustration of different mental pictures of reality is shown on pages 109–111. Three schoolteachers from the southern African nation of Zimbabwe were asked to draw, from memory, a map of Africa and then a map of the world. All were well-qualified teachers from the same language group.

The sketches show strikingly the **social and political** priorities of the individuals. London is the only city placed on the map; England is much larger on the maps than it should be on a world map drawn to scale. Both points show the dominance of Great Britain in the politics of Africa, even in the postcolonial period. Other aspects of social and political ideas held by the teachers are evident in both the positioning of geographical features and their relative sizes. These sketch maps give a glimpse of the individual mental worlds that shape the teachers' role as communicators.

Even considering all the individual physical and psychological variations is not enough to understand the communicator. We must know the society of which the communicator is a part. The communicator is not a solitary individual but acts within a social setting as part of a social network. "There is no autonomous self," state James A. Andersen and Timothy P. Meyer in their study of communication theory *Mediated Communication*. It is as we relate to others that we develop communication; indeed, communication could not happen if we were not in association with other people. Not only do others make up audiences, but they also influence our understanding of surroundings, activities, and ideas. What we say (or communicate in any way) is always done in the setting of a social group. To understand what one person communicates, we need to know that person's social setting.

We are involved with others, and communication is the way we establish, maintain, or adjust those relationships. Sharing information—"facts"—only appears to be the primary reason for interaction. The unspoken and basic need is for relationship with people. These relationships directly and indirectly influence everything we seek to communicate. This is the *social meaning* of communication, something that lies beyond the words or signs used.

This social meaning is more easily seen in formal communication such as writing or preaching. The work of other writers and preachers stimulates new ideas, gives

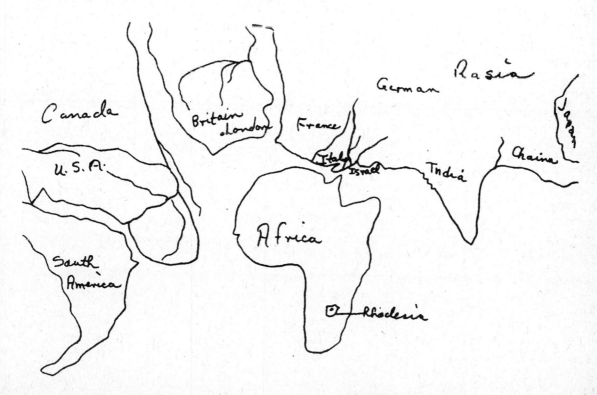

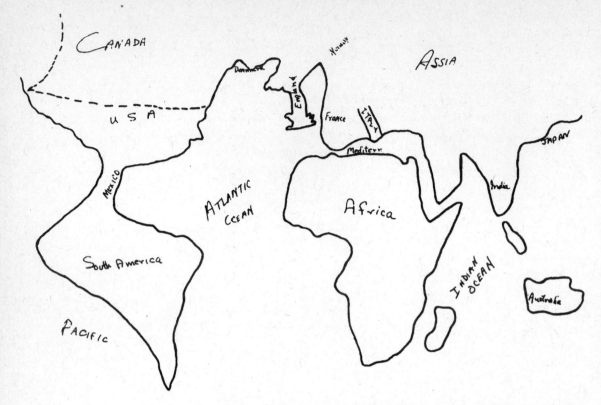

needed background information, and influences the way in which the sermon is preached or the article written. The social influence of other communicators is often shown in references cited and footnotes given. The "independent work" is, in fact, developed from a social context, much as a carpenter develops a piece of furniture from pieces of lumber. The individual is critically important but cannot function apart from a social setting.

A remark stimulates a reply, and the resulting discussion modifies our grasp of a subject or our judgment of a situation. We listen to a news report about rioting; that information affects the way we react to an unexpected crowd in the streets of our city. A neighbor's comment that "there are more robberies than there used to be in this town" increases our concern for personal safety. As a result, we are cautious about helping a stranger.

Memories affect present behavior. A teacher discovered that a student had turned in someone else's work for a final examination, pretending it was his own. Indignant, the teacher imagined how she would threaten him:

> "You cheated on your final exam. Do you realize I could flunk you!"

110

John would be terrified. "I won't be able to graduate," he'd say.

"You should have thought of that before you plagiarized, before you cheated."

But then the teacher began to remember an experience of her own in fifth grade. She had deliberately failed two examinations because of a quarrel with her father. She wished she had not acted in anger, but it was too late. Two days later, however, her teacher made her stay after school and gave her the history exam she had failed.

"I want you to do this again," she said quietly. "And tomorrow we'll do geography."

I, no less than John, had cheated on an exam, even if I'd gone about it in a different way. But Sister Louise, from some prompting of her own, had decided to give me a second chance.

Continuing my walk across campus, I was aghast at what I'd been thinking about John. And worse, what I'd been feeling. True, plagiarism is very wrong, and to cheat is something that can't be dismissed. But my student John . . . was so utterly defeated by my imagined confrontation that I knew I'd been wrong. And Sister Louise had rushed in to fill the vacuum in my thoughts.

—Frank Kerwin, "The Right Answer"

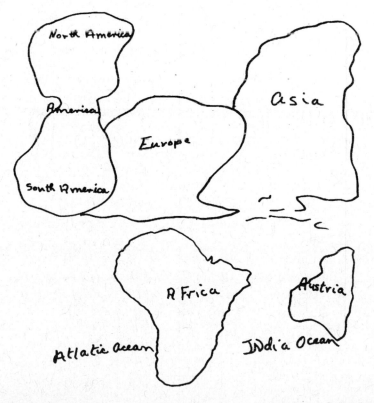

The point is not what was right or wrong in the teacher's dealing with John, but rather why she acted the way she did. Her present communication was shaped by the memory of what an earlier teacher had done for her. It is not only the people around us at the moment that shape our communicating, but also those who are still present in memories. (John did admit that he had plagiarized, and the teacher gave him a second chance. He wrote an excellent story—and passed.)

The editor of the *Illustrated Weekly of India* wrote in the issue of 2 October 1977 of his personal discouragement. His depression resulted from what he saw happening in the society of which he was a part.

> The world has begun to depress me. . . . I am convinced that my depression . . . is due to the shattering of the dreams of my youth. . . .
>
> In my younger days I dreamt that, within a matter of a decade or two, people would be free, there would be no tensions between nations and no wars, everyone would have enough to eat, drink and live in comfort; gifted men and women would enrich our lives with good books, pictures, music and dance. For some time things seemed to move in that direction. . . .
>
> Alas! Racial prejudice not only continued as it was in the medieval ages. . . . The Soviet treatment of Jews is an even more sinister development than the treatment of blacks in South Africa. . . . Being an agnostic, I looked forward to a world where the new generation would free itself of the mumbo-jumbo of archaic religious practices and yet be truthful, helpful and decent towards each other. Religion too has re-erupted . . . all over the globe. Catholics fight Protestants, Copts fight Muslims, Muslims fight Jews. . . .
>
> In Pakistan, General Zia-ul-Haq reintroduces chopping of limbs and flogging in public. No one protests.
>
> I take a look at my own country . . . zealots . . . bigots. . . . I must not write anything critical. . . . All these are beyond argument. This is not the India I dreamt of 40 years ago. And I find it utterly depressing.

An intensely personal statement, this is nevertheless a product of the particular society and time of which the writer is a part. To understand the editor's dismay fully, it is necessary to learn of the society within which he writes. The message is inevitably shaped by the personal experiences of the one communicating the message.

The revelation of himself that God has given in Scripture did not come at one time, in one place, through one kind of person. It began through seminomadic tribespeople living on the edges of great empires of the

---

I graduated from a city high school, and now I was working with high schoolers in a small town. I had had difficult emotional adjustments during the first years of high school, lacking a feeling of basic security. Consequently, I carried "emotional baggage" into my teaching role.

Although we used a standard curriculum, we were free to modify the lessons. I changed them in ways that I felt would have been important to me (as a youth).

On Tuesdays I spent my lunch hour at the high school, eating with the youth from our church. What an experience! I recalled all the feelings, sounds, smells, and actions of my high school days. This made me *very* uncomfortable for the six months or so that I visited there.

I instinctively spoke not only to the youth, but also to the phantom images of my former high school classmates.

Middle East. God showed more of himself to an adopted son of a great Egyptian ruler, the man who became Israel's greatest leader—Moses. Through military leaders, a civil servant, herdsmen, farmers, priests, prophets, scholars, a medical doctor, and fishermen, God continued to teach humankind about himself. These communicators expressed the truth they perceived in the images and experiences of their lives. Inspired by the Holy Spirit, the message was nevertheless shaped by the containers into which it was poured. We can still find those shapes in the various biblical books—the view of a medical doctor or scholar, the images and thoughts of a herdsman, the vivid power of the apocalyptic imagery of the Hebrew people.

And the message continues to be shaped by the individuals carrying it to every ethnic group in the world. It is the same truth, but it looks and sounds different in the Asian vessel, in the African, European, or Latin vessel. Many forms, but one message.

Do these individuals need to be anything special to carry the message effectively? No and yes. No: The Spirit of God uses any kind of person from any place and any language to show his truth to the world. There is no *preferred type* of person. But yes: The character of the person is crucial.

"For God . . . made his light shine in our hearts to give us the light of the knowledge of the glory of God in the face of Christ. But we have this treasure in jars of clay to show that this all-surpassing power is from God and not from us" (2 Cor. 4:6-7). Even though a jar of clay is not something of great beauty, it cannot have cracks or holes if it is to be useful. James L. Johnson warns,

> Spiritual language by itself [does not] cover any of the sins of wrong motivation or shallow purposes which creep in. . . . The roots for insincerity can creep in rather subtly. . . . The lack of proper concern for the content of any production leads to insincerity.
>
> The attitude of sincerity or insincerity . . . [pertains] to the inner character of a person and must be what the communicator allows or disallows for himself in terms of the disciplines that govern or motivate his life. . . . No one can measure for another what is sincere or insincere. That is a final judgment of God himself. But it is safe to say that when any communicator of the message of Christ begins to sense boredom with what he is handling, insincerity is creeping in.

Paul warned about "handling the Word of God deceitfully" (II Cor. 4:2). Our attitude in handling it, then, is just as critical as our concern to preserve its accuracy.

— "The Shadow That Hangs over the Communicator," 3–4

A television preacher sensed his own frustration rising during unexpected delays. In fact, he says,

I was seething. It had been one hour since I arrived on the set, fully made up and ready for taping a series of four half-hour broadcasts. . . . But now . . . time was evaporating.

The reason for the tie-up wasn't easy to pin down. . . . My temper was starting to bubble and almost everyone around me knew "Jack is getting uptight." . . . While my mind was racing with possible responses, my spirit was being assaulted with conviction:

"How dare you even think of using your authority over these people to intimidate or incriminate them, as though they were chattel merely salaried to serve your exalted eminence?

"How can you even think of taping this teaching you are about to do in Ephesians 1 without this very moment living out the acceptance and grace that it reveals?"

And when it's all over, I'll be tempted to smile with sickening magnanimity (presumably undetected as superficial by the interviewer and his cameraman) only to be broadsided by the Spirit of God:

"Words may be filled with truth, but if flowing from an undisciplined spirit indulging itself in anger, pride and pettiness, the result isn't multiplication, but subtraction—activity minus the Spirit of Christ."

—Jack W. Hayford, "Character Before Communication"

Hayford has very concisely summed up the importance of the clay jar that holds the Light of the Gospel. The individual character does shape the message that is perceived by others.

Russell Stendal, a Christian pilot, was kidnapped by guerrillas in a South American country and held prisoner for many months. He tells how he began to understand mercy during that imprisonment:

What a difference a merciful mentality could make on our actions and reactions every day. . . . These guerrillas have taken away my wallet, my watch, even my comb, and have me tied up with a rope. They have separated me from my family. They wrecked my airplane. They are asking ten times more money for my release than my family is able to pay. Yet through this whole experience, up until now I have found that if I put Jesus' merciful mentality to work and refuse to let my mind dwell on negative thoughts of hatred, bitterness, resentment or revenge, no one has been able to take away my inner peace and happiness, no matter what they do. . . .

"Blessed are the peacemakers for they shall be called the sons of God." There seems to be an acute shortage of peacemakers in our world today. As you learn to use mercy, the golden key, you can be a peacemaker in your own home with your family, or maybe at work. If you put Jesus' teachings to work in your life, you can influence everyone that you come in contact with.

—*Rescue the Captors*, 136–37

The author correctly emphasizes that effectiveness is a matter of applying Christ's teachings *in your life*. It is in the individual that the message is made visible, and through the individual that God's truth can be perceived. It does make a difference *who* says it; character inescapably colors the message.

SUMMARY

A message changes as the messenger changes. Though the content is basically the same, the way it is expressed will be different with different bearers of the message.

The communicator's personality, social group, personal spiritual life—in fact, all that he or she is—shapes the message.

8

IMAGES AND REALITY: WHO REALLY IS THE AUDIENCE?

PROPOSITION 8: The communicator's image of the audience and understanding of the context are primary factors in shaping the form of the message.

The missionary was delighted; he looked forward to an interested group for the Sunday morning service at a girls' boarding school in Kenya. The Christian headmistress warmly welcomed him, inviting some of the staff for prayer with him before the service. Everything indicated a good meeting.

But after about five minutes, girls at the back began talking—at first softly, then louder as the small wave of noise crept steadily forward. Their disinterest in the talk on Romans 8 was audible.

Rather desperately, the missionary began to tell a story, then another. Each of them had a "gospel point." The wave of murmured conversations receded, until finally even the back rows were quiet. The closing story directly showed the relevance of Christ to the students' lives.

Afterward, the headmistress was pleased. She explained that only the students were required to go to the Sunday chapel, for the majority of the teaching staff were not Christians. Consequently, the girls registered their objections by deliberately disturbing the services. But due to the speaker's change in style and subject, the Sunday chapel had actually ended more quietly than it had begun.

What was happening in that situation? The speaker had assumed an eager, ready-to-listen audience. His expectations did not agree with the reality that he faced. The headmistress had not thoroughly informed him of what to expect, and he had been "too busy" to do more than prepare a general talk on the Bible. Only quick recognition of the true nature of the congregation had averted disastrous results from this double failure.

▼ YOUR IDEAS ARE IMPORTANT

It is not the *reality* of the audience that determines how you will prepare and shape the message, but the *image* of the audience you hold. Raymond Bauer has said it well: "The communicator says what he has to say because of his notions about his audience(s). In most cases, his notions of his audiences and their expectations and understandings are more or less correct" ("The Communicator and the Audience," 66–77). These expectations are correct, or nearly so, because of shared experiences within similar backgrounds and cultures. When cultures are sharply different, however, the image will not be very close to the reality of the audience. The message will inevitably be shaped inappropriately.

Your opinion of an audience will influence what, and how, you speak to that group. If you feel positively toward them, your message also tends to be positive. If you expect your audience to be hostile, you will tend to be defensive. Beware if your image is largely negative! An incorrect image of the audience often leads to their negative reaction to you. In turn, that may lead you to become more negative about the audience. The downward spiral shatters effective communication.

A group of Japanese university students became angry and shouted at their visiting American professor because he was "too familiar, too egalitarian." He sat on

"This is my fourth sermon on the transforming power of the Gospel. Why do you look like the same old bunch?"

117

the front edge of the lecture table, did not wear formal dress to lectures, and tried to act as a "buddy" to the students. His behavior offended the students' expectations of a professor. Their image of a professor was of someone above themselves socially, who maintained a certain distance from them. Only in such a relationship did they feel they could learn. But the American's image of a good professor's approach was to be a friend to the students, to emphasize that he was just like the students. Only in that way, he thought, could he teach effectively.

Each side held an incorrect image of the other's expectations. The result was a communication disaster.

A minister was invited to conduct student devotions at a fine college in his town. The sermon he gave was full of difficult words and expressions that hardly anyone understood. No one really knew what he was talking about. He did not use such language when preaching in his own church. Why did he change?

The minister changed because of his image of the students and the strong academic reputation of the school. To him, they were well-informed, unusually well-educated, and interested in Christian issues. But they were actually ordinary university students who were not particularly interested in Christian issues. They were more interested in their friends than in major intellectual questions.

How can an intercultural missionary know when an audience is ready to receive the Christian message? There are three choices of action:

1. Don't worry about it. Give the message anyway, and do not be overly concerned about the results.

2. Realize that you do not know the audience and give up; withdraw from new and demanding situations.

3. Carefully study the audience. Commit yourself to the audience, and cross any cultural barriers to become involved with them—despite the emotional cost.

© Rob Portlock, 1983

118

The minister failed to interest the students because his mental picture of the audience he desired to reach was incorrect. The image the communicator holds is critical. Even when the essential content does not change, the manner of presentation changes because of our mental pictures of the audience.

At best, the communicator's image is a shadowy approximation of reality, even though it is the controlling factor in the selection of material and preparation for presentation. To prepare adequtely, we must recognize the image we hold of our audience.

▼ RECOGNIZING THE IMAGES YOU HOLD

Five simple questions can help us see better the shadowy images we hold:

- What is their spiritual interest?
- Do they desire to help in God's Kingdom, or are they simply looking to be helped?
- Are they well-informed and educated? Are they interested in current affairs? World? National? Local community only?
- Do you consider the audience to be antagonistic or friendly?
- Are they interested in your subject?

These questions do not give a full picture of the audience. They simply help to identify our hidden internal images of the audience. If these mental pictures are mostly negative, look for the positive things—and concentrate on those in preparing the communication.

The next step is to learn how close the image is to the reality that is the audience. For most communication, involvement with the audience gives a sufficiently clear understanding. More accurate information can be gained informally by conversations with others who know the audience or who are part of that group. Listening and careful questioning are the most practical ways to develop an accurate picture. What others have written or said about the group can be very helpful, especially when it is confirmed or corrected through personal contact.

But if the communication outreach represents a major effort, or if communication is attempting to reach a group that is foreign and unknown to the communicator, a formal study is the most efficient way to develop a correct image. A careful ethnographic study or a probing sociological survey can be an immense help in painting a more accurate picture in the mind.

First . . . we must find out where a person stands, what he really believes. Is he a realist or an escapist? Is he exclusive or tolerant? That's important. Not that you want to compartmentalize people, but you must have some idea of their position. Or else you're shooting in the dark. Sometimes you may hit the target that way, but generally it's sheer luck.

Jesus listened to people before he made any attempt to speak to their condition. Even so, some accepted what He had to say; others refused Him. That means Jesus did not enjoy one hundred percent success. If we really believe this, it will free us from the compulsion to succeed.

—H. S. Vigeveno, *The Listener*

The most important aspects to be learned are usually these: (1) home language and cultural self-identification, (2) socioeconomic position in the society or nation, (3) major social networks and the way decisions are made individually and within the group, (4) what is highly valued: the nature of their real beliefs, their "folk religion" as distinct from the formal system, and (5) their aspirations and felt needs.

Each of these areas is clearly very broad and often difficult to learn accurately, especially when one is beginning communication with a group culturally and socially distant from one's own group. Undertaking a formal study requires special preparation in appropriate information-gathering skills.

The fifth point—that is, the correct identification of dominant interests and concerns—is particularly useful in improving communication. In other words, what are their felt needs—not what others think they need, but what they themselves feel are needs? A wrong idea about audience concerns and felt needs will almost certainly lead to communication failure.

▼ COMMUNICATING TO RESOLVE TENSION

Virtually all communication is for the purpose of resolving a tension, often identified as a felt need. Communication does not just happen. It is stimulated by tension in the communicator, the audience, or both. It is part of a process that tries to meet physiological, psychological, or spiritual need. Tension can be compared to the motor that moves a car, and communication to the driver who controls the car. The driver's actions that are not related to controlling the motor and directing the car are irrelevant, and they could even be dangerous. Similarly, attempted communication unrelated to resolving tension

"Not many of this world's poor-'n-oppressed are the kinds of Christians we radical types like to imagine," commented the coeditor of *The Other Side* in January 1978. "Again and again we've used them to justify our revolutionary rhetoric, our obsession with structural evil, our flirtation with liberation theology, and our proclamations of a holistic Gospel.

"But among the poor-'n-oppressed there's little if any interest . . . in finding the root causes of oppression, building 'intentional community' or in developing new patterns of economic sharing. . . ."

"We've got to get back to servanthood. . . . We seek to stir up the poor for our own . . . causes. But being a servant to the poor-'n-oppressed means meeting their needs as they define them."

CATHY

© Rob Portlock

not only will fail, but could also mislead people into think-ing some help is being given when it is not. Clearly it is essential to develop the correct image of the audience's felt needs, those tensions that involve them in the com-munication process.

Knowing the audience is basic. But that knowledge must be used with, and for, the audience, or communica-tion becomes merely manipulation. Study the audience, it is often said; learn their felt needs, interests, and ways of expressing their concerns. Then reshape the message to capitalize on their susceptibilities. The formula is straightforward: Find areas of felt need and vulnerability, then exploit them to achieve the objective.

This exploitative approach to communication is not limited to commercial advertisers and politicians. Similar efforts sometimes mar Christian ministry. Church out-reach efforts grandly offer solutions to life's problems—health, social acceptance, harmonious families, and mate-rial prosperity. The promise of meeting these felt needs stimulates interest, and the church grows, at least for a time. These things may be by-products of reconciliation with God through Jesus. But when they are promised pri-marily to promote the church's self-interest, that is dis-honorable manipulation. The church's self-interest may merely be rapid church growth, a good professional credit for the church and its pastor.

The resulting failure is at the very core of communication. Transmission has been substituted for involvement. The church may grow numerically and become a well-functioning organization, but still not fulfill its promise to resolve major tensions. The predictable response is a kind of detached appreciation for the program, but ultimately indifference to all that the church appears to represent.

The success of marketing techniques in reaching sales goals misleads Christian workers. Advertising methods work to sell products—a very limited goal. The goals of Christian workers are much different. We do not merely seek to "sell" a message, to stimulate a desired response. We are providing a framework within which the total life commitment can change. Compared to that, how trivial to switch brands, change styles, or get people to spend more by impulse buying. Manipulation sells; involvement opens the way for transformation. What is called Christian communication too often ignores this difference in goals and method.

▼ KNOW THE AUDIENCE

It is basic to know the audience, but meeting only their felt needs often ignores deeper spiritual needs. Beginning with felt needs, growing involvement develops communication that touches the spiritual core. Stopping with the satisfaction of shallower desires may achieve limited goals but is not truly Christian communication.

"Every marriage can be better! Give it a boost. . . ." The advertisement is to sell a book on Christian marriage. The book may give some marriages a "boost," but basically it is motivated by a desire to sell books. The success of the book is measured by total sales figures, not by the number of marriages that are helped. The publisher probably has a correct image of audience felt needs, but is using that to meet a limited goal of selling books.

"Yes, you can serve the Lord and earn fine financial rewards, too." Many Christians want financial security and at the same time an easy conscience concerning their "total dedication" to Christ. The advertisement promising wealth and Christian service at the same time meets felt needs. But where is the call to involvement with the Way of Christ? To count everything but loss in order to know Christ?

In practice I am never concerned with Buddhism, but with a living person and *his* Buddhism, I am never in contact with Islam but with a Moslem and *his* Mohammedanism. If I seek to take a man by storm with general rules and norms derived from books, it is possible that I may miss the mark, and what I say may go over his head, because what he himself finds in his own religion, and the way in which he lives it, is something entirely different from what I had originally thought. . . .

It is not enough for me to know what a man teaches, I must also know how he experiences it. . . . What is this man actually doing with God in his innermost parts? . . . I must feel a community or fellowship with this man; I must know myself to be one with him. As long as I laugh at his foolish superstition, I look down upon him; I have not yet found the key to his soul.

—J. H. Bavinck, *An Introduction to the Science of Missions*, 2:240, 242

A desire for better marriages or a better income is not wrong. But when such desires are used primarily to promote organizational self-interests, that is dishonorable manipulation. A correct image of the audience is a trust, to be used with great care.

How should we regard our intended audience? With compassion, and a readiness to put our own attitudes toward the audience under the penetrating scrutiny of Christ's love for that audience. As we gain compassion, we will long to know people as they are. We will lay aside our personal and cultural self-confidence so that we are open to learn the truth of others' lives.

SUMMARY

It is not the reality but the image of the audience that determines how communication occurs. The communicator chooses both content and communicative style based on his or her ideas about the audience—who they are, what they are interested in, and how they will respond.

Normally, these ideas about the audience are approximately correct because of shared experiences and similar backgrounds and cultures. But when these backgrounds are sharply different, then the image will not be very close to the reality of the audience, and the message will be inadequately shaped. Often the communicator's image of the audience is a shadowy distortion of reality, even though it is a controlling factor in the selection of content and presentation.

A first step in improving communication is to gain a more accurate understanding of the audience. Identify where your image differs from the reality through formal study, supplemented by careful observations and involvement with the life of the audience. As these steps bring the image closer to the reality, communication effectiveness increases.

▼ BIBLIOGRAPHY

Baehr, Theo. *Getting the Word Out*. San Francisco: Harper & Row, 1986. See especially chapter 4, "Who Is My Audience?"

Bavinck, J. H. *An Introduction to the Science of Missions*. Translated by David Hugh Freeman. Part 2. Philadelphia: Presbyterian and Reformed, 1960.

Engel, James F. "What Is Communication All About?" *Contemporary Christian Communication: Its Theory and Practice.* Nashville: Thomas Nelson, 1979. 37–62.

Lippman, Walter. "The World Outside: The Pictures in Our Heads." In *The Process and Effects of Mass Communication.* Edited by Wilbur Schramm and Donald F. Roberts. Urbana: University of Illinois Press, 1971.

Smedes, Lewis. "Preaching to Ordinary People." *Leadership* 4, no. 4 (Fall 1983).

► Secondary groups, . . . usually internalized and often imaginary, . . . at times
play a decisive role in the flow of communications. (Raymond A. Bauer, "The
Communicator and the Audience,"
127)

How Many Audiences?

PROPOSITION 9: A communicator almost always communicates with multiple audiences.

In *Cry, the Beloved Country,* Kumalo, a pastor whose son has committed murder, returns to his church, bringing his son's girlfriend and stepson.

> And Kumalo must pray. He prays, Tixo, we give thanks to Thee for Thy unending mercy. We give thanks to Thee for this safe return. We give thanks to Thee for the love of our friends and our families. We give thanks to Thee for all Thy mercies.
>
> Tixo, give us rain, we beseech Thee—
>
> And here they say Amen, so many of them that he must wait till they are finished.
>
> Tixo, give us rain, we beseech Thee, that we may plough and plant our seed. And if there is no rain, protect us against hunger and starvation, we pray Thee.
>
> And here they say Amen, so that he must wait again till they are finished. His heart is warmed that they have so welcomed him, so warmed that he casts out his fear, and prays that which is deep within him.
>
> Tixo, let this small boy be welcomed in Ndotsheni, let him grow tall in this place. And his mother—
>
> His voice stops as though he cannot say it, but he humbles himself, and lowers his voice.
>
> And his mother—forgive her her trespasses.
>
> A woman moans, and Kumalo knows her, she is one of the great gossips of this place. So he adds quickly—

Forgive us all, for we all have trespasses. And Tixo, let this girl be welcome in Ndotsheni, and deliver her child safely in this place.

He pauses, then says gently—

Let her find what she seeks, and have what she desires.

And this is the hardest that must be prayed, but he humbles himself.

And Tixo, my son—

They do not moan, they are silent. Even the woman who gossips does not moan. His voice drops to a whisper—

Forgive him his trespasses.

It is done, it is out, the hard thing that was so feared. He knows it is not he, it is these people who have done it. Kneel, he says. So they kneel on the bare red earth, and he raises his hand, and his voice also, and strength comes into the old and broken man, for is he not a priest?

—Alan Paton, *Cry, the Beloved Country*, 219–20

Kumalo is consciously addressing at least three audiences—God, his congregation, and the young woman who had lived with his son. God is his primary audience, but the priest is also particularly sensitive to the people in his church.

Almost always there are such multiple audiences in communication. Sometimes they are "invisible" because they are present only in memory, or because they will listen to a recording or hear what was said from those who were present. At other times they are visible and present but not directly involved in the communication. Still, their presence can influence, even intimidate, those who are communicating.

The primary audience is the visible, or declared, audience, the apparent chief target of the message exchange. The secondary audiences are other individuals or groups who listen to or see the message even though it is not primarily intended for them.

These secondary audiences are often not even consciously identified as an audience. Nevertheless, the secondary audience may have greater influence on the message content and presentation than does the primary audience. It is important to identify the secondary audiences and to be aware of their potential influence. If this is not done, they can exert a pull on the communication process that causes it partly or completely to miss the primary audience. A simple view of communication assumes that it is direct and not influenced by other groups:

A wedding is a private ceremony; the pastor gives his message to the couple as the primary audience. They repeat their vows to one another.

However, relatives and friends that attend can number hundreds—the secondary audiences. What is the purpose in inviting them? Is it to build accountability and commitment into your marriage? Are you planning to entertain them? What you want to communicate to them will make a difference in the music chosen, the kind of decorations, and the place and time of the ceremony.

Family is also a significant secondary audience. Involving them says "thank you" for the role they have played and asks them to continue playing an important part in the marriage.

By identifying these secondary audiences and clarifying goals with regards to them, the bride and groom are able to focus attention on one another as the primary audience.

—Dianne Walker

Another diagram helps to show how these other groups exert unseen influence over the communicator's delivery of the message:

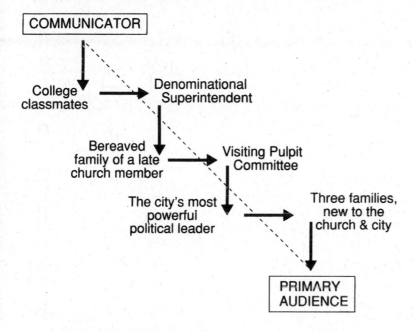

The primary audience must be clearly identified and the secondary audiences recognized, as well as the influence that each may have on the overall process. It is much easier to control known influences than to keep true to purpose against unknown or unexpected pressures.

Priorities must be set for each situation. A small segment of the visible group may be chosen as the primary audience, or even some who are not present. Diplomats and politicians, for example, frequently make press statements that are not intended primarily for the newspaper readers: They are for the leaders of another nation to "overhear." Winston Churchill's wartime speeches made before fellow parliamentarians were actually intended for the nation and the enemy. John F. Kennedy spoke to the American public of his determination to prevent Russian missiles from remaining in Cuba, but the primary audience was Premier Nikita Khrushchev of the Soviet Union.

Within my junior high-age Sunday school class there are many smaller groups. There are students from church families who have attended Sunday school and church most of their lives. Some are from nonchurch families, brought by friends or left at church by their parents. There are both boys and girls in each group. Each of these four different teenage groups must be remembered as I plan the lesson.

When we talked about great warriors in the Old Testament, the boys were much more interested in the battles than the girls. But I had to plan activities which would involve both groups, since the goal was to have all the class learn from the Bible. I also could not assume that they knew the story, since those raised outside of a church environment had no background knowledge of the Bible. Each lesson was planned and presented to present all necessary facts in a way interesting to each of the four audiences in one class.

—Martha Hurlburt

The influence of the secondary audiences is not primarily related to size. Often the smaller group is considered the secondary audience just because it is smaller. But communicators may be more influenced by the smaller group if it represents power in some form—for example, approval, funds, or influence. Or the smaller group may be colleagues or supervisors whose approval is very important to a communicator. At such times, a "mass" audience "out there" may be apparently addressed, but the so-called secondary group shapes the message much more significantly.

Both primary and secondary audiences must be clearly identified and their influence in shaping the message recognized. When that is not done, communication goals may be either ignored or unconsciously changed, and the content may well become distorted.

Answering some basic questions in advance helps clarify the formal communication situation:

1. What audiences will be aware of the communication?

2. What is each audience like? In chapter 9, five questions were suggested to help describe an audience. These will help if used for *each* of the identified groups, so that the audience is not treated as if it were homogeneous. Your analysis may not be correct, but it will be a correct summary of your *image* of the audiences.

3. How could each audience affect the presentation? Do any of the groups have control, directly or indirectly?

Which audience do you *primarily* wish to reach? This group is the true primary audience, even though it may not constitute the largest number present. Consider how communication can best be established with that group. What content should be selected? Is there a way to organize the content for better comprehension and response by that group? Which methods of presentation will be most suitable?

Also remember the probable secondary audiences. Will their real or anticipated response cause a change in the communication? Is that change likely to defeat the purpose of communication with the primary audience? Is there a way in which both audiences can be satisfied at the same time?

Even where you fear that the influence of the secondary audiences will distort the primary communication, you cannot ignore those secondary audiences. It is not realistic simply to say, "I'm not speaking to them. If they don't like it, they can forget it!" They do have an influence, even when you pretend to ignore them. It is far better to recognize that influence and what it could do to communication than to pretend that it does not exist.

James Engel describes an unfortunate situation that can develop when Christian communicators attempt to reach outside the church:

> It was a brilliant idea, or at least it seemed to be from the response of the audience, to introduce a youth-oriented program with a contemporary sound during prime time on a Christian radio station. But it wasn't long before there was feedback of a different sort in the form of a deluge of calls and letters from "the faithful." Some even threatened to withhold their financial support unless such "non-Christian junk" was taken off the air.
>
> Does this sound like fiction? Unfortunately it describes two precise situations which happened in the past few years. The response of management in both cases was to take the program off the air, throwing the staff into a dilemma. This kind of donor veto power can effectively thwart the leading of the Spirit, giving rise to the question, "whom do we serve, the sheep or the shepherd?"
>
> —"Whom Do We Serve?" 5

The cultural style and understandings of the youth and of the ministry supporters were quite different. Both groups were important, but youth were selected as the primary audience. The secondary audience was initially ignored—but later proved to be the critical audience. The secondary audience had the primary power.

It is often essential to have the support of a secondary audience in order to be effective with a selected primary audience. In most evangelistic communication this can be a problem; in intercultural missions it is a major difficulty. What is needed if one is to be effective in one culture will frequently not be understood in another. Audience expectations are shaped by their culture; thus when a supporting secondary audience is from a different culture from that of the primary audience, misunderstanding will often result.

Engel cites another example—a coffee house sponsored by a central city church, intended to be an aid in evangelistic ministry to street people. The music is contemporary—a style of music not acceptable in the sponsoring church but very acceptable to the group for which the coffee house is intended. Non-Christians come and enjoy the place with its relaxed and casual style. Many op-

Our pastor gave two messages on abortion because of the many young people and young marrieds in our church. He addressed the issue honestly, squarely, and biblically. The young adults were grateful for the presentation.

However, a number of older people complained at the selection of such a topic for a message from the pulpit. Even though the pastor was aware of the possibility of such a reaction, he chose not to allow others, in effect, to censor the message.
—Joan Collett

129

portunities develop for relaxed discussions of the Gospel; the effort is effective.

But who is going to pay the rent? electricity? equipment? The leaders ask church people to visit and see how well the ministry is going, for these enthusiastic leaders expect that such visits will lead to donations. But when church members come, they are horrified. They find a "godless atmosphere"—popular music, low lights, visitors who act as if they might be on drugs or drinking and who use occasional swear words. And Christians are sitting around talking with such people. No "devotions" are planned.

So the hoped-for supporters refuse to donate. They criticized the coffee house so severely that it must close.

Clearly the two important audiences needed different communication. But since the purpose was to reach street people, should not they have been the "controlling" audience when leaders determined the kinds of communication to be used? Paul followed that principle, "To the Jews I became like a Jew, to win the Jews. To those under the law I became like one under the law . . . so as to win those under the law. . . . To the weak I became weak, to win the weak. I have become all things to all men so that by all possible means I might save some" (1 Cor. 9:20-22). Christians became as street people to win the street people; they were to be commended.

"But there is another side to the story," comments Engel. "The supporting clientele do have a legitimate stake in our activity. After all, this often is an important phase of their ministry." What can be done to avoid such an impasse?

The secondary audience in such cases must be informed. They need to understand why and what you are doing, and why it is necessary. You dare not destroy fellowship with them; they are also part of the body of Christ. You and they may hold different ideas, ideas so different that it is possible only to agree to differ and ask God's blessing on one another. But before that point is reached, effort must be given to inform these others fully and to be open to hear their viewpoint.

If people are told *in advance* who will be the primary audience and why different kinds of communication are needed, they will be prepared for innovations. Prepare them by telling exactly what differences they can expect, and encourage them to bring visitors who are part of the

Speaking at a Bible college while on furlough in the United States, I mentioned the need for more doctors and nurses to come to Ethiopia. I emphasized the need by describing some of the diseases, and by stating that the country people did not have running water, inside plumbing, or latrines.

An anti-missionary Nigerian student became very angry with me and accused me of belittling African countries. I was only seeking to recruit help for Ethiopia and everything I said was absolute fact. But I would have said it differently had I been aware of his presence.

Later a family sponsoring an Ethiopian exchange student phoned to say they were bringing her to church that night, to meet me. I carefully went through all of my slides before the service to be sure nothing would offend her— even if it was true!

—Douglas D. Priest, Sr.

130

intended primary audience. In such ways, the secondary audience can become a support rather than a hindrance.

To summarize, limiting the tensions and distortions resulting from conflicts of interest between audiences requires—

- Identifying and describing each audience involved in a communication
- Setting purposes and priorities for that communication
- Informing influential secondary audiences of the purpose and methods in reaching the primary audience
- Modifying methods (as consistent with the purpose) to avoid unnecessary tension with secondary audiences
- Evaluating the effort (if tension continues) to decide which audience must be lost—the primary or influential secondary group.

SUMMARY

It is a common fiction to believe that there is only one audience for a communication effort. Every congregation, every radio audience, or any other group is, in fact, made up of a number of different groups, each with distinctive interests. If communicators are unaware of these differences, they will be unable to shape the message adequately to suit their audiences. If they know that different groups are in the audience, they may attempt to meet some of the needs of all of the people, with the result that no one's needs are met.

A communicator must identify the primary target audience and develop communication with that group. Even then, the communicator may be unconsciously pulled away from the prime target by secondary audiences. It is as if a steel arrow were caused to veer from the target by powerful magnets. The influence may not be visible, but it is nonetheless powerful.

Good communication strategy demands identification of the secondary audiences and their potential influences, as well as the primary audience.

Tonight I had as a patient a young man, seventeen years old, with lymphoma. I was to instruct the patient in the *action* of chemotherapy—side effects of the treatment, nutrition, and other information. I recognized that this teenager (nonverbal, sullen, feeling guilty over taking ten months to report obvious symptoms) was not ready to hear what I needed to tell him.

So I waited until his parents arrived, and included them in my teaching. Even though I was directly instructing the patient, his parents as a secondary audience were probably more crucial in the conversation. In the months to come, it is they who will provide most of the care.

—Ruth Palnick

▼ BIBLIOGRAPHY

Bauer, Raymond A. "The Communicator and the Audience." In *People, Society, and Mass Communications.* Edited by Lewis Anthony Dexter and David Manning White. New York: Free Press, 1964.

De Sola Pool, Ithiel, and Irwin Shulman. "Newsmen's Fantasies, Audiences, and Newswriting." In *People, Society, and Mass Communications.* Edited by Lewis Anthony Dexter and David Manning White. New York: Free Press, 1964.

Gans, H. J. "The Creator-Audience Relationship in the Mass Media: An Analysis of Movie-Making." In *Mass Culture.* Edited by B. Rosenberg and David Manning White. New York: Free Press, 1957.

Katz, Elihu, and Paul F. Lazarsfeld. *Personal Influence: The Part Played by People in the Flow of Mass Communications.* New York: Free Press, 1955.

Schramm, Wilbur, and Wilber Danielson. "Anticipated Audiences as Determinants of Recall." *Journal of Abnormal and Social Psychology* 56 (1958), 282-83.

➤ He is trying to convince himself.

➤ Saying is believing.

Persuading Yourself

PROPOSITION 10: Communication increases commitment.

"I'll just watch." Every time the Christian club met, the young man watched. He would not take part in the activities and claimed that he was not learning anything. "It's boring," he complained, "and I don't see what difference it makes anyway."

The leader tried to involve him, but he did not share his ideas or respond outwardly, though he did claim to be a Christian. At one meeting, however, he very tentatively suggested that the group perform a skit at a school chapel. Several were enthusiastic, so he wrote the skit, found others to be the actors, and directed rehearsals. It successfully presented the theme of Christians glorifying God by their attitudes.

The leader was surprised to see how well the formerly uninterested young man advised others in the skit, especially since the advice contradicted his actual behavior. An unexpected result of the skit was a change in the young man. He was no longer a nuisance but an asset to the group. He continued to introduce new ideas and often was responsible for carrying them out. The more he communicated in the group, the more he was committed to his responsibilities.

▼ CONVINCING YOURSELF

The young man demonstrated a very interesting and useful characteristic of communication. It is possible to *convince yourself.* By communicating, that is, acting out or speaking a position, commitment to that position develops and increases. When there is active participation, communication achieves its effect not only in the audience but also in the communicator. Communication is truly a participatory action involving equally those that have been called the senders and the receivers. There seems to be a magic in messages; simply handling them has the potential of changing the persons involved. Active participation can be stimulated in several ways; we will look at those ways that are most commonly useful in Christian communications.

Conviction is strengthened through active participation in passing on a message to others. When beliefs are remembered and reviewed in the process of telling them to others, commitment to those beliefs increases. The sharing stimulates an active rehearsal of reasons and arguments that had been convincing to the communicator in the first place. The repetition is reinforcing; positive attitudes are again aroused. Each fresh stimulation reinforces the strength of conviction.

Commitment begins as a mental decision. As it is acted out and communicated, emotional identification with the commitment develops. Thus both the rational and emotional dimensions now support the new position. A nursing instructor explains how this happens in her teaching: "In preparing for class, I find that authorities say that a thing is necessary and true, so I accept it. The information is put into my teaching notes and passed on in my lectures. After I communicate it the third or fourth time, it becomes more than something researchers have found. I personally believe it. It is then easier to stress the importance of the information and its result in students' lives—I even start practicing it myself."

It is not only in positive ways that acting out a feeling or belief makes that feeling stronger. The same thing happens in giving free expression to negative and destructive attitudes. Carol Travis notes, "Expressing anger makes you angrier, solidifies an angry attitude, and establishes a hostile habit." In the same article she reports that children who are permitted or encouraged to play aggressively become more aggressive ("Anger Defused," *Psychology Today,* July 1973).

Some Christian groups in Guatemala have been criticized for allowing a new believer to speak from the pulpit, usually giving his testimony of salvation. Sometimes the testimony does not sound so wonderful to other believers, but it is very important to the person sharing it.

These groups emphasize that even new believers are to share the gospel wherever they are. It is not surprising that those groups are the fastest growing churches in Guatemala. The communication of the gospel not only increases the believer's commitment, but brings other people to become believers.

—Hector Rodríguez

Certainly this calls into question the popularly held idea that "I should say exactly how I feel; to do anything else destroys my integrity," or, as the American idiom puts it, "Let it all hang out." It is not commendable to reinforce frustration, anger, envy, or disappointment by verbal explosions. Far better that the scriptural instruction is followed: "Let your conversation be always full of grace, seasoned with salt" (Col. 4:6); "clothe yourselves with compassion, kindness, humility, gentleness and patience. Bear with each other and forgive whatever grievances you may have against one another" (Col. 3:12–13). Many other passages of Scripture commend, and command, control of the tongue and disciplined action instead of giving free rein to impulse and hurtful reactions. Experimental evidence confirms this wisdom: Concentration on positive speech and behavior internally reinforces positive attitudes and beliefs.

▼ WHAT IS THE ROLE OF CONFESSION?

Openly taking a position reinforces belief in that position. Thus Paul says in Romans 10, "'The word is near you; it is in your mouth and in your heart,' that is, the word of faith we are proclaiming." Both the inner belief and the speaking out of that faith are clearly seen in Paul's quotation from Deuteronomy 30:14. He continues emphasizing the twin reinforcers of belief, "That if you confess with your mouth, 'Jesus is Lord,' and believe in your heart that God raised him from the dead, you will be saved" (Rom. 10:8–10).

True confession of sin is an admission of what is wrong and of desire to be free of that sin. So confession, the naming and loathing of wrong, is a reinforcement of belief in God's standards of righteousness. It is an agreement that God has correctly judged that sin, and an agreement that the thing must be done away with in a person's life. "Therefore confess your sins to each other and pray for each other so that you may be healed" (James 5:16). Genuine confession is not simply a recounting of sin but includes expression of the desire to turn away from it. Disgust with that practice and the desire to leave it behind are strengthened, particularly as the new resolve is stated publicly to friends.

So-called secret sins are often the most persistent, precisely because they are secret. As much as a person may detest the unhealthy practice, he or she continues—each practice reinforcing the habit. Nothing pulls the

135

person away from the sin, because there is no open confession reinforcing any glimmers of repentance.

Robert Webber has written of this aspect of Christian fellowship: "The church as the community of those being healed goes into the world to provide healing in the power of the Holy Spirit" (*God Still Speaks* [Nashville: Nelson, 1980], 198-99). What we believe and receive is confirmed and strengthened as we take it to others. As we act out the result of our inner conviction, we are healed, and others can be shown how to enter into their healing as well. Scripture clearly demonstrates that human beings function in this manner.

▼ THE COMPULSION FOR CONSISTENCY

Can we understand how this communication principle works? If we understand the process of increasing commitment through communication, we can apply it in many areas of ministry.

All people have a drive for consistency within themselves, consistency between actions, feelings, and beliefs. Inconsistencies between what is believed, what is practiced, and what is felt can cause severe internal tensions. Resolving these tensions is necessary for good mental health.

When behavior is acting out a belief, it is like an engine pulling the belief toward itself, reducing the distance or tension between the two. The closer behavior is to belief, the less the person's inner tension.

Leon Festinger developed this particular approach to understanding communication and attitudes in his psychological theory of "cognitive dissonance." A "cognition" is defined as a belief, attitude, value, or knowledge held by someone. When any of the cognitions held by a person disagree with other cognitions held by the same person, the result is "dissonance." "Something is out of sync" is an idiomatic—and imprecise—way of saying the same thing. Disharmony between what is known to be true and what is valued highly, for example, is called "cognitive dissonance."

An experiment by Muzafer Sherif demonstrated the effect of cognitive dissonance in changing opinion.

A group of people were placed in a totally dark room. The only thing they could see was two stationary points of light. There were no visible points of reference.

The people were then asked to decide "which point of light moved up." Some in the audience had been in-

A danger sign in marriage is failure to communicate. While this is a sign of previous problems, it is also a sure sign of further decay.

When tensions come into a marriage, it is difficult to communicate about them. But to fail to do so is to throw the first glass of water on the fire. It may be necessary to force oneself to communicate—and to keep communicating until understanding is achieved.

Through communication, determination is kept alive and the chances of keeping the flame of love alive are greater. Failing to communicate leads to a weakening of commitment to marriage.

structed to emphatically give a deliberately wrong answer. They responded, "The light on the right." After discussion, the others agreed that was indeed so. Actually, neither light had even moved ("Group Influences upon the Formation of Norms and Attitudes").

Knowing that God tells us to control our tongues (as in James 1:26) yet repeatedly exploding with bitter words of anger creates cognitive dissonance. What is believed and valued is contradicted in behavior.

Eventually, the internal demand for consistency will cause change. One's belief will usually change, so that control of the tongue, for example, becomes much less important in one's mind. Change may even bring acceptance of such verbal explosions as a sign of "being a genuine person" ("I just say what I think; I'm no hypocrite"). We tend to rationalize our beliefs, knowledge, or values until they conform to what we consistently practice. Thus behavior can lead to a change in attitudes. When people who "know better" consistently do wrong things, they are forced to change their attitudes to make the wrong acceptable to themselves.

But this dynamic can also work in the other direction. There is much experimental evidence of *causing* attitude shift through forced change in behavior. For example, college debating groups have provided strong experimental evidence that attitudes can be changed through communication. After debaters had argued the affirmative position on a subject, they were found to have attitudes much more favorable to that position than they had held before the debate. The same was true of those who argued for the negative position. For both negative and affirmative debaters, stating a position verbally and defending it actually caused a shift in their attitudes. In the process of convincing others, the debaters had convinced themselves.

At least two other factors are involved in this change through communication: satisfaction and incentives.

Satisfaction with one's own performance is an important factor in attitude shift. The person who loses the debate, who fails in conversation to convince others, or who does not think he or she has performed well will be less likely to conform inwardly to the communicated position. The belittling remark, "He couldn't even convince himself!" may be literally true.

The incentives involved are also important, not merely the fact of verbal conformity with a position. What

Why is it that behavior sometimes is inconsistent with belief? We can all think of examples of the deacon who cheats in business, the evangelist who falls into immorality, or the missionary who shows race prejudice. Their behavior seems to contradict their apparent belief. Emory Griffin (*The Mind Changers*) suggests three reasons.

One, the connection between their actions and the belief that they hold is not apparent to them. They simply do not see that an action they take has anything to do with the belief they hold.

Two, many attitudes underlie a single action. Some of the relevant attitudes may have changed, but not all. Further growth will change more of the attitudes, so that such inconsistent actions are less likely in the future.

Three, even when the connection is seen and most of the underlying attitudes are changed, the apparent cost may simply be too great. The inconsistency of behavior and belief can be tolerated more easily than the social or physical cost of acting as these persons know they should, and often as they inwardly desire. But there is an unrecognized price to pay for inconsistency: an inward anxiety and self-rejection. That price can be met only in acceptance of the grace and forgiveness that is in Jesus Christ.

We are commanded to rejoice. We are commanded to sing to the Lord. Sometimes it seems impossible to rejoice in one's heart. And yet one can always sing hymns of praise to God. Even when circumstances seem really bleak, God has designed us so that our heart attitude tends to follow, and we are, as a result of our obedience, given the capacity to rejoice—even deep down from the heart itself. Thus our communication of rejoicing leads our hearts to be committed to rejoicing, whatever the circumstances.
—James Lucas

does the communicator get out of agreeing? Debaters have good incentive—the credit that comes from winning a debate. Any public speaker values the recognition of sincerity in speaking. A preacher who harbors questions about foreign missions is more likely to change attitude when he or she receives congratulations for a fine message on Matthew 28:19–20 or Acts 1:8. Acceptance of what is said and recognition of skill in saying it are both incentives that enhance the power of communication to change attitude.

At least four components within each individual are involved in any communicating—actions, feelings, knowledge, and beliefs. (The last three are often grouped together as "attitude.") Everyone strives for consistency among these, though there is always some inconsistency. The resulting dynamic tension causes continual shifts in behavior and attitude, feelings and expectations. Often these shifts are slow, even imperceptible.

▼ USING COMMUNICATION FOR INWARD CHANGE

Are there ways to work with this process, causing desired changes in our own attitudes? Definitely. Some Scriptures that command this have already been noted; Philippians 4:8 is another: "Finally, brothers, whatever is true, whatever is noble, whatever is right, whatever is pure, whatever is lovely, whatever is admirable—if anything is excellent or praiseworthy—*think about* such things."

Consciously thinking about what is good is an action that can change attitudes. Conversely, a danger in reading or viewing scenes of pornography, violence, or exaltation of materialistic values is that it increases awareness of those things and stimulates thinking about them. Ultimately such exposure changes attitudes toward the immoral actions, at the very least making them acceptable alternatives.

Public confessions have been forced in some revolutionary Marxist societies. Little concern is shown that the person confessing "wrong thinking" may be insincere. The right words said in public, accompanied by strong incentive to change, have been demonstrated to begin alteration of attitude. The "confession" is often a prepared propaganda statement that is clearly not the wording of the speaker. But the incentives are strong—restoration of some liberties and social privileges, reduction or elimination of mental and physical torture. This is a key part of what has been called brainwashing.

But the same dynamics can be used correctly to stimulate change, without external pressures to manipulate a person's inner world. Two approaches especially valuable in resolving inconsistencies between action and attitude are discussion and role-playing.

Discussion produces greater change in beliefs, preferences, and attitudes than do lectures, documentary presentations, or any other passive exposure to information. Questioning to stimulate discussion develops active participation, the key to attitude change. The Socratic approach to teaching may be less comfortable for students than other approaches, because it forces involvement, but it is more effective in development of student commitment to belief and the ability to put belief into practice.

Inducing a person to state beliefs publicly will not only reinforce beliefs but also stimulate greater consistency between beliefs and behavior. Questions are a useful tool for this: "What is your opinion about this matter?" "Could you tell me why moral standards are necessary in public life?" "On what can standards be based?" "Why should foreigners in our country be treated as guests?" "Why should Christians care what happens to people of other nations?" Every day there are issues to be decided and problems to be solved in which our beliefs should make a difference. Yet because we seldom articulate our beliefs we may be inconsistent with our beliefs. Starting discussion is a stimulus to verbalizing beliefs, an excellent way to develop greater consistency between belief and behavior.

The use of case studies that require development of solutions (in written papers or group discussion) is also a good way to gain active participation. An instructor may introduce a problem, such as how to lead a Buddhist to recognition of a personal God, by telling of a specific person and the questions that person has asked. Issues of ethnic or racial prejudice can be addressed effectively when one describes real people and real situations in which such a problem developed and then asks one's friends or discussion group to propose a solution. A valuable resource for case studies that can be used is Paul and Frances Hiebert's *Case Studies in Missions*. Others can be found in newspaper and magazine reports, as long as one omits the solution or conclusion when one presents them as case studies.

Through the influence of my best friend, I met a man who would change my life. This man became my landlord, business associate, pastor, and semi-guru. The more I expounded his positions to others, the more convinced I became that what he was teaching was true. Within time my entire identity was wrapped up in what this man did, thought, planned, and taught.

But after several years I began to question some of his presuppositions and approaches. The more I questioned him, the less apt I was to speak up for him. My commitment decreased and the strong tie with his programs was broken. In time, I distanced myself from his group and spoke less with those still active in the movement. Eventually I broke away entirely. I left the opinions that I had held strongly while my communication with the group was strong and frequent.

It has been noted that the people who performed in the Oberammergau Passion Play began to live out the characters they were portraying. This magnificent drama depicting the life of Christ is presented every ten years and involves the entire village of Oberammergau, Germany. Through an entire summer season, in daily presentations the villagers dress and act like the biblical characters they are portraying. A strong tendency for the actors to continue acting like the persons they have portrayed, even beyond the end of the season, has been observed.

Role-playing is effective in changing attitudes because it involves active participation, it is enjoyable, and it permits individuals to "pretend" that they are changing without having to admit publicly that they ought to change. The best kind of role-playing (for attitudinal change) stimulates the actors to use imagination and improvise many of the lines spoken. The actors develop the arguments that are most convincing to the key audience—the players themselves. Giving freedom to imagination and creativity develops a powerful experience for changing attitudes, one that is immensely enjoyable. In his delightful study of Christian persuasion, *The Mind Changers*, Emory Griffin comments, "Role play is really a process of self-persuasion. . . . If he has to create his own material . . . he'll usually come up with the perfect argument—the one that convinces him" ([Wheaton, Ill.: Tyndale House, 1976], 91–92).

Role-playing moves a step beyond discussion by requiring that the roles in a situation be acted out, rather than talked about. This increases active participation because it demands mental effort to imagine and portray someone else's attitudes and behavior. When role-playing, one is forced to assume attitudes one may dislike or disagree with. Thus one cannot avoid grappling with issues one may prefer to sidestep. At the least, this creates a sympathy for another point of view.

Several intercultural games use role-playing to help participants understand what happens when different cultures meet and thereby recognize their own tendencies toward prejudice and bias. The case studies mentioned above can be acted out in role-play. Ethical situations can be portrayed in daily life settings, with actors providing alternative solutions to problems presented. Helping a group to understand the stresses felt by foreigners in their land, for example, can be handled well in role-playing. Different students could take the role of a foreigner, each

Eighteen months ago a student named John became a Christian. A month or two later he attended a leadership training conference, but he expressed dismay that he was expected to do personal evangelism! Nevertheless, he was willing to go with me when I was witnessing in one of the school dorms.

On the very first occasion we both shared the gospel with a fellow who prayed to receive Christ! John was surprised and grateful to God for allowing him to have a part. So he continued to go with me, taking more and more initiative. He has led four more friends and colleagues to the Lord. Through regular sharing of his faith, his faith has grown steadily and he has caught a lifelong vision.

—Chris Mabey

showing a different problem and suggesting how it should be solved.

Effective role-playing requires a director to explain the roles and to help in both the enjoyment and adequacy with which differing people and positions are portrayed. The director-leader should thoughtfully select those to play the roles so that maximum opportunity for needed attitude change is given. There is not much point in choosing the class president to role-play a leader—he or she already fills that role every day. Choose individuals who do not act as leaders so that they can experience the behavior of leading.

In the midst of enjoying role-playing, the director may also need to help the actors keep the theme of the minidrama clearly in focus. Sometimes everyone enjoys it so much that joking, clowning, and irrelevant speech and actions can undermine the overall purpose. Even with occasional difficulty in helping people express themselves when playing an unfamiliar role, or as they try to sidestep hard issues by acting like clowns, the role-play is a powerful tool to bring attitudes and behavior to closer agreement.

▼ BEHAVIOR GROWS OUT OF ATTITUDES

Do attitudes follow behavior, or does behavior follow attitudes? Proposition 10 emphasizes that attitudes can be changed by changing communication behavior. That is, however, not the whole story. Jesus said that "out of the overflow of his heart [a person] speaks" (Luke 6:45) and "what goes into a man's mouth does not make him 'unclean,' but what comes out of his mouth, that is what makes him 'unclean'" (Matt. 15:10). Both of these teachings show that attitude (feeling + knowledge + belief) takes priority over behavior. Behavior does indeed grow out of attitude.

But here we have been discussing *changing* of attitude. Inducing behavioral change can bring attitude change, even opening the way for fundamental shifts in attitude such as changing one's deepest commitment from self to Christ. With that new attitude, behavior will change, and this shift in turn will reinforce subsequent attitude changes. Knowledge and beliefs can transform a life through an initial acting out of that knowledge.

To put it another way, the inner person of knowledge, belief, and feeling can be reached through the outer person of action. When action and attitude are in

141

disagreement, in many situations attitude will alter in order to resolve internal tensions.

How can knowledge be "acted out" before it is fully understood? Imitative behavior, as demonstrated in children, is one way. They act out behaviors that slowly become internalized. Another way is to change the setting or context so that different behavior is appropriate and necessary. The changed context requires changed behavior that slowly brings changed attitude, often opening the way to a very basic shift to accept the knowledge of Jesus Christ. A third way is to provide ways that force one to act on knowledge being acquired. Agreement may easily be obtained if no action is required, but that agreement has little or no impact on attitude. When a specific choice or action is necessary, then inconsistency becomes apparent and attitudes may change—or the knowledge may be rejected.

The effectiveness of communication in increasing commitment is seen in a comparison of two Christian groups, one in Brazil and one in the Philippines. Both were ministering in highly responsive situations, and the two churches were growing at approximately the same rate at the beginning of the time of comparison. They were both located in cities.

In the Brazilian church, a training curriculum for new converts required them in the first lesson to give testimony to their faith, and the assignment was repeated *in every lesson* throughout the cycle. In the other curriculum, used in the Philippines, the people were encouraged to engage in personal witness only after the first cycle of eight lessons. By then they had learned the basic doctrines and how to answer questions and objections.

The first group, in Brazil, subsequently grew at a rate more than ten times that of the Filipino group. Not only was there more witnessing, but the young Christians in Brazil also appeared to be more receptive to biblical instruction. During witnessing they had experienced their need for the information.

Similar findings have been made in rapidly growing churches. When this proposition is acted upon, communication indeed increases commitment. The result is both numerical and spiritual church growth.

A group of Maasai men in Tanzania have been going in groups of four to six men to preach and teach at different villages. One or two new men often ask to accompany the evangelists on their next trip, even though they are not yet Christians.

When they all get to a village they are expected to give their names, where they are from, where they are going, and other significant news that has occurred in their lives. With this, the evangelists lead into their teaching.

The new men are also expected to tell their news, so they have a chance to say what they wish about conversion to Christ. Several times a man has who has not yet made a public confession of Christ shares why he is interested and why he wants to believe. In two cases, men have made the final step to Christ through their own testimony.

—John Mpaayei

SUMMARY

Commitment to an idea or a person is not static, but increases or diminishes over time. It is strengthened by public statement of the commitment, increasing inward commitment.

Attitude includes belief, feeling, and knowledge. It is part of living, not separable from activity. Belief is reinforced when it is communicated, allowing it to involve emotions and relationships actively.

Failure to communicate a new belief will weaken commitment to it. Lacking emotional and relational involvement, the belief becomes increasingly irrelevant and may eventually be given up. On the other hand, active participation in communication can lead to change of attitude and acceptance of new beliefs.

▼ BIBLIOGRAPHY

Griffin, Emory A. *The Mind Changers*. Wheaton, Ill.: Tyndale House, 1976. See especially chapter 7, "Role Play."

Hovland, Carl I., Irving L. Janis, and Harold H. Kelley. *Communication and Persuasion: Psychological Studies of Opinion Change*. New Haven, Conn.: Yale University Press, 1963. See chapter 7, "Acquiring Conviction Through Active Participation."

Lerbinger, Otto. *Designs for Persuasive Communication*. Englewood Cliffs, N.J.: Prentice-Hall, 1972. See chapter 5, "Psychological Foundations of Attitude Change Designs."

➤ What you do speaks so loudly, I can't hear what you say.

➤ Where can I see a sermon?

THE SIGNALS WE USE

PROPOSITION 11: All human communication occurs through the use of twelve signal systems.

PROPOSITION 12: Usage of the signal systems is a function of culture; thus they are used differently in different cultures.

William Temple beautifully described the richness of effective ministry when he spoke of worship:

> To worship is to:
> Quicken the conscience by the *holiness* of God,
> Feed the mind with the *truth* of God,
> Purge the imagination by the *beauty* of God.
> Open the heart to the *love* of God,
> Devote the will to the *purpose* of God.

Do we attain such richness of ministry? Are we leading people into genuine worship, or simply an emotional high point? Words alone will never succeed in giving us the completeness of ministry described by Temple. Instead, they may obscure with a blizzard of woolly ramblings the sharp, clear experience of God.

Scripture speaks of *proclaiming*, and proclaiming can draw upon wider resources than words alone. Proclaiming—communicating—can use twelve different systems of

Nature of sermon

144

signals. Almost all human communication occurs within these systems. In these twelve we have abundant materials for rich proclamation of the Gospel.

Social communication is what we are examining, but that is not the only communication with which we are concerned as Christian workers. Our communication with God is fundamental to all other efforts at creating understanding of him. God knows our hearts, he knows our minds, he knows us altogether. God is able to understand what we want to communicate to him when words and all other signals fail us. Our hearts cry to God with words that are not words at all. And he is able to speak to us in ways that we cannot express, limited as we are to signals alone: "The Spirit himself intercedes for us with groans that words cannot express" (Rom. 8:26).

But here we are looking at interhuman communication, not communication between human beings and God. Our visible task and ministry is primarily concerned with communication to other people.

"So it's great music?" commented an African to a Western friend. "It sounds like cats fighting to me!" Only after the Westerner identified the theme and explained what each section of the orchestra contributed did the African begin to "hear music."

My initial reaction upon hearing a large group of African men drumming at a celebration was much the same. It sounded like hopelessly undisciplined rock music, with no discernible beginning, patterning, or ending. Then someone helped me identify one drummer's rhythm, then another and another. There was not a single theme, but multiple, intricately related rhythms. Then I began to "hear music" *à la Africaine.*

In every area of communication it is the same. *Until you know what to hear, you probably will not hear it.* If we know the message intent, it is easy to "hear" a communication. But when we do not know the sender's purpose, how do we analyze the message to determine its content and purpose?

good intros

The twelve signal systems suggested here give a useful way to perceive and analyze messages, even those involving other cultures where signals are used differently from those in your own culture.

Two modes of communication are frequently recognized—verbal and nonverbal. Because systematizing communication according to twelve signal systems is more specific, it offers a useful way to analyze information

To be considered a signal system, a communicative mode should be
- Interpersonal—used by people to interact with other people
- A deliberate communicative device or act, not an essentially uncontrolled general condition
- Commonly accepted within a cultural grouping as conveying specific information, not a solitary signal used and understood by only one or two individuals
- Composed of a vocabulary and syntax—in other words, the individual signals do not stand alone, but carry an agreed-upon meaning and are in relationship to one another (for example, red, yellow, and green lights for directing traffic, or motions of the hand and arm by a traffic policeman)

content in messages. As an analytical tool, the twelve systems constitute a very useful way to begin learning another culture by focusing on the ways of communication in that culture. This can give quicker access to the many subtle clues that guide a person living and working out of his or her own cultural setting.

The twelve systems are

1. Verbal—speech
2. Written—symbols representing speech
3. Numeric—numbers and number systems
4. Pictorial—two-dimensional representations
5. Artifactual—three-dimensional representations and objects, the "things" used in living
6. Audio—use of nonverbal sounds, and silence
7. Kinesic—body motions, facial expressions, posture
8. Optical—light and color
9. Tactile—touch, the sense of "feel"
10. Spatial—utilization of space
11. Temporal—utilization of time
12. Olfactory—taste and smell

▼ THE TWELVE SIGNAL SYSTEMS

Verbal

The most commonly recognized signal system is, of course, speaking—the verbal system. Too often, speaking is the conscious limit of our formal communication. God has spoken audibly to human beings, but this was apparently the least used system recorded in Scripture. Examples of audible speech occurred at the Transfiguration, at Jesus' baptism, and to Paul on the Damascus road.

How many different verbal systems, languages, are there in the world? About five thousand. In addition, there are dialectical modifications in each language. Linguistics is the formal study of Babel!

Within Scripture there are many references to the written system; consider Exodus 28:9, 12, "Take two onyx stones and engrave on them the names of the sons of Israel. . . . Aaron is to bear the names on his shoulder as a memorial before the Lord." And of course the Lord *wrote* the Ten Commandments. Jesus wrote on the ground, and Paul shepherded the churches through writing.

Written

The written system grows out of the verbal, so that people can send information without the restrictions of time and space. Some writing systems express the idea with no relationship to the sound of the word. Others are representations of sound. A single verbal system may be written in two or more ways, as with Japanese.

146

不登高峯、豈能遠視。

If you do not climb the mountains, you will not see afar

ရှိဉ်သေ့ သောင်ပံရယ် ခတ်လေမှ ပျံနိုင်မယ။

To fly, you must not only have wings, but flap them

ท่านหมายตา ณ แห่งใด จะได้บินไป ณ แห่งนั้น

Whither you look, thither shall you fly

百聞は一見にしかず

Seeing once for yourself is better than hearing a hundred bits of news

සමුඵ සැනෙකදීම සංචාරය විවෘතවේ.

At the moment of meeting, the parting begins

यदी आप अपने भालक को पयार करते है उसे सफर पर भेजिह्म

If you love your child, send him on his travels

Numeric

The numeric system uses individual numbers to carry meaning, as well as expressing relationships through numbers in mathematics. The number 7 often represents divine perfection in the Bible, and 6 is the number representing humanity. The number 3 often represents danger in Western cultures, as with three blasts on a horn or three flashes of light. The universal signal of distress is represented in Morse code by three dots and three dashes, . . . --- . . .

Mathematics expresses relationships through numbers and, in some cases, symbols that stand for quantities or qualities. In simple form, $2 + 2 = 4$ shows a relationship with numbers. Statistics expresses relationships with

$$r = \sqrt{1 - \frac{S_y^2}{\sigma_y^2}}$$

own from the above computation

$$r^2 = 1 - \frac{S_y^2}{\sigma_y^2}$$

$$S_y^2 = \sigma_y^2 (1 - r^2)$$

$$S_y = \sigma_y \sqrt{1 - r^2}$$

a combination of numbers and symbols such as a combination of Roman and Greek letters. For example, the mean (one kind of average) score can be described by

$$M = \frac{\Sigma X}{N}$$

Jules Verne's Captain Nemo suggested that mathematics is not only a precise language, but also perhaps the only universal language.

Pictorial

The pictorial system is the special domain of the artist, reflecting cultural perceptions of his or her environment. Pictures not only reveal culture, but also often carry specific messages. Compare the pictorial styles of Africa, ancient Egypt, Renaissance Italy, and the silk paintings of China. By use of symbols, with realistic and abstract representations, a philosophy is expressed, emotional response is aroused, and specific messages are carried—to those who know the symbolism of the originating culture.

Often the assumption is stated that pictorial systems are universal, with the same meaning for all people. Actually, however, the same pictures communicate different

Emphasis on pattern characterizes Islamic architecture and ornamentation, as on the front of the Great Mosque in New Delhi, India.

The elongated figures express human supremacy and dignity in the vivid rock paintings of the Bushmen of southern Africa. These people are also very musical, and their language employs a series of "clicks."

things to different audiences. A universal "pictorial alphabet" does not exist. An elongated human figure is considered grotesque art in Europe; the same style in Africa is used to indicate human supremacy and dignity. Chinese art uses a bridge to indicate death, the transition from this life to the next. When European art uses a bridge symbolically, it often indicates a joining of separated groups or establishment of contact between warring factions.

The embroidery on the inner curtains of the tabernacle is an example of the pictorial system in the Bible (Exod. 26:31). God graphically described the unfaithfulness of his people by showing how pictures aroused lust in them: "She carried her prostitution still further. She saw men portrayed on a wall, figures of Chaldeans portrayed in red, with belts around their waists" (Ezek. 23:14–15).

The written and pictorial systems have been closely related through the centuries. The modern American game Pictionary depends on the ability of simple pictures to carry information. Frank Laubach's literacy teaching method relates letters to pictures of objects as a memory aid. Pictographs on stone walls of hills and caves throughout Africa are thought to have been a kind of prayer for success in hunting.

Over time, pictures that carried messages developed into symbols representing objects and ideas. Those pic-

Traditional Chinese art often expresses a philosophy of life as a pilgrimage through successive lives. Rivers, paths, bridges and distant mountains all show elements of a Chinese Buddhist view of life.

149

ture-symbols became pure symbols representing either ideas (as in Chinese characters) or sounds of speech (as in the Roman alphabet).

Calligraphy joins the pictorial and writing systems, using letter shapes to create designs. Ornamentation may be added, developing a beauty different from that of either pictures or the letters themselves. Arabic script is frequently used as pure ornamentation on Middle Eastern buildings, in books, and in other places where something more than the writing itself is desired. For Muslims, pictures of humans or animals are idolatrous, but glorifying the written word honors Allah.

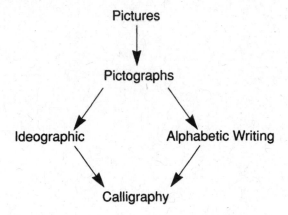

Perhaps all alphabets in use are sometimes ornamented or redrawn to emphasize the beauty of the written character. The Roman alphabet has hundreds of forms beyond cursive and printed or block letters. It is used for representing the sounds of more languages than any other form of writing. But the other approximately forty alphabets in use—such as Hindi, Amharic, Cyrillic, Greek, Thai, and Hebrew—also vary their forms and ornamentation to capture the mood of the message contained in letters and words.

Artifactual

When a third dimension is added to pictures, the artifactual system is introduced. Some art objects—carvings, sculpture, mobiles—are used for deliberate communication. Many are simply "things I like" that nevertheless indicate much about lifestyle and values.

Biblical worship made extensive use of artifacts designed specifically to help worshipers "see" unseen spiritual truths. Some of the more common such artifacts were

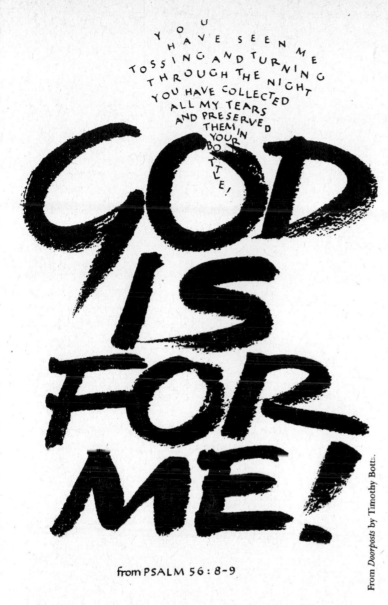

YOU HAVE SEEN ME TOSSING AND TURNING THROUGH THE NIGHT YOU HAVE COLLECTED ALL MY TEARS AND PRESERVED THEM IN YOUR BOTTLE!

GOD IS FOR ME!

from PSALM 56 : 8-9

From *Doorposts* by Timothy Bott.

water, oil, lamps, lampstands, fish, bread, the tabernacle, and later the temple. The prophets often used objects to proclaim profound spiritual insights: Jeremiah's potter and clay (Jer. 18), Ezekiel's cooking pot (Ezek. 24), and Zechariah's flying scroll and four chariots (Zech. 5, 6).

Our immediate environment has many objects that carry messages, quite apart from those objects that are consciously used to convey information. These "incidental" objects, from books to utilitarian items, all communicate to the observant person. It is helpful in observation to recognize four different groups of artifacts: (1) clothing and personal jewelry, (2) furnishings of a room, building,

151

or garden—books, art objects, mementos, furniture, (3) transportation items—bicycles or kind of car, for example, and (4) equipment used—appliances, telephones, computers, tools.

Architecture, of both building and landscapes, is a use of very large "objects" to communicate as well as to provide shelter and beauty.

Artifactual communication is not always as deliberately used as words are, but it is nonetheless an accurate way to understand an individual's or group's preferences and priorities. What does the Rolls Royce communicate regarding the owner? The old Volkswagen "beetle"? Or a shirt and tie versus dirty, patched jeans? What signals show wealth and high status, or poverty?

Audio

A blurred boundary lies between some signal systems, such as between the written and the pictorial. The audio system often overlaps with the verbal. Music is a well-developed form of audio communication often combined with words in singing. In speech, the tone frequently plays an important part in the information carried. Perhaps the verbal becomes audio when some people "speak" with a series of grunts, groans, or shrieks. Some singing, too, loses the verbal component completely!

The use of sound has two subsystems: structured use in music and sound-symbols such as whistles and sirens. In addition, silence—the absence of sound—can be a very powerful signal, and thus it is grouped with the audio system.

Music of different countries is quickly recognizable. Tuning across a shortwave band on the radio, one may comment, "That's a program from the Arabic world," "That's Africa," and so on. The different forms of music express particular ideas, or series of ideas, and feelings.

The sound pattern of voices during speaking can have considerable significance. Sometimes during a misunderstanding, we may ask, "Why are we angry with one another?" The reply may well be, "You said you didn't like what I was doing!" Indignantly, a reply is shot back, "I said nothing like that. I simply said, 'Are you sure that's what you want to do?'" Those were the words, but something else carried a message—the tone of voice. This is the audio system coupled with the verbal.

All over the hills of Burundi a simple advertising sign is used, even though most of the people are not literate. A stick about three feet high is stuck into the ground with three yellow strips of banana leaf attached to the top, pointing like an arrow to a building where beer can be bought. Most Burundi beer is made from bananas. Even the illiterate traveler can discover quickly where he can get a drink.
—Elizabeth Cox

152

Whistles to stop a game; sirens to speed up ambulances or slow down drivers; bells to mark a change in classes or call people to worship or tell time—all these represent audio communication. In nearly every part of the world there is an explosion of devices, such as tape recorders, television, dictaphones, stereos, and telephones, designed to aid audio communication.

Audio communication is commonly spoken of in Scripture. Psalms 149:1, 3 and 150:3–5 are examples of both music and individual sound-symbols:

Sing to the Lord a new song. . . .
Let them praise his name . . .
and make music to him with tambourine and harp.

Praise him with the sounding of the trumpet,
praise him with the harp and lyre,
praise him with tambourine and dancing,
praise him with the strings and flute,
praise him with the clash of cymbals,
praise him with resounding cymbals.

Aaron was instructed to wear golden bells around the hem of his robe when he ministered in the tabernacle. "The sound of the bells will be heard when he enters the Holy Place before the Lord and when he comes out, so that he will not die" (Exod. 28:35). Frequently in Scripture the audio system is incorporated in worship, in daily living, and in communicating truth, as in the Revelation of John.

"That awful, compelling silence" is the way Donald Hustad described the time of invitation at Billy Graham's West Berlin meetings in 1966.

To allay fears that hymns such as "Just As I Am" would unduly influence emotions, it had been decided to have no music during the invitation.

But the response was as great as ever, and critics said it was because of the silence.

153

Kinesics

Kinesics, body motion, speaks loudly even when no words are spoken. People seldom realize what they are saying with their motions because motion is used unconsciously. Persons who cannot stand still, who rock back and forth, twiddle their thumbs, or tap their fingers, are indicating impatience or nervousness. The person who is tired and bored sits in a chair differently from the person who is really interested in what is happening. The nervous and unsure person sits very straight, looking quickly around at many things. Hand motions, facial expressions, and body postures clearly give information, but here too, the information given by the same signals differs from culture to culture.

Beckoning with the hand, palm toward self, means "come" in some cultures and "go" in others. The height of a child is shown by height of the hand, palm down, in European cultures. In parts of Africa, only the height of a crop would be shown that way.

A systematized, conscious use of kinesics, commonly called "sign language," permits fuller communication with the hearing impaired.

While every culture has its own set of kinesic signs, few have developed as full a set of signals as the Italians. I once watched a housewife on a fourth-floor balcony purchase her family vegetable supply from a vendor on the street below. Because of traffic noise, neither could hear the other. Nevertheless, bargaining proceeded through only body language, a price was agreed upon, then a basket was lowered with the money. The vendor filled it with vegetables, and the housewife pulled it up to her balcony. She signaled her satisfaction to the vendor.

The wave offering before the Lord, described in Exodus 29:24, is one example of kinesics in the Bible. There are many others—kneeling, raising hands in praise, dancing. Ezekiel was told to use particular body positions to act out God's message to Israel, lying on his left side for 390 days and on his right side for 40 days (Ezek. 4).

This sign in one culture in India means "It is a taboo. Don't talk about it!" What might this gesture mean in your culture?

Shades of color can be used to describe emotional moods, as in this newspaper comment on the decade 1970–80:

"Clearly, these are not the best of times nor the worst of times. Mostly, the color is gray, a stubborn, frustrating gray we can't seem to shake."

Optical

The eighth system is optical, the use of light and color. Darkness and light both communicate information, with different meanings attached in different cultures. Biblically, colors and light itself are frequently modes of communication—red, black, purple, black, white, and gold. The four horsemen of Revelation are white, black, red, and "pale," each color signifying the kind of judgment to come. Another use of color to give information is in Isaiah 1:18, "Though your sins are like scarlet, they shall be as white as snow."

"In him was life, and that life was the light of men. The light shines in the darkness, but the darkness has not understood it" (John 1:4–5). The light is to be *understood,* showing that it is, at the most basic level, giving us information to be acted upon.

Color does not carry the same information for all cultures. The Zulus, for example, traditionally have considered green a neutral color with no real content and force: "It's just not attractive." Red expresses vigor and force for them, so they prefer reds, oranges, and yellows. By contrast, among another African people, Nigeria's Yoruba, green and blue are royal colors because they express strength and force. The psychological effect of color is quite apparently not universal. Red among the Chinese is the color of good fortune; thus Chinese restaurants are frequently decorated predominantly in red. White is the color of mourning; black carries that information in most Western cultures.

Tactile

The tactile—the use of touch—is the ninth system to consider. A man holding hands with another man is a sign of friendship in some cultures, while in others it is an indication of homosexuality. In traditional Africa, to touch or hold hands in public is never considered "moral" for a husband and wife; in Europe and North America, never to do so could be an indication of marital trouble. Americans do not shake hands frequently; Europeans shake hands both in greeting and in farewell. The slap, a blow

BETTER OR WORSE

with the fist to express anger, the touch of caution—all are uses of tactile communication.

The sins of Israel were put on the scapegoat in a ceremony in which tactile signals were central. In the New Testament, the laying on of hands was a powerful signal of identification with the person and of sharing with him or her the gifts of the Holy Spirit. Christian believers were commanded to greet one another in a tactile manner, "with a holy kiss."

Temporal

The use of time, the temporal system, has at least three subsystems. First are the units of time named and used in a society—seconds, minutes, hours, days, and the like. Northern European cultures are noted for their precise use of time, with schedules planned down to minute-units. There two minutes after the agreed time is late, but in many areas of southern Europe, nothing shorter than a five-minute unit would even be noticed. Among one group of people in south India, time was formerly broken up into only eight units for the whole twenty-four-hour period. Each time was named after a particular flower

Cartoon by Hagler

that opened up at that period of the day or night. In many subsistence societies, units shorter than days have no name, time being reckoned only by the relative position of the sun. A year is not numbered and is remembered only if something very significant happened, in which case the year is named "the Year of [the happening]."

Second, how is time used to convey information? In parts of Africa, if you are starting a really important meeting, it should begin about thirty minutes late. If the meeting is announced for 8:30, and you are there at 8:30, you may be considered overly eager or domineering, and antagonisms may be aroused. A 9:00 arrival shows courtesy and readiness to cooperate, but not an attempt to control. The European complains, "Why can't Africans ever be on time?" They are—the issue is *whose* time, and what is being communicated.

Western cultures use time deliberately to give messages. For example, if a woman is ready for her date exactly on time, she says something quite different from the message conveyed by a half-hour's delay. To emphasize their power, business executives have been known to keep salespeople waiting even if they are not busy with another appointment.

Third, the time orientation of a culture should be observed. Is the culture focused on the past, preoccupied with its own history? Or is it impatient with the past and primarily interested in what will be or could be? England and Vietnam are two widely separated cultures sharing the same orientation toward the past. The United States and the contemporary Soviet Union share an orientation toward the future, giving priority to change instead of continuity.

Time was significant in the giving of offerings, as shown in Exodus 29:38–39, "This is what you are to offer on the altar regularly each day: two lambs a year old. Offer one in the morning and the other at twilight." Other examples of using time and timing occur throughout Scripture. Aaron was to burn incense every morning, feast times were fixed throughout the year, the disciples met together on the Lord's Day, and periods of time are mentioned in books such as Daniel and Revelation.

Spatial

The tenth signal system is spatial—personal space, working space, and living space. In Latin countries, friends stand approximately eighteen inches apart when conversing. But in North America, thirty to thirty-six inches is the "comfortable" distance for friendly conversation. What happens when two men of these different cultures begin conversing without a prior understanding of this use of space?

Immediately the North American would feel that the Latin is too familiar, too pushy. "He's getting too close to me," the North American reacts subconsciously. "I don't like this." So he draws back physically.

The Latin will not verbalize his reaction, but he feels strongly, "Why is he not friendly? Why is he so distant from me?" And so the Latin moves closer. And the North American again moves back. Each experiences an unconscious reaction of discomfort. Unfriendliness, arrogance, trying to be too dominant and insistent, forcing ideas—all these stereotypes can develop because of differing use of the spatial signal system.

All of us have a personal space surrounding us that varies in size, depending on our culture and particular circumstances.

You walk into a business office and find an individual who is helpful, but is sitting at a small desk in a crowded office. Consciously or unconsciously, you think, "Thank you very much, but I want to talk to the boss." You want to talk to the person at the big desk in the big office, because *that* person, you sense, is the one with influence. Working space communicates status.

Compare the spatial communication involved in the typical layouts of a village in Kenya and a village in Nigeria. Given the same amount of land, each cultural group builds quite differently. In Kenya (upper photo), the houses are situated as far from one another as possible, with open land separating them. In Nigeria (lower photo), the houses are set close together, with large open spaces left around the tight clusters of houses.

Note the use of space in the biblical commands on how to build the tabernacle, and later the temple, as well as the location of the furniture each contained. The multitudes before God's heavenly throne, with angels and seraphim thronging close around the throne, speak of the arrangement of space to show glory and authority. In the new heaven and earth, the space separating God and humankind is taken away: "Now the dwelling of God is with men, and he will live with them" (Rev. 21:3).

The Swiss have long had a keen sense of how close together you can sit without feeling crowded.

We Swiss live at close quarters because our country is small and thickly settled. This has made us sensitive to close quarters. We have developed a keen sense of how many people can sit on one park bench, one observation bench, one bench by the tile stove without feeling cramped or getting on each other's nerves.

Possibly our decision to put seats in our DC-10s and B-747s a bit further apart than others was motivated by this feeling.
—A Swissair advertisement

158

Olfactory

The last signal system is the olfactory, the sense of smell and taste, which is frequently referred to in Scripture—incense, the sweet savor of a burnt offering, and spices (Exod. 29:18; 30:23–24, 34–38). The wise men brought precious spices to the child Jesus; the disciples ate with Jesus; and at their last meal together, Jesus insti-

159

My grandfather died three years ago, and his image in (a photograph), caught in a moment of posed reunion, often reminds me of my boyhood, when he doted on me as his hunting and fishing companion. Yet the recollections are vague and distant.

Recently, however, I took his old deerskin hunting vest out of the closet and on an impulse pressed it to my face and sniffed. Abruptly there came over me a rush of emotion and memory as intimate as it was compelling. No longer was I an adult squinting across a chasm of years at dim events: Suddenly I was a boy again, and there in all but the flesh was my grandfather, methodically reloading his shotgun as the flushed quail sailed beyond the mesquite.

This was no hazy reverie. I could feel his whiskered cheek against mine and smell his peculiar fragrance. . . . Momentarily I was once more on the floor of my grandparents' breakfast room, the linoleum cool against my belly as I sketched (airplanes).
—Boyd Gibbons, "The Intimate Sense of Smell"

tuted the Lord's Supper—Communion—by eating bread and drinking wine as symbols of his body and blood.

To express the goodness of the Lord in a powerful way, David uses the language of the olfactory system: "Taste and see that the Lord is good" (Ps. 34:8).

Women use perfume. Of course men do not use perfume, but after-shave lotion. Why it is more manly to smell like a pine tree than a violet is not clear. But in American culture, information about one's gender is carried by the scent one uses. Very definite values are assigned to different smells as well as to different tastes.

Particular portions of food may convey a message of status. The act of eating together is often deliberate communication, conveying a message of binding friendship. Giving a cup of drinking water to a defeated enemy (in the Middle East) is a signal that one will give that person protection.

A clear example of olfactory communication is shown by the story of Mary, who "took about a pint of pure nard, an expensive perfume; she poured it on Jesus' feet and wiped his feet with her hair. And the house was filled with the fragrance" (John 12:3). In many religious ceremonies, specific fragrances are used to symbolize suffering, joy, or thankfulness.

▼ USING THE SIGNAL SYSTEMS

These signal systems are the materials of communication, the things we shape and manipulate. To share human experience, we must use these signals. The presentation of the Gospel must be done within these systems. If we fail to use the signal systems in a way that is appropriate and understandable to the audience we want to reach, we will fail to create understanding.

Signal systems are living elements of a culture, separating one cultural grouping from another. Usage of these signal systems in a commonly accepted way knits a diverse group of people together. On the other hand, signal systems can divide a large group if they are not used in the same way throughout the group. Because signal systems are the observable parts of culture, being able to identify them and how they are used is very useful for learning to function in a new culture.

Knowing the basic components of communication within any culture, and how they fit together, will lead to more effective use of the communication arts. The skills of preaching, of storytelling or writing, and of art and

160

music can be effectively used in another culture only by using the signals in a way that is accepted by that culture. To be understood in Africa, the North American musician must learn how rhythm is used there. The Chinese artist needs to paint using the pictorial symbols of India if he or she wishes to communicate with Indians. The preaching style of Italy may annoy people in Norway; the Latin preacher in Japan may be considered oddly out of touch with people. Recognizing the twelve signal systems, learning how they are used in each culture, and consciously using them in the appropriate way is the basis of effective intercultural communication.

Learning the signal systems of another culture requires conscious attention and patience. Not everything is different between any two cultures, but there must be careful observation to find out which things are the same and which are different. Consider how many combinations and permutations of signals are possible, given that there are twelve basic systems, with hundreds to hundreds of thousands of signals possible within each system.

For an understanding of our use of these basic symbol systems, one must grasp three key principles.

First, we rarely use one system in isolation. In normal interpersonal communication we use two or more of these systems at the same time. Each of the systems usually complements and supports the other systems.

When we use several signals so that they complement each other, more information can be transferred, and the impact of the message is increased dramatically. Using several signal systems in combination is similar to adding more pipes to a water system. A larger number of pipes carries more water. Similarly, each added signal system increases the information load carried. If one system fails to be understood, there is not a total loss of communication, because other signal systems are carrying the same or related information.

Different media emphasize different signal systems; books and newspapers are essentially the written system, with the pictorial also used. Radio primarily uses the verbal and audio systems. Television combines several—pictorial, verbal, and audio, and others to a lesser degree. A well-planned communication campaign will utilize several media so that the strength of each reinforces all.

Even more significant than the way we receive our information is which information we can best recall at a later time. When only audio information is given, 70 per-

During our furlough, I noticed that those meetings which gave time not only for a spoken report but also a humorous role-play and a video of the work left the audiences much more enthusiastic and apparently committed to our ministry

When I was able to sing several songs, the reception seemed to be even better. People left meetings where several different media were used saying, "For the first time I feel I really understand what you're doing over there!"

—Anonymous (a missionary serving in a restricted-access nation)

cent is recalled after three hours, but only 10 percent after three days. When information is given visually, the figures are 72 percent and 20 percent for the same periods. But when the two are combined, 85 percent is recalled three hours later, and 65 percent three days later. Although different studies report differing figures, the relative strength of combining seeing and hearing in teaching has been confirmed over and over again.

Second, it is possible for one system to contradict the other systems. This contradiction between symbol systems is the cause of many misunderstandings in interpersonal communication. One system says one thing, and another system says something else.

For example, "Really? Did you find that interesting? Well! Isn't it nice that you enjoy that!" What was communicated? The words said, "I think it's great that you like it." The audio system—the tone of the voice in this case—implied, "That's a silly thing to like!" When two or more signal systems support one another, we believe the message to be sincere. When the signal systems contradict each other, we believe the person to be insincere.

This brings us to a general principle. We tend to believe the less consciously used system. If while the verbal system is being used, the audio or kinesic system contradicts the verbal, the less consciously used system (audio or kinesic) is more likely to be believed. The person with perception in interpersonal relationships is often the person who has learned to read the signals of these less consciously used systems.

When we say, "Mr. X is a person I don't trust; don't always believe what he says because you can't be sure he really means it," what are we saying? Simply that his verbal system is repeatedly contradicted by the less conscious systems of communication.

This often happens in cross-cultural communication. A person may genuinely mean what he or she is communicating verbally, but the people to whom the communication is directed interpret the audio, kinesic, temporal, or spatial message in a way that the speaker does not at all intend. As a result, they do not believe what he or she says. "You can't trust an American... or an African, or an Indian, or an Arab." Often such destructive charges are leveled because of an unintentional and inadvertent contradiction of systems.

Third, within all the systems there are two levels of information, the rational and the emotional. Some signal

---

Which signals bring the most information?
- 1% from taste + 3.5% from smell = 4.5% from **olfactory** signals
- 1.5% from touch (**tactile** signals)
- 11% from hearing (**verbal** and **audio** signals)
- 83% from seeing (**written, pictorial, artifactual, numeric, kinesic, optical,** and **spatial** signals)

162

systems carry more emotional information, while others are more heavily rational. The written is heavily rational. But emotional response to writing is nevertheless present. In some cultures the message will be believed *because* it is written or printed, while in other cultures it will be disbelieved because it is printed.

In most cultures the spatial, olfactory, and temporal systems carry much emotional information. Misuse of space can cause a person's temper to rise without the person understanding why he or she is becoming angry. If one person walks close to someone and then keeps moving closer, the second person will soon become very antagonistic to the first—a strong emotional reaction that comes with little or no understanding of what is happening.

Both emotion and reason are necessary in effective communication. All twelve signal systems carry both elements, though the proportion of each in a particular system varies from situation to situation and culture to culture.

We are attempting to communicate clearly an infinite message to finite human beings. We must communicate that message in thousands of widely different cultures and subcultures, each with its own way of seeing the world. The very least we can do is understand the raw materials of communication with which we must work.

Only very basic principles have been touched upon here, but they can free you from simple imitation of others' approaches and help you create the best combination of signals to communicate the love of God in Jesus Christ in your particular cultural situation.

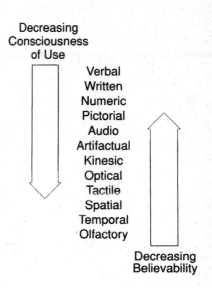

Decreasing Consciousness of Use

Verbal
Written
Numeric
Pictorial
Audio
Artifactual
Kinesic
Optical
Tactile
Spatial
Temporal
Olfactory

Decreasing Believability

SUMMARY

Most human communication happens through twelve different systems of signals. Each system is virtually a language in itself, with its own vocabulary and grammar. The systems normally reinforce one another, but they can also be contradictory. When this happens, not only is it difficult to understand the message, but the messenger also seems insincere.

The twelve systems are verbal, written, numeric, pictorial, audio, artifactual, kinesic, optical, tactile, spatial, temporal, and olfactory. The specific signals used and the meaning assigned to signals vary from culture to culture.

Participating in another culture requires learning more than the verbal language. Other systems may be learned sooner, making interpretation of the verbal a simpler task—and communication in the new setting more effective.

▼ BIBLIOGRAPHY

General Readings on Nonverbal Communication

Adler, Ron, and Neil Towne. *Looking Out/Looking In: Interpersonal Communication.* San Francisco: Rinehart, 1975. See chapter 6, "Nonverbal Communication: Messages Without Words."

Fabun, Don. *Communications: The Transfer of Meaning.* San Francisco: International Society for General Semantics, 1988.

Hickson, Mark L., III, and Don W. Stacks. *NVC: Nonverbal Communication.* Dubuque, Iowa: Wm. C. Brown, 1985.

Ruesch, Jurgen, and Weldon Kees. *Nonverbal Communication: Notes on the Visual Perception of Human Relations.* Rev. ed. Berkeley: University of California Press, 1972.

Signal Systems

Hundreds of articles and books examine or illustrate one or more of the signal systems. The titles given here are some that expand their subject beyond the possibilities of a single chapter in this book. Some of these references are highly entertaining; all are valuable for the reader who seeks a fuller understanding of particular signal systems.

Verbal

Rheingold, Howard. *They Have a Word for It.* Los Angeles: Jeremy P. Tarcher, 1988.

Written

Logan, Robert K. *The Alphabet Effect.* New York: Morrow, 1986.

Numeric

Ifrah, Georges. *From One to Zero: A Universal History of Numbers.* New York: Penguin, 1988.

Kinesic

Lamb, Roger. "Reading Facial Expressions." In *Eye to Eye: How People Interact*. Edited by Peter Marsh. Topsfield, Mass.: Salem House, 1988.

Marsh, Peter. "Using Body Language" and "Making Eye Contact." In *Eye to Eye: How People Interact*. Edited by Peter Marsh. Topsfield, Mass.: Salem House, 1988.

Spatial

Marsh, Peter. "Keeping a Distance." In *Eye to Eye: How People Interact*. Edited by Peter Marsh. Topsfield, Mass.: Salem House, 1988.

Tactile

Thayer, Stephen. "The Language of Touch." In *Eye to Eye: How People Interact*. Edited by Peter Marsh. Topsfield, Mass.: Salem House, 1988.

Olfactory

Gibbons, Boyd. "The Intimate Sense of Smell." *National Geographic* 170, no. 3 (September 1986).

Gilbert, Avery N., and Charles J. Wysocki. "The Smell Survey: Its Results." *National Geographic* 172, no. 4 (October 1987).

Marsh, Peter. "Reacting to Scent." In *Eye to Eye: How People Interact*. Edited by Peter Marsh. Topsfield, Mass.: Salem House, 1988.

➤ If we don't use the media, we cannot complete world evangelization.

➤ The computer was right! The most effective way is just to talk to people! (Os Guinness, *The Gravedigger File*, 62)

MULTIPLYING AND EXTENDING THE MESSAGE

PROPOSITION 13: Mass media extend the range of a message, but inevitably distort the message.

The special ability of mass media is to *extend* a message far beyond the range of unaided human abilities—beyond the sound of speech or any of the human sense organs. The mass media extend the message not only geographically, but also in time. Through printing technologies we are able to enjoy the words of Shakespeare, Chaucer, Dante, and thousands of others across the boundaries of time and space. Electronically based technologies give the same barrier-breaking qualities to sight and sound, so we see people and happenings from the other side of the world, hear great orchestras in a concert hall on another continent, and listen to speeches of great figures who long ago left this life.

There is virtually no limit to the potential audiences through these technologies. Whereas a crowd must press close to hear an open-air speaker, through radio, television, or printing each person can hear as if he or she were face-to-face with the speaker or performers. Ten thousand or a million individuals can have a "private" hearing without taking anything away from others' ability to hear and see. The technical marvels of the mass media can extend communication potential beyond all normal human limits.

It is more satisfactory to view the phenomena as *extending* media rather than "mass" media. Communication is still achieved through use of the basic signal systems. Nothing is added—no new signal system, no work of magic—to give power to an impotent message. The signals, normally restricted to unaided human sensibilities, are multiplied, magnified, empowered so they can be extended far beyond human sensory limits. It is the incredible extension of these signals that is the special quality of mass media.

The term *mass media* also gives a false idea about the audience. There is not a new group called the "mass audience," but rather a large number of clusters of individuals who are now within the range of signals because of the extending effect of communications technology. These clusters (or networks) must be attracted, informed, and persuaded with the same dynamics used in face-to-face communication. It is more difficult to do so through the media, however, because the very act of extending the signals through mechanical and electronic means leaves out some signals altogether, while emphasizing others. This fact inevitably causes distortion or skewing of the original message.

Certainly if there is not a clear and comprehensible message to begin with, using the media will not make it a message. If you begin with 0, multiplying it with powerful media will still give 0. Extending media cannot be useful tools in Christian witness when they are consciously or unconsciously a substitute for a personal witness with individuals.

$$0 \times 1,000 = 0$$
$$0 \times 100,000 = 0$$
$$0 \times 1,000,000 = \text{still } 0$$

Too many grand assumptions are made about the power of mass (extending) media. Advocates claim that only by using extending media can we complete the task of evangelizing the world. Without extending media, it is argued, we cannot hope to teach the Gospel adequately to new millions who are entering the church. The extending media are very useful but have inherent limitations, factors that change the way communication happens.

Why is television appropriate for mass evangelism, and are the results worth the cost?

The church should use any vehicle that has the potential to reach large numbers of people for Christ. As for cost, I can speak only for (my network). Some 70 million people have access to our programming. It costs about a penny to give a Christian witness to each potential viewer.

—Paul Crouch, "Taking Television to the World, *Christianity Today*, 16 October 1987, 209

The technology that makes the various mass media awesomely powerful also limits the ways in which these media communicate. Radio, for example, is almost entirely limited to verbal and audio signal systems. Pictorial, artifactual, and kinesic systems can only be referred to and not directly used. The same limitations apply to audio recordings, even though these do surmount the restriction of time. Television has greater power than radio for many communicative purposes, but it too is limited by inability to utilize tactile and olfactory signals—two of the most emotionally potent ways of communication.

The total context of extending media communication is different from that of face-to-face communication. Context is an important part of building understanding. How carefully a young American man develops the context—quiet dinner, flowers, soft music, a beautiful setting—before he asks the woman of his dreams to marry him! Coffee houses, because of their ambience, frequently stimulate more serious conversations on spiritual issues than formal Sunday services in church.

Context is an important part of the communicative process. But when one uses extending media, one has very little control over the context within which the message is received. The intended audience bring their own contexts; an audience will have almost as many contexts as there are audience members. Since the understanding developed is partly a function of context, the variation is nearly as diverse as the audience.

The lack of immediate feedback, or even full feedback, also causes distortion of the communication process. Without some idea of how the message is being understood, one cannot send corrective signals, and the total process is hindered. It is not enough to assume that if the signals are being received, the message is being heard. Volume does not ensure understanding.

A pastor preaching to a congregation is speaking to a captive "mass audience," but much feedback still occurs. The pastor can know if the people understand, if they are paying attention, or if they are resisting what is being said. With that feedback—which in a formal service is received primarily from body language—the pastor can alter the manner of speech and even content. This interaction keeps the communication process alive.

But the same preacher (and message) extended to a larger audience through radio lacks immediate feedback and possibly never receives feedback. Alterations cannot

A representative of a large Christian radio station wrote to *World Christian* magazine regarding his organization's "outreach to 80% of the world's population, including more than two billion who cannot be reached by any other means than superpower radio. . . .

"A missionary laboring face to face for a whole lifetime could not begin to reach the people reached by superpower radio in just five minutes! . . .

"Without minimizing the ministry of any missionary or mission organization, I must affirm my conviction, based on solid evidence, that no other tool God has given us can reach the most number of people in the shortest span of time for the least investment as superpower radio!"

And the editor responded: "At issue is what you mean by 'reaching' people. No doubt (your) broadcasts 'reach' 80% of the world and
(continued)

be made in the presentation; if it is not acceptable, the pastor is simply turned off. It is much easier to turn the radio dial than to walk out of a church service.

Despite the limitations of the extending media, if used appropriately they have great value. Unfortunately, uninformed enthusiasm overstates what media can do and thus diminishes effectiveness by obscuring weaknesses.

The people who are "reached" within the extended range given by the media are not necessarily paying attention to the communication. Suggesting that the number of people living within broadcast range, or near a bookstore, is synonymous with the number of people reached simply is not valid.

"Where else can you get a 100,000-watt transmitter at so low a price . . . moreover, reaching so many millions, estimated at 80 million-plus souls in what is recognized as the greatest missionary field?" says material from an advertising agency selling time on Gospel radio. But how many of the 80 million are actually listening? Accurate figures are available from the United States for the total population and the regular viewing audience for religious television. The total U.S. population is 250 million, all of whom live within areas covered by television transmitters—equivalent to the figure often called "reached" by the promoters of Christian radio or television. However, regular viewers of religious programming (watching at least fifteen minutes per week) were only 13.3 million people, or 6.2 percent of those living in households with a television set. When the standard of "regular viewing" was raised to one hour or more per week, fewer than 7 million were in the actual audience—3.14 percent of the population. (This study, carried out through the Annenberg School of Communications, University of Pennsylvania, and the Gallup Organization, directed by George Gerbner, was cited in *The Good Newspaper* 2, no.15 [23 May 1984].)

Specialists in Gospel literature have sought to provide every family in the world a printed piece that presents the way of salvation, or to send New Testaments and Bibles to every home, as *the* way to evangelize. Many other plans aim to send literature where people cannot go; the suggestion is that it is not necessary for people to go if literature or other media can. "This new satellite will enable television programs to reach every village in Latin America," enthused one promoter. Another agency says that a

(continued)
we rejoice that multiplied millions do indeed listen. Further, there is abundant evidence that many respond in faith and obedience to the Gospel message. But for a people group to be 'reached' in the sense that is generally agreed upon by a broad base of Evangelical churches and missions, there must be within that people group a cluster of dynamic churches which are aggressively growing and multiplying that promises that the entire people group will indeed be evangelized for generations to come. These kinds of churches usually take a lifetime of labor. . . .

"In many parts of the world, at this time, doors are indeed closed to standard career missionaries. . . . The global Church must, and we believe will, find ways to make disciples in peoples who have yet to hear and see the Gospel demonstrated persuasively among them.

"We want to believe that the Church will begin to use any and all means and not restrict itself to the path of least investment. May a wave of church planters and 'need-meeters' follow the first witness by air!"
—"Letters to the Editor," *World Christian* 2, no. 1 (January–February 1983): 2

satellite can be used to transmit radio programs to every village and every home throughout Africa, India, and Southeast Asia.

Whatever the medium used, certain signals are extended far and wide. But life cannot be reduced to even widespread media signals. There is no substitute for personal fellowship, for sharing in the life of Jesus Christ expressed in the church. The church is necessary; it is the body of our Lord Jesus Christ present in the world today. Literature, radio, television, or any combination of media disseminates facts, simulations of real experience, but it is not the experience itself. By assuming that the experience of salvation and new life in Jesus Christ can be encompassed within those signals that can be extended widely, we reduce the Gospel to a simplistic formula. The Gospel is the very life of God brought to humankind. It can be partly described through media, but can be fully experienced only in the body of Christ.

The second issue to consider in Christian use of the media is the matter of appropriateness. Even if the presumed audience is actually reached, is it possible to evangelize by distributing literature and broadcasting electronic signals? Are the media appropriate for portraying God's self-revelation in Jesus Christ?

Extending media must narrow the signals employed. Literature cannot extend kinesic, olfactory, temporal, tactile, or audio signals. Radio is even more limited. Television can extend a wider range of signals, but there is still an inevitable narrowing that results in something different from the original experience. The transmission may be so condensed, due to the restrictions of time alone, that the result is a caricature of reality. Complex issues, emotional questions of loyalty and commitment, simply cannot be fully portrayed.

Jerry Mander sums up the difference between tangible and intangible on television:

> It suddenly became obvious to me that a product is a lot easier to get across on television than a desert or a cultural mind-set.
>
> Understanding Indian ways enough to care about them requires understanding a variety of dimensions of nuance and philosophy. You don't need any of that to understand a product, you do not have problems of subtlety, detail, time and space, historical context or organic form. Products are inherently communicable on television because of their static quality, sharp, clear, highly visible lines, and because they carry no informational meaning beyond

---

The purpose of our broadcast, as is the purpose of many religious programs, is to strengthen and support the church, which is doing the work of Jesus Christ where it must be done—among people, where they live and where they work.

Focusing the TV cameras on the expressions of people does not fulfill the need for Christian community where people are baptized and where they receive the Lord's Supper for themselves, not just watching and wondering why other people, as they say, go to church.

God is certainly using the electronic media for the proclamation of his grace and glory as you see it in the face of Jesus Christ. The electronic media can never be a substitute, however, for the local congregation.

Paul makes this very clear. He instructs Christian people to get together, to meet, not to neglect this coming together.

— Oswald C. J. Hoffmann, "The Electronic Church: An Extension, Not a Substitute," *Religious Broadcasting,* November 1983

what they themselves are. They contain no life at all and are therefore not capable of dimension. Nothing works better as telecommunication than images of products.

Might television itself have no higher purpose?

—*Four Arguments for the Elimination of Television*, 42–43

Mander continues by pointing out that technology is not neutral, that the nature of the medium determines the kind of information that is carried by it. "The argument goes that television is merely a window or a conduit through which any perception, any argument or reality may pass. . . . Far from being 'neutral,' television itself predetermines who shall use it, how they will use it, what effects it will have on individual lives, and, if it continues to be widely used, what sorts of political forms will inevitably emerge" (Mander, *Four Arguments*, 43–45).

The power of extending media is very real. Each form of the extending media has its specialists and advocates who claim that they alone can do the whole job. Each group has too narrow a view, because they have not grasped the full nature of the media.

Four points need special attention:

1. The primary effect of extending media in most situations is reinforcement of existing attitudes, rather than changing of attitudes.

2. When extending media do bring change, it is often a broad social change that has little to do with the specific content of the media.

3. The greater the area covered by extending media, the greater the possibility that the audience will merely listen passively without involvement or personal reaction to the message.

4. The immense coverage of extending media can lead to ignoring cultural differences within the audience, differences that deeply affect basic understanding of the content we seek to share.

▼ REINFORCING EXISTING OPINION

One of the best-established facts about mass communication is its reinforcement or polarization effect. When mass communication seeks to persuade its audience to change an opinion or attitude, these are the usual results:

No change	65–75 percent
Existing opinion strengthened	10–20 percent
Opinion changed	3–5 percent

In most cases, as many who originally agreed with the persuasive message change their opinion to disagree as those who change from disagreement to agreement.

Sometimes major changes do occur, and under particular conditions the changes may be widespread. But in normal circumstances, change of attitude is the rarest result of mass communications. Joseph Klapper comments, "Persuasive mass communication normally tends to serve far more heavily in the interests of reinforcement and of minor change" (*The Effects of Mass Communication*, 15).

Anyone can prove by illustration that conversion to Christ can result from the use of extending media. But have we evaluated the true effectiveness of the way in which we use mass media? Have we considered the possibility that the indiscriminate spread of the words of Christianity may sometimes have the opposite effect to that which we anticipate? For every illustration of conversion, how many illustrations of antagonism do we not know?

▼ WHAT KIND OF CHANGE?

Many plans have been put forward to blanket areas, even the whole world, with radio, with literature, with television, by the use of satellites and elaborate programming techniques. These ideas are good, perhaps even excellent, but they do not guarantee evangelism, and they may not even approach the basic task of evangelism.

The media greatly increase the flow of information, bringing isolated peoples into the flow of national and world affairs. This increased information, even Christian information, may merely stimulate broad change. The kind of change media bring about is determined by many factors, only one of which is content.

Increased flow of information results in greater awareness of alternatives to present beliefs and ways of living. Exposure to media messages becomes more selective, with a much greater probability that only those messages are selected that agree with existing beliefs. Media provide an important social service by increasing information flow that relates groups to other societies and the world outside their immediate surroundings. Social change is stimulated as a result—change that has little or no relationship to the actual content of the media. Thus, simply increasing the flow of Christian communication may only make the audience more resistant, more indifferent to the basic message of Christ.

Lerner reports that when Radio Cairo comes into a remote village, "in terms of personal aspirations nearly everything happens." But nothing really changed except the people's expectations. "The mass media have been used to stimulate people . . . by raising their levels of aspiration—for the good things of the world, for a better life. No adequate provision is made, however, for raising the levels of achievement. Thus people are encouraged to want more than they can possibly get, aspirations rapidly outrun achievements, and frustrations spread."
—Wilbur Schramm, *Mass Media and National Development*, 130–31: quoting Daniel Lerner, *The Passing of Traditional Society* (Glencoe, Ill.: Free Press, 1958)

The right content does not ensure the desired results. Inserting a pattern of words into a society through extending media does not guarantee that we have accomplished Christian communication. This semimagical utilization of extending media may not be communication at all. It assumes that the truth is simply a set of facts that can be shipped to people en masse because of the power of extending media. Presentation of a set of facts to a huge audience is not communicating Christ, even if the words are orthodox. Even if a good portion of that audience recalls the words, and can even repeat them, that does not prove that true Christian communication has occurred.

The primary change we want is not social change, but a change in people's relation to God. Conventional use of mass communications may stimulate only social change, leaving the heart untouched and Christ unknown.

▼ PASSIVITY INSTEAD OF INVOLVEMENT

Christian communication is a process demanding some reaction, some involvement by the listener. In Marshall McLuhan's terms, it demands a "cool" medium, one in which there is considerable exchange between the message-giver and the message-receiver. An exchange, a transaction, is necessary for God's truth to be apprehended. Mass communications can be useful tools for ministry when involvement is part of the process. But if involvement is not developed, mass communication becomes only a telling of facts.

It is possible to code and feed into the computer an accurate statement of the Gospel. The computer will remember it perfectly, and when the appropriate question is asked, it will perfectly recall the content of the Gospel. It can even print it out on request. Because it has remembered the Gospel, and can give such an accurate and "clear testimony" of the Gospel content, could we say that we have converted the computer?

No, the computer is not a Christian because it is not involved. It has no concept of commitment, no reaction, no internal appropriation.

Christian communication is a process demanding involvement, a personal reaction to the person of Jesus Christ. It is not enough to convey a set of facts from one mind to another. We seek to stimulate in another heart the experiencing of God in Christ. Mass communications, thoughtlessly used, merely transmit facts that demand no involvement, no reaction.

Normal use of the electronic media requires little involvement, little response from the audience. The "hot" media bombard the listener-viewer with strong images, portraying emotion dispassionately, so that little room is left for imaginative involvement. The fitting of Christian facts into mass communications does not necessarily change the nature of the tool. As a result, the Christian experience is not communicated, though a feeling of religiousness may be developed. That religiousness may shield people from a shattering contact with God in Christ. Religiousness without serious commitment can be a protection against the demands of real faith.

▼ TOO MANY CAN MEAN TOO LITTLE

Modern extending media can cover a remarkable geographic area. A dozen tribes, or a hundred, may be within range of a powerful radio station. A mass-circulation magazine may have subscribers in twenty or thirty nations. The diversity in this audience is difficult to imagine. And that is precisely why mass communication can easily fail at its point of greatest potential strength.

Culture is the screening device through which messages pass. They may be eliminated, they will be altered, and only occasionally will they pass through the cultural screen intact. What effectively communicates with one group of people may be ineffective with another, even if they are all considered to be the same audience. The wider the coverage of the media, the larger the number of different groups within the coverage area. Differences in habits, values, and beliefs among these groups will vary from minor to major. The effectiveness of communication will likewise vary from good to poor or nonexistent.

When people within the same culture communicate, it is usually successful, because they share a common cultural framework. But when people who have derived their meanings from different cultural experiences try to communicate, misunderstanding is common. The more differences there are within the audience, the less likelihood there is of success in communication. Huge audiences may, in fact, be a mirage.

Mindless entertainment becomes for most North Americans an increasing addiction that gradually diminishes them as persons and prevents their taking seriously the ultimate issues of guilt, death and afterlife, purpose, themselves.
—*The Way* 18, no. 9 (September 1974)

▼ DOES MASS COMMUNICATION EVER WORK?

In certain conditions, mass media can be tremendously useful. When people are dissatisfied with their present situation, they are much more open to receiving messages that call for personal and group change—such as the message of Jesus Christ, which demands a total reorientation of life.

In times of rapid change, people often do not know how to adjust to that change. Familiar patterns of behavior no longer bring the positive results expected. New conditions require new knowledge, so people will know how to respond appropriately to the new needs and opportunities. The familiar social system has become dysfunctional; it no longer works as it should. In such situations, mass communication can be highly effective. People are looking for new information, new ways to satisfy old needs that are not being met in the changing environment. Mass communication can provide that information, and people's use of it increases in times of change and crisis.

When a devastating earthquake struck Managua, Nicaraguans turned to whatever media were available to learn "the news." Their physical world was in shambles, and they did not know how to relate to the changed circumstances. In that situation, the extending media were both powerful and valuable.

Vast changes occurred in China under the leadership of Mao Tse-tung and after his death, creating a classic situation in which extending media can be very potent. The resulting openness to the media was not permanent, but would continue until new stability was achieved.

When President John F. Kennedy was assassinated, listenership to all news and analysis programs increased dramatically. Americans were eager for the full story of what happened, but even more fundamentally, they showed their need for information so they could adjust appropriately to the changed circumstances in the leadership of the United States. After the new president was visibly in charge and normal routines had returned, listenership lapsed to its normal levels.

In such situations, extending media play a particularly valuable role. The alternative is the spread of information by word of mouth, friend talking to friend, a message's being overheard by someone who repeats it inaccurately, or a frightened person's imagining the worst and talking about it—creating a rumor that may be repeated as fact by the next person. Under stress and conditions of ignorance, responsible use of the media gives critically needed information and guidance. It can have a calming and stabilizing effect.

When a society is stable, no crisis threatens, and the population is generally satisfied, how are mass communications used? As said, the dominant *effect* is to reinforce existing attitudes. The audience is active, making selections among the media and deciding what they will pay attention to. People commonly choose to view or hear things with which they already agree, and to ignore messages or message sources with which they expect to disagree. This is one of the primary reasons that mass communications usually reinforce opinion. When there is no opinion, or new information shows the situation has changed, mass communication is effective in forming opinion.

The media are consciously used for entertainment. What is chosen because of its presumed entertainment value fills other functions—giving new information, showing how to deal with familiar but frustrating circumstances, teaching how to respond to unfamiliar situations. The active audience does not consciously select media with these goals in mind, but finds entertainment satisfy-

When the volcano Mount St. Helens exploded, I was with my high school band nearly three hundred miles away. We were to return home the very day that the volcano erupted. But we were unable to go because of dangerous driving conditions. We all gathered around the television to watch reports on what was happening in our home, only fifty miles from the volcano and in the path of the dust and debris from the explosion. There were so many conflicting reports that we didn't know whom to believe.

The media increased our anxiety by its constant message that our home town was "a disaster area." We thought of buried homes, people dead from suffocation—total devastation. In reality, clouds of dust had settled on our home, but there were no deaths.

We depended on the media in the crisis, but by omitting reports that showed normal things and emphasizing the huge explosion, the media warped our understanding of the situation.
—Dan George

ing when those unidentified needs are being met.

Through such entertainment, and the selection of information that is poured out through media, we modify our images of the world and how we should relate to it. This process of restructuring our perceptions of life and forming new opinions and beliefs does not happen *because of* mass communication. It is always happening through the experiences of daily life. The process is greatly accelerated, however, through the feast of media information from which we can select vicarious experiences.

A striking illustration of mass communications effect on our thinking is provided by the *Issues Management Letter*. This exclusive subscription service "presents a measure of the use of all media space (print) and time (broadcast) as national news." The publishers say, "Measuring exposure is a rough gauge of what's going into the public mind. People may or may not act on it." But the analysis of media content has been shown to predict what people will be thinking about, and even how attitudes will develop in the general public. "Politics . . . offers the clearest evidence. . . . Over the past six years we have found that changes in the President's approval rating could be foreseen solely by looking at the level of media criticism of his domestic policies." Media analysis was also able to predict the winners of the 1984 primary elections. Its accurate prediction of behavior and financial trends came only "from measuring the volume of news messages" (*Issues Management Letter*, 10 September 1987).

To trace the formation of particular attitudes directly to the effect of mass communication, however, is nearly impossible. The long-term results are nevertheless real, with very visible consequences. Relationships between behavior and repeated exposure to violence or sexually oriented programming have been established, *but not a direct cause-and-effect relationship*. It has not been possible to establish beyond question whether that kind of programming is selected because of a predisposition to sexually deviant or violent behavior or whether the programming itself has caused the behavior. Either way, there is no question that a Christian's use of the media should carefully exclude input whose results are questionable.

There is little question that the long-term effects of mass communications do subtly but surely shape the way we structure our image of the world. The media are a way by which we learn to relate to what surrounds us. Not

I was on my first trip to China. . . . As I was unpacking some gifts for my relatives, one of my cousins began asking me about my life. Finally he asked me straight out, "Did you bring a Bible for me?" All of my other cousins also asked for Bibles after I had witnessed to them. . . .

I thought I might have difficulty communicating spiritual matters. But they understood me. Yet they had been indoctrinated in atheism. "Where did you hear about this before?" I asked my relatives.

One cousin replied, "Once a week we listen to the overseas Christian radio programs." I found there is a real curiosity and interest in the Bible because of the Christian radio programs they hear from the free world. They need people to visit them and confirm what they have been hearing on the radio.

—*Open Doors*, May–June 1978

everything can be included in mass communication; selections must be made. What we are told, and what we are not told, determines *what* we think about even if it does not control *how* we think.

Editors and producers choose content because of what they think the audience will accept, but some potential content is not even considered. The audience has no chance to develop a desire for things of whose existence they have not been made aware. The gatekeepers of mass communications make an initial choice of gates to open and roads to follow. After that, they tell the audience about those gates and roads; other roads might as well not exist.

When unacceptable values in some programming are challenged, the common defense is, "If the audience didn't want it, we wouldn't give it to them." That statement is correct, but it does not address the issue of how preference has been developed or how it might gradually be changed through different programming.

Christian impact in extending media could be most significant if believers developed secular programming that consistently portrayed Christian values within the marketplace of ideas and entertainment. Christian participation in the media for primary evangelism will seldom be effective. The active audience will select what it wants, and the very people for whom evangelistic programming is intended are most likely to choose *not* to listen. Win Arn confirms this: "In a survey we conducted of 40,000 church-related Christians, only 0.01 percent said they attend church as a result of mass evangelism, including religious radio and television." He points out, "Each year, about 2 million religious television and radio programs are beamed over some 7,000 stations. These programs have made little impact on non-Christians. More than 70 percent of Americans either have no religious affiliation or are Christian in name only" (Win Arn, "Is T.V. Appropriate for Mass Evangelism?" *Christianity Today*, 16 October 1987, 50).

In nation after nation, people are dissatisfied. We can use mass communications to build an awareness of Christian values, to develop an openness to the supreme message of change, the Gospel. But the media must be used appropriately. They must be used to gain involvement instead of passive acceptance of words. And the media must extend a vital personal witness rather than being used as a substitute for personal relationship.

Andrew Meltzoff, a psychologist at the University of Washington in Seattle, has conducted a study that indicates television has a wonderful and previously unsuspected effect on children under the age of two—children at their most vulnerable and impressionable age.

Dr. Meltzoff put infants in front of a TV set and allowed them to watch a tape of an adult disassembling and then reassembling a toy. Ater the tape ended, a huge percentage of the babies grabbed that particular toy and did just what the adult on the screen had done. Babies who hadn't seen the tape just kind of drooled on the toy or banged it around.

Here's what this means: . . .

Those who said babies couldn't understand two-dimensional images were wrong. . . . It also means TV can dramatically change the behavior of a very small child.

Based on "Imitation of TV Models by Infants," 1221–29

SUMMARY

The mass media are essentially multiplying and extending devices. Through electronic and mechanical devices, the basic signals of human communication are reproduced many thousands of times. The area where those signals can be seen and heard is vastly extended, even to covering the entire world. If there is an effective message or messenger in interpersonal communication, the mass media can multiply that impact.

But in the multiplication, certain parts of the message are unavoidably dropped. Mass media are able to use fewer of the signal systems than do face-to-face interpersonal relationships. With the loss of some signal systems, there is a loss in the information given and, usually, in the impact of the message.

Mass media also have constraints on their overall effectiveness that must be remembered. For example, the primary effect of mass media is reinforcement of existing beliefs. Mass media messages are normally perceived as impersonal and not demanding involvement. Such hidden characteristics diminish the impact of the Christian message in mass media. The marvels of mechanics and electronics may powerfully assist the spread of the Gospel, but at other times they may hinder true understanding and response to the message of Christ. There is no magic in the media.

Sitting on the Moscow subway, I was conversing with the man next to me. "Why do the American mass media treat us Soviets as if we were primitive bears in the forest?" he asked me. "We are flesh-and-blood human beings like any other people."

Later that same week, I met with the editorial staff of . . . the multilingual magazine of the Soviet Peace Committee. One staff member said to me, "You Americans talk a great deal about the importance of living in a free society. Yet why do Americans know so little about the Soviet Union? What does freedom of the press mean when you get such one-sided treatment of our country?"

—Richard Deats, *The Other Side* 23, no. 10 (December 1987): 26

▼ BIBLIOGRAPHY

Hoover, Stewart M. *Mass Media Religion: The Social Sources of the Electronic Church.* Newbury Park, Calif.: Sage, 1988.

Horsfield, Peter G. *Religious Television: The American Experience.* New York: Longman, 1984.

Klapper, Joseph T. *The Effects of Mass Communication.* New York: Free Press, 1960.

McLuhan, Marshall. *The Medium Is the Message.* New York: Bantam, 1967.

_____. *Understanding Media: The Extensions of Man.* New York: McGraw-Hill, 1964.

Muggeridge, Malcolm. *Christ and the Media.* Sevenoaks, Kent, Eng.: Hodder and Stoughton, 1977.

Schramm, Wilbur. *Mass Media and National Development: The Role of Information in the Developing Countries.* Stanford, Calif.: Stanford University Press, 1964.

Schramm, Wilbur, and Donald F. Roberts, eds. *The Process and Effects of Mass Communication.* Urbana: University of Illinois Press, 1971.

When Less Is More

PROPOSITION 14: Communication effectiveness normally decreases with increasing size of the audience.

Suppose permission were granted for a powerful Christian radio station to be sited on an island off the coast of Asia. All of India, Pakistan, Bangladesh, Burma, Nepal, Sri Lanka, Thailand, Cambodia, Malaysia, Singapore, Afghanistan, the southern provinces of China, the Central Asian republics of the Soviet Union, and several smaller nations would be within listening reach of the station. As many as one-third of the world's total population would be within broadcast range.

What kind of programs would best reach people in the target area? If we are to answer that question, preliminary questions need to be addressed. Which language will we use? What religious beliefs does our intended audience hold? What are the economic level and way of life among the people who will be listening? At least a basic understanding of how to participate in the audience's life and communication is necessary for program planning.

A quick survey of India alone shows that there are ten major "regional" languages, each with more than ten million speakers. Nearly fifty additional languages are spoken by approximately one-half million people each, with more than seven hundred languages and dialects each used by one-quarter million or fewer people. While

Hindi and English are widely used, they would not be suitable for communication with tens of millions within the broadcast area. The wide "potential" audience of the station is subdivided by language into many separate groups. The farther the signal reaches, the more linguistic divisions appear in the audience.

A simplified map shows the situation.

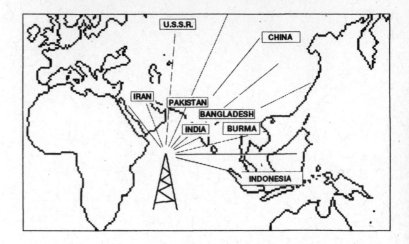

The problem of covering many languages can be partly solved by transmitting only in the most widespread languages and using simultaneous broadcasts on different frequencies. But then there is the question of religious beliefs.

Hinduism is dominant in the geographical area, but Muslims constitute at least 10 percent of the population in India itself. In Pakistan, more than 90 percent are reputed to be Muslim. There are even higher percentages in Afghanistan and some republics of the Soviet Union. Another 5 percent of the people are Christian, Sikh, Jain, Buddhist, and Zoroastrian. Within Hinduism there are sharp differences between the beliefs of so-called philosophical Hinduism and the beliefs and practices of popular Hinduism.

If our map displayed the areas where each religion has its greatest concentration, we could see how religion further subdivides the linguistic divisions within India.

Even in a broad overview of the potential audience, we must consider the great differences in way of life between the villagers and the urban dwellers, between the economic elite of the land (5 percent) who hold more than 90 percent of India's wealth, and the poor, who are deeply in debt. There are many great universities in India, with hundreds of thousands of hardworking students, yet 65 percent of the people are functionally illiterate.

Singapore is a compact, prosperous city-state trading with the world. It is far distant from the harsh struggles and warring groups of Afghanistan, or the narrow horizons of a farmer in the rich lands of Thailand.

It is clearly not possible to communicate with all these audiences at the same time and with the same approach. Even if the problem of language could be solved, each group has different concerns and felt needs—and thus different beginning points for any attempt to create understanding of the Gospel.

The mass media appear to surmount such social boundaries with ease. Many and different audiences can listen to or see the message. But the great diversity means that a smaller and smaller proportion of the audience is truly part of mass media communication. A diagram can help us visualize the problem.

The circle represents one group of people, one audience with which the message producer wishes to establish communication. As the range over which the message can be distributed is increased (through greater radio power or better literature distribution, for example), other audiences can be covered as well. But how much do these audiences have in common? What they share is illustrated by the overlap between the three circles

When communication is desired with *all* groups at the same time, then clearly it can take place only within the area of common concerns. If the groups are quite similar, there will be many things in common and communication is relatively easy. With each group added to the desired audience, however, less and less is shared by all the groups in the potential audience. Communication is limited to a smaller and smaller area of each group's experience.

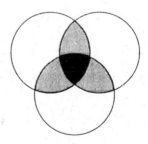

To reach a large, widespread, and diverse audience it is necessary to narrow the content of the communication. For as the potential audience grows, the message producer will find it increasingly difficult to make the message seem relevant to all.

When widely differing groups receive the message, are they being "reached"? What understanding has each created from these signals?

Instead of a vast audience, a much smaller number, self-selected from the whole population, is actually the listening audience. A narrow band of people listen. They are, in effect, a new "group"—a few from here, one or two from there, people for whom the message seems to have value. This elusive audience is really a group only while they are listening and reacting to the same communication.

Where is that audience? Who is it? How can we describe it, so we can better shape our messages for communication? Kinship groups or geographical areas may be identifiable. But audiences are often not fixed, not a particular group of people that can be identified, counted, and described. Particularly in urbanizing areas, they are shifting, fluid groups. They are labeled "audience" only because they temporarily are involved in communication to meet a need.

But surely it is possible to find those basic parts of the message that apply to everyone. Can the message not be simplified so that it will be equally suitable to all in the mass media audience?

Yes, the message can be reduced to basics, and some will still understand its relevance to their lives. Certainly it cannot be presented richly, and seldom with attractiveness. It is instead a matter of finding the lowest common denominator among diverse groups. The lowest-common-denominator approach eliminates most illustrations that would make a teaching point easy to understand and remember. Colorful idioms must be dropped in favor of simple and straightforward language.

"But," object many mass media users, "when the audience hears of God's love, they will respond to that, even if other things are not understood." That would be so if communication were simply a matter of transmitting information—but actually communication is also the receiving and interpreting of that information, as we have already discussed.

Information sent from one context is received in a very different context. What is clear to Christian broadcasters may be a mystery to villagers listening at the end of a day's work in the fields. The same language may be used by both parties, but experience is so different that understanding is absent. Making sense of signals is a social action, so different social settings will result in different meanings given to the same message. Content cannot be shipped; it is recreated within the social group. "The act of sense making is . . . a social action. . . . Sense making as a social action is performed in, and as appropriate to, some context of the social matrix" (James A. Anderson

Mass communication (1) finds the lowest common denominator in order to build or keep a mass audience, and/or (2) stimulates audience self-selection, narrowing the audience to a special interest group.

and Timothy P. Meyer, *Mediated Communication: A Social Perspective*, 119).

The producer is absent from the villages, or from the apartment houses in huge cities, so he or she cannot correct misinterpretations, alter signals, or give more information. The producer's intention in the program does not concern the listeners. They are concerned only about what the media message means to them in their setting. So the two most important parties in the communication process—the producer and the listener—have only very limited common ground for interaction.

That lack can be partly overcome if the resourceful producer shares the experience of the listeners. Then what is transmitted will fit into their setting. When message and message styles are matched between producers and receivers, the intended meaning is more likely to be formed by the audience.

> The people who write the programs and the people who record them (sometimes, but not always, the same people) are not easy to find. They must, of course, speak fluent Russian as it is spoken in the Soviet Union today, and they must be familiar with daily life in the USSR as it is lived today, not as it was twenty or even ten years ago. Program writers must, of course, be thoroughly grounded in the Christian faith and very often have some other specialist knowledge as well.
>
> —Jane Ellis, "Broadcasting to Russia"

However, which social experience will be shared from the many represented in the wide audience? If the producer enters the lives of villagers, how will he or she communicate with the urban dweller? If the producer speaks so the Muslim will understand, what will happen to communication efforts with the Hindu or Jain or Buddhist?

The technical power of radio, television, or print carries the signals far beyond the group from which the signals originated. Some of those other groups have little in common with the originating group. Communication becomes increasingly difficult.

At the very point where mass media appear to have greatest strength, then, they may fail. That failure is not the fault of the media, but of the way such marvelous technology is misused.

The same programs on television were shown to carry *opposite* messages to different socioeconomic groups in India:

"For landless laborers, the moving pictures were like fairy tales, not helping towards a better living. They remained high sounding ideas without any practical consequence.

"For the small cultivators in the village, most of the agricultural practices were capital intensive, meant for rich and large cultivators. For them it was a state of helplessness in which the new knowledge could not be used due to a lack of finances.

"The opinion of rich cultivators was characteristically opposite to this view. They viewed television as an instrument of instigation of the poor against the rich. They saw the television message as an evil force for destroying the existing status quo and the so-called harmony of the village.

"In a nutshell, nobody seemed to be satisfied."

—Arbind K. Sinha, *Mass Media and Rural Development* (New Delhi: Concept Publishing, 1985); quoted in *Media Development* 1 (1985)

▼ LOCALIZE THE MEDIA

Instead of mass communication, mini communication is often a better strategy. Effective communication will often come through use of localized media ("mini-comm") rather than through far-reaching media ("mass-comm").

How does mini-comm differ from mass-comm? They both use extending media and often the same technology, *but with different goals in view.*

Mass-comm concentrates on gaining the largest possible audience; mini-comm seeks to build involvement extensively within a group. Mass-comm is horizontal in its outreach; mini-comm is vertical. In other words, mass-comm develops an audience by skimming some from each of many groups; mini-comm strives for involvement of nearly all in a single group.

Mass-comm usually speaks *to* an audience, and only limited feedback is possible. Information is given out, but there is little or no awareness of how that information is interpreted in the listeners' social settings. It is almost entirely one-way. Channels for feedback are designed into mini-comm programs, so information flow is truly two-way.

Localizing the media with mini-comm makes possible greatly increased feedback. Feedback is part of normal conversations. The expression on the face of the person with whom you are talking is feedback, as well as responses to your questions and comments on your statements. In face-to-face communication, we adjust our message according to such feedback. Mini-comm can use feedback as well, so communication effectiveness can be increased. Close attention to audience response results in changes in audience attitudes. If we can stimulate feedback, we are more likely to stimulate change in minds and hearts.

Media in developing nations have a special need to keep close contact with their audiences. Because the audiences are changing rapidly, the media must change rapidly as well. There is no tradition to guide the changing use of media in developing nations. Mini-comm makes possible the close links between producer and audience that are especially important in rapid change.

Typically, mini-comm uses less sophisticated technology so it is often lower in cost and simpler to use. One result is greater participation and control by a local community, frequently resulting in less polished writing or production. Even though the "Big Media have been the glamour boys of the field," as Wilbur Schramm says, the mini-media stimulate greater involvement and satisfaction in local communities.

The basic step in developing mini-media is to get the producers to participate in the communities with which they are trying to build communication. An important part of the success of a noted development project in Pakistan, the Comilla Project, lay in requiring instructors and producers to visit villages frequently. Farmers were invited in groups to the training academy, where instructors learned *from them* about their problems. "Gradually the faculty broke out of its academic shell and established direct contact with rural reality" (Wilbur Schramm and Daniel Lerner, *Communication and Change*, 78).

Living with the people is the ideal way to begin building communication with a group, but that is not always possible. Perhaps frequent visits are possible. The message producer can spend time where the people gather for friendly discussions—the coffee bar, restaurant, village well, or blacksmith workshop. Opinions of the "average person" can be sought and used. Forums can be developed, using as participants members of the desired audience. Local speakers, musicians, or leaders can be employed. Encouragement, possibly even awards, can be given for letters to the editor. Discussion groups centering on specific magazine articles or radio programs have been used with success in many countries.

Long-distance communication can easily become merely transmission. But when the producers and receivers are members of the same community, the potential of mass media is much more likely to be realized. Unfortunately, the requirements of mass-comm often separate producers from the community they are trying to reach. They need to develop special skills, working closely with other specialists. While producers are increasing their ability to use mass-comm, they can spend little time with the desired audience. Unintentionally, mass-comm becomes a substitute for personal participation.

The sacrifice of personal involvement may seem worthwhile. A wider audience is reached through mass-comm, an audience that would not be touched through mini-comm alone. However, a much higher percentage of the community becomes involved in community-centered mini-comm than in normal mass-comm. For example, a mass-circulation magazine distributed in twelve countries

An international Christian radio station was perceived as isolated and uninvolved with people in the nation in which it was located. It was no surprise to learn that listenership was far lower than expected.

A local citizen commented, "Those people at Radio Village don't know (our country). They have their little town," she said as she made a small circle with her hand, "and they don't know anything else. Why can't they come and talk to the people, find out what's happening, and what people would like?"

of eastern Africa had a total readership of approximately 250,000. Its distribution was widespread since it used the one common language of those twelve nations—English. But another mass-circulation magazine published in the same city gained a readership of nearly one million, using only the Zulu language. It was distributed in only one country—in fact, in only one region of that nation.

Both publications were considered mass-comm. Where one used the trade language (English) to gain the widest possible readership, the other made its impact by becoming part of a single community, the Zulu people. If the extending potential of the media is to be fully utilized, they must become "citizens of the community"—in other words, follow the mini-comm approach.

▼ USING THE EXTENDING MEDIA

The most significant points to remember in using extending media are to make the magazines, books, radio, television, or other media fit strongly felt local needs, and to ensure that the listeners can do something about the advice they get from the programming.

Mini-comm has a great advantage in both of these areas. The programs can be shaped to fit specific felt needs, and local conditions can be taken into account in demonstrations of how the felt needs can be met. When attempts are made to reach many different communities through the same programs, planning for the communication cannot be specific; only generalities are possible. And generalities rarely make for interesting communication. While what is said may relate vaguely to felt needs in a community, most often the broadly oriented program does not seem relevant to listeners. It seems to talk about someone else's problem, never directly to a specific listener or reader.

The effectiveness of various forms of mini-comm has been demonstrated. In Zimbabwe, for example, among the Matabele people, literacy was increasing rapidly, but there were indications that new literates seldom used their reading ability. Reading matter was too expensive, unavailable in wide areas of the countryside, irrelevant to the lives the potential readers lived, too difficult to read because of difficult writing styles and foreign thought-patterns in translated material, and unattractive in appearance.

A periodical in the Ndebele language (spoken by the Matabele of Zimbabwe) seemed a promising way to begin encouragement of a reading habit. Periodicals are repetitious, can include a great variety of subjects, and make topicality and relevance possible. Short, readable stories and articles give a sense of satisfaction that encourages more attempts at reading. Periodicals also make possible a flexible format to meet changing conditions and interests. A periodical was designed and tested using an informal approach to subject matter and layout that made possible a very low selling price.

Content was relevant to social patterns and concerns of the audience, often gleaned from conversations and discussions in public places. Writing was carefully graded to ensure that new literates could handle the material. Production was unsophisticated, so relatively untrained personnel could produce the periodical within their own community.

In a test period, the periodical outsold more sophisticated national magazines by approximately a 100-to-1 margin. The mini-comm approach actually gained a much larger audience than its competitors, even though it circulated in a restricted area (Donald K. Smith, "Developing and Testing of a Low-Cost Periodical for Use in Developing Areas of the World," Ph.D. diss., University of Oregon, 1969).

The medium can be changed and the same results achieved. The essential features of relevance, affordable price, involvement in and production by the local community, entertaining ways of dealing with felt needs, and language that is understandable can be repeated with posters, wall newspapers, or low-power FM radio stations.

Audio cassettes are an excellent tool in mini-comm. They encourage repetition of the message, permit flexibility of programming so that specific groups can be targeted, and can be produced at relatively low cost. Close contact between the producer and audience is possible during times of distributing new cassettes and collecting the used cassettes. While this can be done through postal services, person-to-person contact strengthens communication. Viggo Sogaard tells of many cases in which audio cassettes proved valuable:

> A Thai Christian regularly took his cassette-player to a friend's house. Some neighbors often came in to listen, too, and after a time three of them accepted Christ as their Savior. They said later, "We heard about Christ before, and we read tracts, but we did not understand the Gospel until

To reach American high school youth with the message, "Don't do drugs!" many TV and film messages feature an "admired personality" (from sports or films, for example) telling of experience with drugs and that drugs can kill. Some mass media messages have been well received, but sadly, they rarely create change. Those youth who were taking drugs still take them. Those who felt drugs were bad have had their beliefs reinforced.

But bring the "admired personality" face-to-face with youth, and notice the difference! The face-to-face talk about drugs, and what they do to destroy life and health, creates change within the audience. The mass media star becomes real, relating to a particular group of people—who respond with acceptance of the change message.
—Tom Sager

now." The cassette had broken through literacy barriers. . . .

One man in Maseod had been a Christian for two years. Extreme shyness kept him from even smiling at others. Then he borrowed a cassette-player and played it every day at full volume. In a short time his life changed, for he won two neighbors to the Lord and opened up a new village to the Gospel. A cassette made the difference.

—Viggo Sogaard, *Everything You Need to Know for a Cassette Ministry,* 19

Others spoke of how cassettes permitted them to "hear the message again and again" so that they could understand it for the first time. Technology does not need to dominate the communication process, but especially with a mini-comm approach, it can aid in creating understanding.

Video cassettes are being used widely for mini-comm, in classrooms, at home for how-to-do-it instruction in thousands of skills, and as part of retail stores' marketing through demonstration of products and how to use them. The uses of such a flexible form of audio and visual presentation are almost endless. At least one seminary—Western Conservative Baptist Seminary in Portland, Oregon—has prepared its core curriculum on video cassettes, enabling students to complete as much as two-thirds of their seminary training while remaining at their homes—thousands of miles from the seminary campus.

While Sogaard's comments have to do with audio cassettes, they apply equally well to video cassettes:

The cassette is a personal medium or tool. It is used by a person to improve or expedite his or her work. . . . There exists a very high motivation and desire to learn. The cassette is used . . . as a teaching media. . . . The cassette tool can be used by the person any time he wants it. . . . These people are INVOLVED. They are not just passive spectators. It is a cool communication that requires a lot of input from them.

—Sogaard, *Everything You Need,* 97

A creative linkage of mass-comm to local networks occurred in New Guinea.

"In New Guinea when a village leader is ignored by his people, the Papuan Government sometimes records his speech on tape, then releases it on radio, to be heard by now respectful villagers, played to them by the village leader himself."
—Ted Carpenter, *They Became What They Beheld*

This well summarizes the distinctive nature of good mini communications.

▼ HOW CAN MEDIA BE LOCALIZED?

For media to be of greatest value, they must be part of the existing communications networks of a group. For media to have necessary social power, they must be tied in to local groups. Otherwise, all the technology results merely in sound and lightning.

A study in India identified the failure of the producers and teachers to be part of the local situation as the underlying cause of the overall failure of a development project.

> The paramount obstacles to effective functioning of these organizations is the . . . inadequate participation of the clientele groups; the lack of continuous two-way communication between the field and the secretariat; and the presence among administrators of values, attitudes, and motivations not conducive to effective action.
>
> —Uma Narula and W. Barnett Pearce, "Development as Communication: A Perspective on India"

In other words, what the development workers were doing had little or no relationship to the people they were supposedly helping. Two networks were side by side, but not linked together to make possible effective communication.

Mass-comm can help to create awareness of alternatives. It can suggest possible solutions. But that information must be considered within the society before it will be acted upon. "The mass media," says Wilbur Schramm, "can feed the interpersonal channels." But for mass-comm to do that, it cannot express opinions or give information that is strongly opposed by the intended audience. If mass-comm antagonizes by using materials considered objectionable by its audience, it certainly cannot fulfill its potential of linking to the networks.

Mini-comm can more readily integrate with local communication networks, because it is able to meet four conditions for appropriate media usage:

1. Involvement in planning and production is developed at the local level.

2. Both the content and the style of presentation are relevant to the social patterns and concerns of the local audience.

3. Content and presentation are understandable and acceptable to the local audience, even when this results in production quality not considered suitable for mass audiences.

4. The media effort can be partially or fully supported by personnel and funds at the local level.

The Central African Republic has one government-controlled radio station, Radio Bangui. Most homes have transistor radios which are on most waking hours. Anything on Radio Bangui is almost like the gospel. To question Radio Bangui is almost like questioning God, "But on radio Bangui they said —!" And that settles the discussion.

But a few scorn the station, "What, Radio Bangui? You mean Radio Manioc! I *never* listen to Radio Manioc." Regardless of the message, if it was delivered by that medium it was simply not considered seriously.

The media will connect only with those networks where Radio Bangui has credibility.
—R. Bruce Paden

▼ INCORPORATING FOLK MEDIA

Mini-comm can readily build links within the community by the use of *folk media*—that is, the styles of communication already within use in that community. Folk media take hundreds of forms: painting, carving, dance, song, drama, the many traditional ways of expressing values used in ceremonies, daily life, and recreation. No list could be complete because of the immense diversity possible, as pointed out in introducing the signal systems under proposition 12 of this book.[1] It is important, nevertheless, to learn what folk media are used by the audience and then to use them as much as possible.

Folk media involve members of the audience in production as well as use of the media, a process that does much to strengthen communication. Since audience members are already part of the society's internal communication system, their involvement largely eliminates the barriers present when any message is introduced from the outside. Further, since the symbols used in folk media are familiar to the audience, comprehension of the message is enhanced.

Drama is frequently an effective folk medium to use. Varieties of folk drama range from simple monologues to complex productions in professional theaters. Some is impromptu, a more developed form of storytelling, while some is highly stylized, not permitting deviation or innovation.

The dance drama of Thailand and neighboring nations beautifully portrays traditional Thai stories, usually from the Buddhist tradition. A creative Christian dance-drama troupe in Thailand uses the same type of costuming and movements to present biblical truth.

In India, dance is similarly used to tell stories, to recount the legends of Hinduism. This richly beautiful folk medium uses every motion, ornamentation, and costume color to represent details of the myth. As in Thailand, a group of Christians has formed a company to present the Gospel through Indian dance, with wide acceptance given by audiences that are usually anticipated as being antagonistic.

Both of these creative uses of folk media have been very effective. Caution must be exercised, however, when

---

1. Leonard Doob, in his pioneering work *Communication in Africa: A Search for Boundaries,* came as close as anyone to a comprehensive listing of communicative modes.

the message of the Gospel is put into traditional forms and media. There is always the possibility that the association with non-Christian messages is so strong that the Christian message will be overshadowed or even lost.

Textiles with portraits and messages printed on them can be folk media. In one African nation, it was strongly urged that women make dresses to be worn on the national independence day from cloth printed with the president's picture. A political party in one West African nation printed cloth with its slogans and voting symbols and sold it at a subsidized price in the traditional markets.

Many cultures use song for much more than entertainment: to teach values, to instill courage in warriors, to teach children proper behavior, to stimulate worship. Praise songs are used to enhance a leader's reputation. Ballads recount highlights of the people's history or retell legends intended to inspire.

Communicating for Development by Karl-Johan Lundstrom, Donald K. Smith, and Samuel Kenyi shows ways folk media can be utilized effectively in development work. Practical guidance is given for drama, song, cassettes, flip charts, handbills, storytelling, and demonstration as tools for communication even where technological resources are limited.

Folk media include differing speaking styles. A particular style of preaching characteristic of Afro-American churches is a stylized question-and-congregational-answer that is sharply different from the lecture style used in Anglo-American churches. The question-and-answer technique builds a sense of participation and full communication between preacher and congregation. Another distinctive pattern for speech characterizes serious community discussions among the Lotuho people of southern Sudan. The speaker makes his points, sentence by sentence. Each point is restated by an appointed "orator," who rephrases what is said so that it is more appropriately spoken. The audience reacts to the "orator's" words, ignoring the initial speech.

Folk media are not the total answer to effective communication, of course. Effective mini-comm requires planned integration of folk media with the technology of extending media.

The "griots" are a caste of storytellers and musicians that one still finds, particularly in Senegal and Mali. They are the custodians of oral history, they transmit from father to son the accounts of great leaders, of famous battles, of all the events worth recounting. But they tell only what is favorable, and their principal gift, the one from which they derive their income, is a gift for flattery. . . .

Griots are respected and even feared because of their knowledge and their capacity to do mischief by spreading malicious gossip about their enemies. Their services are appreciated, and they are called upon to officiate at the important ceremonies of life—marriage, birth, circumcision. They play their songs and celebrate the virtues of whoever is paying them. No family wants to have a ceremony less grand than its neighbor, and hiring griots is like hiring the best orchestra and the best hotel. . . .

Clearly, the griots were the first media men.

▼ BUILDING BETTER LINKS
WITH THE AUDIENCE

Mass-comm can improve its audience relationships, even though it cannot build links as closely as a mini-comm approach can. Many different techniques are used to link mass-comm deliberately to social networks, such as radio listening clubs and radio forums in which discussion and debate follow presentation of a topic on a radio or television program. Readers' clubs have been successfully promoted to enhance the communication of mass-circulation magazines. Such approaches are effective to some degree in localizing even mass-comm, but they require continuing support and supervision if they are to have continuing value. They do increase significantly what is learned and acted upon from the mass-comm messages.

Talk shows and letters-to-the-editor features build audience involvement. Many other types of articles and programs can help focus mass-comm in its relationships with specific audiences. For example, regular features on geographical areas or cultures stressing their distinctives, showing reasons for community pride, and featuring local people build local identification with the mass-comm. Local news, alongside national and international, draws attention. It is especially valuable to use local talent, in music, art, or writing, even if it is considered less developed than talents normally used in mass-comm.

▼ MEDIA IN RELATION TO THE LOCAL
CHURCH

There is a critical need to bridge the gap between mass-comm and local churches. Often the mass-comm ministries are controlled by and feature people from outside the local area. These organizations, often called parachurch groups, too often conduct their ministries as if the local church were irrelevant to the evangelizing and discipling of the nations. How can this problem be lessened?

Large media groups need to reconsider the theology underlying their efforts and to develop a local church orientation. It is important to rethink the nature of the local church and its role in the process of communicating the Good News. The church universal is expressed in specific local congregations where repentance, believing, and growing up "into Christ" occur. Sidestepping local churches can lead to fragmenting the body of Christ under the guise of being more effective in extending it. Following the biblical pattern of equal concern for each other will mean placing high priority on the church and its needs as well as on assisting Christian media to fulfill their part of the task.

Planning of media usage and development of overall strategy can be done with local church representation. Local church involvement could perhaps be partially achieved by using the local churches as a forum in which to test ideas, programs, and materials designed for the Christian audience. The producers would need to listen to the critiques given and demonstrate good faith by acting on as many as possible.

Cultivate local church participation in the creation of programs. It is better to gain input early in program development than only to present the finished result for reactions. Participation at an early stage increases the sense of involvement and thus the readiness to become part of the program's long-term audience, encourage others to do so, and talk about the program with them.

Regular joint sessions, in which church leaders and media leaders explain to one another their needs, problems, and ideas for meeting those problems, increase respect and trust. As the leaders jointly seek solutions, relationships are deepened—and better solutions are usually the result.

▼ GUIDELINES FOR MEDIA USE

No single approach to communication can do the whole job. Used appropriately, both mini- and mass-comm are needed. The principal medium cannot do the job alone. It must be built into a teaching system, which might include radio, television, textbooks, other books, charts, a newspaper, magazines, a study group, and field representatives (see Schramm, *Big Media: Little Media*, especially 274–76). Some general conclusions from research and experience can help in better media usage:

1. A well-planned campaign will use whatever media it can command that will reach the audience it wants to reach. The important variable seems to be not so much the characteristics of the media as where they go and who uses them.

2. A combination of media is likely to accomplish more than any medium by itself.

3. Interpersonal communication, whether from change agent to potential adopter, from friend to friend,

or within a group, is the indispensable element of development communication, regardless of the mass media used.

4. A combination of media and interpersonal communication is likely to be more effective than either alone; and information in any medium is likely to be passed along by interpersonal channels.

5. Regardless of the pattern of media and interpersonal communication, the social situation must be favorable for the desired kind of change.

SUMMARY

The larger the audience, the greater the diversity of interests and cultural patterns existing within that audience. Communication effectiveness depends upon commonality between the sender and the receiver, but such diversity makes it very difficult to achieve commonality. It is easier for two people to share understandings than for two hundred or two thousand. The more people involved, the smaller the overlap of interests is likely to be. Areas of commonality may be found, but effective communication is clearly reduced to only those areas.

An efficient strategy is to localize the media. When the aim is to reach a smaller but distinct audience, more complete coverage and greater audience involvement are possible. "Mini-comm" (mini communications), in which both form and content are relevant to the audience, often creates a greater impact than "mass-comm" (mass communications).

▼ BIBLIOGRAPHY

Engle, James F., Roger D. Blackwell, and David T. Kollat. *Consumer Behavior.* 3d ed. Hinsdale, Ill.: Dryden, 1978.

Lundstrom, Karl-Johan, Donald K. Smith, and Samuel Kenyi. *Communicating for Development: A Practical Guide.* Geneva: Lutheran World Federation, 1990.

Schramm, Wilbur. *Big Media, Little Media: Tools and Technologies for Instruction.* Beverly Hills, Calif.: Sage, 1977.

Sogaard, Viggo. *Everything You Need to Know for a Cassette Ministry.* Minneapolis: Bethany House, 1975.

➤ Can media evangelize the world in this generation?

➤ If I can identify the audience, and describe them, can't I just use media to win them?

WHAT DETERMINES MEDIA EFFECTS?

PROPOSITION 15: The effectiveness of a medium is largely determined by factors other than the medium itself.

The lion raised his great golden head to roar out frustration. He struggled to stand, but could not walk, let alone charge the impala warily grazing nearby. Tangled in a brown net that had dropped around him like a confining cloud, Simba could neither hunt nor eat. He could only rage and roar.

Wild hares flattened their ears. The anger of the impotent monarch had frightened them into their holes. They didn't know that the roaring was not a warning—that the lion could do them no harm.

Unseen by the lion, the hares, and the impala, a family of tiny field mice began to chew on strands of the net. They found the soft cord to be just what they needed for their nests. The mice cut with their tiny teeth, chewing apart first one strand, then another.

Exhausted by his futile anger, the lion lay down for sleep. Hours later, he was awakened by noises of hunters returning. With the coming of danger, he gathered his muscles to spring. As the hunting party came nearer, Simba tensed with anger, then sprang. The astonished hunters jumped aside as the great lion came free from the net and bounded into the dense, head-high grass.

197

Now for the moral of the story: Was it the strength of the lion that gave it freedom, or the unnoticed nibbling of the mice? The mice prepared the way, but the lion had to jump and tear the net apart itself.

Is it the power of the media that brings change in a society? Or are there "families of mice" that are actually of greater importance? Many generally unnoticed factors determine whether media will have an effect, and when they do, what kind of effect. Ignoring the less visible reasons for media effectiveness or failure could result in unwittingly working against desired goals.

Media do have impact. But there is seldom a direct cause-and-effect relationship between the media message and audience response. Media are not like a hypodermic needle—inject a pattern of words and a particular effect is obtained in someone's life or in a society. Unfortunately, the hypodermic-needle approach still characterizes too much Christian use of the media. The value of a program is measured by the letters of response; evangelistic outreach is evaluated by counting those who openly respond to an invitation to become Christians. A missionary's career is considered successful if he or she can point

Bill Schorr/Kansas City Star

The mass media are only one of many influences operating in the audience.

to large numbers of converts or to a chain of churches started. Missionary radio or publishing is assessed according to the number of conversions reported through its programs or literature. These are indeed important results, but almost never is it possible—or accurate—to show that these things happened because the message was given in a particular style, using a specific channel or medium.

Many, many different factors come between the communicator and the listener. Those things that come between—intervening variables—are often more important than the message itself in causing response or lack of it.

These intervening variables are like photographic filters that diffuse light, change its apparent color, or block out part or all of it. There are many screens in communication, and each influences the ultimate effect of the message.

Suppose a photographer wants to take a picture of an ocean scene. She decides that the blue-greens need to be darkened, so that the white foam of the waves will be clear in the black-and-white picture to be made. A yellow filter is put over the lens. What begins as "white light" reaches the film with some of the blue blocked out. The blue waves seem darker as a result, and the foam whiter. The filter has changed the message before it reaches the film.

To change the analogy, the whole process can be compared to a pinball machine. The ball's path from the top of the playing board can be generally predicted. It will roll down the sloping surface, but which path will it follow? It will strike springs, levers, walls, troughs—each of which changes the path of the ball on its inevitable downward course. Even when the ball begins at precisely the same point each time, the combination of things it hits as it rolls downward is different each time, and so the score earned by the player is different each time.

And so with communication. Even with the same message, given in the same way, there will be different results each time it is shared, because of the many changing factors that affect both the communicator and the listener. "No one can step into the same river twice," they say—a proverb that holds true of communication.

What, then, are *some* of the more important factors or screens (intervening variables) that influence message effect? These can only be stated and briefly explained

1. Mass communications ordinarily does not serve as a necessary and sufficient cause of audience effects, but rather functions among and through a nexus of mediating factors and influences.

2. These mediating factors are such that they typically render mass communication a contributory agent, but not the sole cause, in a process of reinforcing the existing conditions. . . .

3. On such occasions as mass communication does function in the service of change, one of two conditions is likely to obtain. Either (a) the mediating factors will be found to be inoperative, and the effect of the media direct; or (b) the mediating factors, which normally favor reinforcement, will be found to be themselves impelling toward change.

4. There are certain residual situations in which mass communication seems to wreak direct effects, or to directly and of itself serve certain psychophysical functions.

5. The efficacy of mass communication, either as contributory agents or as agents of direct effect, is affected by various aspects of the media themselves or of the communication situation (including, for example, aspects of contextual organization, the availability of channels for overt action, etc.).

—Joseph T. Klapper, "What We Know About the Effects of Mass Communication," 453–74

here, for each factor could well be the subject of a chapter, if not a book.

Clustering the wide assortment of factors in three groups—individual, social, and contextual—helps to bring some order to a potpourri of influences.

▼ INDIVIDUAL FACTORS

The individual factors are characteristics of participants in the communication process—the listener, receiver, viewer—in other words, members of the audience for mass communications.

Individuals have *predispositions* to listen to particular messages and reject others. These predispositions are based on previous experiences, their current psychological needs, and their personal needs for food, shelter, acceptance, security, information, internal peace, or spiritual understanding.

Based on their anticipation of satisfaction from particular messages, individuals *self-select* what they will pay attention to. They may be incorrect in their view of what will be said or how satisfying they will find a particular message, but whether or not they listen is a result of their own selection. Only in a totally controlled situation can exposure of individual audience members be guaranteed.

Even then, the message may be only partially perceived. No other external messages may be present, but receiving is still not a sure thing. Individuals *selectively perceive* incoming messages, choosing those parts that prom-

A community college successfully used television advertising to increase its enrollment. "We're not spending a lot more on advertising; we're just spending it differently." Their use of media centered on interests of potential students, with the theme "The typical student is you." The ads show a cross section of students ranging from a young man in tennis shoes to a well-dressed businesswoman. It ends with the message that everyone is college material. "As we paid more attention to what the needs were in the community, we increased our enrollment," a college official reported.

© Rob Portlock, 1979

TODAY'S SERMON: TITHES AND OFFERINGS

"Welcome!"

ise satisfaction of a need and rejecting portions that seem irrelevant. It is important to realize that this rejection is not conscious, but simply a failure even to perceive that a particular message is available. Of the hundreds of thousands of stimuli physically received by an individual, it is those that seem to be relevant to a felt need that reach the level of consciousness. The difference between simple hearing or seeing and perception is similar to the difference between the presence of invisible ultraviolet light and being able to see this "black light" with the use of special instruments. Selective perception turns on an internal selector, as it were, that permits only a few of all incoming signals to be consciously recognized.

Repeatedly Scripture speaks of God's messages to persons being "screened out"—that is, not perceived. At the end of the message to each of the seven churches in Revelation 2 and 3, it is repeated "He who has an ear, let him hear what the Spirit says." And in 3:20, hearing is again seen to be selective, "I stand at the door and knock. If anyone hears my voice and opens the door, I will come in." The point that everyone can hear (mechanically) is made in Romans 10:18: "But I ask: Did they not hear? Of course they did: 'Their voice has gone out into all the earth, their words to the ends of the world.'"

Paul shows that the inability to perceive what was heard was a result of willful disobedience: "All day long I have held out my hands to a disobedient and obstinate people" (Rom. 10:21). God then sent a "famine of hearing" (Amos 8:11) and took away the ability to perceive. Since the people refused to do what they knew, "God gave them a spirit of stupor, eyes so that they could not see and ears so that they could not hear" (Rom. 11:8). Hearing and perceiving are separate things. Perception is selective both in spiritual issues and in material matters.

> Often times a felt need is the open door that prepares a person to acknowledge his deeper, real need and Christ's solution to it.
> —Anonymous article, *Common Ground*, April 1987

Sometimes even when the message is perceived, it is not understood because of *reinterpretation*. The signals are received and mentally perceived, but in the process different meanings are given from those originally intended. This often happens in ordinary conversations. A statement or request is made, and it is perceived in a way that is completely at odds with the original intention.

As churchgoers were gathering for Sunday services, a friend was asked, "Are you moving your truck to free those parking spaces?" The truck owner reacted with apparent annoyance, silently went to the truck, and drove away. Only later that afternoon did he explain the difficulty: "I heard you say, 'You've done it again and caused difficulty for others. You're the "bad person," and the parking of your truck confirms it!'" None of that was in the mind of the questioner. The truck driver later came to understand: "I heard your words and they 'plugged in' to things that have happened in the past. I gave your question the wrong meaning." He had *reinterpreted* the words.

Neville D. Jayaweera points out a much broader and more serious example of reinterpretation, when the intended message of Christian workers is reinterpreted by the hearers.

The message transmitted is intended to be of God's love, forgiveness, and salvation in Jesus Christ. But the many factors influencing media effectiveness frequently cause that desired content to be reinterpreted:

> While the Gospel promises salvation in Christ and a release from our "Adamic" selves, the Third World sees Christendom as being built upon some of the worst characteristics of the Adam in man—individualism, acquisitiveness, greed, conflict, exploitation, oppression and war. Behind the tinsel niceties and superficial "liberalism" of western civilization, the Third World tends to perceive what it believes to be its true nature—a ruthless and insatiable acquisitiveness and a readiness to throw its "Christian" pretensions to the winds when the life styles built upon acquisitiveness and greed are seriously threatened.
>
> —Jayaweera, "Christian Communication in the Third World"

Jayaweera has also pointed out other factors that determine media effectiveness, particularly the *image of the source*. The media presentation may be superb, the content may be accurate and true, but the overall message will still be rejected. Rejection results if the listeners do not trust the source, or if they already oppose the source. In countries whose government controls the media, for example, the general public tends to disbelieve whatever is said in official news releases. Even when government statements are true, the people have an image of the source as self-serving, therefore not to be fully trusted.

Just as the communicator's image of the audience shapes the way the message is presented, the audience's image of the communicator shapes its reception. When the communicator is considered to be of high status and of considerable importance to the audience, the message is more likely to be accepted. If the audience distrusts the communicator or does not consider the communicator

What I am trying to say is that when we look at the overall situation . . . we cannot avoid coming to the conclusion that the Christian communication effort in the Third World . . . may even be counterproductive. . . .

Why is this so? The answer is simply that the Gospel has lost credibility! This is not intended as a statement about the Gospel. The Gospel itself can never lose credibility. . . . Through a lack of understanding of the history, the culture and the consciousness of the various social groups to whom the Gospel is being communicated, through a persistent and appalling insensitivity to the social, economic and political realities that shape their beliefs and values, and through a naive adherence to the assumption that western models and styles are applicable universally, Christian communicators have all too often succeeded only in concealing the Gospel and generating prejudices towards images that are really only caricatures of the Gospel but which, in the minds of the local groups, are mistaken for the true Gospel.
—Neville D. Jayaweera, "Christian Communication in the Third World"

"I see our next speaker needs no introduction. . . ."

likely to say anything valuable, the message will be at least initially rejected or ignored.

Yet that is not necessarily the end of the story. The message itself may be remembered even when it is not acted upon. If the message promises to meet a need of the audience, it may be remembered and acted upon *later*. Thus, an important message brought by an unacceptable messenger may in fact be later accepted, after memory of who the messenger was has dimmed or disappeared.

An unacceptable messenger can take advantage of this latent message effect by "seed planting," giving small, low-key suggestions of a needed change until people seem to think of it on their own. "Seed planting" requires patience, just as it takes time for seeds to sprout. But practiced with patience and skill, it is effective in introducing change.

Based on past treatment of Native Americans by whites, Native Americans frequently reject the white missionary. As one explained,

> Christianity is a white man's religion. Look at what has happened to the Native American in the name of Christ and Christianity. Christianity has contributed to the assimilation process, the removal process, the suppression of tribal religions, the dividing up of the reservations for various denominations, the allotment policy which resulted in a loss of millions of acres of Native American lands, the notion of the racial inferiority of Native Americans—and so on. We want no part of Christ or Christianity.

A Native American Christian worker would improve initial acceptability of a Gospel message.

It is not unusual to see people accept the judgment of a visiting "expert" on a problem, when in fact the "expert" has no more expertise than local personnel. When working on construction of refineries, I noticed times when local people were truly authorities on the subject, but someone from out of town was treated as if he were the authority! The outsider's opinions were considered authoritative.
—P. B. Shaw

Advertisers frequently employ well-known personalities to say how good a particular product is. But how much does a prominent athlete know, for example, about motor oils? His knowledge does not matter if the public know his name and admire his skill. Their image of the athlete is very positive, so they tend to believe what he says even in areas outside his expertise.

At a time when two prominent televangelists were discovered to have committed immoral acts, respect for all radio and television evangelists dropped. This change in image of the source affected contributions sharply, causing difficulty even for ministries that were in no way related to the discredited televangelists.

The same message heard at the same time by listeners sitting side by side will have different effects on each listener. Each audience member has *different personality patterns* and so will perceive different things and apply them in different ways. Personal needs vary just as personalities vary. Some people are optimistic and others pessimistic; some have a hunger for God, while others apparently "couldn't care less." Many learn best by seeing, through visual messages, and others are most able to learn by hearing.

Individual levels of frustration and uncertainty are different.Thus a message that seems remarkably timely and important to one person will attract little or no interest

MESSENGER — forgotten
MESSAGE — remembered,
IF felt needs will be met by the
message.

"Yeah, I knew I was going to receive a real blessing the minute I saw his picture on the album cover."

© Mary Chambers, 1983.

204

from someone else who appears (on the outside) to be the same kind of person. Changes in our personal lives affect our receptivity to messages. The newly married woman normally shows far more interest in a magazine article about making an attractive home than the single man living by himself. But there is clearly no way to be certain that this will be true of all newly married women or all single men. Such individual differences are another reason for differences in media effectiveness.

▼ SOCIAL FACTORS

Societies differ in frustration and uncertainty levels, much as individuals differ. During times of crisis that force people to adopt different living patterns, there is much uncertainty. People do not know exactly how to respond to the new demands. They feel uncertain of their ability to relate to the environment satisfactorily. And so they turn to the media to learn what is happening, how they ought to react, and how to cope with new situations. As the crisis diminishes, use of the media also lessens. In normal times when most happenings are expected or predictable, the media have far less impact.

In periods of social discontent and frustration with the status quo, media usage is high and messages are carefully heard. How well the message is presented, the quality of programming, the brilliance of the speaker, the beauty of the music—all are ultimately less important for message impact than the level of uncertainty and frustration in a society.

How highly does a particular individual *value membership and acceptance* in a group? If such acceptance has importance, then the group's attitude toward the media and its messages will greatly influence the individual's response. If a group has little significance, then other factors will be more important in determining response to media messages.

Someone may appear to be part of a group, but his or her mental and social orientation may be toward a different group or a purpose not shared by all of those in the social setting. Such is the case with Christians, who are "in the world but not of the world." Or, as expressed by the writer of Hebrews, "Here we have no continuing city." The biblical Christian's values, goals, and purposes in life are not gained from the social setting but from the patterns shown in the Word of God. The biblical Christian

On the first Sunday after the death of Kenya's first president, Mzee Jomo Kenyatta, thousands of nonchurchgoers attended churches in Kenya's capital city, Nairobi. Newspapers sold nearly twice as many copies as normal, and close attention was paid to news broadcasts. Media that gave any information or help to Kenyans for the uncertain transition to a new president were heavily used.

When I trained technicians, we explained correct, required procedures and the technical reasons for them. We convinced the men that they should do what we taught them.

To my surprise, when I visited job sites I found that technicians we had trained were using inadequate methods. In fact, those wrong methods required additional time and effort!

Almost always, the reason for doing the work incorrectly was that the technician was convinced that his immediate supervisor wanted the work done in that way. The technician usually knew that the method he was using was incorrect, but the opinion of the supervisor was more important than doing the job according to correct methods.

—P. B. Shaw

seeks to obey God rather than being pressed into the mold of the surrounding society.

In the flow of communication, we have already said that it does not work like a hypodermic needle—push in so much message, and there will be a proportionate response. *The message is always mediated*—that is, passed through the mind and experience of each listener and then shared with others for verification and acceptance, alteration, or rejection. Messages flow within networks, like electricity flowing through a power grid from power station to house to store to other houses. It is always flowing but not always utilized; whenever a switch is turned on, it flows into that particular use, where it is modified into light or heat or energy. Outwardly a motor and a light bulb seem to have little in common, but they both are mediating the electrical power, changing it to perform different functions. The effectiveness of electrical power ultimately depends on how well motors, heaters, and light bulbs function. The power generator is essential, of course, but it would have no useful purpose if its power could not be converted to a useful function.

The electric power analogy is close to the way media function in communication. The newspaper publisher and press or the television station is like the power generator. Needs and information that can be used to meet those needs function like the electric power. The people who listen, discuss within their personal networks and then act as seems appropriate are like the light bulbs, motors, and heaters driven by electricity. Always the ultimate effect of the media is determined by the receivers at least as much as by the transmitters.

▼ CONTEXTUAL FACTORS

The *social context* within which the message is heard affects how it is understood. In June 1989, Chinese army troops had just moved against the thousands of students who occupied Tiananmen Square in Beijing. Hundreds and perhaps thousands were killed. During those early days of June, an issue of *National Geographic* featuring China sat on my table. It has been there for fourteen months, but only in June 1989 did I pick it up and carefully read the splendid article telling of train journeys throughout China. The magazine (a medium) had not changed, but the context had, so the magazine's message suddenly became relevant. My interest in the article was greatly increased.

> In Africa, human relationships are the focal point of existence. Impersonal events and abstractions do not fit easily into African mentality. Interpersonal relationships play a key role even in rather straightforward business transactions. It is inadequate to designate those who listen regularly simply as "listeners." This is too cold and impersonal. In a very real way, the listeners are friends. Though they may have never seen Hoodibbo Manikasset or Ahmadou Djika or Babuba or Peter, they know them by name, recognize their voices, know which programs they speak on, and feel a personal debt of gratitude to them for having helped them in so many ways through the broadcasts. They do indeed call them their friends.
>
> —Ron Nelson, "Radio for the Fulani"

The passage of *time* may be necessary for a message to be adequately perceived. Something new may be so unfamiliar that it seems threatening to stability or personal security. Or the new information may be so unexpected that it is immediately disbelieved. People almost always prefer the familiar to the unknown, even if the unknown promises to be more desirable. In such cases, time is needed for the new and startling to become familiar. Time will allow people to adjust mentally to changes that may come. Time softens the disturbing sharpness of some messages.

If no *way to respond* is open to the intended audience, it is probable that the message will be discarded, even when it is correctly perceived. A continuing stimulus that cannot be acted upon at first is annoying, then causes frustration and perhaps anger; finally, people try to ignore the stimulus. Inability to respond to a message received stiffens resistance to the message.

To invite people to be followers of Christ, yet not tell them where they can get spiritual help, is to encourage frustration. If an appropriate way to respond is not available to media users, they cannot act on the message. They may become "Gospel-hardened" (to use a common description) simply because they have perceived the message and would like to act on it, but do not know how. To avoid further frustration, they will simply ignore the message in the future.

Cultural appropriateness is a major factor in media effectiveness. This use of media should take into account not only differences between major cultural blocks, but also less obvious differences within major groups of people. A single message prepared for several different groups will not be equally effective in all groups. Some forms of media are useful in one culture but not in another.

Often media take distinctive forms in a culture, forms that can be utilized for Christian proclamation. Kathleen Nicholls tells of one:

> Some 15 Christian poets for two hours recited their poems in praise of Jesus in the Urdu language and the couplet form beloved in India. The hall full of Muslim men listened attentively and many more stood outside. Afterward, members of the audience talked to the poets about

The mission once had the idea of starting a radio program. Hours were spent putting together some attractive programs, and the tapes were sent to the government-controlled radio station. The mission was at the mercy of the radio programmers for the time of broadcast. The time chosen by the station was around 6:00 in the evening. This was just the time that working men left their places of work and started to head for home. Before going home, however, many stopped off at one of the bars in Bangui to relax. No sooner did they reach the bar than—you guessed it, the solemn sound of the mission broadcast!

The radio station was besieged by angry calls and letters protesting such a broadcast at just the hour when Bangui's hot, tired, and *dry* office workers were seeking a few moments of escape at their favorite bar. So much for the broadcast! The radio station insisted that this was the *only* time they had, and since it wasn't appreciated, they could not continue to broadcast it.

—R. Bruce Paden

the content of the poems. Had these been evangelist preachers there might have been violence.

—"Tell the Story Powerfully in
Local Cultural Forms"

How culture affects communication is considered more fully in the subsequent chapters of this book.

What determines the results of a particular mass media message? Primarily the audience, not those who are controlling the media. This means that response to a media message is determined by virtually the same influences that affect a message shared in face-to-face communication.

The popular image of mass media as a powerful force changing unsuspecting people's ideas and ideals cannot be supported despite thousands of research studies and years of effort. The mass media are not a pervasive presence causing individuals in a widespread audience to think new thoughts and hold new values. Instead, people normally select the media to which they pay attention. The media they select and the messages they hear are acceptable to the audience, at least partially, or those media would not be selected. The media messages are consistent with existing opinions and commitments. Messages that force consideration of existing beliefs are ignored or reinterpreted so that the message appears to agree with what the audience members already think.

Why then, do we have so much that is objectionable on television and in some popular music of Western nations? Why do unpopular governments seek to control the media in order to build support for themselves?

If the audiences did not accept what the media offered in Western nations, the media would offer something else. Despite strong objections to content and the shifting of values through the mass media, the majority of the people still watch and listen. Even when they feel they should not like or accept what is presented, it is accepted or it would be turned off. People may wish to strive for something better, but at the same time they are often satisfied with programming that caters to secret lusts. The media's pouring out of rubbish will be controlled when individuals control their taste for rubbish.

Media in many nations are tightly controlled by the government in an effort to control the information received by the people. With the limiting of knowledge, acceptance of the status quo is more likely. When alternatives are unknown, there will be little effort to bring about

---

Since radio is the chief medium of highlands people in Guatemala, it was common to see groups of people clustered around a small transistor in shops and on the sidewalk. Through radio they learn of the personal God of the Bible. . . . Some who still meet in "radio churches" plan trips a year ahead of time to see the station and to meet Oscar and "the little people inside the radio." With them they bring fruit from their fields, handmade crafts, and flowers. They want to be a part of God's work at TGNA.

Guatemala City is unlike the rural areas. . . . Here the FM band is tailored for the smaller population of middle and upper classes. Literature, telephone calls, and personal visits accompany the normal broadcast ministry. Interspersed with classical music, easy listening, news, and cultural programs are short evangelistic messages and micro-sermons. The Gospel, clear and uncluttered, is aired at least thirty times in TGNA's twenty-one-hour day.

—Peggy Wehmeyer

change. In societies that are held within a fortress of ignorance, information becomes very powerful. When information about alternatives does reach the people (and with contemporary technology it cannot be kept out for long), an explosive reaction against repression is probable.

As we have noted, under some conditions the media do help to form opinion and perhaps even change it. When a crisis confronts an individual or a society, they turn to media to gain necessary information to understand and handle the crisis. If a society is unstable and undergoing rapid change, the media will be more extensively used. There are also times in any society when groups feel a need for reinforcement of their beliefs, especially when they are under pressure that would cause change.

Thus, media are useful—but primarily for reinforcement rather than conversion, except under special and often short-lived conditions.

Paul (points) to the Christian revelation as being the only means of making eyes truly see, and ears truly hear; of, as it were, bringing into sync the crazy world of Nero's Rome. By the same token, I am more convinced than of anything else that I have ever thought, or considered, or believed, that the only antidote to the media's world of fantasy is the reality of Christ's kingdom proclaimed in the New Testament.
—Malcolm Muggeridge, *Christ and the Media*, 24

Summary

The effectiveness of a mass media message is normally determined by factors apart from either the message or the media carrying the message.

The mass media do not simply inject information into a passive group of listeners, who then respond to that information as the communicator desires. Individuals functioning as a part of groups, within a social network, actively sort, select, and reject messages. This active audience is the first influence operating on the individual listener.

Some of the other factors determining effectiveness of mass media, apart from the media themselves, are the personality of listeners, the frustrations (or lack of them) present, whether or not the media fit naturally into the existing communication patterns of the society, how highly individuals receiving the message value membership in their social group (and whether or not that group is in sympathy with the message), provision of ways for the audience to act on the message, what the audience thinks of the message source, and the simple factor of allowing enough time for change to occur.

To make adequate use of media, one must recognize that they are one part of the total context, not the solitary influence on an audience.

▼ BIBLIOGRAPHY

Engel, James F. *Contemporary Christian Communications.* Nashville: Nelson, 1979.

Klapper, Joseph T. *The Effects of Mass Communication.* New York: Free Press, 1960.

Schramm, Wilbur. *Men, Messages and Media.* New York: Harper & Row, 1973.

► The classic Outsider's request faced with a new society: "Take me to your leader!"

► Who really is the leader?

Hearing Through Other Ears

PROPOSITION 16: Messages are mediated.

It is said that the Mogul emperor Shah Jahan, who built the fabulous Taj Mahal of India, was overthrown by his son and then confined to rooms in a guarded palace a few miles away. The magnificent white marble building was visible from the balcony of his rooms, but Shah Jahan could not see it. He had become so nearsighted that anything more than a few feet away was merely a blur of light and shadow. So he placed a mirror in a stone pillar of the balcony, positioned to reflect the image of the Taj Mahal. He could then see the glorious monument to his wife by looking into the mirror. The mirror "mediated" the image so that Shah Jahan could see his beloved building instead of a confused jumble of light.

Similarly, interpersonal networks mediate the messages that come to us. We may hear what is said or see what is happening, but generally we do not interpret it until we have talked with others about the message. Through interaction, we "make sense" of the message. The meaning and significance are thus developed socially. Our interpersonal networks function like Shah Jahan's mirror, helping us to interpret the world around us. For this reason it is said that meaning lies in the group, not simply in the individual. Messages are mediated by the group, through interpersonal networks.

211

© 1960 by United Feature Syndicate.

The mirror of our interpersonal networks may not, however, be accurate. The group may unknowingly give an incorrect meaning to new information, the mirror may be dirty with self-interest, or it may distort the image with its biases and prejudices. Having chosen the wrong meaning, we will find it very difficult to understand accurately. Further information will be interpreted, or reinterpreted, so that it agrees with the meaning already given.

In a fluid and open society, it is clearly important whom we choose for friends. How we understand something depends on our friends as well as on our personal perception and intelligence.

In closed, traditional groups there is little personal choice in friends; a person is simply part of networks that shape his or her understanding and interaction with the world. Individuals are so molded by interpersonal ties that they normally perceive only what is socially acceptable.

The exchange of information in interpersonal networks is the normal, day-to-day way in which new ideas

Accuracy of understanding is at least as much determined by interpersonal networks as by personal perception.

212

and new information are discussed, tested, evaluated, and accepted or rejected. A decision may be expressed individually, but it is usually made as a result of network processes. Conversations, formal and informal meetings, letters and telephone calls, parties, weddings, funerals—all these are the places where networks function. Networks are simply the people we know and with whom we interact.

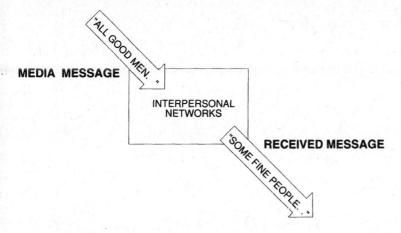

Information is almost always mediated—that is, it is passed from one person to another so that information is received from others rather than directly from the information source. Studies of information flow in both small and large groups find the same thing: People are seldom able to say where they heard something; they know only that "somebody" told them. Only rarely is the specific source named. Fewer than half of those who can name the source say that it was one of the mass media. Virtually all say that they heard the information through conversations, even those who identify one of the mass media as being among their sources.

▼ THE WAY COMMUNICATION FLOWS

Communication flows through networks like signals through the human nervous system, linking one part to another, exchanging information, and guiding relations with the external world. Signals of some kind are always passing along the nervous system, so the body can change, adjust, and interpret the surroundings. Tracing the nervous system would give a fairly good idea of a person's size and shape; though it certainly would not be as recognizable as a photograph of the same person, it would provide better understanding of how the individ-

Communication, as used here, refers to a social process—the flow of information, the circulation of knowledge and ideas in human society, the propagation and internalization of thoughts. It does not refer to electronics, roads and railways, or vehicles.

It is through communication that people can learn about new ideas, can be stimulated by change . . . and what it means, and can understand what is going on around them.
—Y. V. Lakshmana Rao, *Communication and Development*, 6–7

ual functions. Similarly, if the flow of communication were traced in a group, important knowledge about that group would be gained—which individuals are included, how and where decisions are made, and how the group adapts to changing circumstances. Communication takes the form of the society itself.

Though it oversimplifies the process, a partial picture of what happens with new information helps to show the importance of interpersonal networks and how they mediate messages:

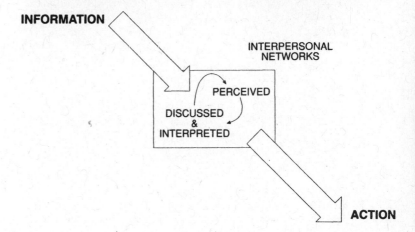

Information is seldom directly acted upon by an individual. When received, it is normally processed through an interpersonal network. Or putting it another way, a message is not really "heard" until it has been cycled through the group. "What do you think of ——?" and "Did you hear ——?" are two common indicators that the interpersonal network is mediating a message. Even when a matter is not openly discussed with the group, or is kept secret, group attitudes and anticipated reactions are very much in mind as an individual responds.

Personal decisions are very rarely made in solo fashion; usually they are made with reference to a small group or network. The group contribution may not be direct at the time, but its attitudes deeply influence the individual. Social approval and acceptance are not lightly discarded.

▼ BASIC BUILDING BLOCKS

As long ago as the early 1950s, Elihu Katz and Paul Lazarsfeld began to point out the great importance of interpersonal networks. Yet many of us still cling to ideas of communication that are not supported by either research or practical experience. The audience is considered a mass of individuals that can be reached only through mass media. The "mass" can only make decisions one by one. If groups within the audience are recognized, they are regarded only as channels for the message.

Actually, these groups are *active* shapers of the message as well as shapers of response. The interpersonal networks are participants in the communication process.

The correct target of a message, then, is the network, not solitary individuals. It is with the network that commonness must be developed. The messenger must become part of the community, instead of taking the role of an outsider telling others what they need or what they should know.

What are these interpersonal networks like? They are the basic building blocks of society, taking different forms in different social settings. But some things are generally true of networks:

- They usually support the status quo, because that is familiar, and familiarity often represents security. Networks tend to establish social stability.
- The networks cement a society together by meeting the human need for social participation. There are few true "isolates"—hermits who never interact with others. Small groups make up the social world in which we live.
- Through interaction within networks, the values of a society are learned and maintained. Group pressures, whether implicit or explicit, powerfully shape individual values and attitudes.
- Individuals are supported in their social roles through interpersonal networks. When individuals are not doing what is expected, the interpersonal networks shape the individual to fill the role in a way that satisfies the group.
- Resources, information, money, and goods are exchanged through the networks. Such exchanges often act like glue, holding the networks together for the mutual benefit of all participants.

Seemingly private opinions and attitudes are maintained by an individual in conjunction with small numbers of others with whom he is motivated to interact. (Therefore) the success of an attempt to change an individual's opinion or attitude will depend, in some measure, on resistance to or support for the proposed change which the individual encounters in his group.
—Elihu Katz and Paul Lazarsfeld, *Personal Influence*, 130

▼ HOW MANY ARE INVOLVED IN A NETWORK?

Trying to count the number involved in a network is somewhat like asking the proverbial question "How long is a piece of string?" It is as long as necessary: short one time, and very long and tangled at another time. In the same way, different ways of describing networks will lead to different numbers.

Most individuals have from twenty-five to one hundred significant social ties—that is, with intimate, close friends and frequent associates at work or school. Some contact is maintained with as many as one thousand persons. At least two factors may alter these estimates significantly: (1) the overall nature of the society within which the network operates, and (2) how "significant ties" are defined.

In a rural or face-to-face society, individuals may have more extensive involvement with fewer people. In that type of social setting, one person may fill several roles—farmer, church elder, mechanic, school board member, neighbor. Since the pool of individuals available is limited, the relationships become greatly intertwined. People know each other better because they have more frequent contact. Relationships are given high priority; good relationships bring prosperity and may even be crucial to survival itself.

In an urban setting, a different individual probably fills each of those roles. Thus the contact with each person is much less, but there are ties to more people. Many urban ties are temporary and superficial because they are limited in content. The only contact with the store clerk is to buy groceries or other goods. In most cases, the topic of conversation is limited to that one function. The pastor only deals with church affairs, the bus driver with which bus stop you need, the mechanic with your car, and so on. In societies where business and technology are dominant, little time is given for broadening relationships: "Time is money, and I make no money talking to you."

Even with these differences, the maximum number of people involved in a single extended network among either rural or urban dwellers remains fairly constant at approximately one hundred. Anthropologist Carol Stack reports that helping networks among urban Afro-Americans typically involve ninety to one hundred people (*All Our Kin: Strategies for Survival in a Black Community*). Suburban dwellers of the same cities are in touch with eighty to ninety people. The number drops to between fifteen and thirty-five individuals when a network is defined as those with whom "significant" or "important" ties are maintained.

In management theory, it is said that twelve is the largest number that can function as a single unit, report-

---

In urban African life, traditional rural networks have become part of urban life.

"There are a number of invisible . . . networks, such as, landowners' associations, secret societies, herbalists' associations, town unions, religious groups, dispute settlement committees. . . . These bodies complement rather than contradict formal government institutions."
    —Frank Okwu Ugboajah, "Cultural Factors in Communication for Rural Third World Development: The African Case," 35–47

ing to one manager. With twelve individuals, there are already an immense number of possible relationships to manage, because of the interaction among the twelve as well as with the manager to whom they report. The possibilities are expressed mathematically as 12! (12 factorial), or 12 x 11 x 10 x 9 x 8 x 7 x 6 x 5 x 4 x 3 x 2 x 1, which equals 479,001,600—nearly half a billion different ways of relating to one another within just a group of twelve!

Clearly, there is a practical limit on the functional size of networks: What is it? One hundred, mentioned above, or twelve? Or somewhere in between, say thirty-five?

These different numbers are referring to different things. Networks do not all have the same intensity of relationships. A useful model shows a network centering upon one individual as a point of reference, whom we will label EGO. Four rings surround that person, showing less and less involvement between that individual and others as the rings are further from him.

Beyond those concentric rings is the general population, with whom the individual has little specific involvement beyond knowing the names of up to one thousand individuals. (Some, with special attention, learn the names of even more than one thousand people.) In our diagram, each ring represents a level of involvement, or closeness to the central individual.

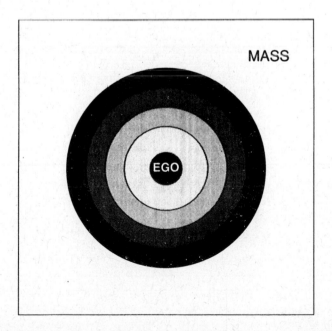

217

The first ring, as the next diagram illustrates, includes those who are *intimates,* with whom personal matters are shared; here there is a high level of trust and extensive involvement. Normally one's husband or wife, children, and very special friends are included in this innermost ring. It usually includes one or two people, almost never more than three; there is simply not enough time to develop intimate relationships with a larger number.

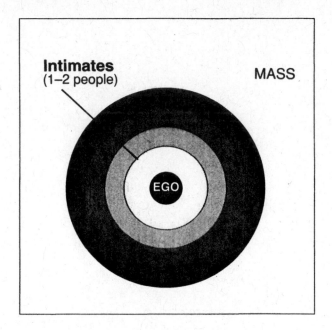

Less time is spent with good friends who are not intimates, represented by the second ring. There are more close friends than intimates, but less time is spent with them. They are a *small group,* usually numbering between seven and ten people. Much of our work and many of our responsibilities are carried out within such small groups. This is the basic unit of interpersonal relationships, the maximum number of people with whom one person can successfully maintain close relationships. (See the illustration at the top of the next page.)

Next is the *medium-sized group* of twelve to twenty-five individuals. Full intercommunication is not possible with this large a group, but it is an optimum number for directive leadership or teaching. The medium-sized group is suitable for a classroom situation with some discussion.

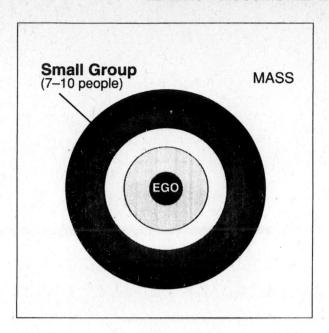

Discussion within such a group will often be dominated by a smaller number within the group, reducing effective interaction to the small group (close friends) level. Others become observers and infrequent participants.

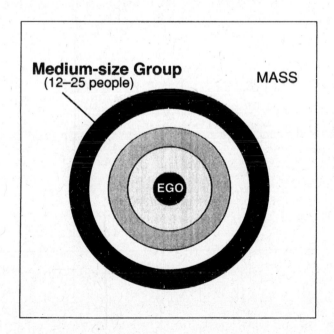

The *large group* of twenty-five to seventy-five people represents the normal limits of personal acquaintance—people about whom we know something more than their names. There is limited social interaction and an aware-ness of a few salient points about each person in the large group.

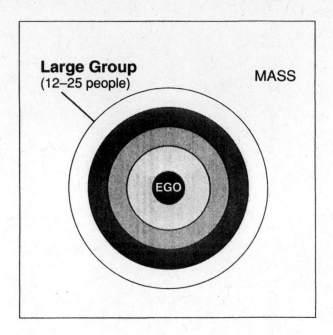

Beyond seventy, we are soon dealing with a mass of *acquaintances*. Personal involvement between leader and group member is impossible, except for brief and limited contacts.

▼ NETWORKS: MODELED IN SCRIPTURE

The ministry of Jesus modeled these network rings. He kept time alone, in direct fellowship with his Father. That time had priority over sleep and even striking op-portunities in public ministry.

Although he understood all persons, he nevertheless selected three to be his special *intimates* on earth—Peter, James, and John. They were brought by Christ into pri-vate and very special occasions such as the Transfigura-tion (Luke 9:28–36) and when he prayed in Gethsemane before his betrayal (Mark 14:32–42).

The *small group* of close friends were his twelve disci-ples, who spent three years traveling together, learning from him, and sharing his life. Why were there only twelve designated as his disciples when there were others who also went about with him? We are told not only that some women traveled with them, helping to support the disci-ples with their own funds (Luke 8:1–3), but also that others were there, from whom Judas's successor was chosen: "It is necessary to choose one of the men who have been with us the whole time the Lord Jesus went in and out among us" (Acts 1:21). The Twelve were not the only ones who were with him during his ministry on earth.

There are explanations for the number of Jesus' apostles, such as the parallel with the twelve tribes of Israel. But it is also worth noticing that Jesus was teaching us and modeling for us the most productive pattern for ministry. A group of twelve is still a small group, making possible close interrelationships for accountability and support. A group larger than this will almost certainly subdivide into at least two sections.

In the third ring, a *medium-sized group* associated with Jesus, walked with him throughout the land, saw his healings, and heard his preaching. They loved him no less than those in the first and second rings, but their relationship was different. Some were wives and mothers (Acts 8:1–3), and others were involved with the religious and political councils and rulers of the land (John 3:1–10; 19:38-40). With those responsibilities, they were unable to give their total time to following Jesus literally. Thus they became part of the third ring instead of the second.

In the fourth ring was a *large group*, at least seventy in number, who were committed to learning from Jesus and obeying him. We do not know them by name, only that Jesus sent these seventy out to tell that the kingdom of God was near. They obeyed, and when they returned, they reported to Jesus, but again we see them only as a group (Luke 10:1–17).

Beyond even the large group were the crowds, the *mass* of people who were acquainted with Jesus. They sometimes followed him, sometimes listened, and were often deeply impressed with what they heard and saw. They discussed and debated whether or not Jesus was indeed the Messiah; some believed, but others found the issue too demanding and turned away. The personal relationship was negligible. Instead, consideration was given to ideas, signs, or political implications. The crowd was aware of Jesus and his teachings, but chose not to give themselves to knowing him more closely (Luke 12–14).

▼ IDENTIFYING AN INTERPERSONAL NETWORK

Networks can best be identified by choosing one individual and then tracing relationships with other people.

In beginning to understand networks and how to trace them, it is a good plan to start with yourself as Ego. Begin by asking, "Who are the people I feel closest to?" These could be your family, other relatives, friends, and neighbors.

A further step will give a more accurate picture. By direct observation (a cooperative subject may keep a simple diary that will be useful), collect this information:

- With what people is there contact?
- How frequently is contact made?
- How much time is spent with each person?

This information can be diagramed, with Ego in the center, so that those who have spent the most time and who are most often in contact with Ego are located nearest on the diagram. In making the diagram, you may combine the last two items (frequency and length of contact) as total time.

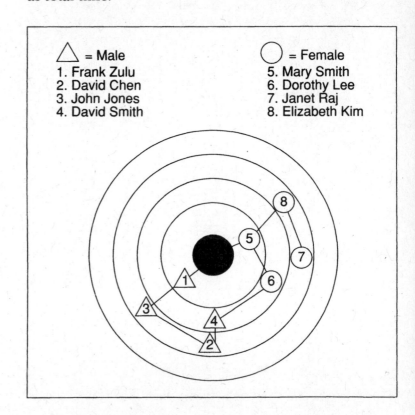

In the above figure, the intimates and close friends (small group) can be identified; these constitute the personal network for Ego. If the same thing is done for each individual, interrelationships between the personal networks will be shown by the lines that link those who are in frequent contact with each other. This diagram then represents the interpersonal networks that are basic building units of a society. Networks are seen most clearly in how one person relates to others. Centering on others in turn, the complex web of relationships (the term used by Win Arn of the American Church Growth Institute) is revealed.

These interpersonal networks shift and change. More time is spent with one person and less with another; a new person becomes a part of the social setting, causing "ripples" in the networks—a realignment of relationships. Needs and new opportunities arise, both of which require help from different people. Disagreements trouble a relationship, and sympathy is gained from a new acquaintance. Interpersonal networks are dynamic, except possibly in small societies where relationships are controlled by survival requirements.

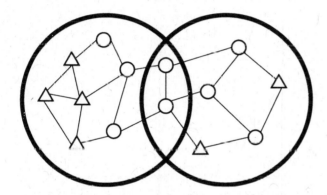

One person's primary network is relatively small, almost never including more than twelve people (at one time) in the intimate and close-friend rings. When the number grows larger, some will slip away to the third or fourth ring of relationships, through lack of Ego's time. A person's capacity to handle interrelationships seems to be reached when there are about twelve in the small group.

Within the group of twelve there is always a group of intimates in which especially strong relationships bind two or three together closely. These intimates are usually interdependent and mutually supportive.

Cells are the dynamic structure of society. Though shifting in membership and activities, these small groups (seven to ten people) are the way people function and survive. Examples of such small groups are seen among hunting and gathering peoples, such as the Khoisan Bushmen of the Kalahari Desert in southern Africa or the

It must be the interpersonal networks that are critical in dissemination of information, else why would it tend to spread outward from a point of origin? Mass communication which . . . reaches the entire area at once, would promote an equal growth, not an expansion across space in ever-widening concentric circles. . . . Dissemination through conversation easily outbalances other means of communication.
—Torsten Hagerstrand, in *Handbook of Communication*, ed. Ithiel de Sola Pool and Wilbur Schramm, 432

Gurung honey hunters of Nepal. The Gurung honey hunters are limited to nine men, each inheriting the right from his father. "'Like the many fibers of our rope, our hands are united,' says Mani Lal, interlocking his fingers. 'Together we can go where one man alone could not travel'" (Eric Valli and Diane Summers, "Honey Hunters of Nepal," 663).

In larger, technologically oriented societies, these networks have been found to be a vital link in health care. When individuals lose personal relationships or are socially marginal or in a minority position, they are more likely to have both poor physical and mental health. Research has documented this relationship between social disorganization and health (L. E. Hinkle, Jr., and H. G. Wolff, "Ecologic Investigations of the Relations Between Illness, Life Experiences and the Social Environment," 1373–88). In other studies, adverse health consequences were found to be the result of social isolation and disorganization. The highest incidence of schizophrenia, for example, was concentrated in the most disorganized zone of a major city. This finding was repeated in further studies of minority neighborhoods and areas of transition and high mobility.

The ability to develop new relationships when old ones are disrupted is critical in maintaining personal health. Interpersonal networks are fundamental not only in the social structure, but also to individual health.

▼ USING NETWORKS TO BRING CHANGE

All of this points to one practical fact: Small groups of twelve or fewer "units" are the fundamental unit to work with in bringing any kind of change to a society. Begin change within one network or social cell, and participants can spread that change to other networks. Since the networks (social cells) are linked together like a chain-link fence, the innovation will, in due course, penetrate the entire larger social structure, bringing change from within. This dynamic has been recognized and sometimes utilized.

Lenin shook the world by building a revolution on the principles of interpersonal networks. The Communist Party has made many aware of the concept of "cell"—a small, closely interlinked group of approximately ten "comrades" who work together to further the revolution. The cell leader is accountable to another leader; through such linkages, an almost invisible but tightly disciplined

---

God is using a web of family and friendship ties as a network for the Gospel in Mexico City.

Let's trace the workings of one web of relationships. Luis and Mary lived two streets over from the home of Phil and Kathy Banta. Kathy met the young Mexican mother, Mary, while on a stroll. "What does your husband do?" led to a Bible study including Mary and her scientist husband, Luis. Mary was baptized in June, and two months later Luis decided to trust Christ.

Several months later, Luis and Mary moved to Cuernavaca. . . . their neighbors were Enrique and Rocio, who began participating in Bible studies.

After a few months, Enrique and Rocio were baptized and are now a spark of life in the congregation.

The network goes on and on. Contacts . . . go to the second and third generation. Altogether, there have been approximately 300 significant contacts with Mexicans.

Fast paced and impersonal? No, Mexico City is a network of warm, personal, friendly relationships that lead to faith in Christ.

—Ray Giles, in *Impact*, Christian Missionary Fellowship

group becomes a potent force. The manageable size of the interpersonal network (cell) eases the problems of indoctrination, since it is conducted in the optimal-size group for intensive learning and interaction—approximately twelve people. It is practical for someone to be a cell leader even while engaged in other work full-time, because the number for which that person is responsible corresponds to the normal size of social relationship circles. The leader can know the condition of each cell member, so that tight discipline and encouragement can be maintained.

Long before Lenin used the cell structure to launch a revolution and Mao employed it as the organizing principle for the world's largest nation, John Wesley used it to alter the course of English history. In 1742, all Methodists were organized into "little companies or classes—about twelve in each class" (John Wesley, *Journal,* 15 February 1742). Such class meetings, as they were named, made possible the personal supervision of every member of the Methodist societies. They met weekly, men and women separately, under class leaders who were actually lay pastors. Members discussed the most intimate problems of life and encouraged one another in their faith. Confessions of sin and failure were heard, but not repeated—all were pledged to secrecy regarding one another's confessions. "All now were their brother's keepers; all helped to heal the wounds of sin; all strove together to keep running the springs of grace; and however painful were temporary defeats, the note of triumph prevailed" (J. Russell Bready, *Before and After Wesley,* 215–17).

The class meetings were formalized interpersonal networks, the strong backbone of the Methodist movement as it became the largest Protestant church group in the world. Through discipline, courageous Christian action, and steady confidence in Christ, the Methodist movement sparked the Evangelical Revival and led to the abolition of child labor and slavery, ushered in a reform of the English penal code and prisons, laid the foundations of popular education, and so influenced conduct of public affairs that numerous historians have said the Wesleyan revivals saved England from revolution. Conscious utilization of personal networks was at the heart of this movement.

The same concept is used today in the world's largest single church, Full Gospel Central Church of Seoul, Korea. Its cell groups are clusters of church members who

225

meet weekly in homes, offices, factories or any other place convenient for evangelism and Christian fellowship. Leaders are carefully trained, and the cells are firmly guided in their teaching and pastoral care of members. An assistant leader is trained and appointed who then assumes responsibility for half the group. Each cell is kept between eight and sixteen in number. When it divides, the assistant becomes the leader of the new cell, and the process is repeated. In this thorough manner, a congregation of approximately 500,000 not only is cared for, but continues to reach out evangelistically (John N. Vaughan, *The World's Twenty Largest Churches*, 44–47).

Each of these examples uses the basic unit of society first to firmly implant teaching and disciplined action; second, to incorporate others into the larger movement; and third, to win others through division of cells to form new growth points. Evangelism conducted primarily by the cells aids enormously in the discipling of new believers. Through the cells they already have relationships with Christians and a framework for teaching, care, discipline, and encouragement. Cells develop ministry on a "human scale," combining the way people function with the Holy Spirit's power focusing on specific lives. It removes ministry from dependence on star performers who are gifted to convince and teach hundreds or thousands at a time.

Almost never is a society totally isolated from all other societies. There are links between societies through geography, economics, education, religion and other things. The links exist within interpersonal networks and at times are even present within the first or second rings of relationships. Marriage between people of different social backgrounds is one example of such linkage. School classmates, sports team members, buddies from military service, and business partners are other examples of situations where close bonding can develop across normal social boundaries. Through such cross-cultural network links, change and information spread between societies—much as epidemics of sickness spread.

▼ WHAT PRACTICAL DIFFERENCE DOES THIS MAKE?

Two different points arising from this discussion have major significance for Christian ministry throughout the world, especially efforts to reach yet-unreached peoples.

I also feel that in evangelism we have not earned the right to be heard. The people do not know us nor understand us so we are suspect in their eyes. I therefore wonder as to the place of the hit and run methods of evangelism. . . . Earning the right to be heard will mean, apart from other things, a) our living in the area, b) our working in the area so that people see us in normal life, c) our friendships and relationship developed in the area. We have expected to take shortcuts and they have not worked. . . .

Our problem is that we have moved away from the biblical model of communication, which is participatory with emphasis on relationships. The need is to go back to our roots—the Bible—and follow the model of communication outlined there.

—Joseph D'Souza, unpublished paper, 1986

First, only if a group is totally isolated do we need to start evangelism in that group from "zero." There are ways of access to virtually every group in the world through existing social linkages. But, obviously, those links must be deliberately sought and utilized. Communication with the group must then proceed within existing internal communication networks.

Second, the increased flow of information between nations and within nations brings us closer to being a "global village." Few societies are so isolated that they do not receive news regularly from powerful radio and television stations or newspapers. Ideas flow along with goods, or even ahead of them, and the products of technology have spread almost everywhere. Rather than basing plans for world evangelism on reaching thousands of distinct and presumably isolated people groups separately, we should focus primary effort on seeking and then building through existing links. They are the highways for our God that are integral parts of every culture.

In the centuries before communication technology restructured most of the world into a global village, reaching people groups separately *was* the only way. To plan and work for world evangelism in the same way today is, to borrow another phrase from Marshall McLuhan, "looking at the present through a rear-view mirror. We march backward into the future" (*The Medium*, 16).

It is hard even to find those useful links, however, when planners continue to think in restricted patterns, when Christians in a few powerful cultures assume they can do the job of reaching everyone, with some supportive assistance from newer Christian groups. Instead, emphasis should be placed on finding ways to work with and through those involved in networks that include unreached peoples. That will, of course, mean not only new thinking, new strategies, and differently trained personnel, but almost certainly new structures as well.

The isolation of China for nearly forty years was an immense discouragement to Christians. But then to their surprise, it was learned that within Chinese interpersonal networks the Gospel had spread more, and had more response, than ever before in history. Outside input had been almost totally limited to Christian radio. Crucial, of course, was knowledge of the message already present as a result of a century of resident missionary work. A significant lesson is that the Gospel spread without the struc-

Electric circuitry has overthrown the regime of "time" and "space" and pours upon us instantly and continuously the concerns of all other men. It has reconstituted dialogue on a global scale. Its message is Total Change, ending psychic, social, economic, and political parochialism. The old civic, state, and national groupings have become unworkable. Nothing can be further from the spirit of the new technology than "a place for everything and everything in its place."
—Marshall McLuhan, *The Medium Is the Message*, 16

tures, procedures, and outside intervention thought to be necessary for missionary evangelism.

Concentrating on the dynamic process of information flow and change, working *within* a society, would radically change the way most intercultural evangelism is conducted. Workers would become part of existing interpersonal networks, no longer approaching the task with an "us and them" attitude. It would free the message to flow through networks without being anchored to the presence of outsiders. Instead, we are approaching the world's peoples as if they were a wall that we must take apart brick by brick, people by people.

Identifying "people groups" is probably useful as a preliminary step toward evangelism. When we name and attempt to describe overlooked groups, attention is focused on incomplete parts of world evangelization. But the tendency is to assume that these groups are separate and fixed units that must be evangelized one by one. The "homogeneous unit principle" has correctly pointed out that people mostly interact with other people like themselves. Based on this principle, some are making an effort to list all these "homogeneous units" by describing where they live, religion, income, cultural patterns, and similar characteristics. This gives an "average" picture of what the people are like, but little idea of how to relate to the networks that actually are the society. It gives a still photograph on which to draw what the people should learn and do. Instead, a moving picture is needed, showing relationships and tracing the flow of communication within which the Gospel can genuinely be shared.

The practical mistake made by adherents of the "homogeneous people group" idea is to assume self-contained, rigid, separate societies. Attention is centered on visible characteristics of the unit, rather than on how information flows, how decisions are made, and how change happens. Our task basically has little to do with a society's visible culture and external appearance. It is to *communicate,* to make known the message of Jesus Christ. So our focus ought to be on how communication happens. With that perspective, it would be seen that societies are not isolated but dynamically involved with other societies. Linkages that could speed the flow of the ultimate Good News for all people would become apparent.

Social networks are rarely homogeneous; dissimilar people are in contact with each other through work, special interests, and geographical nearness. For example,

The structure of a society determines appropriate communication strategy.

Japanese and American business networks function differently. In America an idea is sent straight to the top and is decided upon at the upper levels. Then it goes down through the ranks. In Japan, however, an idea must start from the bottom levels of management and be sent up, gaining approval at each level before it is finally approved at the top. If a Japanese director has an idea, he will normally get a lower level manager to start the process down where it is supposed to be started.

—Bruce Penner

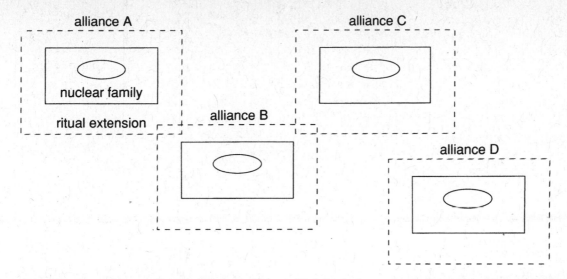

frequently throughout church history, slaves effectively introduced their masters to Jesus Christ.

Even though the idea of the homogeneous unit is inadequately defined and seems to miss the essential understanding of networks,[1] it recognizes *the group* as a valid target. It shows that the group can make a general decision to become Christian, thus opening the way for individual commitment to Christ. It recognizes the crucial concept of "people movements" that can open societies to personal knowledge of Christ. Approaching our task as essentially a task of communication, identifying and working within social networks, makes it more likely that a true people movement will occur.

A people movement is excellent preparation for individual commitment to Christ. In a people movement, there is first much discussion within social networks of the Christian way. In the small groups, the new information is considered, alternatives are weighed, and a consensus is reached. As this process spreads throughout a society, individuals of all kinds participate in the discussions and are prepared to accept the final group decision.

Personal acceptance of that decision, according to research, "is primarily determined by the amount of influence the subject has had over the final decision" (Fred

The strength of Filipino society rests in the linked alliances rather than in the individual alliances. Such linkage of many alliances provides security.
—Marvin K. Mayers, *A Look at the Filipino Lifestyle*, 27

---

1. In his initial writings, particularly *The Bridges of God*, Donald McGavran clearly pointed out the functioning of networks within a society—but not between societies. He called them bridges, but the concept is the same. Later followers of his perspectives seem to have taken a less adequate view of society. (See *The Bridges of God* [Cincinnati: Friendship Press, 1955, rev. ed. 1981]).

L. Strodtbeck, "Communication in Small Groups," in *Handbook of Communication,* ed. de Sola Pool and Schramm, 661). A necessary preparation for personal commitment is heavy involvement in discussions leading to that commitment. Leaders who attempt to enforce a decision unilaterally seldom gain the full support of their followers. Evangelists who work from "outside" to win individuals, separated from their social networks, run the risk of shallow conversions.

▼ HOW DO WE COMMUNICATE WITH NETWORKS?

Talking with a single person is a familiar thing; even talking with a large group can be easily imagined. But how do we talk with a *network*? A network itself is invisible. Its presence is detected only by what happens. It is not only invisible, but also changeable. Even after contact is made with an invisible, changeable grouping of people, how can contact be maintained?

It is seldom possible to chart all, or even most, of the interpersonal networks in a society. But it is possible to learn where information is exchanged normally and how group decisions are made. It is at these *information points* that new messages are shared, like seeds planted in prepared ground.

Among the Turkana people of northern Kenya, a Kenyan missionary noticed that information spread rapidly among the people even though they were scattered widely across the desert. There were no telephones and no visible signaling devices, and they used no cars. But the Turkana women came daily to the water holes dug in dry, sandy riverbeds. There they exchanged news items, which were carried back to their encampments and the inevitable visitors from other encampments. The Kenyan decided to spend several hours each day at a water hole, talking to the people who came. After several days, he was invited to stay in a village where a wedding feast was to be held over a three-day period.

There he met Turkana who had come on foot as far as 125 miles. The men held long discussions about matters of concern and the missionary observed how decisions were reached—who spoke, in what order, and how consensus was reached. By starting at one visible "information point" and listening, he was able to learn outlines of the major Turkana networks.

He was invited to stay with an influential diviner and later led that man to believe in Jesus Christ. As men and women came to this converted diviner for solutions to their problems, they were told of Jesus. They spread the news as they returned to their own places, so more came to learn what the diviner was now speaking about. Within a two-year period, several groups of Christians formed among a people who had been very resistant to Christian witness. The Gospel had been planted within the networks and had spread through those same networks.

Information points differ widely. In some societies, as in working-class England of the twentieth century, the pub or tavern is the major information point. Among international business executives, exclusive social clubs are often significant information points, or golfing excursions at country clubs. Such points may be sporting events, a street corner on summer evenings, the country trading store, a coffee club, the town square or the district market. Some of the information points serve only one society; others draw people from several societies.

In each network there are unwritten and unspoken rules on how relationships are maintained. The accepted procedure may be as simple as buying and selling goods while news and ideas are exchanged. Often there is a gift exchange involved, whether in paying for the drinks in turn or in giving items as gifts. The gift obligates the receiver to a return gift of equal or greater value; in some cultures, failure to give a gift or the giving of a lesser gift closes relationships. Barter may build and maintain social relationships as well as economic. Networks continue to function when needs are being met for all those involved.

Becoming part of interpersonal networks is the surest way to proclaim Christ, leading to new churches. It is also the most emotionally costly way, because it often requires changing one's own ways of living. Media can be used to raise the level of information and to build familiarity with and credibility for the message. But entering the personal networks, with the possibilities of give-and-take that shape the form of the message, enables the Christian to be a participant, not merely an observer of evangelization.

An Afro-American family provided a home base for anthropologist Carol Stack, "a place where I was welcome to spend the day, week after week, and where I could sleep. . . . My personal network expanded naturally as I met those who visited each day. Ultimately I was welcome at several unrelated households. . . . I found extensive networks of kin and friends supporting, reinforcing each other—devising schemes for self-help, strategies for survival in a community of severe economic deprivation. I became poignantly aware of the alliances of individuals trading and exchanging goods, resources, and the care of children, the intensity of their acts of domestic cooperation, and the exchange of goods and services among these persons. . . .

"The process of exchange joins individuals in personal relationships. These interpersonal links define the web of social relationships"
—Carol B. Stack, *All Our Kin*, 43

SUMMARY

The primary audience to be reached is interpersonal networks, not a mass of unrelated individuals. Individual perceptions, attitudes, and values are shaped within these networks, not in solitary, rational contemplation.

Message effect depends (among other things) upon its perception in these networks. The networks intervene, as it were, between the message source and the individual. It is within the network that the message is assimilated through discussion and decisions are reached.

A flow of communication links individuals to one another within the networks. This "network communication" cements a society together by maintaining individuals in their social roles, assuring social participation, and reinforcing identification with the values of a society.

The networks filter messages. The individual hears the message, then considers and discusses it with friends. That individual will react to the message heavily influenced by the understanding and evaluation of the message in these interpersonal networks. In most societies, an individual decision apart from the group or network is unlikely; group-think is the normal pattern for decisions.

Individuals often participate in several networks simultaneously, thus forming the many links that tie groups together to form a society. Through these interrelated networks, a message or idea spreads, with or without the use of mass communications.

▼ BIBLIOGRAPHY

Burt, Ronald S., and Michael J. Minor. *Applied Network Analysis: A Methodological Introduction.* Beverly Hills, Calif.: Sage, 1983.

Chu, Godwin C., Syed A. Rahim, and D. Lawrence Kincaid. *Communication for Group Transformation in Development.* Communication Monographs 2. Honolulu: East-West Communication Institute, 1976.

De Sola Pool, Ithiel, and Wilbur Schramm, eds. *Handbook of Communication.* Chicago: Rand McNally, 1973. Specifically note "Mass Media and Interpersonal Communication."

Engel, James F. *Contemporary Christian Communication.* Nashville: Nelson, 1979.

Gottlieb, Benjamin H., ed. *Social Networks and Social Support.* Sage Studies in Community Mental Health 4. Beverly Hills, Calif.: Sage, 1981.

Hopler, Thom. *A World of Difference: Following Christ Beyond Your Cultural Walls.* Downers Grove, Ill.: InterVarsity Press, 1981. See especially chapter 9 "Networks of Communication."

Katz, Elihu, and Paul F. Lazarsfeld. *Personal Influence: The Part Played by People in the Flow of Mass Communications.* New York: Free Press, 1955.

Mayers, Marvin K. *A Look at the Filipino Lifestyle.* Dallas: SIL Museum of Anthropology, 1980.

Padilla, C. René. "The Unity of the Church and the Homogeneous Unit Principle." *International Bulletin of Missionary Research,* May 1982.

Stack, Carol B. *All Our Kin: Strategies for Survival in a Black Community.* New York: Harper & Row, 1974.

Vaughan, John N. *The World's Twenty Largest Churches: Church Growth Principles in Action.* Grand Rapids, Baker, 1984.

17

➤ If one doesn't know how to exercise a cross-cultural ministry at home, he is not likely to do so overseas. He is more likely to slip into a missionary subculture with colleagues. (Ada Lum)

Patterns to Shape Communication

PROPOSITION 17: Cultural patterns of a society fundamentally influence the form of communication.

"No, you don't sit on that!" Surprise and consternation showed on the Zulu woman's face. "That is an eating mat!"

The American couple looked at each other with puzzlement, but said nothing—until they were alone. "Can you see the difference between this 'eating mat' and the 'sitting mats' that we use before sitting on the ground?" the husband asked, in private. Both were made of a tough grass and were about the same size. But after careful examination, the couple found some differences and took note of them so that they would not again make the mistake of sitting on the dining table.

Tourists seem to go everywhere nowadays, and experts in every conceivable subject are living for months and years in cultures different from their own, in order to share their skills and knowledge in religion, farming, mechanics, or computers. With so many short- and long-term visitors, how do the local people react?

Two young men were trying to decide what to do with their day off from work. Finally, one suggested, "Let's go down to the market and watch the tourists. That's always good for laughs!"

The tourists, of course, went to the market to satisfy their omnivorous appetite for souvenirs. *They* wanted "local color," collecting photos of the "natives" along with their carvings, feathers, and colorful clothing. They went home to tell their stories, and the local people went home to tell theirs.

Culture differences provide hundreds and hundreds of anecdotes to amuse friends. Some are amusing, some are sad because the misunderstandings result in anger and distrust. Where the mark of a tourist is description of scenery, festivals, and food, the mark of a traveler is the collection of cultural anecdotes. This at least shows awareness of people, but still falls short of the ability to understand shown by a genuinely bicultural person.

How can we become bicultural in our communication skills? Probably the first step is to show respect for those who act differently, recognizing that what we see is only the thin skin of the outer layer of a culture. While we all have the same fundamental human needs, those needs take different forms, and we satisfy them through a wide variety of practices. Some ways are good, some are not, but valid judgment cannot be made only on the basis of the differences. Beginning with respect and an attitude of learning, a person can slowly proceed into another culture, until he or she becomes bicultural—comfortable in the second culture as well as the first.

The goal of functioning effectively within another society is never reached quickly or easily. It is something like learning to play a sport—soccer, basketball, or tennis perhaps—except that this "sport" is learning to communicate in another culture.

First you review what you are trying to do—throw the ball into the hoop, or kick it into the net, or hit it with a racket so that your opponent cannot hit it back. Then you learn the rules. There are actions that might work but are not permitted; you cannot throw the ball with your hand in tennis, you cannot kick it in basketball, but you must kick it (or hit it with your head) in soccer.

Then someone shows you the best way to throw, hit, or kick, and all the other motions that can make you a good player. Even after you learn all those things, many hours of practice remain before there is much enjoyment of the sport. The motions are uncomfortable at first, and your muscles ache from the practice. Concentration is necessary just to throw, hit, or kick correctly, and there is no thought of such things as a game plan and strategy. It

If a missionary is basically a servant, many common problems are eliminated or at least more readily worked out. For instance, the ability to cross those invisible but rugged mountain frontiers of racial feelings, cultural strangeness, climate and diet changes. To shift mental and emotional gears to a different pace of life. To adjust to a different standard of life with varying ideas of hygiene and sanitation. To empathize accurately with people in their personal dilemmas. To communicate Jesus Christ so he makes sense to needy men and women. To persist in the face of inevitable opposition. These are almost impossible without a servant's heart.
—Ada Lum, "What Does It Take to Be a Missionary?" 11

235

is enough just to hit the ball and hope it ends up somewhere near where it should. There is not much fun yet, only a great deal of frustration.

The motions must be gone through again, and again, and again. After a while, to your delighted surprise, you find that the correct motions are becoming a habit. No longer is it necessary to concentrate totally on the ball. Habits have been formed, and they begin to control your actions so that response is quicker and easier. You actually begin to think about enjoyment, perhaps even winning occasionally.

There are many further levels to be achieved before it can be said that you are skilled, or that you are outstanding. And beyond being a player, there is much more about the game to learn before you can become a manager or coach.

The stages in learning to communicate in another culture are similar. First is learning how to handle basics, the signals that can lead to food, water, shelter, and safety. Chapter 12 deals with the raw materials of communication that are the beginning point in learning how to function in another culture. The signal systems must be learned, and the appropriate time and situation in which to use them. Does "mmmmm" mean yes, no, maybe, or let me think about it? Is a red light used to direct traffic, to give warning of a danger, or to mark the channel for boats? To show friendliness, is a smile best—or does smiling too much mean that the person is an idiot?

Often, considerable mental and emotional stress goes along with learning the basics in another culture. It is relatively easy to learn *about* the signals from outside the culture, but knowing correct timing and context for signals can be fully learned only within that culture. Uncertainty of the response, because the signals may not be correctly used, causes much anxiety. The more fully a learner is immersed in the new culture, the more rapidly the signals will be learned—and the greater will be the stress and anxiety. But trying to learn how to function in a culture without ever committing oneself to that culture is like trying to learn to swim without ever plunging into the water.

As signals are learned, patterns begin to be seen, such as men expecting to be waited on by the women and children, women controlling the kitchen area and family food, or men and women not mixing in public gatherings such as church services. Perhaps smiles are not appropriate during discussion of serious topics, or a joke should be

A hard, but essential, lesson to learn is that "different" doesn't necessarily mean "inferior" or "wrong." . . . The first time I was in a prayer meeting in Korea I was horrified to hear seventy-five people praying aloud and calling on the Lord at the same time. I thought it was irreverently noisy. A brother who had been abroad must have noted my disturbed reaction and in kindness remarked, "Your churches are quieter, aren't they? I think that's why so many fall asleep during the sermon."
—Ada Lum, "What Does It Take to Be a Missionary?" 12

told before starting an important meeting. The learner discovers that the people who have patiently helped to teach the signals are friends. Times to relax or joke can be shared; enough signals have been formed into habit patterns to become comfortable in another cultural setting. Even though the basic signals are learned, communication is not yet easy. The newcomer is still an outsider, because motivations are not fully understood and values are not shared completely. Over time, the traditions will be learned. The values will be deduced by what is accepted and rejected, and the inner world will begin to take shape through seeing rituals, hearing explanations, and sharing in reactions to the joys and discouragements of daily living. Acceptance of the outsider increases and the outsider finds it increasingly easy to function within the second culture.

The demanding process of creating understanding across cultural boundaries is outlined below, perhaps too simply. The purpose, however, is to review the major steps so that we can better see the many ways culture affects communication. The progression of learning can be summed up thus:

How could I establish rapport with the people? I observed that (1) few facial expressions were used (recognizable by me, at least), (2) head and eye position has significance, (3) facial expressions of whites are not understood, (4) touch is important, shown by the length of time they hold on after a handshake. I tried to imitate these things while visiting a coffee shop for about an hour. I was told by my local host afterwards that I seemed to be at home with the people!
—A student of intercultural communication

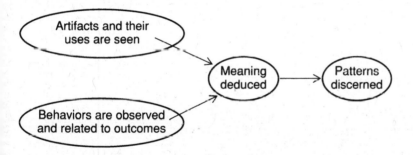

Almost the first thing that happens in learning other culture patterns is to note different objects (1) and how even familiar objects may be used differently. The kinds of houses built, the way space is used, what food is eaten and when—the signal systems are used as a checklist to help in looking for clues to meaning and the building of patterns.

Using the signal systems as a guide will help in noting specific actions (2), kinesics as well as work, play, discussions, the giving and receiving of messages. Motions of the body, particularly facial expressions, at first seem the same everywhere. But no kinesic signal has yet been noted that has the same meaning and same usage everywhere—even the smile. Space, temporal and tactile systems may use the same signals but with different meanings, and it is the same with each of the signal systems. Which signals are used most frequently, the occasions when they are used, and who uses each kind of signal must be noted in order to interpret the meaning correctly and to use similar signals appropriately. A missionary describes well the uncertainty as new ways are learned:

> Suddenly the spell was broken as we entered a large village. People were everywhere. Ahead we could see hundreds more seated on the ground around several African dignitaries.
>
> "Do we have time to stop?" one of my fellow missionaries asked.
>
> "Sure," said the driver. "What an opportunity to preach!"
>
> Everyone bounded out with enthusiasm . . . except me. I had so much to learn about this land and its people. Would it be proper to meet the dignitaries unannounced? Maybe it wasn't allowed. Maybe . . . Maybe. . . .
>
> I approached with the others, but hesitantly, carefully studying the crowd. I watched in fascination as the villagers greeted their leaders. Gracefully and silently they slipped out of their sandals, crouched low, and finally, on bended knee with head bowed and eyes averted to the left, they extended their right hand to each leader. With their left hand they held the forearm of their extended right arm. After being recognized by the leader, they quietly turned, picked up their sandals, and joined the crowd seated on the hot, dusty earth.
>
> There was a stir among the people as our group of three whites, four blacks, and myself, the only woman, approached. One by one, in standing positions, the men in our group shook hands with the leaders.
>
> I had already been seen, so I had to go on. Should I do as the men in our group had done? Or should I follow the example of the Africans who had preceded them? The agony of that decision was momentary, but unforgettable. I chose the African way, feeling strange as I slipped off my sandals and bowed, all the time praying that I was just showing respect and not worshiping.
>
> I greeted each individual with the words, "I see your heads." I wasn't positive if those words were appropriate, but I had heard them during a funeral ceremony in my home village. The dignitaries seemed to be of similar rank. . . .
>
> Hours later, the oldest, most respected African in our group quietly told me I could return to that village any time I wanted. The people would listen. "Because you showed them respect, the chief asked me to tell you," he said.

Truly learning a language is more than learning grammar and vocabulary. Early in my overseas experience I realized I wasn't learning the language at my desk. I got permission to live with an African family. Despite wanting to give up many times in those early months, the hidden personality of the African language and life-style eventually began to become a part of me.

—Sandra Banasik, "A Living Language"

Actions and objects can effectively build communication. New meanings can be introduced or reinforced in nonverbal ways. Unfortunately, old meanings can be unintentionally strengthened through the use of particular objects or actions. Use of debatable practices should normally come only after thorough observation and discussion with insiders who understand the hidden messages of particular behaviors and objects.

It is most natural to learn the verbal system, spoken language, along with the other signal systems. It does not replace the other systems, despite its overall efficiency in sharing information. It is enriched by the parallel "languages." Learning all of them *together* lays a sound foundation for communication within that culture. The nuances of language are often lost unless the whole context

is understood, along with the particular usage of that culture.

The third step (3) in the learning process comes when accumulated observations and thought are brought together—mentally collated. Meanings behind objects and actions begin to be understood. At the same time, language is being learned: Language, objects, and words come together to clarify meaning.

An assortment of isolated meanings is collected. As these are compared and contrasted, patterns of culture behavior will begin to emerge. This step (4 in the diagram) will be very tentative at first, but as more patterns become apparent the "sense" behind the culture will begin to emerge.

Because English is spoken so widely and by so many different cultures, what is thought to be clear may not be if one does not know the local culture. "I'm finished" seems a straightforward statement. But does it mean that the job the speaker is doing is completed? Or does the speaker mean that he or she is totally exhausted physically? Both meanings are possible, the first being the standard dictionary meaning and the second common in East African use of English. Without knowing the total setting, one could well miss the intended meaning.

Beyond the straightforward meaning of language, the matter of language form and style is affected by culture. In a traditional African court hearing, a complex issue of responsibility for damages may well be discussed by means of proverbs. The same kind of matter would be argued in European or American courts by referring to previous rulings in similar cases. Proverbs and precedents—both are built on experience, but language form and style are sharply different.

One language may use concrete expression, while another tends to the abstract. Written Chinese is particularly concrete, reflecting Chinese thought. The English *hydrogen* is literally *water dust* in Dutch, an example of an abstract name's being made concrete in another language. Hydrogen is a gas that remains when water is broken down to its components—the "dust" left behind when water is demolished.

Direct translation from one language to another is virtually impossible because of different connotations and experiences carried in words that are superficially the same.

An Indonesian middle-class boy wanted to marry an upper-class girl. The boy's mother went to the house of the girl's mother for tea. A banana was served with the tea, which was a most unusual combination. The women did not discuss the marriage during the visit, but the boy's mother knew the marriage was unacceptable—bananas do not go with tea. The relevant information had been communicated nonverbally, but nobody lost face. (A person) unaware of the significance of this symbolism might have picked up the banana and started to peel it while discussing the marriage date!

—Muriel Wall, "Cultural Factors Cause Insight to Affect Eyesight"

240

Special dialects are often in use among particular interest groups. Conversation with a knowledgeable sailor of small boats may sound like English, but the words are unfamiliar or have a different meaning from that used in more familiar settings. *Clew, tune, raking, jibe, boom, sheets, beam reach, broad reach, luffing*—just a few words from sailors' English that require more than knowledge of linguistics to be understood. Baseball has its own set of terms, some of which have carried over into daily English in the United States: *sacrifice, fly, first base, double play, bunt, out, home run, out of the ball park,* and idioms such as *two strikes against you* and *he threw me a curve.*

Language may be used purely for the beauty of its sound, as a preparation for serious matters to be discussed. Through repetition, alliteration, onomatopoeia, and other devices of spoken language, a poetic effect is achieved that is untranslatable but effective in the original setting.

An elderly Zulu was brought to testify in a white-controlled court in South Africa. A translator was present, but for the first five minutes of the Zulu's testimony he translated nothing into English. Finally the judge interrupted and urged the interpreter to tell him what the Zulu was saying. "Your honor," the interpreter responded, "he hasn't said anything yet!" The witness had spoken, but the effect of great courtesy created by beautiful use of language was completely untranslatable.

Learning a language sufficiently to pass a language examination is only a bare beginning in learning how to use the language in a culturally appropriate way.

Then there is the question of what form the message should take. It will use the language of the group where communication is being developed. But should it be spoken or written? Should it be presented as a series of propositional statements or in a story? It certainly must use the patterns of communication already present within the society, even if the medium itself is new to the group. Let's consider how communication patterns can affect some of the major media.

▼ USE OF THE WRITTEN WORD

The written message has many advantages. It is not bound by constraints of time, distance, or personal contact. It does not change with each reading, so it can remain authoritative as a check on the correctness of what is spoken. Missionaries of the nineteenth century wanted

What special knowledge is needed to understand the language often used among Christians? *Redemption, washed in the blood, hallelujah, getting into the Word, preach the Word, quiet time, sinner,* "Praise the Lord" as a comment on almost everything, *speaking in tongues, saved.* . . .

Is it, then, necessary for a person to learn this dialect before becoming a Christian? If the person does not, how can he or she understand what is being said? Or should Christians translate their ideas into everyday speech?

Most languages have a word that is used to translate *bread.* But do the words carry the same package of experiences and function?

Even in English, the word may mean a food that is eaten, or it may mean money.

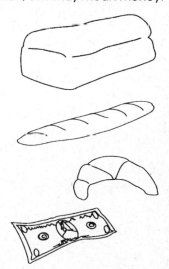

the power of reading and writing to be part of the new churches, so literacy was at times made a requirement for church membership. Should we always focus primarily on using the written system because of its advantages and history?

No. Even though languages have a developed written system, writing may be used very little by the people. Literacy rates might be very low, limiting the audience. Even where 40 percent, 50 percent, or more of the people can read, do they read? And do they learn from reading? The technique of reading may be known, but the use of reading to gain needed information may still not be a cultural pattern.

A missionary was showing Zimbabwean friends some small agricultural developments on his land. Waste water was being reused (important in a semiarid area), compost was prepared and added to the thin, rocky soil, and varieties of fruit trees especially developed for that climate were planted. Most of the family food was being grown on one acre of what had been unproductive land.

"Have you studied farming?" the Zimbabweans asked.

"No, not in school."

"Is your father a farmer, then?"

"No, he is a university professor."

"Where did you learn these things? We've never seen them here before."

"From books." The missionary explained how by reading he found answers and learned from successful farmers he had never met.

"You mean you have learned things like this from books?" Though each of them had completed twelve years of schooling, the use of reading to help in their daily lives was a new thought. In further conversations, it became clear that reading was for passing examinations. It was not used for solving problems or for entertainment.

It was not a question of ability, or even being part of the contemporary world. All the Zimbabweans had done well in school, and they held jobs in offices or as researchers. It was a question of cultural patterns. Important information was shared orally in their society, and skills were learned in person-to-person sharing. Successful communication had to fit within the patterns already followed.

A reading habit can be developed to the great benefit of a society. But literature must be relevant to the peo-

---

What would you think if you were taking your baby for a walk, and a total stranger stopped to admire your baby, then very seriously and forcefully said, "There is a breeze. You *must* put socks on your baby!"

This happened often in Germany. We were told that we *must* give our dog a different kind of food, that we *must* air out our apartment at a certain time of day, and so on.

Toward the end of our two-year stay we began to realize that what was being expressed was not what we were "hearing." To us, it sounded like an ultimatum—we must comply or we would be rude, implying their advice was poor.

We began to notice, however, that another German would respond to such statements very differently from our timid response. "No, it's not very breezy and a little air is good for the baby." Something which sounded like an argument would follow. At the end nothing would have changed as far as the baby was concerned, and the people would still be friends.

It seems that the German word *mussen* (translated "must") is used in a sense closer to the English word *should*. What we heard as a command was meant as a suggestion.

—James Lucas

ple's concerns, and it must be readable—readable at the skill level of the intended audience.

What format will be used depends on cultural patterns. Are newspapers common? Are they carried and read in public as a badge of the intellectual? Is a book used—picked up and read? Or is it only a display of education? The variety in magazines may be more attractive and stimulate more discussions in interpersonal networks. Do pamphlets and tracts seem authoritative, trivial, or perhaps even objectionable?

Then there is the question of the preferred writing style. The clever use of impressive words can enhance a message in some places, but completely obscure the meaning for another group. Letters and discussions (in writing) between readers and a columnist may be attractive. A different culture will prefer an objective, carefully reasoned summary of what is known on a topic. Talking about people so that they convey the facts to be communicated is still another approach of value. Which approaches should be used? Only by examining existing styles of communication can one discern indications of appropriateness. Then careful experimentation (using simple but adequate research methods) will allow the best formats and writing styles for each audience to be determined.

This effort will not quickly turn an orally oriented society to a reading-oriented society. An enlarging group within the culture, however, will be able to expand the group's information pool and then share this information through the existing communication networks.

▼ PICTURES MAY HELP

Where reading is not a habit, will pictures help to communicate? Perhaps. Comprehension of two-dimensional pictures is also a learned skill. Where pictures are plentiful, children seem to learn to comprehend them almost as early as they learn to comprehend speech. But lacking such experience, even adults have considerable difficulty.

Teachers in a teacher-training college were given flannelgraph to use in teaching Bible stories. When they attempted to use these aids, however, a figure might be placed so that it appeared to stand on another figure's head, the idea of perspective was absent, and when only part of the figure was available (as when Jesus was shown speaking from a boat) it was not even perceived as a

One out of three people passing the street corner news vendor was literate. Hundreds passed daily but few sales were made. As far as the publishers were able, they had used proven Western techniques in creating their magazines and newspapers— slick, bright covers, calling attention to fiction stories and reports of contemporary situations. What else could the publisher do to produce a good- selling periodical?

Four of the best-selling periodicals were examined. . . . Content was not relevant to daily life in the target group. The magazines were well-written but not readably written for the intended audience.

human shape. It was evident from the way these teachers manipulated the flannelgraph during the telling of the story that the pictures had no significance: The figures were being used because the teachers had been told to use them, but they really had no idea why.

When pictures are used, they should accord with the artistic traditions of that culture. Pictorial literacy is high within India, for example, but the pictures are of a very different style from the European. Patterns are more important than perspective, and different pictorial symbols are used. Symbolic clues to meaning and pictures are culturally rooted. Symbols unconsciously accepted in Western cultures may be meaningless or distracting elsewhere.

Illustrations may distract or confuse, requiring special explanation if they are not culturally oriented. They must be prepared with the experiences, symbolism, and total culture of the receiving people in mind.

In employing illustrations in a cross-cultural setting, always be careful of these things:

• Perspective might not be understood, though perspective recognition increases with increased exposure to Western pictorial styles.

• The manner of dress associated with biblical characters is unknown in many areas. Where possible (as in parable portrayals), the artist should represent the dress, customs, and appearance of people in the immediate culture. The purpose is to deepen understanding and application of the text. This will best be done if puzzling and foreign elements are eliminated.

• Beware of symbols—rays of light, splashing water, music notes, silhouettes of presumably familiar objects like trains, city skylines, and trees.

▼ ORAL COMMUNICATION

Even though the values of written and pictorial communication are great, they are not always the best media to use. It has already been pointed out that oral communication is more familiar in many cultures. There is little point in striving to change an oral culture to a literate culture. It is more effective to work within existing oral patterns. Oral channels are efficient in carrying information. They have bound societies together for thousands of years, mediating and preserving knowledge essential for group survival.

What are the ways information is shared? When are public speeches made, who makes them and what orator-

---

Where there is little experience with printed pictures, check these things:
- Background must be reduced to a minimum.
- Include essentials only. One point should be expressed in one picture, not an assortment of points to make a "study picture." Viewers may concentrate on nonessential details instead of the main message.
- Detail in scenery may be of little value, but detail in the human face and figure is appreciated. Emotion can be shown in faces and bodily postures, as used in that culture. Action in the human figure is usually appreciated.
- Avoid abstractions. Use true shades and realistic portrayals. Abstractions may be liked by some, mostly for design and color values. But if comprehension is the goal, abstractions, even of familiar objects, will not help.

ical style is used? Is there a particular acceptable form for each different kind of topic? All these questions have answers that are specific to each culture. Sweeping statements about communication are often wrong, simply because communication happens within a specific culture. That culture shapes its forms and influences comprehension. Communication must be developed within each setting.

Formal speeches that affect the community's future are made at an annual festival of thanksgiving among the Lotuho people of southern Sudan. Anyone can speak, but greater weight is given to those who have already earned community respect by being outstanding cattlemen, farmers, or wrestlers. Issues of concern are raised as the men stand in a huge ring, spears at the ready for the ceremonial hunt that immediately follows. The speaker gives his view, but nobody "hears" him until his idea is repeated, sentence by sentence, by one designated as the "orator." The "orator" does not exactly repeat the speaker's words, but rephrases them to "make them sweet"—in other words, more acceptable to the assembled men. He is, very visibly, mediating the message. But his role also makes it easier to retain everything said, since each speech is heard twice, in the original and then the paraphrase.

New ideas, suggestions for change, political viewpoints, and tribal quarrels are all proclaimed in this arena. But no action is taken at that time. After the celebrations are complete, the men remember as they discuss events with their closest friends while watching their livestock return home in the evenings. Pros and cons are brought out until a consensus is reached among these friends.

Members of these small groups meet informally at a central square in their town during periods of rest. Again subjects of concern are raised and considered. When all the men once again assemble for a decision on any of the topics, usually the choice has already been made. It is now a matter of listening for the differences, modifying positions, and arriving at a consensus that includes the whole group. The elders sense when agreement is reached and typically have the final words, expressing the common position.

This is totally an oral process. Any new information, a new belief, a proposed change that would affect all—these are shared orally, and through a long oral process a decision is reached that unites the people rather than risking division (a risk that is present in the Western practice of individual voting).

Another society will handle oral communication in another manner. Change agents (whether in economic or in spiritual spheres of life) must learn and work within each system to share their message effectively.

Among the Matabele of Zimbabwe, it is improper for concerned parties to discuss a major matter directly. Whether the issue is marriage, purchase of property, discipline of children by the schoolteacher, or a dispute over damages by uncontrolled livestock, mediators are used. Oral communication is used in a carefully structured manner. Telling a message directly, even an important message, invites incomprehension. If it really were important, the hearer unconsciously responds, it would come through mediators.

But using mediators instead of talking directly is considered by most Americans evasive and insincere. There are almost endless varieties of oral communication patterns. Those that are appropriate in each culture must be learned before effective communication can be achieved.

▼ MODERN MEDIA, BUT TRADITIONAL STYLE

Since radio is new in many cultural traditions, how does its programming relate to existing oral communication? Can radio disregard existing patterns and use its "own style" in timing, program structure, and speaking? No, not if its message is to be seriously considered in the target society. Passing the words through electronic circuits does not change the need to be culturally relevant in style.

Music styles should be suited to the receiving culture, not the sending group. For example, the gospel men's quartet is accepted as Christian music in America, but neither the group nor the style of music sung has a precedent in India or Iran. The African emphasis on rhythm is not understood or appreciated in many traditional American churches, nor is the antiphonal style of singing a message or story familiar to most Americans. While there has been an internationalization of music and speaking styles, that is understood only by the small group in each society who have had international exposure. For most of the population, comprehension and appreciation go along with familiarity with the style of communication.

The morning hours between ten and noon usually found Busian seated on the low wall in front of my house, taking his morning tea and rolling the day's cigarettes. I made it my habit most days to sit in the morning sun with this neighbor and exchange jokes. One morning our conversation drifted to religious topics, as it so easily does when talking with a Muslim. This looked like the moment I had been waiting for to share Christ with this man.

Interspersed with my life story, I told Busian how I had come to realize that Christ had come from heaven to die as the substitutionary sacrifice for sin, that my sin was now forgiven and a new heart had been given to me by God. His response was immediate and outright rejection. These were thoughts a Muslim could never accept, he told me.

A period of several days passed, and another opportunity arose with the same neighbor. This time, however, I chose to communicate my message with two stories—one from the Muslim and Christian scriptures, and the other a modern-day parable. Busian's interest and attention were immediate and undivided. As the stories concluded, Busian was smiling and nodding his head in enthusiastic agreement to the very ideas he had rejected only days before. What had made the difference? I believe it was the use of a story rather than a propositional presentation of the message.
—Paul Steven

Talk shows, with listeners phoning the station in order to share their viewpoints on a radio program, are popular in the United States. The master of ceremonies asks them leading questions, often encouraging controversial statements to stimulate other listeners. A kind of open discussion is held between widely separated people by the use of telephone and radio. Such a program would be impossible where telephones are less easily used. But substitute approaches can be found, such as tape recording a discussion in a public meeting, interviewing people in public places, or inviting group representatives to the station for a broadcast discussion.

But a controversial discussion would not be helpful (or even permissible) in a politically closed society. Where the people are accustomed to being told through radio what they need to hear, radio listening clubs have been successful. A group gathers to listen to a particular broadcast that tells them of new farming methods or public health measures that should be followed. A discussion follows, and consideration is given to what was said, whether the method can be used, and how it might be changed to be more useful. Often, an appointed discussion leader sends group questions to the radio station to be answered in later programs.

In places where stories are used to teach important truths, stories should be the emphasis in oral communication. Drama has great value, especially where dramatic storytelling is part of the oral tradition. Drama has been combined with traditional dance styles in India and Southeast Asia to portray the Gospel stories in a form acceptable and understandable to the non-Christian populations.

▼ SUCCESSFUL AND BIBLICAL

"Just preach the Word," many Christians say—simple advice whose very simplicity commends it. But when have we successfully "preached"? For many, preaching has come to mean one-way lecturing. That is not the primary biblical meaning of the word, which would be better translated "proclaim" or "make known." There are certainly occasions when biblical figures stood before an audience and lectured—Peter at Pentecost, Stephen before the Sanhedrin, and Paul before rulers, before the crowd at Ephesus, and on Mars Hill in Athens. Sometimes, however, the proclamation was a dialogue, even a heated debate. Old Testament prophets lectured, but also used drama (Jere-

"Feasts of Repentance" have become the accepted way to make a public confession of faith in Christ among the Maguzawa people of northern Nigeria. Having resisted Islam for many years, recently they have responded in large numbers to the Gospel.

The Feasts of Repentance hold great significance for the Maguzawas, being patterned after the celebrations that Muslims hold when a person is initiated into Islam. A report from the Sudan Interior Mission describes such a feast: "About three to four hundred people gathered in a huge circle under a large tree to celebrate with the new converts. In the middle of the service, the 130 new believers marched right into the circle and sat down—identifying themselves with the Christians of the area."

247

miah, Hosea), stories (Samuel), dialogue with the audience (Moses), music (David), and object lessons (Amos, Jeremiah). David, Ezekiel, and John (in Revelation) saw as well as heard God's message. Jesus lectured on occasion, but primarily he taught using dialogue, stories, examples from daily life, and objects, as he did in telling us to remember his death in Communion.

An Afro-American seminary student complained, "I can't use what I'm being taught about preaching! That just isn't the way my people will understand." The homiletical devices of three points, alliteration, and holding audience attention through illustrations, gestures, and tone of voice often have great value. But they are culture-specific, not universal in their usefulness. The Afro-American student probably should not use techniques that have proved their worth outside his own culture. He should instead shape the form of his message by patterns familiar to the Afro-American culture. Each culture is rich in oral and visual ways for sharing information. Those patterns are the ones to learn and use in building communication within that culture.

Failing to use those patterns may result in serious misunderstandings, more than simply a loss in the messenger's effectiveness. Gordon Molyneux explains,

The Philippines has witnessed numerous evangelistic campaigns of all kinds—"healing miracles," "gospel explosions" to name two. However, the results have been quite frustrating. Many of the endeavors created very little (if any) impact on the non-Christian community.

The language used can only attract church people. Most efforts used "church" music that can only be appreciated by Christians. Some have a total disregard of the Filipino culture. To illustrate, during a "gospel explosion" an evangelist preached on God's power over witch doctors and voodoo—neither of which exists in the Philippines.

—"Pop Music and Celebrities: An Evangelistic Strategy?" *Asiacom: Asian Institute of Christian Communication Newsletter,* January–March 1989

> There is a feeling shared by many Africans that Christianity, as it has been brought to Africa from the West, is "alien" or "foreign." For many, Christianity is an ill-fitting, outer cloak; the Gospel has not reached the heart and mind. The result has been the multiplication of groups that are not biblical, even though professing to be Christian. They are not solely responsible for a Christianity that is only marginally Christian. The bringers of the Christian message often expressed the truth in Western languages in teaching those who would be leaders.
>
> —Report on a talk in Zaire
> about 1970

Western cultural patterns of teaching and church organization were followed with very little adaptation to African patterns. Communication styles, methods, and channels used were primarily those familiar to Westerners.

How can the message reach hearts and minds? How can distortions of biblical truth be guarded against? Not by squeezing God's message into exclusively Western communication patterns. While useful for the West, they hinder other people's comprehension. It is like attempting to fit a square peg into a round hole. Western modes fit Western needs; Africans or Asians or Latin Americans need different communication patterns.

The issue is more than a question of efficiency in communication. It is an issue of fundamental comprehension. Biblical truth has often been masked by the style of presentation and by cultural practices associated with the messengers. Careful attention to appropriate communication patterns would be a major step toward avoiding hurtful distortions of the Gospel message.

Beyond the matter of structure of the message, methods for delivering it, and channels to be used is the question of content. That is the subject of the next chapter.

SUMMARY

All people share many basic needs, such as needs for food, shelter, acceptance, security. But the ways in which those physical, social, psychological, and spiritual needs are met differ widely. Each group's successful ways of meeting needs become patterns that are repeated, because they have worked. They ensure survival and a sense of well-being for all in the group. The patterns that make survival and comfort possible are interwoven to make the fabric of culture.

Each culture has unique opportunities for presentation of the message of Christ. Effective communication seeks out those opportunities, building the form of the message from within the culture rather than seeking to find a lowest common denominator between cultures through adapting an existing message form.

Even though the content remains the same, the form must alter in each culture to have comparable impact.

Within every culture will be found keys to the culture, or, as they have also been termed, redemptive analogies, bridges to understanding. These existing keys within a culture are often witnesses that God has left to himself, and they make possible teaching the fullness of his revelation in Christ. If these are ignored and a message is simply adapted from another culture, the opportunity designed by God is lost.

▼ BIBLIOGRAPHY

Klem, Herbert J. *Oral Communication of the Scripture: Insights from African Oral Art.* Pasadena, Calif.: William Carey Library, 1981.

Mayers, Marvin K. *Christianity Confronts Culture: A Strategy for Crosscultural Evangelism.* Grand Rapids: Zondervan, 1987.

Olsen, Bruce. *Bruchko.* Carol Stream, Ill.: Creation House, 1973.

Richardson, Don. *Peace Child.* Glendale, Calif.: Regal, 1974.

Samovar, Larry A., and Richard E. Porter, eds. *Intercultural Communication: A Reader.* 4th ed. Belmont, Calif.: Wadsworth, 1985.

Saunders, Denys J. *Visual Aids for Village Workers.* Mysore, India: Christian Association for Radio and Audio-Visual Service, 1960.

Schramm, Wilbur. *Mass Media and National Development: The Role of Information in the Developing Countries.* Stanford, Calif.: Stanford University Press, 1964.

UNESCO. *New Educational Media in Action: Case Studies for Planners.* Vols. 1–3. Paris: United Nations Educational and Scientific Organization, 1967.

18

> As Christians we all are cross-cultural. We live in this world, but are only so-journers, for our citizenship really is in heaven. (Akiko Kugita in *AIM Journal*)

BELIEFS: THE INVISIBLE FILTERS

PROPOSITION 18: Existing beliefs and value systems are a major factor in building communication.

A pastor should not stand in front of a group and preach in a loud, clear voice. An admired spiritual leader must be humble and willing to sit on the ground with shoes off and head covered. Certainly the hymnbook should not be used, nor should the pastor read Scripture verses. Hymns should be sung and verses quoted from memory to show that they are "written in the heart."

The godly pastor will share his faith quietly, using songs interspersed with lively, short illustrations—all learned by heart. "For instance, belief in many gods is like a many-headed snake trying to escape a forest fire. Each head hides in a separate hole—leaving the body outside unprotected." A similar illustration can be used to show that the proud and mighty miss God's richest blessings: "An elephant will search in vain for sugar dropped in the sand, but an ant feasts on its sweetness" (Fred and Margie Stock, letter, November 1977).

These illustrations show how the culture in the Sindh area of Pakistan has shaped communication. To be effective, communication must follow those patterns. In the Sindh, a Christian singing team uses instruments common to local religious services: the sitar, drums, and small cymbals. They share in all-night song fests in which leaders of Hindu sects proclaim their beliefs through song. The Christian singers present their faith in an appropriate way and are heard with respect and interest.

Why is it necessary to change the externals of gospel proclamation in this way? It is necessary to adjust the externals in order to avoid unnecessary offense, remove strangeness that can make a message incomprehensible, and ensure emotional understanding of the Gospel's relevance to the hearer. Only the external expression—behavioral patterns—changes, not the content.

A basic model of culture will help to show more clearly what can be changed and what should not be changed in proclamation of the Gospel. Culture is often viewed as a huge potpourri of customs, social structures, and beliefs. The outsider probes and describes this tangled mass of needs and traditions, trying to understand how to build relationships. Everything is not equal in value, but what is important and what is trivial? It is simple to assume that "everything should be changed, because it is heathen." It is equally simplistic to take the other extreme, "Don't change anything—it is all valuable culture." But culture is not a fixed thing. Parts of culture are changing quickly, and parts change only over a span of generations. Some parts are necessary for survival of the people, and other parts are detrimental to their way of life. How do we begin to sort out the tangle?

Consider an onion.

What happens when you try to peel an onion? It brings tears to your eyes, and it is hard to tell where the papery outside layers end and the fleshy, edible layers of the onion begin. With tears misting your sight, it is difficult to know when you have cut away enough or too much.

An onion can be a good model of culture. The dry brown skin both conceals and reveals what is underneath. It protects the moist fleshiness of a good onion, and the shape of the outer skin comes directly from the shape of the inside layers. Similarly, the outer layer of culture indirectly shows much about a culture.

The common reaction of many missionaries is expressed in three statements:
1. The Filipino culture is pagan and therefore should be discontinued.
2. The Bible provides a better culture, a "Christian culture."
3. The Western culture is better than the Filipino culture; therefore the Western should be adopted.

There are better principles, however, to correct these misstatements:
1. No culture is unfit to accept or accommodate the Gospel.
2. No culture is better than another culture.
3. The only ethical and fruitful way of working with another culture is to work within the culture.
4. Success in bringing cultural change is only possible if it starts from within.
—Danny Villa

▼ BEHAVIORAL LEVEL

This visible outer layer is the patterns of behavior in a culture, including the artifacts (objects) used. These elements are by no means all that make up a culture. In fact, behavioral patterns and the uses to which materials are put are largely determined by nonvisible layers of culture.

External Behavior

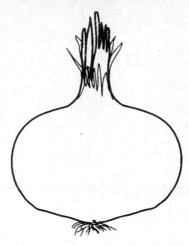

The forms of communication used are a part of the behavioral level of culture. Reading from left to right, for example, is a learned behavior. Studies have shown that in cultures where reading is from right to left, or from right bottom to top, children learn that kind of eye movement, not what is considered "natural" in another culture. These learned behaviors are manifestations of deeper levels of culture. By learning and using the appropriate behavior patterns, we can begin discerning the underlying layers.

But again there is a parallel to an onion. Probing beneath the surface of a culture is a tearful process. To understand the deeper levels of another people's way of life requires sharing in that life. That sharing means putting aside some familiar things and leaving the "comfort zone" of our own way of life. Learning even outward behaviors, such as language or new kinds of food, can be stressful; going beyond those to learn the inner shape of another cultural world initially increases the stress—and tears. But we peel onions because they are enjoyable to eat. And so we go beyond the tears to the satisfaction of entering another cultural world.

▼ SOCIAL AUTHORITY LEVEL

The many layers of an onion merge into one another so that it is sometimes difficult to know where they separate. In culture it is much the same. We can describe behavior patterns separately from the next layer, social authority, but sharp dividing lines exist only in models, not in real life.

Social Authority

Much of our behavior rests on social authority—that is, the approval of the group to which we belong or wish to belong. Certain behaviors are approved, such as standing when a woman enters the room (Western), sitting in the presence of important people (south-central Africa), or eating with knife, fork, and spoon (Western), but with the fork in the left hand and the knife in the right (British). If a member of a society fails to act as expected in such matters, the disapproval is clear. Patterns and "standards" are accepted throughout the society by common consent and are enforced by social pressure.

Those who do not act acceptably are outsiders, mentally incompetent, or discourteous and subject to correction by some kind of social sanction. The authority of the group enforces group patterns. At least temporarily, such individuals are not considered fully functioning insiders;

instead, they are "odd" or "misfits." Continuation of culturally inappropriate behavior leads to placement in a category of people who cannot be taken seriously. Permanent exclusion could follow. The fear of rejection haunts most people. Rejection from the group is a severe sanction, to be avoided at almost any cost. Acceptance by a group can be such a pleasurable, even necessary, thing that an individual will voluntarily change behavior to conform to group patterns.

The Davis family (a fictitious name) were active in their local church. Their oldest son, Dan, was elected president of the youth group during his senior year in high school. He was a good leader; the young people enjoyed him, for he always seemed to know how to do "the right thing." The older people appreciated seeing him at church in almost every service, sitting with the other young people. Everyone expected him to do well at the state university.

When Dan came home after his first year, he did not bother going to church for the first three weeks. He was uninterested in the youth group activities. Everything seemed to bore him; he was critical of the pastor—"not a good thinker, irrelevant, out of date." Naturally, his parents and church friends were dismayed. What had happened? It was easiest to blame the university, but the university was only indirectly the cause. At the university Dan, had met new people. Away from his home and friends, he needed acceptance in a group. He had found it with some fellow students who did not value church attendance, were fascinated with existentialist thought, and had little contact with anyone older than they. Within a few months he had begun acting as they did.

Had Dan "lost his faith"? Perhaps one should ask instead, did he ever have personal faith? It is likely that both at home and at university he was only conforming to the dominant social authority. His "faith" was in social acceptance, not in Jesus Christ. For faith to stand when others disagree and social pressures push away from the church, it must be rooted much more deeply.

Peer pressure is not the only form of social authority. The authority figure, the "hero" who is to be imitated, the holders of institutional authority, and the abstract structure itself are part of this sphere of culture. In most Western countries, it is said that the rule of law is supreme. Law is the authority for controlling society, enshrined in tradition, a constitution, and law-making bodies, and administered by police officers, judges, and lawyers. Although this system has been superimposed on many other societies, in those societies the functional authority is not always law. It is frequently relationship, both kin relationships and fictive relationships established through an intricate system of favors and obligations.

Social power may come from the ultimate authority recognized in a society. Thus in Islamic societies the final authority is the Qur'an. In predominantly Christian groups it is the Bible. For many in both democratic and Communistic societies, only human beings themselves determine what is ultimately good or bad, righteous or evil.

▼ EXPERIENCE LEVEL

Hidden under the layer of social authority is experience, both collective and personal. The collective experience of a group is history, which powerfully shapes current culture. The Armenians and the Turks come from the same part of Asia Minor but have quite different cultures. They have sharply different experience as peoples, and that history lies underneath the ultimate authority that each group strongly holds. The Armenians were the first people to become Christian as a body and have held to their Christian tradition since. The Turks migrated from Central Asia and after settling in what is now Turkey developed the great Ottoman Empire. The Islamic religion was a major bond holding that empire together for centuries. Though these two cultures are side by side geographically, two very different histories underlie great differences and bitter antagonisms.

Experience

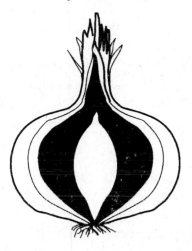

Even as experiences shape societies, they shape individuals. Where there has been emotional involvement, seeing, feeling, it is useless to say that a remembered experience did not happen, or that it is "not the way you think it is." Personal experience is powerful, and argument will not change an individual's perception of it. It is essentially emotional, so rational discussion does little to alter beliefs based on experience.

The brilliant Guinean writer Camara Laye went to Paris with great anticipation of what he would learn and of becoming acquainted with the "Queen of Cities." But his personal experience changed his evaluation (*A Dream of Africa,* 65):

255

After several months spent at my hotel in convalescence, I realized once and for all that Paris is not a French city but an international centre in which human beings are grouped solely according to their intellectual affinities. I had not had this kind of feeling at all when I first arrived in Paris; what had struck me then was the surface appearance, the grey walls and skies—on the whole, the least important aspect of the place. I still knew nothing about the spirit of the city. . . .

Once having entered this world of intellect and money, everything seemed to me not only different, but contrary. What had always seemed to me unimportant in Africa here held the centre of the stage. What had until then seemed to me important was relegated to the background by the Parisian populace. What I considered evil in Africa was here considered good, and vice-versa.

But I did not wish to lose myself forever in this different world, and while I lived there I was intent on preserving my identity. In that Paris where the cold, especially in winter, was so piercing, I would often put on my African boubou [an outer garment].

A French friend objected to the African dress, considering it a rejection of Paris and Western culture: "I do not think that rejecting everything he finds in Paris is the correct attitude."

An older friend defended Laye: "I fail to see why a blind acceptance of occidental civilization should be a better attitude. If it were, he'd have to eliminate his entire past, which would mean sacrificing his identity. No one can reasonably be asked to make such a sacrifice." Laye's defender recognized the strength and value of personal experience in shaping behavior.

Laye's personal experience shaped his response to Paris and the way in which he behaved. Consequently, he did not accept the social authority of the French. Personal experience was more significant than the social authority of the group within which he was now living.

▼ THE CORE OF CULTURE

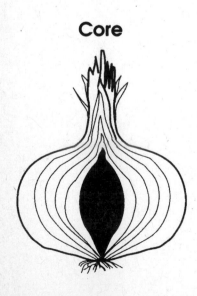

Core

As we peel more and more of the onion away, what is left? Just the center. The brown outside layers can be taken away, the next layers can be peeled back and eaten, but if the very center is left the onion could still reproduce itself.

At the very center of the invisible layers of culture is the core. It is the core that determines the shape of the other layers and of the culture itself. The core dynamically shapes the whole culture; it is the heart, the essence

256

of a culture. More than dress, food, or language, this is what makes a Korean different from a Kenyan, an Italian different from a Peruvian, an American different from an Indian.

The core in culture is like the cell nucleus in any living thing. That nucleus contains the chromosomes and genes that control the biological characteristics of the plant or animal. The genes control height, flower color, and all the other things that distinguish a fir tree from a maple or a bougainvillea from a lily. The genetic pattern determines whether the plant can survive in a swamp or a desert, at the seacoast or on a mountaintop.

The core contains the values and assumptions from which a culture develops. These come from the accumulated experience of a society, explanations and actions that seem to have worked for the society's survival. They interpret puzzling phenomena and provide an understanding of the ultimate mysteries of life, death, and eternity. These values seem necessary for maintaining the group and life itself.

Various terms are used to label this innermost core of the culture—worldview, value profile, core beliefs, presuppositions, assumptions, and themes.

In the model of culture presented here, *worldview* is equivalent to *the core*, an overall term embracing values and beliefs. It includes the culture's ideas about the nature of reality, the nature of God, of humankind, of the universe, and of the relationships between God, the universe, and human beings.

Themes are recurring expressions that point to a basic aspect of the worldview. Water, for example, is a dominant concern of the Lotuho people. The most powerful individual among the Lotuho is the rainmaker, whose sole responsibility is to ensure that water is plentiful. "He is responsible for ensuring that relationships are tranquil so that rain will not be withheld." So he is called to be the arbiter in arguments.

> The saliva of the rainmaker . . . is held to be especially valuable. . . . It is an important ingredient in the invocation of rain. The rainmaker spits on the rainstones and into a calabash of water or beer. Spitting is also done by elders at weddings. They spit into a calabash of water used to wash guests' hands before the feast to indicate that the families have become mingled as the saliva and water are mingled. The water is sprinkled on the bride as an invocation of fertility. People may spit on a relative's forehead

as a token of blessing when greeting him after a long absence.

—D. Vance Smith, *The Way of Fire and Water*, 43

Water is a recurring theme in the culture, pointing to basic values. Values are often shown by such repeated emphases on a subject, particular behavior, or form, especially on ceremonial occasions. Values are ideals and priorities that express what is desirable or undesirable. They are a mental framework for development of attitudes, from which behavior develops. "I consider a value to be a type of belief," explains Milton Rokeach, "centrally located within one's total belief system, about how one ought or ought not to behave. . . . A value is a disposition of a person just like an attitude, but more basic than an attitude, often underlying it" (*Beliefs, Attitudes and Values*, 124).

Some examples of values are ambition, intellect, independence, love, honesty, helpfulness, creativity, politeness, courage, pleasure, wisdom, and beauty. It has been suggested by researchers in the field that there may be no more than fifty values held in varying degrees by all cultures. But all cultures do not hold all of them equal in importance. One culture may value courage most highly, another pleasure, and a third wisdom. The ranking of values by different cultures gives each a distinct value profile.

Why are values considered differently? Why do not all cultures value the same things equally? Cutting still deeper into our cultural onion, we find the very center: unquestioned core beliefs. These beliefs are simply assumed to be reality. Any right-thinking person *knows* that these things are true. These core beliefs can well be called presuppositions or assumptions, since no proof is necessary, nor is discussion possible about these things. It is simply this way.

If these core beliefs are seriously questioned, the first reaction will probably be to ignore the question: "Anyone who says that can't be serious." If the questioner presses the point, he or she meets laughter, even derisive laughter. Further disagreement leads to anger and possible violence against the person who is skeptical of a core belief.

Challenging core beliefs directly brings rejection of the message and often of the messenger as well. Clearly, it is of great practical importance to learn the assumptions on which a culture rests. It is particularly crucial in intercultural communication, where the assumptions may be unknown. No matter how valuable a message may be for people, if it is shaped so that it violates core beliefs it will be rejected, perhaps violently. When a message challenges deeply held values, the most likely result, in fact, is rejection of the messenger.

Reasons given for rejection are often incorrect, because the people may not themselves understand why they are angered and antagonistic. They may be reacting to superficial irritants but feel (rather than know) that fundamental values are threatened. It may be impossible to articulate, it may appear irrational, but nevertheless the strength, and fury, of a cornered leopard may be aroused. Outbursts may be dramatically severe, as in the Boxer Rebellion of 1900 in China, or restricted to one church's rejection of a leader.

Old Church had well over one hundred years of emphasis on personal evangelism, featuring in each of its Sunday services a public invitation to receive Christ. When a new pastor came, he stressed that evangelism should be done outside the church. Church services, he emphasized, were for Christians. He stopped giving pub-

© 1987 Leadership.

"I tried to tell him not to change the order of service."

lic invitations. The explosion came after only eighteen months of rising tension. The pastor resigned, and the church split. Even the angriest persons did not really know what the issues were—though of course all thought they knew.

Essentially, it was a conflict of core values. The people valued evangelism and stability. Evangelism was not considered complete until someone responded publicly to an invitation. Changing that pattern seemed, to many, a challenge to evangelism in that church. Similar changes in other areas created a feeling that fundamental values were being challenged.

But these were not the issues brought out in the meetings that led to the pastor's resignation. Value conflicts were touched upon, but were not directly named. Issues of practice dominated arguments. Underlying questions could not be discussed rationally because people were highly upset over particular issues—not enough visitation, using the wrong version of Scripture, inappropriate dress, and on and on. Hurt feelings and disagreements all pointed to values of which the participants were not consciously aware. Much was learned of those hidden values by noting the most sensitive areas, where reason gave way to emotion.

▼ WHEN IS THE CORE LEARNED?

It is always difficult to learn the core beliefs of a culture. Those beliefs are seldom verbalized and indeed for most people cannot be verbalized. They are so basic that there is no need to talk about them—"everyone knows." How are core beliefs, including both values and presuppositions, learned?

Core beliefs are largely learned during babyhood and childhood, in the process of enculturation. As a baby learns how to meet his or her needs, interact with people, and become a valuable member of society, the baby learns very fundamental values and beliefs. They are almost entirely learned nonverbally, from observation and listening, from rewards received for acceptable behavior and punishment for what is unacceptable. The socialization of an infant consciously and unconsciously teaches the core values and presuppositions of a culture.

Two-thirds of an individual's knowledge is gained this way, by the time the child is seven years old. This includes fundamental knowledge about the nature of reality, God, humankind, and the world—mostly learned

---

I've had a concern for witnessing to Muslims and seeing them come to Christ, but have I been effective? For example, I had very close contact with two men from Saudi Arabia. I was of genuine help to them and their families. After a while it seemed to open up for me to witness to them. As time progressed, every time we got together our discussions turned into arguments. What was happening?

In seeking to present the Good News to my Muslim friends I have threatened their worldview, their core beliefs. I've often been intense in discussion, pushing them into a corner. That caused them to react, to cover up and respond in a negative way. The two men often strayed from the point to avoid the implications of some point that I was trying to make.

I have determined before the Lord to make much more effort to relate to my audience, to talk in their terms and to take the time and effort necessary to communicate in love. There is one major obstacle to carrying out my plans—it's me. I love to argue! But if my rightness is at the expense of the other person, I can't expect the other person to respond positively when I am tampering with his core values and beliefs.
—Max Kershaw

© United Feature Syndicate

nonverbally. Since it is learned without words, it is seldom put into words. When, and if, people try to articulate these matters, they are frequently unable to do so. It remains for various kinds of philosophers to seek to express these basic assumptions of their society.

In no way does verbal inability indicate that those values and presuppositions are questioned or held lightly. On the contrary, they are strongly and emotionally held. When they are attacked or threatened, especially by outsiders, an emotional reaction may be the only defense available for cherished and fundamental principles.

When someone criticized one mother, she clearly expressed how core values and beliefs are learned:

"If you really love your children, how can you allow your house to become so messy and then go out and drink?"

She replied angrily, "You have no business asking me that. Who do you think you are? You are no good. I hate children! They come between me and my husband. I hate them! I hate God." She used curse words against God. "He is no good. He doesn't care." A pause followed and she cried. "You are right. I can't love my children. I have never learned to love. Neither have my brothers and sisters. Ever since we were small, our parents fought and drank.

261

And whenever they did, we had to find someone to stay with. We went from house to house. I cannot love because I have never experienced love."

—Tom Claus and Dale W. Kietz-man, *Christian Leadership in Indian America*

The core of a culture is not a miscellaneous collection of beliefs and values. Instead, it provides a largely consistent interpretation of life. The nature of the core may better be seen when one contrasts different cultures. This is not an attempt to give a complete view of any culture's core, but simply to illustrate what it is, though at the risk of overgeneralization.

Comparing Cultures: The World

In Africa south of the Sahara, the traditional view is that the world is something like an organism. It is not simply an inert mass, but is infused with power or force. Outstanding physical features—high mountains, great boulders, rivers—focus more of that force and are thus to be treated with caution.

The common view in the Western nations is that the world is machinelike. It is to be used, exploited, for the benefit of human beings. The world functions according to fixed physical principles or laws, so mastering the world requires discovering and utilizing those principles for human benefit. No question arises about spiritual forces in mastering the earth, since it is without any shadow of life.

Comparing Cultures: Time

The concept of time is understood and used differently. Asia is considered to be future-oriented; thus skilled artisans in that part of the world may spend years in masterful hand-carving of tough jade—not for immediate benefit, but as a lasting expression of beauty. In business, this future orientation is evident in willingness to accept long-delayed returns.

The United States is a present-oriented society, where efficiency is measured by production in the shortest possible time. Business profits must be rapid; even entertainment is fast-moving and assumes a short attention-span.

Some travelling Indians having in the year 1777, put their horses over night to pasture in my little meadow, I called on them in the morning to learn why they had done so. I endeavoured to make them sensible of the injury they had done me, especially as I intended to mow the meadow in a day or two. Having finished my complaint, one of them replied: "My friend, it seems you lay claim to the grass my horses have eaten, because you had enclosed it with a fence: now tell me, who caused the grass to grow? Can *you* make the grass grow? I think not, and nobody can except the great Mannitto. He it is who causes it to grow both for my horses and for yours! See, friend! the grass which grows out of the earth is common to all; the game in the woods is common to all. Say, did you ever eat venison and bear's meat?"—"Yes, very often."—"Well, and did you ever hear me or any other Indian complain about that? No; then be not disturbed at my horses having eaten only once, of what you call *your* grass, though the grass my horses did eat, in like manner as the meat you did eat, was given to the Indians by the Great Spirit. Besides, if you will but consider, you will find that my horses did not eat *all* your grass. For friendship's sake, however, I shall never put my horses in your meadow again."

—John Gottlieb Ernestus Heckewelder, in *A Book of Travellers' Tales,* ed. Eric Newby, 401

262

Comparing Cultures: Relationships

Between Western cultures there are often sharp differences. In Italy, it is assumed that power decides social issues and stabilizes society. But in the United States, law and justice are expected to be the stabilizing force, regardless of power.

The real, permanent unit in Italian society is the extended family, and its good has priority over the desires of individual members. But in the United States, an individual's rights supersede group or family rights.

Technical mastery of the environment is at the core of Western belief systems. Personal relationships are secondary to technological competence. In contrast, many Asian and African societies place personal relationships in the core. Avoidance of disharmony is vastly more important in Afro-Asia than technical mastery.

The American Core

In the mid-twentieth-century, Cora DuBois of Harvard University proposed a succinct statement of the "Dominant Value Profile of American Culture" (1232–39). It included four basic principles:

1. The universe is mechanistically conceived.
2. Man is master of the universe.
3. Men are equal.
4. Men are perfectible.

▼ HOW CAN ANYONE BE CONVERTED?

What hope is there that the Good News of Christ can ever be fully received by non-Christians? The only point of access to what is essentially a closed system is personal experience. Personal experience is powerful, and when it comes into conflict with the authority and behavior levels, experience will win. What is known by firsthand experience can be debated, explained, and argued with, but it remains with the person. An experience such as near-death is hard to describe, but may lead to the choice of different social authorities and changed behavior. Is there any way that Jesus Christ can be experienced?

Jesus can be experienced initially in the lives of others. As the living Christ becomes evident in a friend, the reality of the Gospel begins to be understood. Teaching, winning debates, using slogans—no such approach genuinely *shares* the life of Jesus Christ. Without sharing, how can people know that he is living? Reducing Christian experience to a set of propositions moves consideration to

Within every culture will be found keys to the culture or, as it has also been termed, redemptive analogies—bridges to understanding. These existing keys to a culture are witnesses that God has left to himself that make possible teaching the fullness of his revelation in Christ. If these are ignored, and a message is simply adapted from another culture, the opportunity designed by God is lost. *Eternity in Their Hearts* by Don Richardson (Ventura, Calif.: Regal, 1981) gives many examples of this.

the level of authority and behavior. What is needed is to see Jesus living in others, to experience his life through them.

"Praying Hyde," the Reverend John Hyde of India, could not master the language of the people where he was ministering. In great discouragement, he sent in his letter of resignation from the mission. But the village people in his area immediately sent their own letter, asking that his resignation not be accepted: "If he never speaks the language of our lips, he speaks the language of our hearts." Hyde was deeply involved with the people: He cared for the sick in their homes, he washed dirty children, he would forget committee meetings because he was talking with the people—and he prayed for the people. They experienced the life of Jesus through John Hyde. Of course, many came to Christ as a result.

Myra Scovel sums it up, "We searched for ways to tell the students of the uniqueness of Christ. . . . Over the years we came to know that it was not so much what a missionary said, as what he was, that spoke to people about Christ" (*Richer by India*, 78).

Our opportunity is to let Jesus be known in us. Ultimately the Spirit of God brings recognition of truth. It is the Spirit that gives new birth so that Christ is known within the very core of a person. Then beginning from the very innermost, he teaches and brings a conviction of right and wrong, gradually changing the core to conform to the image of Christ.

Not everything is changed. An Indian remains Indian, a Japanese is still Japanese, an American is American. There are three kinds of values and beliefs in the core: those that are unbiblical, those that are approved by the Bible, and those that are neither approved or disapproved in Scripture. Every culture includes elements that are already in agreement with the teaching of God's Word, such as hospitality in Africa or the greatness of God recognized in Islamic cultures. Those things are not to be changed. Many other values and beliefs are not a biblical issue, and they also need not be changed. But in *every* culture there are things in the core that are ungodly and that are condemned in the Bible. Greed, the worship of spirits and false gods, lying, sexual immorality—these are universally wrong.

With the new birth, the Spirit of God begins his work within each person so that those things that are wrong are steadily removed. At the same time, the commendable

In a real sense evangelism is culture change at the core level. The task therefore calls for a great degree of sensitivity, study of a people's culture, and an awareness of where culture change is wanted. Since many aspects of culture are neither right nor wrong, when we bring the Gospel we do not force culture change on them.
—Joseph D'Souza

qualities are strengthened, until the believer grows into maturity, showing Christ to others in his or her society. Paul speaks of "being confident of this, that he who began a good work in you will carry it on to completion" (Phil. 1:6).

From the innermost out, God does change people. Through changing people, cultures are steadily changed. Authorities are altered, and behaviors come to reflect the presence of Christ. It is his work; ours is to simply share the living Christ with those around us.

SUMMARY

How an audience reacts to a message depends upon both the audience and the communicator. The first problem is comprehension. The audience can understand new information only in relation to existing beliefs and values. The new information will be related to previous knowledge, sometimes leading to correct, other times incorrect, interpretation. An effective communicator knows what the audience has previously known and relates the new to the old in such a way that the audience can give the intended meaning to the new message.

Second is the question of reaction to the message as understood. When the message directly challenges deeply held values, the most likely result is rejection. If it seems to threaten deeply held values of the audience, explosive rejection is probable. On the other hand, if it is understood as in agreement with those values, acceptance is more likely.

Understanding the core of a society is the necessary foundation for effective presentation of a message. When basic beliefs are not known or understood, the communicator risks unwittingly causing a premature rejection before the message has been truly understood.

Messages are not all equally threatening. Change is continual at some levels of culture and strongly resisted at other points. To understand differences in reaction, it is helpful to consider a four-level model of culture—a "culture onion." Visible culture, the behavioral level, is constantly changing; no major confrontation is likely when change is suggested at this level. The behavioral level includes things like the style of clothing, the kind of house preferred, the games played, and the kind of transportation used. These are the visible patterns of living, differing from culture to culture.

The authority level depends upon authorities outside of the person for the strength of beliefs. That authority may be a schoolteacher, the church minister, the village headman, the structures of society, or the authority of a book such as the Qur'an. Beliefs and values at this level can be changed only when the controlling authority is changed.

Closer to the heart of a culture lies the experience level of beliefs. These beliefs are not subject to reason primarily, nor do they rest upon what someone else has said or taught. They are developed from individual and group experience. That which is personally experienced leads to very persistent beliefs.

The deepest level is the core, or the basic assumptions of a person or a society. Often the individual is unaware of these basic beliefs because they are commonly held within the culture. They are not subject to challenge. In fact, questioning these beliefs will often cause a violent reaction. They are learned through enculturation—that is, through the socializing process of infancy and early childhood. They are maintained by group pressure.

As we watch and participate in behaviors of a particular culture, we are soon able to see recurring patterns. We can "peel away" those patterns, look through them to see why they are the way they are. Under those behavior patterns lies the layer of social authorities and the structures that formalize them. Under the authority level lies the collective experiences of that group, reinforced by personal experiences of its members. And at the heart of a culture are its values and beliefs, the core.

Change is not the same in all, nor does all change involve the same degree of difficulty. Change at the behavioral and authority levels does not necessarily mean change at the core. A full response to the Gospel will open the way for change at the very core of a person, such a profound change that Christ called it the new birth.

▼ BIBLIOGRAPHY

Hiebert, Paul G. *Anthropological Insights for Missionaries.* Grand Rapids: Baker, 1986.

Kincaid, D. Lawrence, ed. *Communication Theory: Eastern and Western Perspectives.* Human Communication Research Series. San Diego: Academic Press, 1987.

Lingenfelter, Sherwood G., and Marvin K. Mayers. *Ministering Cross-Culturally: An Incarnational Model for Personal Relationships.* Grand Rapids: Baker, 1986.

Luzbetak, Louis J. *The Church and Cultures.* Maryknoll, N.Y.: Orbis, 1988.

Mayers, Marvin K. *Christianity Confronts Culture: A Strategy for Crosscultural Evangelism.* Grand Rapids: Zondervan, 1987.

Padilla, René. "The Contextualization of the Gospel" and "The Unity of the Church and the Homogeneous Unit Principle." In *Missions Between the Times.* Grand Rapids: Eerdmans, 1985.

Rokeach, Milton. *Beliefs, Attitudes and Values.* San Francisco: Jossey-Bass, 1970.

Petersen, Jim. *Evangelism as Lifestyle.* Colorado Springs, Colo.: NavPress, 1980.

Smalley, William A., ed. *Readings in Missionary Anthropology.* Vol. 2. Rev. ed. South Pasadena, Calif.: William Carey Library, 1978.

Webber, Robert E. *God Still Speaks: A Biblical View of Christian Communication.* Nashville: Nelson, 1979.

➤ I can't hear you because of what I expect you to say.

Hearing What You Want to Hear

PROPOSITION 19: The interpretation of messages is related to experiences and needs.

"Will my house in heaven have a corrugated iron roof, too?" I was dumbfounded by the question. In my Nigerian study group we were discussing the future state of the believer and the glories and grandeur of heaven.

What a strange question, I thought, and I almost reproved my earnest African friend for entertaining such an idea. As I gave him a more likely description of heaven, the realization dawned that I was to blame, not him, for his impression that heaven was something resembling the good life he saw me living.

—R. J. Davis, *Africa Now,* 45

Two men in the same place, talking about the same thing—but with vastly different concepts of exactly what they were discussing. When straightforward Bible teaching is given, how can there be such divergent understandings? The missionary separated the message he brought from the way he lived and what he had. The African saw all of it as a whole, not separating between the parts, each of which was equally new to him.

People are concerned about similar things and have similar needs. So it is expected that receivers and senders in a conversation will give shared messages essentially the

268

same interpretation. As the foregoing example shows, that is not always so.

There are always differences between the experience of the sender and that of the receiver, sometimes great differences. Differences in interpretation of the same message are the usual result of these differences.

Sometimes more than different interpretation may result. A message may be completely unperceived, even though it is apparently heard or seen, if the message has no apparent significance for the intended receiver. The senses—sight, hearing, feeling, taste, and smell—may detect the signal, but the brain does not consciously interpret the signals. They remain, in effect, unperceived.

If every signal in the world surrounding us were consciously perceived, we would be reduced to a state of helplessness. We simply cannot respond to every message that clamors for our attention. If we did, the confusion in our minds would cause psychological disintegration. Thus the apparently troublesome screening the brain practices helps maintain mental and emotional health. Unfortunately, this protective pattern also screens out messages that could be helpful, but seem to have no direct relevance in meeting felt needs.

Initially, perception is individual. I see with my eyes, not a group's eyes; I hear with my ears and feel with my fingers. The sense organs that structurally perceive signals around them send those signals to the brain, not to some kind of group consciousness. The first challenge in accurate communication, then, is the individual mind. It is the individual's concerns and needs that largely determine what is actually perceived. Perception, in other words, is self-centered, even when it is modified by our friends and the society of which we are a part.

The problem of self-centeredness in communication is well summarized by the man who said, "Famine in Ethiopia; earthquakes in California; the collapse of communism in Eastern Europe; racism in New York and London; AIDS—and all I'm really concerned about is that my hair is getting gray!"

▼ REINTERPRETING MESSAGES

Even when a message is perceived, it may be reinterpreted by the individual. When a message is in disagreement with an existing belief or commitment, the message may be altered as it is received so that it agrees with previously held belief. This is an unconscious process in most cases; the receiver is not aware that he or she is actually altering the intent of the message. The receiver is aware only that this new message supports his or her existing position.

For example, Christian teaching concerning angels might be used to support belief in the intervention of ancestral spirits in human affairs. Someone else could understand it as a validation of séances and messages "from beyond." Similar reinterpretations underlie many heretical beliefs and explain the ability to "screen out" clear biblical teaching.

The meaning given to a picture, story, or fact strongly depends on past experience and knowledge. Seeing, hearing, and feeling are as much in the brain as they are in the eyes, ears, and skin. Perception involves two things—structural perception and functional perception.

▼ STRUCTURAL PERCEPTION

Structural perception is the biological or mechanical part of seeing, hearing, or feeling. In hearing, for example, the sound waves can be observed (with the right instruments), and the way in which the ear reacts to them can be described in detail. A particular sound wave will be received by all normal ears in exactly the same way. The musical note C will always be a C. An extremely high sound will not be heard by anyone, simply because no human ear has the equipment to hear that sound. When we know how the ear is constructed and we know about the physics of sound, we can predict what will be structurally perceived. The same principle is true for the eyes and the sense of touch.

So why do some people listen to music and then sing off-key? If they all hear the same thing, why do they not sing the same thing?

While teaching science, I once blindfolded a volunteer student and told him we were going to see how much heat he could tolerate on his arm. When he told us that it was too hot, we would stop. We then lit a burner and rattled various instruments on the science table while supposedly heating them in the burner flame. To show they were hot, we pressed a piece of metal against some uncooked meat. The smell of burned meat filled the room.

The student said that he was ready for the test, and we began by holding heated metal several inches from his skin—he could easily feel the heat. Then suddenly another student hit the subject's arm with a piece of ice and

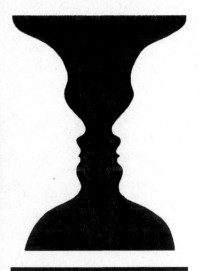

What do you see? A lovely, black marble vase—or two people looking at each other? Perhaps you see both.

Which is correct? Did you see one of those first, and then the other after the question was asked?

What you see, or don't see, helps to show how the mind controls perception. This process is called functional perception.

exclaimed about his clumsiness. The test student jerked and cried out as if he had been burned. Yet only ice had touched his arm, and that very briefly.

We then took off the blindfold and explained what we had done, while the student continued to rub his arm in pain. Even two hours later, he felt the pain of a burned spot on his arm.

Clearly the student was misled, but even a careful explanation of what had occurred did not remove the feeling of pain. How did structural perception go so wrong?

▼ FUNCTIONAL PERCEPTION

The second part of the perceptual process had taken over. Functional perception, which happens entirely in the mind, interpreted the touch and temperature signals in a completely reversed way from their true nature. The student felt what he had expected, even though the real signal sent was very different. Expectation caused functional perception to miss what actually happened.

Can that happen in other matters as well? Can "facts" be so distorted that not only wrong meanings but even contrary meanings are gained?

Yes. Absolutely clear presentation of information may lead to absolutely confused understanding—or off-key singing. Teaching, or preaching, that concentrates on presentation in no way guarantees correct reception of the message. Communication is a fifty-fifty matter; both parties in the communicative process are responsible for a satisfactory result. Poor communication is not always the fault of the "sender," nor is it necessarily the failure of the "receiver" to understand.

Nevertheless, Christian communicators have a special responsibility, because we bring the message on behalf of Someone else. Failure to achieve good communication is a failure to fulfill a trust. We are told to go the second mile, to make the extra effort to ensure that those who do not even want to hear the message nevertheless understand it.

Knowing how the mind interprets the signals received (functional perception) helps us structure the message to increase the likelihood of understanding. Six axioms of functional perception summarize its most significant aspects:

1. Experience: Perception operates from experience.
2. Social: Perception depends on social confirmation, especially when structural perception is unclear.

A company sent a form letter to all its clients announcing an upcoming seminar. However, the owners accidentally put their home telephone number in the letter instead of their office number. When this was brought to their attention by a client, they showed a copy to the secretary and asked her to read it and see if there were any errors.

When the secretary read the letter, while looking at the home telephone number, she recited the office number without even realizing what she was doing!

271

3. Selective: Perception is always selective.

4. Surprise reduction: Perception seeks to reduce surprise.

5. Wholes: Parts are perceived as parts of a whole, whether or not the whole is present or real.

6. Proximity: Items close in time and space are perceived as parts of the same structure.

▼ EXPERIENCE SHAPES PERCEPTION

Experience largely determines how signals are perceived. New stimuli are related to a store of memories in the effort to make sense of incoming signals. Previous experience becomes the translator between the world outside and the world inside our heads. For new experience to be meaningful, it must be associated in some way with previous experience. Again, this is recognized in one of the basic principles of educational method: Proceed from the known to the unknown.

A photograph reminds us of an earlier time, of friends, or of a particular place. Souvenir industries are efforts to sell items that will remind people of their experiences. It is not a carved elephant that is purchased, but a memory. The elephant is a signal that prompts the mind to recreate experience.

Experience has taught some people to pay very close attention to details of plants and animal life, because their survival depends on it. One early study suggested that Papuans and South Indians had exceptional sensory powers because of their ability to see minute differences in landscape and vegetation. But structurally they could not actually see any more than other people. Instead, their experience had taught them that such discrimination was a necessity for survival. Differences in surroundings could be noticed because of their experience of what was normal. The mind's ability to interpret was sharpened in a particular area, based on experience.

In another instance, experience taught people in a country newly introduced to Western ways that the pictures on a tin can showed what was inside the can. A picture of corn showed that corn was in the can; a cup of coffee showed that coffee was inside. Eventually stores began displaying jars that sported a picture of a baby to show that they contained food for infants. Rioting broke out as rumor spread that human flesh was being sold and that Europeans were cannibals, for the jars had come from Eu-

The study of language . . . shows that the forms of a person's thoughts are controlled by inexorable laws of pattern of which he is unconscious. These patterns are the unperceived intricate systemizations of his own language. . . . And every language is a vast pattern-system . . . in which are culturally ordained the forms and categories by which the personality . . . communicates . . . channels his reasoning, and builds the house of his consciousness.

—Benjamin Lee Whorf, quoted in John B. Carroll, *Language, Thought, and Reality*, 252, 257

rope. Experience in this case was a false guide, but still it controlled functional perception.

How can a communicator determine what meaning will be given to his or her message when it is received by an audience that does not share the communicator's experience? Clearly it is necessary to understand an individual's or a group's experience in order to communicate adequately.

The communicator must learn the receiver's frame of reference: what physical, social, and mental experiences are common among the intended audience. Only with this knowledge can a communicator reasonably predict what meaning will be developed when the message is received. The emphasis in achieving effective communication must be on learning the audience's experiences and comprehension, rather than on the communicator's use of techniques.

Failure to do this can lead to rejection of what is presumed to be the message. Even where a Christian message is apparently accepted, a dilution or distortion of biblical teaching may well occur. Why should this be so? Why does clear telling not guarantee clear perception?

A message is always received in a different setting from the one from which it is sent. Individuals and groups have different experiences and hold different mental models of the same things. So even when the message is

THE FAMILY CIRCUS By Bil Keane

correctly stated, those different experiences will result in different interpretations. New information is inevitably related to past experiences, and that of course affects interpretation of the new material. The understanding developed by the receiver may be very similar to, or very different from, the intended meaning.

Consider prayer. Prayer is conversing with God, made possible by the Mediator Jesus Christ—Christians know and practice this straightforward truth. When prayer "in Jesus' name" was taught to some African peoples, the people understood this as a better way to pray. They already prayed through their ancestors, so they knew about prayer. Since white people were teaching them to pray through Jesus, it was obvious to the African that Jesus was the white people's ancestor. The whites had demonstrated much power in their way of life, so clearly Jesus was the most powerful of all ancestors. No reason could be seen to stop praying through their own ancestors; Jesus was added to existing and unchallenged beliefs.

This is often called syncretism, adding to or taking from scriptural truth. The truth is obscured, and Jesus' lordship is challenged. But who is at fault for this syncretism and the misunderstanding that was behind it? The ones who brought the message of Christ.

The missionaries needed to understand the mental model of prayer held by their listeners, then begin their teaching at that point. The missionaries needed to dialogue with the people until their understanding of prayer was clearly known. Then the differences between that and the biblical portrayal of prayer should have been discussed, building on the old mental model so that the new information could change that model. Subsequently, as more was taught about prayer, perception would have been much closer to the intended meaning of the teacher.

To proclaim the Gospel while ignoring the experiences of people is to invite misunderstanding and risk sharp rejection.

▼ SOCIAL INFLUENCE AFFECTS PERCEPTION

Sometimes new information is a seeming jumble that makes little sense. We hear facts, but they do not fall into a discernible pattern. So we ask, "What does it mean?" Or the communication is clear, but we do not know whether it is true. There is no way to confirm what we have heard. At such times, how do we determine "truth"?

When our own physical senses cannot confirm or deny the incoming information, we depend on social confirmation. What our friends think greatly influences how we think. What they accept largely determines what we accept, particularly when there is no direct way to validate a message.

Even when there is direct physical sensing, we may reinterpret what we perceive so that our perception agrees with what those around us say. The constraints of social relationships skew what our senses have reported. This social influence is seldom recognized, which actually increases its power in shaping our perception and thinking.

This social power can even control which things we see, not only how we see those things. It is an old trick, but it still works: Stand on a busy corner and look intently up at something—anything—and soon others will stop and look up to see what you are looking at. Once several have begun looking, walk away. The others will keep on looking, trying to figure out what there is to see.

If two people are looking at a man in the distance, a third person with them will shift view to look at the man as well—even if the third is busy reading a letter or examining something else.

This behavior is called "co-orientation." While it is interesting for its effect on physical perception, it also points to the importance of the companions with whom you spend your time. If your friends focus their attention on a matter, you will also become interested. If they are interested in good and positive things, you probably will think more of those good things. If their attention is centered on rubbish—or worse—it is likely that your own interests will descend to the same level.

▼ PERCEPTION IS ALWAYS SELECTIVE

It would be impossible to identify, let alone respond to, all the stimuli that bombard us every minute. Some shield must be put up so that we are not overwhelmed. This shield must not exclude all stimuli; it must exclude irrelevant signals, yet permit those that seem to be helpful or to meet a need to be consciously received. And the selection must be accomplished with great speed, because new stimuli pour over us every second.

Look quickly at this picture, and then describe in writing what you saw, without again looking at the picture. Ask a friend to do the same thing; then compare what you and your friend have written. It will rarely be the same thing. (If it happens to be the same, try it with one or two other friends and then note the differences.)

It is the same picture, but there are different reports. Why? Our eyes structurally saw the same things, but something happened as the signals reached the brain. Only some of the signals were selected as significant, while other signals were ignored and probably cannot even be remembered.

This shield is selective perception, an unconscious process that powerfully affects what we consciously see, hear, and feel. The process does not work perfectly. Useful messages are often lost along with the clutter of unneeded signals. We functionally perceive those things that meet a need or promise to meet a need. As needs change, so do the things that we selectively perceive.

The scene on this page of a bus terminal in Bulawayo, Zimbabwe, will be seen in different ways by people with different needs. A man going home will give close attention only to the destinations indicated on the front of the buses, as he tries to find the right bus for his journey. Someone selling food for the trip will try to find passengers who appear to have money—and who are going on long journeys where they must take along their own food. A third person might be looking for a friend. She would pay little attention to the buses but would concentrate on the people as she tried to pick out her friend from the crowd.

Structurally, all have perceived the same things. Functionally, however, their individual needs or interests have determined what they really "saw."

The significance of this should be clear. No matter how valuable the message, no matter how much it is needed, it will not even be "heard" if the message does not seem to meet any felt needs. If it does, at the very least the result will be positive attitudes toward the message.

When information does pass the shield of selective perception, it may be reinterpreted, which usually means distorted. The original meaning may be lost because the person perceiving the information gives it new meaning,

meaning that is based on his or her own experience and needs.

The tragic shooting down of Iran Air Flight 655 in July 1988 by the *U.S.S. Vincennes* clearly shows reinterpretation at work. A newspaper account explains what happened as determined by a military inquiry.

> The investigation of the July 3 incident over the Persian Gulf, in which 290 people were killed, found no malfunction in the sophisticated radar technology aboard the Vincennes. . . .
>
> The inquiry found that in the stress of battle, radar operators on the Vincennes mistakenly convinced themselves that the aircraft they had spotted taking off from the airport in Bandar Abbas, Iran, was hostile and intended to attack the Vincennes.
>
> With the perceived threat fast approaching, *they wrongly interpreted what they saw on their radar screens in a way that reinforced this preconceived notion,* the inquiry said.
>
> These misinterpretations were passed on to Capt. Will C. Rogers III, the ship's commanding officer, and led him to conclude that his ship was in imminent danger.
>
> —New York Times News Service
> (italics added)

The inquiry attributed the psychological stress to the fact that the ship's crew were operating under combat conditions for the first time. The experience of the crew and the events occurring immediately before the tragedy show why signals were functionally reinterpreted, even though they were correctly received structurally.

▼ PERCEPTION SEEKS TO REDUCE SURPRISE

My friend settled into the airplane seat. He thumbed through a magazine, at ease and relaxed even though he had never been in an airplane before. He had not been to a large town until he was in high school, for he had lived his whole life in the rocky hills of southwestern Zimbabwe. The only public transportation he had known was country buses, packed full with people and produce, speeding along dirt roads in clouds of red dust.

"Well . . ." I could contain my curiosity about his thoughts no longer. "How do you like traveling by plane?" His nonchalance at being thirty thousand feet in the air was remarkable.

"Oh—it's fine. Just like a country bus, but not so many people."

A missionary once came to Luhyaland, Kenya, to preach and start churches. As he preached in English, a follower translated into the Kiluhya language. He preached the Good News of God, but nobody listened. Children were begging for food, and others were just talking. Most people had not heard of Jesus Christ and didn't have any idea what he was trying to tell them. So they told him, "Stop him from talking about Europeans and their weather."

This missionary did not know the people's experience or needs, so they thought he was talking nonsense. He was unable to gain their attention.
—Zelika Liyosi

Our group visited an Asian home that was filled with statues and pictures of various gods and idols. We were all surprised when one of the women in the home commented that Christianity was very similar to her beliefs. She thought that the Trinity was three separate gods—Father, Son, and Holy Spirit. She thought we worshiped them in a way similar to the way she worshiped her idols, even though we tried to explain the differences.

I was amazed. This jet was not at all like a country bus to me, but then, how else could he have perceived this experience?

My friend perceived his experience in a way that minimized surprise—a normal way to handle new situations or new stimuli. Something new is seldom perceived as totally new; it would be practically incomprehensible or even frightening. So new stimuli are related to memories, to previous experience, in the attempt to interpret their meaning. When new things are related to something older and more familiar, they are much less surprising and therefore easier to understand and assimilate.

It is difficult to bring a surprising, totally new experience to anyone. Structural perception passes the signals to the mind, which sorts through them with extreme rapidity. Many are discarded and never reach the level of consciousness; a few are familiar and so are quickly processed. Others are unfamiliar and together create a new, strange reality. But the mind will modify that strangeness so that it is less surprising, making it seem familiar and therefore understandable and tolerable. A simple and humorous example of this is shown in a "Hi and Lois" cartoon.

A Sudanese Christian leader tells of an evangelist who preached in a traditional Muslim area. He illustrated his preaching with a song. Translated, the words said this, "There is a sweeter thing, sweeter than money: It is Jesus Christ." Some Muslim men listened quietly, and the evangelist was pleased. He thought he had put the Word across well.

Two days later the Sudanese leader met some men who had been among the group. They told about their time with the evangelist, starting by singing the song he

had taught. They sang it this way, "There is nothing sweeter than money. . . ."

The men had found the message surprising—and unacceptable to their existing beliefs. They had liked the evangelist, however, so the message was functionally perceived in a very different way from that intended. They "heard" nothing new; surprise was eliminated and thus the real message was not perceived.

▼ PERCEPTION FUNCTIONS IN WHOLES, NOT PARTS

Are these three separate dots, or dots marking the corners of a triangle?

If we add five dots to the diagram, is the result a circle, an octagon, or simply eight dots?

People tend to perceive in "wholes," mentally "completing," or filling in, information that is actually lacking in the signals received. Because of this behavior, most people will "see" a triangle in the first series of dots and either a circle or an octagon in the second series.

If part of an action is shown, the viewer will functionally "see" the entire action. If the subject is familiar, the total setting will be filled in mentally—even the temperature, the smells, and the sounds. This closure enables us to perceive and apparently understand many things when we have really not received enough signals to complete the action. It is an extremely valuable quality. But it can also be extremely misleading.

It is valuable in storytelling, whether by verbal, written, or pictorial signals. The good storyteller uses words or pictures that suggest a mood, a feeling, and the setting of the story. The reader, listener, or viewer supplies the rest of the scene and the emotion. That is why a skilled communicator needs to use only a few symbols to create a desired reaction. Closure, the human tendency to perceive in wholes even if only a part is there, is an essential part of most communication.

But it can also be misleading. A conclusion about what is being perceived can be made too soon, based on incomplete and insufficient information. Functional perception tries to complete, to gain closure, to see in wholes even when only a part is present. And when it does that too quickly, a wrong conclusion is often the result.

Some testing in school uses this fact of perception—completing the blanks. For example, try to fill in the correct word in the following statement:

The sting of death is _____.[1]

It requires knowledge of Scripture to complete the statement correctly. Sometimes in completing such statements there are clues in the internal structure of the sentence, as in the following example:

"You have heard that _____ was said, 'Love your _____ and hate your enemy.' _____ I tell you: Love _____ enemies and pray for _____ who persecute you" (Matt. 5:43).[2]

The structure of the sentence itself gives many clues as to the missing words, and the ability of the mind to "complete" what is missing makes it possible to fill in the blanks.

A signal received by one of the senses can suggest a much larger meaning, even a meaning that would normally be perceived by another sense. A sharp blow to the face immediately brings closure—this person is angry with me! Or a soft touch on the hand is functionally perceived as showing concern or love.

Without closure, communication would be greatly impoverished. But the difficulties and barriers also raised by closure must be carefully avoided if correct meaning is to be achieved.

▼ PROXIMITY CREATES A PERCEPTUAL RELATIONSHIP

Parts close to each other, either in time or in space, are perceived as if they were related to each other—or were even the same thing. For example, an athlete chooses a new kind of socks to wear when she competes, and to her delight she performs very well. Her conclusion

---

1. Sin.
2. The missing words are *it, friends, But, your, those.*

is that the new socks brought her good luck. There is no true relationship between the socks and athletic success, but since the two things were close together in both time and space, a belief develops. It is false, but strongly held.

Many superstitions develop in exactly this way. Reason may prove that there is no relationship, but because two events were perceived together they remain bound together in people's minds. Closeness in structural perception misleads functional perception. It is not only in popular "superstitions" that proximity has deceived, but also in careful scientific studies. Careful research design is necessary to avoid confusion between possible causes for a particular effect that has been noted. Two or three things may happen at the same time, and the consequences are recorded. Statistics may show whether or not the change was significant, but cannot untangle perceptual confusion of the causes behind the change unless there has been careful advance planning.

We fall into this perceptual error almost daily. A church may be struggling to survive, but the congregation calls a new pastor, who leads the church to substantial growth in membership. Was it the pastor who resuscitated a failing church? Or the new factory that began in town at the same time and brought new employees (Christians among them) to live there? Or the combination of the two things?

When the Gospel was first brought to Hawaii, the missionary women wore long dresses, which were the style of that era. The Gospel was certainly their primary message, but the clothing they wore set styles in the church for a century afterward. The men preached while holding the Bible in front of them, while stressing its content and relevance to the lives of their congregation. For many, many years that pose was considered the only proper one to take for preaching in Hawaiian churches, even when the preachers were illiterate.

Even though the Gospel (A) was the primary message, clothing (b) and the holding of the Bible while preaching (c) were seen by the people as equally important messages. So the total message as it was perceived can be expressed in a simple mathematical formula:

$$A + b + c = \text{Gospel}.$$

The missionaries assumed the following:

$$A = \text{Gospel}$$
$$A > b, c.$$

That is, the message alone, as preached, was the Gospel, and it was much greater than *b* and *c*, which were secondary in importance. Many stories have been told of how the early missionaries to Hawaii equated American civilization with being Christian. Actually, their intention was simply to proclaim the Gospel. They did not realize that the Hawaiians perceived the Gospel to include clothing and speaking styles as well as Jesus Christ. The Hawaiians did not separate the different elements, because all of them came at the same time and from the same source. Proximity caused them to be perceived as equally important parts of Christianity.

Exactly the same mistake has been made repeatedly in many other parts of the world. Can anything be done to avoid this? The confusion between the substance of the message and the way in which it has been delivered is the cause of problems in evangelism and church-building worldwide. It may be a confusion between the forms used and the message itself, or a confusion of understanding because those bringing the Gospel were not only Christians but also colonialists, or socialists, or capitalists. They may have come from a powerful nation, so that Christianity is confused with national power. Or they may have come from a nation very proud of its long history and traditions; Christianity is then perceived as simply a part of those traditions.

Perception is both a messenger's and a receiver's problem. But it is the messenger's obligation to phrase the message so that it is perceived distinctly and not confused with his or her culture. That is not an easy task. It requires ability in three areas: knowing the message, knowing the receiver's culture, and understanding one's own culture. Otherwise, the messenger will unknowingly present cultural elements along with the message. The receiver will unavoidably perceive all of the parts as equal, and the uniqueness of the news of Christ is lost.

The heart of the Gospel is not the forms in which we contain it. The forms can, and must, change. Christianity in essence is not any more indigenous to the West than it is to the East, to the North than it is to the South. Its universality will be perceived only when the messengers clearly distinguish between the Gospel, which came from outside this world, and their culture patterns, which are of this world. Early in his missionary career, E. Stanley Jones of India saw this problem, as related in *Sacred Stories:*

Christ indeed had been offered to India, but not Christ alone. So often there were other issues or culturally-bound institutions that obscured Christ, and he [Jones] vowed that in his own preaching he would focus on Christ alone. . . .

"The Christ I presented would be the disentangled Christ—disentangled from being bound up with Western culture and Western forms of Christianity. He would stand in his own right, speaking directly to the needs of persons as persons without any canceling entanglements."

Following on the evangelist's message, a Hindu principal of a coolge stood to make the closing remarks . . . :

Jesus has stood four times in history before the door of India and has knocked. The first time he appeared in the early days he stood in company with a trader. He knocked. We looked out and saw him and liked him, but we didn't like his company, so we shut the door. Later he appeared, with a diplomat on one side and a soldier on the other, and knocked. We looked out and said: "We like you, but we don't like your company." Again we shut the door. The third time was when he appeared as the uplifter of the outcasts. We liked him better in this role, but we weren't sure of what was behind it. Was this the religious side of imperialism? Are they conquering us through religion? Again we shut the door. And now he appears before our doors, as tonight, as the disentangled Christ. To this disentangled Christ we say: "Come in. Our doors are open to you."

—Ruth Tucker, *Sacred Stories,* 145:
quoting E. Stanley Jones, *A Song of
Ascents* (Nashville: Abindgon,
1979), 109–10.

It is irresponsible for the message-bringer to say, "Well, I told them!" and accept no responsibility for communication failure. Neither is it responsible for the message-receiver to excuse perceptual failure by saying, "I didn't understand because I didn't get the message." There is coresponsibility in communication, well illustrated by the difficulties surrounding adequate perception.

Clearly, the ways in which functional perception operates can form major barriers to creating understanding. The difficulties seem even greater when we realize that the initial perception tends strongly to shape and fix the meaning assigned. Once a meaning is assigned, other information is interpreted to confirm the initial meaning. New information that would alter that meaning is often filtered out or only partially received, so that there is little possibility of forming a more nearly correct meaning.

Barriers must be recognized and strategies used that help new information get past the barriers. Styles of communicating that command attention must be used. The appropriate style is different in each culture, and sometimes for each individual.

Again we come back to basics—know your audience. All effective communication begins at that point.

SUMMARY

Perception acts in two stages—structural (the physical reception of signals by the sense organs) and functional (the mental interpretation of those signals). Functional perception is usually the critical element in achieving effective communication. Functional perception acts like a porous shield against the overwhelming array of signals coming to an individual. It selects some for conscious recognition and discards others. Some may be reinterpreted to agree with expectations. A few are accurately perceived.

What happens functionally to signals that are structurally perceived is determined by experience, the social context, and felt needs. Functional perception also seeks to minimize surprise, to complete fragments so they are perceived as wholes, and to organize signals in relationships—real or presumed.

To anticipate how a message will be perceived, it is essential to know the audience in its social, physical, and historical settings. With that knowledge, a message can be clothed in a form that increases the probability of correct functional perception.

▼ BIBLIOGRAPHY

Claus, Tom, and Dale W. Kietzman, eds. *Christian Leadership in Indian America.* Chicago: Moody Press, 1976.

Guerry, Vincent. *Life with the Baoulé.* Translated by Nora Hodges. Washington, D.C.: Three Continents, 1975.

Kincaid, D. Lawrence, ed. *Communication Theory: Eastern and Western Perspectives.* Human Communication Research Series. San Diego: Academic Press, 1987.

Lingenfelter, Sherwood G., and Marvin K. Mayers. *Ministering Cross-Culturally: An Incarnational Model for Personal Relationships.* Grand Rapids: Baker, 1986.

Mayers, Marvin K. *Christianity Confronts Culture: A Strategy for Crosscultural Evangelism.* Grand Rapids: Zondervan, 1987.

Padilla, René. "The Contextualization of the Gospel" and "The Unity of the Church and the Homogeneous Unit Principle." In *Missions Between the Times*. Grand Rapids: Eerdmans, 1985.

Petersen, Jim. *Evangelism as Lifestyle*. Colorado Springs, Colo.: NavPress, 1980.

Rokeach, Milton. *Beliefs, Attitudes and Values*. San Francisco, Jossey-Bass, 1970.

Scovel, Myra. *Richer by India*. New York: Harper & Row, 1964.

Tuan, Yi-Fu. *Topophilia: A Study of Environmental Perception, Attitudes, and Values*. Englewood Cliffs, N.J.: Prentice-Hall, 1974.

Webber, Robert E. *God Still Speaks: A Biblical View of Christian Communication*. Nashville: Nelson, 1979.

> Rejoice with those who rejoice; mourn with those who mourn. (Rom. 12:15)

> Mankind cannot live by logic alone, but also needs poetry. (Mahatma Gandhi)

BECAUSE I FEEL, I KNOW

PROPOSITION 20. All communication has simultaneously rational and emotional dimensions.

Some things simply cannot be understood through reason. Even with full explanations, comparisons and contrasts, descriptions, or counting and measurement, we may learn all about something but still not understand it. Love, for example, largely defies rational explanation.

What purely intellectual explanation can completely, or even adequately, describe the apostle Paul's care for the churches? They were scattered across the Roman Empire, were made up of many different national groups, spoke different home languages, and lived within different cultures. Some of the churches were indifferent to living for Christ; others tolerated gross and repulsive sins in their midst. They had no power and were harassed by the Empire, rejected by Jewish nationalists, and internally troubled by divisions and heretics. Nevertheless, Paul cared, and cared deeply. "Then, besides all this, I have the constant worry of how the churches are getting along: Who makes a mistake and I do not feel his sadness? Who falls without my longing to help him? Who is spiritually hurt without my fury rising against the one who hurt him?" (2 Cor. 11:28–29 LB).

Something happened in Paul' s communication with the churches that was more than the rational content of

Discipleship is not limited to what you can comprehend—it must transcend all comprehension. Martin Luther said, "Plunge into the deep waters beyond your own comprehension (God says), and I will help you to comprehend."

"My sermon this evening is entitled, 'Divorce and Remarriage among Christians.'"

his letters. He showed a quality of empathy that is inexpressible through reasoned discourse. It was expressed through the sufferings he endured on their behalf, his concern for their correct understanding and their physical well-being. He did not try to prove his concern with argument, but with his life: "I have plenty to boast about and would be no fool in doing it, but I don't want anyone to think more highly of me than he should from what he can actually see in my life and my message" (2 Cor. 12:6 LB).

How can we explain this pervasive kind of communication—communication that is not neatly packaged in words? Much of the wonder and joy of communicating seems waiting to surprise us beyond the limits of our rationality. Better than merely explaining, how can we *use* this unseen dimension to enrich our communication?

Clearly, there are two elements in all communication, the rational and the emotional.

The rational is a conscious act, carried out deliberately and with at least some understanding. It uses our ability to grasp the surrounding world and then marshals that knowledge for achieving particular goals. "Being rational" is essentially an intellectual activity.

The emotional is not conscious, in the sense that it is involuntary. Communication is felt rather than reasoned. Emotions are aroused, being essentially a physiological

One does not improve through argument but through example; one does not excite love except through love. Be what you wish to make others become. Make yourself, not your words, a sermon.
—Henri Frederic Amiel

response instead of a mental response. Perception and action are not controlled by the intellect.

Various popular and technical words refer to the distinction between rational and emotional: cognitive versus affective, intellectual versus emotive, denotative versus connotative, thought versus reaction, cerebral versus intuitive, thought versus feeling, rationalism versus emotionalism, uninvolved versus involved, knowledge versus sentiment, facts versus "vibes." A contrast is usually drawn by these words, as in an illustration from *Webster's Dictionary:* "She writes straight from the emotions; nothing mental ever gets in her way."

It is a fundamental difference, a difference recognized in Christ's teaching, "True worshipers will worship the Father in spirit and truth, for they are the kind of worshipers the Father seeks. God is spirit, and his worshipers must worship in spirit and in truth" (John 4:23–24).

Spirit and truth are two different things, and both are necessary. The rational understanding of God and his ways is necessary on the one hand, and on the other there must be involvement of the emotions. Reason and emotion together make the whole being. Emphasizing one di-

"They're Christians! They go to church all the time. They're not supposed to be happy."

mension of communication or the other results in partial and inadequate communication. If either the cognitive or the affective dimension is omitted, John 4:23 suggests that worship has not occurred, regardless of the forms used.

Much that is traditional in worship can easily be meaningless. Attendees at church services can "feel good" about their experience in the service, without any involvement of their mind. Or it is equally possible to consider very carefully the theology of worship, then preach and hear correct biblical doctrine, using appropriate music in a beautiful sanctuary, without opening the emotions and truly worshiping. Worship involves all of a person, both the mind and the feelings, the cognitive and the affective aspects of communication.

The problem is discussed from a different perspective by Ralph Otte:

> The lights dimmed slowly. The organ music throbbing in the background demanded my attention. Conversation subsided to a whisper.
>
> A dignified figure strode to stage center and conducted a community sing. The congregation lustily sang the benefits of Christian living and exhorted each other to new and greater deeds for Christ.
>
> Then came a grand moment. The organ began its tonal meanderings and a deep hush covered the room. The pastor began to pray. His voice dropped two levels in pitch and receded some 300 years in time.
>
> Next, the song leader rose and gave a welcoming speech urging all to attend again and to feel right at home. Future events were profusely enumerated for ten minutes.
>
> Then the big moment arrived: The Sermon. The minister held everyone's attention for the allotted 20 minutes, making skillful use of dramatic words and gestures. Then he closed with an illustration worthy of any radio serial. His voice lowered dramatically and the prayer tone was called into play as he pronounced God's blessing upon all. It was all over.
>
> I had just spent one hour in worship of the Almighty and Everlasting God. Well, perhaps, one half hour—or was it 15 minutes? Very little of all that went on was directed towards God. I sang three songs, but only one was directed to Him; the others were directly pointed to my Christian brothers. The pastor did all the praying for me. The choir sang to me and the sermon was preached at me.
>
> Could it be that in our evangelical zeal to restore truth to worship, we have forgotten how to worship?
>
> —"Are We Worshiping or Watching?" 54

It might help if we thought less of the dignity of divine worship, and more of the sheer fun of it; if we took over all God's pleasures of body and mind and showed how, rightly used, they are faint foreshadowings of the supreme pleasure.
   —Joy Davidman, *Smoke on the Mountain*, 58

Worship is something for the whole congregation. Scripture shows us that believers participated—in Corinth, too enthusiastically. Participation does much to restore the almost-absent element of emotion to worship.

Participation was certainly not absent in six churches observed along a two-hundred-yard stretch of beach in Nigeria. One was a group of four people clustered around a leader. At various times they went into a trance and shook from head to toe, as a physical expression of their ecstasy. Further along the beach a sign proclaimed the "Unity Church Mission, the Church of Positive Thinking." About fifty people shuffle-danced to the beat of drums. Another group of ten sang nonstop for nearly thirty minutes, repeating the same tune and words while swaying to the rhythm of the music. Each of the groups was physically involved in their service. Outbursts of excited preaching from the leader were interrupted by singing, started from within the congregation. At no point in the afternoon was there any sustained sermon or teaching in any of the groups. There was much expression of emotion, through dancing, singing, loud praying, crying, and sounds of joy.

Certainly the groups needed teaching, and teaching was almost totally lacking. But teaching would not have answered the needs met in the emotion-loaded services. An exclusive concentration on the rational is not a suitable antidote to overemotionalism. Neither is meeting people's emotional needs alone truly building them in their "most precious faith." Both elements are essential.

Frequently there is a mental appraisal of something before an emotional response. The evaluation may be very rapid, virtually subconscious, screening the signals to interpret more accurately what is happening. But emotions also affect the screening process, causing some signals to be missed and others to be "perceived" that are not even present. (See chapter 19.) Emotions do influence our response to the environment. The emotional dimension of communication strongly affects the rational. It is a badly misleading fiction to assume pure rationality in any human communication.

▼ DEVELOPING THE EMOTIVE DIMENSION

How do we develop emotional response in communication? Emotion seems like the smell of spring flowers, or fall's burning leaves. A mood can be enjoyed, but cannot be captured and recreated on demand. To say we

---

'AMEN' SAID HIS FLOCK TO PRIEST'S CLEANSING PRAYER

THE VILLAGE PRIEST knelt reverently in the crowded church of Bad Aibling, Germany With folded hands and sunken head he recited a washing powder advertisement from television.

"Amen," the Catholic congregation murmured dutifully when he finished.

Father Johannes Engels was carrying out a test on his parishioners after he had reproved them for paying no attention to what was said in church on Sunday mornings

"You don't pray at all," he thundered from the pulpit. "You just mumble some words without thinking and you say 'amen' automatically"

The church elders were aghast at such plain speaking and took the father of the flock aside

"I'll prove it to you one of these mornings," replied the priest—and he did —SN Corr

"It's amazing how much guilt can be packed into the two little letters 'N' and 'O'!"

should have more emotion or more reason is not the same thing as having it. But are there ways to introduce emotion?

Human communication is almost totally contained within twelve signal systems (see propositions 11 and 12). Both factual knowledge and emotional cues are carried by these signals. Some of the signals convey facts, so-called straight information. Others are cues that stimulate feelings in the recipients.

The emotion is in the respondent, however, not in the signal itself. The signal or group of signals contains information that triggers emotional response in one person but not in another. That makes it very difficult to say accurately what is emotive and what is rational. All information, taken apart from people, is rational. But when people perceive that information, the reaction is emotional at least to some degree.

Simple statements of fact can carry depths of meaning unsuspected by communicators. This emotional significance is personal and internal. The only way to anticipate what it will be is to know the individual very well—background, desires, fears, likes, and current felt needs. Even then it is difficult, because these factors are mixed together in the individual in a unique way at any given time.

In my country you see many Christians in traditional churches leaving their church because change is forbidden. They go to churches where they don't only listen to sermons but also have time to express all their feelings in singing, clapping, and even dancing. After services there is fellowship where people pray together, confess their sins, sometimes crying, singing, and drumming as much as they wish. This gives them opportunity to share how the Word of God works in their lives—with much emotional expression.
—Sudanese Christian worker

There are general patterns, of course, and we must learn those with each group of people in order to strengthen our use of emotive communication. Once again, we are challenged with the absolute necessity of knowing people in order to communicate, to create understanding. No techniques, no standard methods can substitute for knowing people through involvement with them.

▼ EMOTIONAL CUES VARY CULTURALLY

Not only does the rational and emotional content of the same signal vary among individuals, but it may also vary sharply from one culture to another. Certain signal systems tend to be highly rational in cultures of North America and Europe—the written, for example. That same signal system has much greater emotive impact in a nonliterate culture where the mystery of the written word is highly valued.

An international Christian ministry decided to use women social workers in new projects within an East African country, since they had proved to be sensitive and responsive to people's needs. Well-qualified women were assigned to work through local churches. But prominent church leaders reacted very negatively to the women, de-

"Admit it, Madge. You're angry with me, aren't you?"

spite the care and competence shown. No specific reason could be found for the objection, until the organization's administrators realized that the area was predominantly Islamic. Though Christian, the church leaders lived within an Islamic culture, where women are never at the forefront and certainly never give orders to men, as was necessary in the aid projects. Dissension and quarreling stopped when the women were removed, even though they were rationally the best suited to direct the work. Their presence was interpreted emotionally, a fact that had to override other considerations.

▼ USING EMOTION TO MOTIVATE

In political campaigns, emotion is highly important. Voters seem uninterested in reasons and facts, preferring to vote for candidates with whom they identify emotionally.

A medical doctor was accused of causing the death of a member of Parliament under cover of his medical practice. In the courts, he was declared innocent of the charge. The doctor was later appointed to the vacant seat in Parliament. But in the next election, an opposing candidate produced cartoons portraying the doctor pointing an injection needle at the deceased man. The opponent opened his meetings by asking the people to pause for a period of silence in memory of the late M.P. Having made no direct accusation, he appealed to people's emotions only through nonverbal suggestions. It is not surprising that he won the election.

While this use of emotion seems extreme, the same kind of communication approach is used regularly in persuasive campaigns of many kinds—politics, sales, and sometimes religion.

A presidential candidate is able to make his opponent seem personally guilty of water pollution and indifference to violent crime.

Through the juxtaposition of two photographs, a senator is shown talking confidentially to somebody considered a traitor.

A happy, prosperous family—handsome father, beautiful mother, and two lovely children—is shown participating in an activity of a religious group, thus distancing the group from its history of polygamy and dictatorial rule.

In each of these cases, nonverbal signals are used to build an image that is not the same as the reality. When

> Mankind makes far more determination through hatred, or love, or desire, or anger, or grief, or joy, or hope, or fear, or error, or some other affection of mind, than from regard to truth, or any settled maxim, or principle of right, or judicial form, or adherence to the laws.
> —Cicero

293

words are used, they are also emotive, reinforcing the other signal systems.

Do you know what motivates people emotionally? Yes, at least partially. Some of the important emotional motivating factors are the urge to conform, the desire for security, and the desire for reward and recognition. Communication can be strengthened through use of these motivating areas, and by building an atmosphere of trust. There are many ways in which these emotions can be built into communication. Each group and perhaps each individual presents different opportunities.

Products are often sold emotionally. "You want the customer to fall in love with your product and have a profound brand loyalty when actually content may be very similar to hundreds of competing brands," marketing expert Pierre Martineau has said. "To create this nonlogical loyalty, the first task is one of creating some differentiation in the mind" (quoted in Vance Packard, *The Hidden Persuaders*, 47). In other words, sell emotionally; rationality may support emotion but does not make the decision.

Vance Packard quotes a research report that stressed how emotion can be manipulated through symbols. "A car can sell itself to different people by presenting different facets of its personality. . . . Advertising is a multiplier of symbols." In 1989 a new car was introduced to the American market with extensive prime-time advertisements on television. For several weeks the car was not shown at all—only the beauty and power of the ocean, waterfalls, autumn leaves, and similar scenes. The name of the car was repeated often, so that when it was finally shown it had been given the aura of the majestic and beautiful outdoors.

"When the image analysts know a few of the images we buy, they can project our behavior in other buying situations" (*The Hidden Persuaders*, 55). The analysts concluded that the sale of billions of dollars' worth of products hinged to a large extent upon successfully manipulating or coping with our guilt feelings, fears, anxieties, hostilities, loneliness feelings, inner tensions (*The Hidden Persuaders*, 57).

What is the difference between motivation and manipulation? How do we harness the power of emotive communication without simply imitating the media image-makers? These issues will be addressed later in the chapter—but first, let's consider the source of emotional communication and why it has such power over us.

Gandhi had a compelling need to communicate with the hearts of men; he had an artist's genius for reaching the heartstrings of the inner man. But how does one communicate with one hundred or two hundred or three hundred million persons, most of whom are illiterate and only five thousand of whom have radios? Gandhi's fasts were means of communication. The news of the fast was printed in all papers. Those who read told those who did not read that "The Mahatma is fasting." The cities knew, and peasants marketing in the cities knew, and they carried the report to the villages, and travelers did likewise.
—Louis Fischer, *The Life of Mahatma Gandhi*

▼ EMOTIONAL COMMUNICATION BEGINS IN CHILDHOOD

What tools are used in emotive communication? The most effective one was suggested in proposition 1—involvement—for it stimulates both thinking and feeling. Involvement will use nonverbal signals, ten of the twelve signal systems, and they are the primary triggers for emotion. Why is this so?

Why do words play a relatively small role in emotive communication? Basic attitudes and fundamental awareness of love, security, God, and life are learned by the time a child is five or six years old, perhaps even earlier. They are learned almost entirely without the use of words. What is learned nonverbally becomes the basis for the verbal abstractions used throughout life. *Love, hate, work, play, father, mother*—the meaning of these crucial emotion-laden words is learned by observation and participation, not explanation. The meaning of crucial signals is acquired before spoken language is learned; thus emotion is largely triggered by nonverbal signals for the rest of one's life.

> Concepts like love, acceptance, faith, justice (fairness) and dependability are based on real experiences with actual people, particularly those people of most significance to [children]. This combination of concepts and feelings based on relationships is the very foundation for their basic experience of God's mercy, forgiveness, and the witness of the Spirit.
>
> —David Seamands, *The Healing of Memories,* 109

Emotive communication is particularly important to very young children because of their dependence on it. This means greater vulnerability, and the possibility of long-term emotional damage, even if the child does not apparently "understand" what is happening around him or her. When formal teaching is inconsistent with what the child sees in parents and other significant adults, the contradiction can destroy the foundation for healthy emotions. The child is of course not consciously aware of the damage, even when he or she becomes an adult.

▼ HEALING DAMAGED EMOTIONS

Dealing with persons who have sustained serious emotional damage dating from childhood is often a costly task for Christian communicators. When adult behavior exhibits serious problems or is antisocial, talking will do little to change behavior. Emotional damage must be

---

Words are needed, but they are not enough, even for God Himself. The Word became flesh. . . . He has become one with us by becoming one of us.
—David Seamands, *The Healing of Memories*

A man came to me for counseling—he wanted to talk about the death of his wife. As long as she was alive, their home was busy with people coming and going. There was always someone visiting.

When his wife died and the funeral was over, he thought people would keep coming, but they didn't. He went back to his home and waited, but no one came to talk with him. He had no company. The hours went by, and still he was alone. Finally about ten o' clock in the evening, he couldn't take it anymore. He was filled with such anger at the coldness of the people who left him to handle his grief alone that he had to strike back. He put on his jacket, headed down to the liquor store and began his drinking. The end result was his eventual commitment to the treatment center where I worked. . . .

If it was pathological grief that triggered the alcoholism in the first place, then we need to deal with the grief as well as the addiction.
—Arthur H., *The Grieving Indian,* 49, 57

dealt with on the emotional level, through emotive communication. True feelings must be somehow uncovered and dealt with before there will be emotional healing.

Simply discovering the feelings that lie behind wrong behavior, however, is of little help. Although the damaged person is not to blame for having been hurt as a child, he or she is responsible for the way the pain was dealt with. Often there is a problem of bitterness, resentment, unforgiveness, or determination to protect the self at all costs. Such attitudes are sins, and they must be confessed to God in order to receive the cleansing and healing that he alone gives. "If we confess our sins, he is faithful and just and will forgive us our sins and purify us from all unrighteousness" (1 John 1:9).

Some confessions of individual actions may evade the root of the problems, which may actually be unknown to the person. Until the root is identified, it is not possible to confess it. Confession is agreeing that a specific wrong is present, so evasive generalities will not help. Finding and confessing the problem is often a very emotional experience. The help of competent Christian counseling may be necessary for the adult to discover the feelings that need to be confessed and cleansed. If the damage has been serious, the healing process can be long and difficult.

> It is amazing how tenaciously people will deny their feelings because "Christians are not supposed to feel that way, especially not Spirit-filled Christians." This is denying reality and is a form of untruthfulness. Until it is brought up and out into the light, it cannot be healed by the One who is called the Spirit of Truth.
>
> —David Seamands, *The Healing of Memories,* 135

This emphasis on becoming aware of true feelings is not just some modern psychological "feeling therapy," which brings about an emotional catharsis so that people will feel better. It is the bedrock Scriptural reality of confession, repentance and forgiveness.
—David Seamands, *The Healing of Memories,* 135

▼ EMOTION AND LEARNING

Despite the contrasts we are accustomed to drawing between emotion and reason, the two are not sharply separated. Instead, they are intertwined, so that in practice it is nearly impossible to divide them. Even the learning of so-called plain facts is affected by emotion. Many studies have shown that memorization of multiplication tables, vocabulary lists, and similar material tasks is severely hindered by emotional disturbance. The child who has quarreling parents or who experiences anger and abuse at home rarely will do well in learning tasks. In addition, of course, the child's social development is twisted, and his or her relationships with others are often troubled.

Emotion can erect a high barrier to learning. Specific subjects may forever seem difficult or dull, if early experience with them is associated with emotional stress. The teacher who seems distant and forbidding unknowingly creates that kind of emotional response to the subject in pupils.

By contrast, emotion can enhance learning. In one study, students who were consistently poor spellers did not improve their spelling skills after study and many repetitive drills. But when they were frequently complimented on their achievements in other areas, then asked why they thought their spelling was not equally good, their spelling began to improve without formal drills. Self-esteem has been shown to be directly related to academic achievement.

Basic intelligence is seldom the reason for good or poor learning. Attitude toward learning is a much more important determinant of what is commonly perceived as intelligence. Frequently what is called aptitude represents positive emotions toward a subject or a skill. The potential of every person is vastly greater than normally shown in educational achievement and the level of mastery of other skills. The significant factor in the development of particular interests and abilities is emotion.

▼ IS EMOTION LEGITIMATE IN COMMUNICATION?

The use of emotion to aid communication is too often considered irrational, impractical, and an inferior way to reach a conclusion. Devaluing emotion is like devaluing water in a river. Without water there is no river, just a dry riverbed. It cannot float boats, give home to fish, or irrigate nearby lands. A river without water is of very limited usefulness. Communication without emotion is equally dry and of limited usefulness.

At least 80 percent of the information content in human communication is emotive. That is, probably 80 percent of the signals in normal communication are emotive cues, triggering feelings instead of just stuffing us with facts. Some researchers say as many as 95 percent of all signals are primarily emotive; most estimates vary between 85 and 95 percent. Since most emotive cues are nonverbal, great attention must be given to appropriate and extensive use of the ten nonverbal signal systems.

Attempts to distinguish crisply between logical and emotional appeals have been problematic. . . . Almost all ordinary language conveys emotional overtones. . . . Persuasive discourse is an amalgam of logic and emotion, (with) particular messages differing in the relative amount of each element.
—Gerald R. Miller, "Persuasion," 43

297

Limiting communication largely to the verbal and written systems sharply reduces its effectiveness, simply because some 80 percent of communicative resources are unused.

Words are efficient tools of communication; we cannot advance far without them when we seek to explain principles, ideas, and commitments. Anyone who has played the game of charades knows how much we need words for sharing factual content. Yet words rarely convey facts only. They can be highly emotive cues. Consider the stirring speech of Martin Luther King, Jr., "I Have a Dream." In the following excerpts I have italicized some of the particularly emotive verbal cues:

> Five score years ago, a *great American,* in whose symbolic shadow we stand today, signed the Emancipation Proclamation. This momentous decree came as a *great beacon light of hope* to millions of Negro slaves who had been *seared in the flames of withering injustice.* It came as a *joyous daybreak* to end the *long night of their captivity.*
>
> But one hundred years later, the Negro is still *not free;* one hundred years later, the life of the Negro is still *sadly crippled* by the *manacles* of segregation and the *chains* of discrimination. . . .
>
> *I have a dream* that one day on the red hills of Georgia, sons of former slaves and sons of former slave-owners will be able to *sit down together at the table of brotherhood.*
>
> *I have a dream* that one day, even the state of Mississippi, a state *sweltering with the heat of injustice, sweltering with the heat of oppression,* will be transformed into an *oasis of freedom and justice.* . . .
>
> So *let freedom ring* from the prodigious hilltops of New Hampshire. *Let freedom ring* from the curvaceous slopes of California. But not only that. *Let freedom ring* from Stone Mountain of Georgia. *Let freedom ring* from every hill and molehill of Mississippi. From every mountainside, *let freedom ring.*
>
> —James Melvin, *A Testament of Hope,* 218–20

If we examined every line of the speech as we have these few excerpts, it would be apparent that over and over, emotive cues are built into the speech. Abstract words like *injustice, oppression,* and *freedom* become emotionally alive when coupled with stirring images—*withering, chains, manacles*—and with phrases and metaphors that evoke strong memories—*let freedom ring, sweltering with the heat, oasis.*

It has been said that Winston Churchill was worth tens of thousands of soldiers to Britain by his oratory alone. Less imaginative speakers might have clearly de-

"Rabbit's clever," said Pooh thoughtfully.

"Yes," said Piglet, "Rabbit's clever."

"And he has Brain."

"Yes," said Piglet, "Rabbit has Brain."

There was a long silence.

"I suppose," said Pooh, "that that's why he never understands anything."

—A. A. Milne, "The House at Pooh Corner," 270

scribed what was ahead for the nation in World War II, speaking of inevitable sacrifices, shortages of goods, and the grief of separation and death. But Churchill used simple words that triggered emotional reactions in his national audience: "I have nothing to offer but blood, toil, tears, and sweat." Historians have speculated that without his moving speeches Britain might have lost the war.

We cannot explain with words and reason alone that which is learned emotionally. Basic ideas of love and forgiveness, for example, are learned in very early childhood, when no words are available. How can we learn, or relearn, such fundamental things when we are adults? It is the same way as in childhood—through nonverbal cues, through participation in experiences.

▼ WAYS TO DEVELOP EMOTIVE COMMUNICATION

Role-playing is effective because it involves many signal systems at one time and the learner is participating in a desired experience. Simulating racial prejudice, oppressive political structures, and cultural conflict can become a deeply emotional experience because of participatory use of signal systems. Simulation games in schools have been known to create such intense emotional reactions that the games had to be stopped. Because of emotional power, potentially explosive subjects should be role-played only under the guidance of experts.

Drama is similar to role-play in communicative effect. When a play is well acted, the audience identifies strongly with the characters portrayed and "learns" through emotion. Music conveys meaning and significance beyond the ability of words and reasoning. Similarly, dance can say things (through kinesics—body language) that cannot be put into words. In combination, these forms of communication carry unusual power to communicate at the emotional level, often preparing the way for verbal summary of the truths depicted and communicated.

It is striking that the biblical prophets often acted out their message and used objects to give God's message. They sought to touch emotion, to challenge the heart. The prophets gave clear verbal proclamation, but their overall ministry made powerful use of nonverbal signals. The rational and emotional were combined to achieve maximum impact. Do you remember how Hosea dramatized Israel's unfaithfulness? Jeremiah was given vivid pictures by God—of an almond-tree branch, a boiling pot, bones disinterred from their graves and exposed to "the sun and the moon and all the stars of the heavens." Ezekiel acted out a siege of Jerusalem as a warning to the people and showed the length of the siege by the number of days he lay on his side. Over and over again, the prophets used powerful emotive signals from each of the signal systems.

Why, then, do we hesitate to stimulate emotional response? There is a fear of manipulation, leading people to make a decision that is not based on thoughtful choice. Emotion is considered an inadequate foundation for commitment to Jesus as Lord.

But emotion is not the danger. Danger lies in any communication if the motivation is wrong. When either emotionalism or rationalism is used to cause people to fulfill someone else's desires, that is manipulation. Manipulation is using others to fulfill your desires; if any good comes to others through manipulation, it is incidental to the achieving of your selfish goals.

An advertisement placed in a magazine by the World Home Bible League summarizes the frequent concern. The ad pictures a multibarbed fishing lure under the heading "How to trick somebody into becoming a Christian." The text below the illustration begins with this warning: "The Lord still needs fishers of men, but what about the artificial bait? In their zeal to reach the unsaved, Christians sometimes resort to gimmicks."

The fear of superficial acceptance is valid. However, emotional communication is not the only source of problems. A purely rational decision may be equally superficial. Reason and emotion are both essential parts of complete communication.

SUMMARY

Although much attention is given to the rational content of communication, in fact emotion is the largest part of all human communication. Approximately 80 percent of the information load in typical communication is carried through emotion, and 20 percent or less by reason. Both elements are present at the same time in all human communication, in varying degrees in each situation.

True worship involves both reason and emotion. Neither emotion at the expense of reason nor reason at the expense of emotion fulfills Christ's definition of worship in John 4:23.

Emotion itself is not transferable from one person to another, but is stimulated by emotive cues in communication. These cues are largely from the nonverbal signal systems, though words themselves frequently are powerful stimulants for an emotional response.

Emotive signals prompt people to reject other people, accept political or philosophical positions, buy, sell, or trade both needed and unneeded goods, learn new things well or badly—in fact, they affect our behavior in virtually every area of living. Inner tensions that lead to visible emotional difficulties and conflict with others often arise from learned emotional responses to signals that are neutral in themselves.

The outer levels of culture (behavioral and authority) tend to be based more on cognition than are the two inner levels (personal experience and core). Behavior can be consciously modified when one receives appropriate information, and the strength or acceptance of authorities can be consciously changed. But even in behavior and acceptance of authority, emotion plays the larger part in exchange of information.

When changes are sought at the deeper levels of culture, communication should be primarily emotive. Rational elements are necessary, but these levels are primarily emotional. They will change gradually, if strong negative emotion is not aroused, under the influence of communication that has high emotive content.

▼ BIBLIOGRAPHY

Arthur H. *The Grieving Indian*. Winnipeg: Intertribal Christian Communications, 1988.

Backman, Carl W., and Paul F. Secord. *A Social Psychological View of Education*. New York: Harcourt, Brace, 1968.

Booth-Butterfield, Melanie, and Steve Booth-Butterfield. "Conceptualizing Affect as Information in Communication Production." *Human Communication Research* 16, no. 4 (1990), 451–76.

Davidman, Joy. *Smoke on the Mountain*. Philadelphia: Westminster, 1954.

Fischer, Louis. *The Life of Mahatma Gandhi.* New York: Harper & Row, 1950.

Knapp, Mark L., Michael J. Cody, and Kathleen Kelley Reardon. "Nonverbal Signals." In *Handbook of Communication Science.* Edited by Charles R. Berger and Steven H. Chaffee. Newbury Park, Calif.: Sage, 1987.

Kuethe, James L. *The Teaching-Learning Process.* Glenview, Ill.: Scott, Foresman, 1968.

Littlejohn, Stephen W. *Theories of Human Communication.* 3d ed. Belmont, Calif.: Wadsworth, 1989.

Mehrabian, Albert. *Silent Messages.* Belmont, Calif.: Wadsworth, 1971.

Miller, Gerald R. "Persuasion." In *Handbook of Communication Science.* Edited by Charles R. Berger and Steven H. Chaffee. Newbury Park, Calif.: Sage, 1987.

Otte, Ralph G. "Are We Worshiping or Watching?" *Eternity* 22, no. 9 (April 1971).

Packard, Vance. *The Hidden Persuaders.* New York: David McKay, 1957.

Perse, Elizabeth M. "Involvement with Local Television News." *Human Communication Research* 16, no. 4 (1990), 556–81.

Seamands, David. *The Healing of Memories.* Wheaton, Ill.: Victor, 1985.

Speer, David C. *Nonverbal Communication.* Sage Contemporary Social Science Issues 10. Newbury Park, Calif.: Sage, 1972.

21

➤ No man is an island. (John Donne)

➤ The group is worth as much as the best medication: it spells life! (Vincent Guerry)

CHANGE IS NOT LONELY

PROPOSITION 21: People react to communications as members of social groups.

What do a chicken and a person have in common? They are both strongly influenced by their peers. Put a chicken alone in a cage with ample food, and it will peck and eat until it is satisfied and then stop. When a second hungry chicken is placed in the same cage, it will of course start eating immediately, and the first chicken will resume eating, even though it was already satisfied.

For people it is a matter of "keeping up with the Joneses," "going with the flow," "being a good team member." Whatever it is called, people's actions are modified by the actions of others. The desire to conform goes deeper than actions. It affects values, attitudes, and even the ideologies by which we live.

Those who protest the most loudly about the dangers of conforming to society often most rigidly follow the style of their sub group. The hippies, counterculture people of the 1960s, protested that most Americans behaved like a herd of sheep—simply following the leader. Hippies expressed their refusal to conform to society's expectations by doing the opposite of what was generally expected. In the sixties it was easy to tell who the hippies were: the ones with long hair, beards, dresses like sacks, and insistently informal work clothes at every event. They expressed their nonconformity by conforming to a different standard; there was still little independent individualism.

Such conformity is normal for both chickens and human beings. It may be tuxedos and long dresses for a wedding, formal dress clothes for the opera, rudeness or courtesy to other drivers in heavy traffic: Our conduct mirrors the conduct of those whom we value. We use communication to shape ourselves to fit into the subgroup to which we belong, or wish we belonged. This means that we will usually do what other people around us do, but as we go about it our behavior is a little more complicated than that of chickens.

We will examine the group role in communication, first considering the group as the medium of communication to change individuals, and second, how communication can change the group itself.

▼ THE INDIVIDUAL DEVELOPS IN THE GROUP

Groups are like a protected, well-watered garden in which the emotional development of the individual flowers. It is within groups that attitudes and values are learned. Interaction with other group members develops practices of helping, comforting, sharing, assisting, and giving to others. Personal relationships are formed that provide friendship, support, and help. A sense of personal identity is developed. In fact, it is communication within groups that stimulates nearly all social and psychological development.

▼ GROUP EFFECT ON COMMUNICATION

The group is important to every individual, but how important is it in communication—in the attempt to create understanding? It is a key factor in how we understand and respond in communication. Culture—including the signal systems, the patterns of behavior, the ideologies, and the experiences that affect our perceptions—is shaped and taught *in the group*. To ignore the group effect on communication is to ignore fundamental reality.

The idea of individuals participating solo-fashion in communication is false. We do not function as individual atoms, but as parts of social molecules. Some of the molecules are tightly bound; others are loose, allowing the atoms to shift and rearrange themselves into new molecules.

A fine Singaporean evangelistic group emerged from the close friendships formed during early teen years.

"The Eagles started as a bunch of aimless Anglo-Chinese school boys meeting regularly on weekends—at cemeteries! . . . We gave each other the courage to do the things we would hesitate to do individually. During one outing one of the guys suggested, 'Since we are together so often, why not form a group and give it a name?' . . . Two years after they chose their name (Eagles), one of the boys 'gave my heart to God.' That was to result in the transformation of the Eagles. . . . Eventually, of the ten members, six became Christians.

"It was through no deliberate decision that we stuck together. . . . They completed their exams, then attended a camp where they planned to say goodbye to each other. On the last night, seven members responded to the challenge to go into full-time Christian ministry if the Lord so directed. 'We were about sixteen then.'" . . .

Today they are nearing forty, and the Lord has continued to use them as a group.

—"The Dauntless Eagles," *Impact* (September 1978), Singapore

304

Each new arrangement affects the flow of communication. These social arrangements, in fact, determine the formal and informal flow of communication within and between groups. (See proposition 16, "Hearing Through Someone Else's Ears.") Communication is seldom simply to an individual; instead, it is generally directed to a person filling a particular role or holding a specific status in the group. The same person may react very differently to the same communication received at different times, if that person is filling different social roles at the different times.

▼ DEFINING THE GROUP

What exactly is meant by a group: a culture? a tribe? friends studying together or meeting at the corner café for coffee? There are indeed many kinds of groups, but all demonstrate effective communication among members. Communication is what makes a collection of individuals a group.

In a group,

—members interact with each other,
—influencing each other and
—developing interdependence, so that
—they see themselves as a group, and nonmembers also recognize them as a group,
—the group is rewarding to its members.

Relationships within the group demonstrate

—shared social norms,
—common goals, and
—social roles that are mutually supportive.

Size is not an important issue in determining whether or not a collection of individuals is a "group." Two or more people can be a group. There are nuclear groups (two or three people), intimate groups (three to five), small groups (twenty or fewer), and large groups. A village or a tribe can be a group. Size affects the ways in which the group functions, but does not necessarily change the fact that it is a group.

Since an individual is part of several groups at the same time (for example, family, sports team, Bible class, city, state or province, and nation), which group is important in a given communication? That depends on the subject or purpose of the communication. A message about a game is important to the sports group; an announcement

After gaining independence, Kenya changed the British crown on its currency to a picture of President Kenyatta. People were told to change the old bills for new ones at the banks. Despite many announcements on the radio and in newspapers, people did not believe that the new money would be good. They were suspicious and worried. In my village I could see them in twos and threes discussing the issue. Many went to the local evangelist's house to verify the reports and to seek advice.

Only later, after discussion and reassurance from knowledgeable friends, did they begin to go to the bank twenty miles away to change their money.
—Nicholas Dondi

People live, buy, work, vote, and play as members of groups. They communicate as members of groups, and they receive and react to communications as members of groups. Any conception of audience that does not recognize its group nature will be badly misleading.
—John Riley and Matilda Riley, "Mass Communication and the Social System," 148

A statement is valid in a traditional society if it comes from the right oracle. It is not necessarily everyone's right to judge its validity. There are statements within one's own sphere and there are those which are outside one's proper role.

A study of Cambodia tells us that "information itself is considered sterile by the individual villager until someone of status has interpreted it. The individual does not see it as his role to judge the news."
—Ithiel de Sola Pool, "Mass Media and Their Interpersonal Functions"

of meeting times for a Bible class is of interest to class members. A son's coming home from college for Christmas is exciting news to the family, but probably has only a "courtesy meaning" for neighbors across the street. Different communications are relevant to each group.

▼ RECOGNIZING REFERENCE GROUPS

These groups are all *reference groups*. Each group is a reference point for communication considered related to its concerns. Through an often unconscious process, the group is used to validate, reject, or modify both incoming and outgoing communication.

Reference groups function something like dictionaries or encyclopedias. New information comes, or new information is needed, so the relevant group is involved in confirming or giving that information. Like an inadequate book, the reference group may give poor or inaccurate guidance. But the individual seldom has a way to check this and so can be led to wrong conclusions and wrong reactions.

Objective ideas of truth are frequently unimportant in deciding what "truth" one will accept or act upon. What is accepted by the reference group is, for practical purposes, what is true. The power of the reference group depends not on its accuracy, but on its ability to meet felt needs.

▼ REFERENCE GROUPS AFFECT EXTERNAL COMMUNICATION

Reference groups not only affect what you hear and believe, but also strongly influence how and what you communicate to others outside the group. What you tell others must first be acceptable to members of your relevant reference group. Even when the message is intended for opponents, it must first be considered suitable by your group. If it is not, you run the risk of becoming unacceptable in your own group. Conformity to group opinion is valued more highly than effectively communicating with the target group.

This has been demonstrated frequently in Christian ministry. Evangelistic communication must first be approved by Christian friends, by the church group, or by the missionaries *before* the planned effort can proceed. Often what appeals to them does not appeal to the non-Christian, so communication is never established. Words are thrown around, but very little understanding of the

*"Before you make any snap decisions,
think of the kids he could reach who may
think you're too weird."*

Gospel is created. The home reference group is kept, but the target group is lost.

An innovative manager of a Christian radio station determined that he would redesign the station to live up to its claims of being evangelistic. The format was changed, preaching was nearly eliminated, contemporary music was used, and interspersed throughout the broadcast day were thirty- and sixty-second capsules of Christian truth. Listenership increased, and response from those who had been indifferent to Christianity was high. But the Christians whose donations supported the station objected; they wanted the older-style preaching. So the station was forced to revert to its original format—and lost its desired audience, but did retain the needed donations.

Successful coffee-house ministries and youth programs have often come up against the same dilemma. When the music, decorations, environment, and activities appeal to non-Christian young people, they do not appeal to Christians. The target group is reached at the expense of losing the original supporting group.

Missionaries who become effectively involved with their adopted people may do so at the cost of full acceptance by their fellow missionaries. When the mission

At the heart of the social design, then, is the dependence of a person upon others—for information, a sense of reality, and moving ahead on tasks that require cooperation. As a consequence of this dependence, he is sensitive and vulnerable to their positive or negative social approval.
—Otto Lerbinger, *Designs for Persuasive Communication*, 93

307

group is internally cohesive with high morale, missionaries understandably value those relationships. When some use different approaches to gain more effective communication with nationals, it challenges the easy conformity and can disrupt the cohesiveness of the mission community and culture.

In international affairs, the same mistaken pattern is evident. Establishing fruitful communication with other nations usually demands shaping messages differently from the way one would for an internal audience. Instead, governments often sacrifice external understanding in favor of internal acceptance, even when the internal audience is not the true audience.

Historians suggest that if, upon invading the Ukraine, the Nazis had been able to talk and act in terms of Ukrainian rather than German attitudes, they probably would have defeated the Soviet Union in World War II. The Ukrainians were not enthusiastic supporters of the Soviet Communist government, but Nazi actions antagonized them even more. The Ukrainian reaction was more a matter of rejecting the Nazis than supporting the Soviet government.

▼ THE DANGER OF GROUPTHINK

An undesirable effect of a tightly knit group can be forced conformity of thinking. It becomes more desirable to maintain a strong sense of group unity than to examine all the facts. Some of the facts may not agree with existing ideas; challenging those ideas threatens group oneness. This pattern, illustrated above in government, missions and evangelism, is called *groupthink*. Groupthink "refers to a deterioration of mental efficiency, reality testing, and moral judgment that results from in-group pressures" (Irving Janis, *Victims of Groupthink: A Psychological Study of Foreign Decisions and Fiascoes* [Boston: Houghton Mifflin, 1982], 9).

To maintain or develop oneness in a valued group, members ignore evidence that would call into question existing behaviors or decisions. Instead, leaders introduce rationalizations to justify what is already being done. The group's moral rightness is assumed; thus its planning and actions are also seen as moral and necessary. Any opposition must therefore be wrong.

Group members are discouraged from expressing any other viewpoint, often being told, "Don't rock the boat." At the least, a group member who introduces an al-

In every city of the Orient, there is a thing called The White Community. The color of your skin elects you to its membership, whether you like it or not. It will give you a Welcome Party—just merry games and nice refreshments, and get-to-know-everybody. Very soon John and I had to face the question: How much time were we going to spend at parties and pink teas?

There was an important angle to it—the indigenous pattern to which we were pledged. This suggests that relaxation times be spent *with the nationals.* Do we need a game of volleyball? Call in the Thai neighbors to take part with you. They will love it and you incidentally have made a contact. The same holds for parties and picnics—Thai friends are always available. This does not mean that we never went to a party; it means that this was the pattern to which we felt committed. Or, as Amy Carmichael put it, "We march to a different drumbeat."
—Isobel Kuhn, *In the Arena,* 36–37

ternative viewpoint loses popularity. The dissident member may lose more than popularity. The group may find reasons for disciplining this member—overlooking the person in conversations and in recognition, lowering his or her status, or subtly shifting roles to make the person irrelevant to the group. Formal expulsion may be the eventual result.

By contrast, acceptance in the group is increased when an individual gives strong support to the majority position.

▼ GROUP ACCEPTANCE: A BASIC NEED

The influence of the group on members is expected. Even if not part of some easily identified, special group, every individual needs a sense of group acceptance. It is basic to individual social adjustment and personal achievement.

Rejection does more than simply leave individuals alone. It cuts off access to social learning situations and to potential help. Those who are, or feel, rejected are far more likely to show hostility and disruptive behavior and to reject others. The rejected individual seems to lose his or her bearings, often showing low self-esteem, anxiety, and various forms of emotional illness. Communication is severely disrupted (David W. Johnson and Frank P. Johnson, *Joining Together,* 131 32).

Clearly, groups are central in determining each person's quality of life. To gain group approval, individuals will learn and adopt group opinions. Even before he or she is accepted as a group member, the individual will conform to the norms of a desirable group. After the invisible line of group approval has been crossed, pressure to conform is even stronger.

▼ TO KNOW THE PERSON, KNOW THE GROUP

In short, groups have a powerful influence on individuals. To know the individual, it is necessary to know the group. A study completed in the 1930s by Theodore Newcomb is a classic illustration of group influence. The study showed that 250 students from Bennington College, all politically conservative when they entered the school, had become liberals by their final year at the college. Conforming to the liberal political norms of Bennington was rewarded by the acceptance and approval of fellow students.

When Ishiyama san was deciding whether or not to accept Jesus as his Savior, he worked through the pros and cons of the decision. He understood and believed the message of salvation. He was held back by worry about how his family (the relevant reference group) would react when they heard he accepted Christ. He finally decided that if he had to live outside his group, it would still be worth it to follow Christ.

His parents did what he had feared: They disinherited him, expelling him from their home because of his new faith. He has struggled deeply with this rejection from his reference group, often doubting. He must find a new reference group in a local church to encourage him and help him grow in his faith.
—Bruce Penner

More than two years ago, we escaped the horrors of Lebanon (civil war) and chose a tranquil milieu . . . for children traumatized by the havoc of a decade of protracted violence and random terror.

Little did I know that (our son) was to face, at such an early age, the more subtle terror of American peer pressure . . . and the unsettling dissonance of conflicting norms and expectations.

The family system in Lebanon is, on the whole, intimate, warm and affectionate. . . . The Lebanese are very tactile. Touching, kissing, hugging and the outward display of emotion—regardless of gender—are generously and spontaneously expressed. . . .

I first noticed a transformation (or deformation) a few months after we had settled in Princeton. Normally . . . George would interrupt his play and rush across the driveway to greet me; often, he would literally hurl himself into my open arms. . . . On that day, however, just as he was about to heed his normal impulse as he rushed across the driveway, he suddenly froze in mid-passage, looked in the direction of his watchful playmates and, with obvious hesitation and embarrassment, calmly walked over to greet me with a cold handshake and a casual, "Hi, Dad."

Bit by bit, even this gesture has been abandoned. The most I can expect is a disengaged and distant nod.
—Samir Khalaf, "The Americanization of George," 14

About the same time, Solomon Asch conducted a noted "line experiment" to test the strength of group pressure. Participants were asked to choose the one line (among three) that was closest in length to a standard line given to them. When asked to judge without other people present, the participants almost always made the correct choice. But when asked to make the selection with other people involved in the decision, subjects made a wrong judgment nearly one-third of the time in order to agree with the majority—who had been told to make wrong judgments deliberately.

▼ THE GROUP AFFECTS PERCEPTION

People are so sensitive to the reactions and opinions of others, even in a temporary group, that it affects their perception of reality. Parents are right to be concerned about their children's choice of friends, for our friends do make a difference in what we become.

In some settings, individuals are so group-conscious that they have no real sense of personal identity apart from the group. To be separated from his group—family, village, or clan—is to lose any true sense of identity. The group provides security, cooperates in meeting the needs of life, supports its members emotionally in birth, marriage, and death, and sets the boundaries of proper behavior. These boundaries are crossed only with the certain knowledge that penalties, perhaps even exile, will result.

© Erik and Vicki Johnson, 1983.

"We're in debt, the deacons have all quit, and we've not had a visitor in six months. But thank goodness none of the other churches are doing any better."

Seeking to change individuals in such a setting is almost fruitless; the entire group must be the target for change.

Strong group influence, virtual group control, is especially apparent among many African and Asian peoples. Groups that depend on the immediate environment for survival develop this "groupness" in a particularly visible way. Weddings, celebrations, and feasts include everyone and may last two or three days. Funerals often clearly show the cohesion of villages. Work stops when a death occurs, and people go to the home of the deceased, partly to help but mostly just to be with the bereaved family. Burial may occur quickly but funeral ceremonies may last for one, two, or more weeks.

Similar patterns can develop in urban areas. Intense group cohesion is built, for example, within gangs that frequently follow a dangerous or even violent lifestyle, and within neighborhood groups whose members assist one another against those same gang and drug subcultures. Successful sports teams, fine drama groups, workers who share high risks on the job such as police officers or deep-sea fishermen—such situations encourage a closeness that deeply affects attitudes and lifestyles of the group's individual members.

▼ CHANGING THE GROUP

Seeking to change individuals through the group is excellent communication strategy—*if* the group is in general agreement with the change. The power of this approach has been demonstrated repeatedly in such groups as Alcoholics Anonymous, Weight Watchers, and small Bible studies and church fellowships. But if the group is not in agreement, the possibility of changing individuals is small. When that is the case, the group itself needs to be changed.

Changing the group demands different approaches from those aimed at changing individuals. A group change must be approached with great caution, lest the change destroy more than it helps. Deliberate change is possible, but not always desirable or ethical: Manipulation of group processes is at the heart of what is called "brainwashing," the involuntary change of behaviors and attitudes.

Any group that lasts has achieved enough social stability to provide security for its members. That is a complex achievement and should not be lightly disregarded. A group develops its own culture that regulates conflict-

(The early Filipinos were) tightly organized and highly structured on the local . . . level, but quite fragmented and lacking cohesion beyond the local *barangay*.

This political unit was based chiefly on blood ties, and the in-group feeling and sentiment were so strong as to make external social and political relationships rather restricted. Any dealing with an out-group was primarily concerned with war or a question of marriage. . . .

His kinship web defines for him his world to which he is deeply obligated and from which he can expect support. The picture is very little changed from the earlier periods in Philippine history. . . .

Even today, this mosaic of kinship webs remains basic in Philippine society. Much of the fragmentary nature of Philippine political and religious life can be traced to this basic characteristic of the society. The internal life of the Church with its family factions reflects it. . . . Much of the growth of the Church follows family kinship web lines.

—Arthur Tuggy, *The Philippine Church*, 43, 133, 39

"This recommendation comes as a recommendation of the personnel committee, the finance committee, and the board of deacons. The church staff has approved it unanimously. We also feel it is the will of God. Is there any discussion?"

ing motives, harmonizes relationships, and enables the group to reach its goals. This culture has developed through interaction, in a matter of hours or days in small groups with limited purposes and perhaps requiring generations in large groups. It is not surprising that all groups tend to be conservative, resisting change that in any way appears to threaten its sense of security.

Group conservatism can be discouraging. Individual change is incomplete and perhaps impermanent apart from change in the relevant reference group.

How can communication stimulate productive change, despite this natural conservatism? Here I suggest six steps that not only assist the process of change, but also help avoid damage to the group.

1. *A change agent can help the group recognize needs and stimulate a desire to meet the need.*

When the process begins this way, the source of pressure for change comes from within the group. It is not simply something being demanded by an external change agent.

Conversations are started, questions asked, and ideas planted during discussions. It becomes clear that

One church in our area came into being through a family. A young man heard the Gospel and believed the truth. But he could not take any step forward because he was afraid of his family and his age group. He started talking to two men of his age group about Christianity without giving his opinion. After a considerable time, he accepted Christ publicly. A week later his other two friends joined him. The three men led their families to Christ. After that, it became easy to witness to others in that tribe.
—Harun Arun

the change agent has come to learn as well as to share from his or her experience and training. When the change agent works slowly and within the group communication channels, the change is often accepted as if it were the group's own plan—a highly desirable outcome because it prevents the development of dependency. More detailed suggestions for change agents are given in *Communicating for Development: A Practical Guide* by Karl-Johan Lundstrom, Donald K. Smith, and Samuel Kenyi, resulting from a six-year study of communication and change sponsored by the Lutheran World Federation.

2. *The change agent must know the group.*

As we have learned, the group strongly affects perception and evaluation of new information, and decisions on possible changes. Ignoring the group structure, in what ways it is linked together by communication, and its values is worse than ignorance. It is foolishness. The danger of proceeding without this knowledge is something like a pilot's trying to land at an airport surrounded by mountains on a cloudy night, without navigational aids or charts, with no ground lights. A disaster in such circumstances comes as no surprise.

3. *Intimacy with the group must be developed.*

Many studies show that to change deeply rooted attitudes requires the development of an intense relationship between two parties, in this case between the change agent and the group. Increasing closeness increases the obligation to agree with the opinions of others in the relationship. Skills can be learned from reading, television, or films, but attitude change occurs almost entirely through a relationship with a person important to the learner. (See proposition 1.)

4. *The relationship between the group and the change agent must be voluntary.*

Compulsion, direct or indirect, arouses resistance. When the compulsion is removed, the group will revert to what it was before the effort began.

The group must determine for itself that the change is not destructive and that it is compatible with group interests. When the group believes that to be true, there is no need for pressure. The group will fit the proposed change to group needs and culture. The change is then long-term and permanent.

5. *Individuals who are of high value to the group (sometimes called "influentials" or "communication elites") should be fully informed about proposed changes.*

When the group is used to change individuals, five axioms guide good communication design:

1. The people to be changed and those seeking to introduce change must have a strong sense of belonging to the same group.

2. The more attractive the group is to its members, the greater the influence the group exerts on its members.

3. The closer attitudes, values, and behaviors are to the basis of group attractiveness, the greater is the group influence over them.

4. Individual influence in the group increases with increasing prestige within the group.

5. Change efforts that would cause individuals to deviate from group norms will meet strong resistance.

—Adapted from Dorwin Cartwright, "Achieving Change in People," 381–92

The person valued most by the group has the most liberty to deviate from group norms. That person is most free to try something new. Group constraints on this individual's behavior are significantly less than for marginally acceptable members.

6. *The group's own communication system must be used to spread information, further discussion, and focus the issues clearly.*

It may seem quicker and easier to introduce changes primarily through extending media such as radio, tape recorders, or printed leaflets. But if these efforts are not strongly linked to the interpersonal networks, such an approach is inefficient.

▼ IMPLICATIONS FOR EVANGELISM

Evangelical Christianity is heavily oriented toward individuals. Teaching is typically geared to individual decisions, individual acceptance, and individual perseverance. Daniel in the lions' den is a favorite example of brave and faithful individualism. In this chapter, however, it has been stressed that attitudes, beliefs, and behavior are based in the groups to which an individual belongs. Attempts to change beliefs and values must be concerned with the group, not only the individual. Which pattern is demonstrated in Scripture?

Examples of both group and individual decision and action are plentiful. Individuals with courage to stand against the group come readily to mind: Noah, Abraham, Joseph, Moses, Joshua and Caleb, Gideon, Daniel, the prophets, Paul. Each of these individualists, in fact, was part of a group. Noah seems to have been the loneliest, but he did have his extended family, who in general went along with his actions. Abraham did not go from the city of Ur alone, but with his family and servants. Joseph faced the animosity of his jealous brothers, but had the support of his father. In Egypt, his abilities earned him a place in society, but his individual moral courage got him a place in jail. In prison, he gained a support group (a group that seems to have failed him later). Still, in his exile he was not totally alone. Moses' family kept him alive, another family group provided a home in the desert, and stormy relationships with a group—the children of Israel—were the setting for the last third of his life.

Each of these great men of faith acted with individual righteousness and bravery, but *within the setting of a group*. Values and attitudes were learned in a group set-

The villagers in my home get all their messages at the marketplace, at a definite spot, delivered by an elder in government service.

Then the Ugandan government sent adult literacy teams to rural areas, including my village, so that through reading the village could have better communications. A team member went door to door announcing the opening of adult literacy classes.

However, villagers complained and rejected his work totally. They were not sure who this man was and could not trust him—all because he did not give the message at the right place and time.

—Margaret Ekwan

ting, the group provided the framework for living them out, and often a small group even supported the brave individual's stand. It is not a matter of sheer individualism, nor is it simply flowing with the group. Both elements are demonstrated in Scripture.

In the New Testament, the group setting for decision and action is even more evident. The disciples were in small groups when they were called (note John 1:35–51), and they traveled as a group, were taught, discussed what to do and responded as a group. Left alone, Peter denied Christ. After Christ's crucifixion the disciples regathered in small groups; by the time Christ appeared to them after the resurrection, they were meeting again as a group. A successor to Judas was chosen by the group, and they were meeting "all together in one place" when the Holy Spirit came. Peter preached his first sermon standing "with the Eleven," and the first apostolic miracle occurred when Peter and John were together.

The group-centered quality of Christianity is very clearly seen in Acts 4:32–37, a passage that describes the sharing of possessions among the believers. Paul traveled, taught, and suffered with companions, and together they established further groups of believers throughout the Roman Empire. Group commitment to believe and follow Jesus is illustrated by Paul's response to the Philippian jailer, "'Believe in the Lord Jesus, and you will be saved— you and your household.' Then they spoke the word of the Lord to him and to all the others in his house. . . . then immediately he and all his family were baptized" (Acts 16:31–33).

The church is the body of Christ, much different from a mere collection of individuals who believe the same things. It is a dynamically interrelated group, infused with the Divine Presence. Intragroup relationships are part of the very essence of following Christ.

There is a continuing tension between being group-centered and individually courageous. Depending completely on the group for every decision does not demonstrate strength of character. On the other hand, individual independence is unrealistic and develops incomplete people. It is within the group that our life in Christ is maintained and completed, so that we are enabled to express that life individually.

The individual is bound to the group; life was given him by the village and it is through the village that he continues to live; should he cast himself off from the village he would be but a dead branch. For a while, he may be able to wander away from this source of life but, as the proverb says, "A dog with a broken leg very quickly finds his way home." At the slightest trouble, any Baoulé will come back to the village.
—Vincent Guerry, *Life with the Baoulé*, 51–52

A Muslim friend announced his determination to follow Christ. His decision was taken in the hothouse atmosphere of a Christian camp, and everything in the garden looked rosy to him that day. He was far from home, and none of us really appreciated to what lengths a Muslim father would go to prevent his son (from) leaving Islam. Months later we heard that he had been beaten again and again, and locked up without nourishment in a bare room in wintertime. Finally he escaped and joined a Christian group. He is still with them, but his family count him dead.
—A believer from India

SUMMARY

Humans are social beings. We find our sense of completeness, security, and identity through interaction. We care what our peers think of us. We feel secure when we hold views identical to their views. To ask us to believe or behave contrary to other group members creates a sense of insecurity.

Individuals normally change only as their group changes or permits change. Individual change does not take place in a vacuum, since all individuals are related to groups of one kind or another. Change in the individual produces reaction in the group. If the reaction is negative and the person values group membership above the proposed change, the change will not be made.

This proposition is especially applicable in fundamental matters of values and beliefs that lie at the core of a person. This core is developed in the groups to which an individual belongs, either by birth or by voluntary association. Therefore attempts to change beliefs and values must be concerned with the group, not only the individual.

The group can be the channel for changing the individual; in fact, often the group must be the target of change before the individual can be reached. Normally the group must change or be willing to change before the individual can be open to change. A people movement may prepare the way for individual conversions, and on other occasions individual conversions of key individuals in a society may begin a people movement that in turn opens the door for others to follow Christ personally. Either way, the group must be involved if an effective communication strategy is to be developed.

▼ BIBLIOGRAPHY

Bales, Robert P. "How People Interact in Conferences." *Scientific American* 192 (1955), 31–55.

Bauer, Raymond A. "The Audience." In *Handbook of Communication.* Edited by Ithiel de Sola Pool et al. Chicago: Rand McNally, 1973.

Cartwright, Dorwin. "Achieving Change in People." *Human Relations Journal* 4, no. 4 (1951), 381–92.

De Sola Pool, Ithiel. "Mass Media and Their Interpersonal So-
cial Functions." In *People, Society, and Mass Communications*.
Edited by Lewis A. Dexter and David Manning White.
New York: Free Press, 1964.

Dexter, Lewis A., and David Manning White, eds. *People, Society,
and Mass Communications*. New York: Free Press, 1964. Introduction by Lewis A. Dexter.

Guerry, Vincent. *Life with the Baoulé*. Washington, D.C.: Three
Continents, 1975.

Hovland, Carl I., Irving L. Janis, and Harold H. Kelley. *Communication and Persuasion: Psychological Studies of Opinion
Change*. New Haven: Yale University Press, 1953.

Johnson, David W., and Frank P. Johnson. *Joining Together:
Group Theory and Group Skills*. Englewood Cliffs, N.J.:
Prentice-Hall, 1987.

Katz, Elihu, and Paul F. Lazarsfeld. *Personal Influence: The Part
Played by People in the Flow of Mass Communications*. Glencoe, Ill.: Free Press of Glencoe, 1955.

Keesing, Felix M. and Marie M. Keesing. "Opinion Formation
and Decision-Making." In *Communication and Culture:
Readings in the Codes of Human Interaction*. Edited by A. E.
Smith. New York: Holt Rinehart, 1966.

Lerbinger, Otto. *Designs for Persuasive Communication*. Englewood Cliffs, N.J.: Prentice-Hall, 1972.

Littlejohn, Stephen W. *Theories of Human Communication*. 3d ed.
Belmont, Calif.: Wadsworth, 1989.

Riley, John, and Matilda Riley. "Mass Communication and the
Social System." In *Sociology Today*. Edited by Robert K.
Merton. New York: Basic Books, 1959.

Roloff, Michael E., et al. "Acquiring Resources from Intimates."
Human Communication Research 14, no. 3 (Spring 1988),
364–96.

Schaller, Lyle E. *The Change Agent*. Nashville: Abingdon, 1972.

Westly, Bruce H. "The Relevance of Group Research to Development." In *Communication for Group Transformation in Development*. Edited by Godwin C. Chu, Syed A. Rahim, and
D. Lawrence Kincaid. Honolulu: East-West Communication Institute, 1976.

22

➤ The power of lightning is of greatest use when it is harnessed to wires, switches, and outlets.

COMMUNICATING FOR CHANGE

PROPOSITION 22: A decision to change results from the combined effects of public or mass media and interpersonal networks.

Just how powerful are the media? With control of the media, can we bring change to a nation or culture? Can we overpower people's resistance to new ideas, to doing things in different ways? An immense amount of research has explored these questions. It is one of the most practical issues researched: If the media are all-powerful, control is essential for the health of any ideology or political structure. If not, should the media be simply ignored, or used only for entertainment? Or is there a better alternative between these extremes?

Certainly television, radio, and the press do influence people. If they did not, advertisers would not invest hundreds of millions of dollars in them to sell their products. Yet the media do not sweep all before them—they are also turned off, ignored, forgotten.

Possibly no regimes have ever controlled the mass media as completely as did East European governments after World War II. For forty years, opposition ideas were not broadcast or printed within those countries. Then the wall broke *from within*, and hundreds of thousands of ordinary people collected in the streets before government

318

headquarters, demanding political and social changes. The demonstrations were not, and could not be, organized through the mass media. Yet the governments of East Germany, Czechoslovakia, Romania, Poland, and Bulgaria were toppled without an invading army or civil war. How could that have happened?

In the Soviet Union, organized religion was repressed and virtually banned. Use of the mass media by religious groups was forbidden, and most churches were closed. Children were taught by the schools that there is no God; at times they were encouraged to report any religious observances of their parents. When the full effects of more than sixty years of this public policy became visible, the church was still present. House groups, secret believers, and the few publicly visible churches were thriving. In many ways the church of Jesus Christ was stronger than before. Pastors and bishops had continued to care for their people while employed as factory workers, engineers, or teachers.

Similar patterns have occurred in other areas of the world. The church has often grown deeper and stron-

© 1984 *Leadership*

ger—and sometimes more numerous—when access to the public media has been denied. The spread of the Gospel, the encouragement of people in following Christ, and the building of small, strong groups of believers happened through interpersonal networks.

At times, external media have helped—for example, through radio broadcasting to China and the Soviet Union. People turn to external sources of information when they lose confidence in the reliability of their own national media. Some of those external sources were Christian; what was learned there became part of the unofficial flow of information within otherwise closed societies. But neither radio nor any other medium can be said to have been the sole cause of the church growth in these repressive societies. Nor can interpersonal networks be invoked to explain all that happened.

There is massive evangelical broadcasting in the United States, but very little national gain in church membership. Many (but not all) of the examples of outstanding church growth are simply a matter of borrowing from Peter to pay Paul; already-convinced Christians hear compelling preachers through the media or want an attractive program, so they shift to the new center of growth. The average church with an average program and preacher is the loser, but the larger church makes no real gain for the kingdom of God.

There is endless debate between media enthusiasts and media detractors. "Develop a credible lifestyle and personal witness, then just talk to friends," the detractors say. "Forget media and do it yourself." Or as one bumper sticker puts it, "Just Say NO to Television." Is there no way for media *and* interpersonal networks to be deliberately used for evangelism and church-building?

An introduction to the limitations and strengths of media is given in propositions 13, 14, and 15. Propositions 16 and 21 provide discussions of how social networks function to tie a society together. In this section, we need to see how the media and interpersonal networks *together* make up the all-important internal communication system in any society. Media do have a valuable function, and interpersonal ties are essential. Both are necessary; they accomplish different things in communication. How can we deliberately interweave their strengths for more effective communication strategy?

Communication is to meet needs, and that means change. Change is a constant and continuing thing, difficult to separate into parts. It is difficult to see how decisions to change are made, but if we "froze" the process at certain key points, as if we were taking a high-speed photograph, it would look something like the diagrams that appear on the following pages.

The process does not proceed in a strict order. At times some steps may be skipped; at other times steps may be repeated. But six broad steps have been widely identified that represent the normal way decisions are made both by individuals and by groups. Understanding those steps will make it easier to see how both mass media and interpersonal networks are essential parts of effective communication.

▼ CHANGE BEGINS WITH NEED

Change normally begins with realizing that there is an unmet need. The awareness of a need may have persisted for a long time, or it may have emerged only recently. Making people aware of their own needs is often necessary. The Brazilian Paulo Freire has coined the term *conscientization* for the work of making people aware of their needs and of the fact that there can be solutions. The conscience is aroused, sensitivity to long-accepted conditions is increased, and with it there is a new determination to change in ways that will meet the need.

Part of this first step toward change is developing **awareness** of an alternative. It is one thing to be aware of the possibility of change and quite another to be interested in actually making the change. The primary challenge at this step is to give information—information relevant to the target group, enough information to bring the change to a level of visibility, and information that arouses some emotional **interest.** Change certainly does not happen on a purely rational basis.

A circle is used to represent the making of decisions because it is not a simple linear matter in which one need at a time is met. Almost nothing is decided all by itself; instead, relationships link one need to others, one possible change to consequent changes. The decision-making process is best seen as a continuing process in which one change leads to another, and then to two or five or eight more. Since it is a part of communication, it is best seen as a process with no clear beginning or end. The bold line symbolizes decision activity that includes thought, conversation, and action as it moves through the usual six stages.

A Japanese international student in America was invited to a church while serving as a trainee in the next state. There he gained an awareness of the Christian faith. When he returned to his school for study, he had a number of opportunities to hear about Christ through an English class, a film in Japanese and messages at another church he visited with a host family. He also read Christian books and magazines left by a previous trainee. His interest in the Christian faith grew.

Along with this, he had interpersonal networks that were primarily Christian friends. They were able to answer various questions, helping him evaluate the effect of accepting Christ. The Holy Spirit used all of these things, working together, to bring him to repentance and accepting of Christ.

—Bruce Penner

321

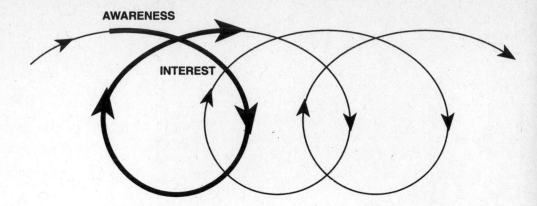

AWARENESS

INTEREST

▼ CHANGE NEEDS CONSIDERATION

When there is awareness and interest in meeting a need and an alternative is proposed that may meet that need, clearly there must be some kind of **consideration**—directly in conversation or indirectly through discussions, questions, and thought. The kinds of issues that must be considered are personal and relational, with a large element of emotion involved:

• Is this change really going to help? Will it meet the need?

• What other changes will be necessary if this change is made?

• Will it affect relationships with family, friends, the community, or other people important to me?

• Are there other possible consequences that might help or hurt me, my family, or my community?

Consideration can be a lengthy process, sometimes even requiring years before a choice is made. Some matters, however, can be decided almost immediately. Some people decide quickly, while others agonize over every change that must be made. When a community decision is involved, there will be not only discussion but also negotiation. Negotiation helps form broad understanding in the community of the change proposal. During the process, the social, psychological, and material costs are estimated. The estimates may not be correct, but they are nevertheless the "facts" used in making a choice.

▼ MAKING THE CHOICE

Often, the most visible part of the whole process is **choice.** At this point, acceptance (or rejection) is apparent. The person or group is able to say what the choice is: A vote is cast, the decision to buy a product is made, a de-

An elderly Hindu villager listened to Christian broadcasts for many months and became convinced of the truth of Jesus the Messiah. He was, of course, deeply committed to the family clan and foresaw that he would have great difficulty in the clan if he accepted Christ. He deliberately sought to broaden his network to include the small local Christian community. They were able to help him lovingly to make the change, which predictably antagonized his family.

The happy sequel of all this came when he was, in turn, able to help develop new networks in the village that now included local Christians. Many bridges were built that led to much wider acceptance of the Christians and to a greater audience for the broadcasts.

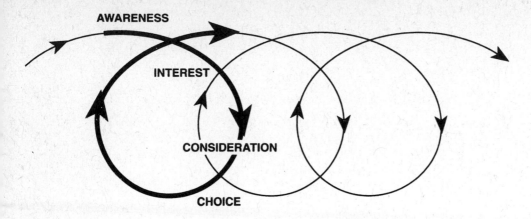

cision is made to accept Jesus as Lord. A wide range of choices is possible, but all come to this pivotal point—I will, or I will not.

Because choice is so obviously a critical point, great efforts are focused on persuading people to "make the right choice." Persuasive techniques are primarily concerned with this stage in the decision process. Salesmanship, in the minds of some, is concerned with getting people to choose a particular product, whether or not they actually want it. Some so-called evangelism does much the same thing, seeking to influence people to make an outward choice to follow Jesus, whether or not they truly intend to do so.

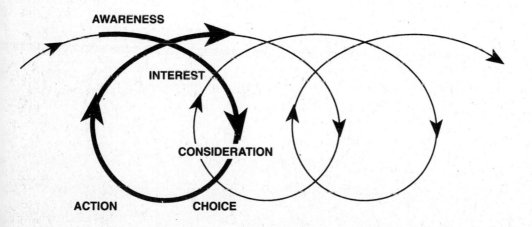

▼ ACTING IT OUT

Directly following the choice must come **action** to implement the choice made. The action is outward and visible; it is the behavior resulting from the inward choice.

323

To paraphrase Scripture, it is the evidence of things not seen, the unseen choice expressed in visible action.

If no outward action results from the choice, has the choice not been made? Or does the lack of action show that the choice was never made? No.

There are times when a genuine choice was made, but no way to implement that choice is available. On a superficial level, for example, an advertisement may convince a homemaker to buy a different brand of soap. But when she goes to the store to buy the soap, it is not on the shelf, and the storekeeper has no plans to stock it. Of course she cannot buy the different brand, even though she had genuinely chosen to do so.

At a much more important level, an individual may be convinced that he or she ought to follow Jesus as Lord. Having chosen to do so, the person then seeks ways to take action that would give expression to the choice. But no opportunity is found to speak publicly or to join with other Christians. Perhaps the person knows that to do so would lead to severe persecution or even death. So the new Christian becomes a "secret believer" and remains silent. Does that mean that a genuine choice was never made? Not necessarily; there is a difference between making the choice and having the opportunity to act on that choice, to implement it. Judging the sincerity of someone else's choice in such circumstances is beyond human knowledge and ability—though it is still attempted by some.

▼ THE CONSEQUENCES OF A CHOICE

Consequences grow out of any choice. The actions implementing that choice may cause little outward change, but they require major **readjustment** of thinking. Or an apparently insignificant mental choice may lead to

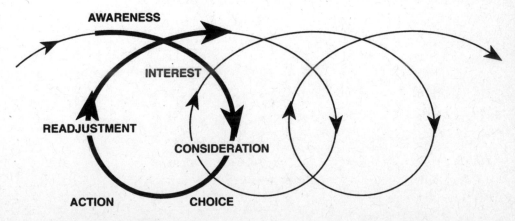

AWARENESS

INTEREST

READJUSTMENT

CONSIDERATION

ACTION   CHOICE

major changes in way of life, friendships, even family relationships. Virtually any choice requires some readjustments.

Efforts to bring change cannot be concerned primarily with the act of choice, as if the process were complete once the choice is made. The action growing out of the choice may well require major readjustments, not all of which will be immediately apparent.

At times these readjustments begin immediately and help is available. Often, however, readjustment does not begin at once. When it does become necessary, enthusiasm about the choice may have faded. Friends may be unaware of difficulties and so are not giving the help needed. A choice made wholeheartedly begins to seem unwise and even impossible to follow. It is at this final point in the whole process that the change may be stopped. Once this has happened, it is very difficult to reintroduce the change. Individuals or groups have gained considerable acquaintance with the change and decided that "it just isn't practical." They are, in effect, immunized against any future change along the same lines.

It is overly simplistic to assume that decision-making moves only in one direction—forward. There often are detours, delays at one or more points in the process, and even backward movement—backward, that is, in terms of the model presented here.

These same stages of change are presented in a different way by James Engel, who has listed the identifiable points through which a person moves from basic awareness of a Supreme Being to a decision and then on to spiritual maturity. Engel's description (see next page) focuses particularly on the different aspects of Christian ministry. Clearly, ministry is not simply gaining decisions; much has happened before that point, and much must happen afterward.

In reality the process is a continuum—that is, an unbroken line rather than distinct steps. One part blends into the next. Sometimes steps may appear to be skipped. But overall, this outline provides a very useful guide to recognition of what is required at different points in the journey to faith.

▼ USING MEDIA IN DECISION MAKING

How best can media be used in the process of change? When is it necessary to relate consciously to interpersonal networks?

Spiritual reproduction

↑

Incorporation into church

↑

Reevaluation

↑

Change of allegiance

↑

Problem recognition

↑

Positive attitude toward
becoming Christian

↑

Understanding of gospel
implications

↑

Knowledge of gospel basics

↑

No awareness

The spiritual decision process

The first two stages in change (awareness and interest) can be accomplished through use of mass or public media. Public media include the usual electronic methods and printing, as well as speech and oratory. Public speeches, drama, debates, classes, and similar forms suitable for large groups are frequently the most useful way of informing large numbers of people where radio and television are not generally available. These alternates to electronic and mechanical means are often considered "group media." Regardless of the name, these public media are effective in increasing awareness.

The public media also can create interest in the alternatives. Barriers to perception can be bypassed or even broken down through constructive use of emotion in the public media. Humor and pathos create interest in changes proposed.

The group, however, will remain a major source of influence for its members. Even where individuals are aware of need and interested in change, group opinion can block change. The group can virtually compel conformity, shutting out change that seems to threaten the group. Lasting change cannot occur if the group is ignored. The two critical stages of consideration and choice happen within interpersonal networks.

326

Even when those interpersonal networks are not visible during consideration of change, they have influence. At times an individual may consider and decide on change without consulting with a reference group. Even then, the remembered ideas and values of a desirable group are weighed, along with other positives and negatives, before a decision is made.

After the choice, which channels can help during implementation, action, and readjustment? Both public media and interpersonal networks are needed. The public media can give information helpful to reinforce the choice already made. Interpersonal networks provide opportunities for discussion of new ideas, new ways of doing things. Again we find that public media are useful for giving new and needed information, while interpersonal networks are valuable for social support.

It is clearly not a question of which are best, public media or interpersonal networks. The question is how to combine the strengths of each to stimulate change most effectively.

Simplifying the change diagrams to a single circle summarizes the primary area of strength for each kind of channel:

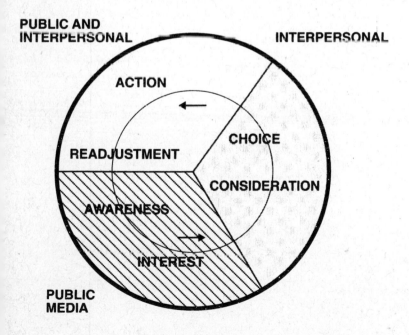

To summarize, the first two stages in decision for change are accomplished primarily through the public media. The next two stages, consideration and choice, normally happen within interpersonal networks. The choice to change usually results from contact with friends who recommend or support the decision. The final two stages draw on both public media and interpersonal networks for carrying out the choice and readjustment in areas affected by the change.

▼ CASE STUDY: COMBINING MEDIA AND NETWORKS

An insightful study of religious change among the Lotuho people of southern Sudan shows something of the relationships between public media and interpersonal networks. Mission work among the Lotuho was conducted by a Roman Catholic order, the Verona Fathers, from 1920 to 1964.

> The Verona Fathers largely made use of their own channels for spreading their message. As noticed already, they saw the education of the young as the main means of converting the Lotuho. Thus the students became the main channel for reaching this goal. The schools were, then, typical of an Exotic Communication approach. They were introduced, run and controlled by outsiders. . . .
>
> Initially the schools were located on the mission stations. These were perceived by the Lotuho as foreign. The invitation to students to come there was initially somewhat threatening. The boys were badly needed to herd the cattle, guard the crops etc., and leaving their homes to go to school put a heavy strain on the households. . . .
>
> It is, however, evident that at some point the communication efforts of the Verona Fathers tied in with a wider indigenous network, otherwise no contact could have been established. How did this happen? . . .
>
> To begin with, the Fathers directed the work particularly towards the *aduri horwong* (teenage boys). In traditional societies this particular group did not have access to the public domain of the adult world. The fact that it was through converted *aduri horwong* that Christianity became introduced conveyed quite emphatically that it was not meant for communal use.
>
> Christianity would not have become universally accepted had it only come through this one channel. . . . The change came when the students had grown up and become catechists or teachers. They had left school and some of them found employment in government or mission service. Quite a number had also returned home to their villages and settled there. They had been initiated, had married, usually in the traditional Lotuho fashion, and were making a living as Lotuho farmers. They participated also, with few exceptions, in the traditional Lotuho festivals and rites. They were part and parcel of the Lotuho communication system. . . . Their teaching, and per-

haps even more their very life, communicated to the Lotuho what it meant to be a Christian, and this information
spread through indigenous channels.

—Karl-Johan Lundstrom, *The
Lotuho and the Verona Fathers*

What does this model of change show us for Christian ministry? Of the many areas it affects, a few significant implications are suggested.

1. *Lay involvement in the church's ministry is not optional,
but essential.*

Full-time or professional clergy may be outstanding
pulpit preachers or superb radio and television speakers,
but may still have little effect in evangelizing the unchurched. How is that possible, especially given the slick
media productions of some clergy?

The "professional" ministry can do an excellent job
through the public media (which include the pulpit)—a
very necessary job of making people aware of possibilities
for change. But the weighing of alternatives—consideration of the change and all that would be required—will
still be done through interpersonal networks. Professional clergy can enter only a very few of those networks,
and most of those will be composed of other people like
themselves. Their personal influence for change is absent
from the very networks most important for evangelistic
impact. Further, the networks including largely unchurched people will probably *not* perceive what the
clergy are saying. The professional preachers will be
"screened out," unless initially they touch on a point
where there is felt need.

> Without lay evangelism, there will be little evangelism.

Christians who live and work with the unchurched
can be an integral part of their networks. From that strategic position, Christians can find opportunities to do
more than make their friends aware of the Christian message; they will be part of the consideration and choice
process. Then when the choice is made to become a follower of Jesus Christ, the Christian is still there to assist in
the action and readjustment stages. There is no way that
a professional clergyperson, no matter how gifted, can do
this critically important work.

The third quarter of the twentieth century strikingly
demonstrated that public media are supplementary in
evangelistic growth of the church. Limited almost entirely
to interpersonal networks because of repression, forbidden from having public meetings, churches nevertheless
grew significantly in numbers in countries where they

> Several non-Christian groups have demonstrated the validity of this model in their rapid growth. A notable example is Soka Gakkai of Japan. In 1950 they had nine thousand members; in 1970, membership was twenty million. Only the president and two hundred publications workers were on the payroll in that period. Their publications concentrated on presenting their beliefs and giving instruction to those who made the choice to become part of Soka Gakkai.

could not use most public media—for example, China, Ethiopia, and eastern Zaire (during days of civil war).

Where outward circumstances forced strengthening of interpersonal networks, response to the Gospel greatly increased.

2. *Media usage does not need to be geared to an immediate decision for its maximum effectiveness.*

A decision, as we have seen, is a process. It does not occur at a single point. The act of choosing to follow Christ follows after other actions that make that choice possible—feeling a need, becoming aware of a way to meet that need, and becoming interested in the Christian alternative. Consideration of what it would mean to be a Christian, usually with close friends, prepares the way for the critical choice to be made. Opportunity to express that choice and help in readjusting commitments, relationships, and lifestyle follow the choice. All these steps together should be considered the decision.

In bringing a person to Christ, which step is most important? No step is more important than another. All of the steps must be made to complete the journey, beginning with a sense of need and ending with a life of faith in Christ. Concentration only on the pivotal step of choice is somewhat like building a bridge over a river by concentrating only on the span over the water. Ignoring the piers that support the bridge or the approaches to the bridge would mean that the center span leads from nowhere to nowhere. If somehow it is suspended over the river, it will collapse under the slightest pressure.

Far too often, evangelism efforts concentrate only on the time of choice, disregarding the essential steps leading to that point and support for the choice after it is made. Where such concentration appears to give numerical results, it is because others have done the preparatory work and stand by to help those who have made the decision to believe.

3. *Media usage must be related to local church ministries if it is to have maximum effectiveness.*

Who is not impressed with great rows of lights, microphones hanging from the ceiling and sprouting from the floor, huge control boards with sliding switches, and glowing lights—all the paraphernalia associated with media use? Think, too, of the vast reach of the signals sent from transmitting towers, or the incredible speed with which high-quality magazines and books are produced on giant presses. It is all overwhelmingly powerful. What

It is commonly admitted that mass communication largely exists to diffuse information. But it does not have to be so limited.

Probably that is the "threat" the so-called electronic church poses for the rest of us. They use television only as a part—I think less than half—of their communication. They may not fully achieve groupness when they add telephones and computers massively to personalise communications between the evangelist or his staff and the individual listeners. Yet without doubt, listeners who not only listen but who use the telephones and write and receive letters feel very strong groupness—they identify themselves with the evangelist's entourage and with his mission. It is a powerful stratagem. . . .

The evangelists, starting with nothing at all except a call to witness, build mass bases that are similar in effect to groups, by intention and thought.

—Robert Cramer, "Many Groups, One World"

possible need is there for the local church, except to channel funds to these megaministries?

Regardless of their might, the media are effective
only at certain points in the total process of bringing a
person to faith in Jesus Christ. The media must link to interpersonal networks for their message to be adequately
considered. The networks that can be most useful for this
are those centered in the local church. The people there
are most likely to be helpful in the vital consideration
stage. If non-Christians or "anti-Christians" are the recipients' major interpersonal contacts, the message will certainly have a far smaller chance of acceptance.

After a choice is made to become a follower of
Christ, the interpersonal networks are critically important in helping the new convert develop in understanding. The strengthening that comes through those networks is also necessary for growth in consistent daily
obedience to Christ. Such interrelated networks in the local church provide the essential fellowship for becoming
established in faith and in turn reaching out to others.

4. *Opportunities for public expression must be given to confirm the choice made individually and privately.*

A choice to follow Christ can be, and often is, made
privately and individually. The choice is certainly real
even though it is not made in a public setting. But if it is
not later confirmed by some public action, two things are
lost: the strengthening of resolve that comes from making
a public commitment (communication increases commitment) and identification with a supportive interpersonal
network.

Public expression of belief is essential if the convert
is to gain a necessary supportive social group. Through
public commitment the believer makes a clear identification with that group, even though the old dominant social
group remains highly influential.

5. *Those who are caring for the new convert, attempting to
establish him or her in the Christian life, must make an active effort to provide new interpersonal relationships to assist Christian
growth.*

Every believer needs a Christian reference group.
That group can model appropriate behavior and discuss
problems in the Christian life, following the biblical command to encourage, exhort, rebuke, and approve. The
believer's growth certainly has its foundation in the private devotional life, but it is worked out in relation to
some reference group. If that group is not essentially

> Unless the average person is
> involved, the message will
> simply not be considered in
> the interpersonal networks. In
> matters of belief and faith, the
> layperson is frequently a more
> effective evangelist than the
> professional pastor.

Christian, even private devotional habits will wither. The stimulus to full and consistent obedience to Christ and his Word will be lost.

A key part of helping a new believer to be firm in the choice to follow Christ is linking him or her to such a Christian group. Formal teaching of the content of faith is needed, as is the establishment of personal prayer and study of Scripture. It must also be remembered that we are, as believers, made a part of the body of Christ. That body has many members, interrelated in worship of God and service for him. The Christian group at the interpersonal level is a basic expression of the body.

Sometimes more change will result from a shared cup of coffee than from hours of public speeches.

▼ CASE STUDY: EVANGELISTIC CONCERTS

Prior to a ministry tour in Europe, the leader of a Christian singing group outlined how the group would deliberately seek to link the interpersonal networks with public media. The public medium in this case was the group's concerts. Following is a condensation of the plan.

An evangelistic music group with high quality music and message can gain entrance to media (recordings, radio, television, and press), drawing large numbers of people to concerts. But there are two closely related problems that need to be solved to improve a group's ministry. First, to be effective media need to be as localized and specialized as possible. Second, the nature of the group's ministry lends itself to a "hit and run" style. The group doesn't become personally involved with a specific situation, so local ministries never benefit from the full potential of the group. Steps can be taken to minimize those problems.

1. Ministry must begin and end within interpersonal networks. The music group must have the framework of an already existing group of believers—a church, a missionary team, any existing group of believers—in order to best perform their ministry.

Well in advance of the first meeting, the sponsoring group will receive from the music group publicity materials, including an album of the group's music. This is to familiarize the sponsors with the visitors, setting the stage for the first personal meeting.

2. Four to six weeks before the concert (or the beginning of the period of ministry), members of the music group come to the area to meet with the sponsoring group. The meeting should be informal and preferably at an already existing meeting time, such as a weekly Bible study or a church dinner. The leader of the sponsoring group should ensure that his working group members are present, who will be doing preparation and follow-up.

This meeting is to become personally acquainted, not to go through a formal agenda. Interaction is the key.

332

Though it is not a time for public performing, some informal music may be done that is suitable for the interactive setting. As a result of this beginning time together, rapport with the music group should be established, leading to increased commitment to the goals of the concert, and motivation of sponsors to share about the music group in their interpersonal networks.

3. Posters and advertisements in press, radio, and TV will support and authenticate the word-of-mouth advertising. The most significant source of audience for the concert is through the networks of sponsoring group members.

4. Arrangements that the sponsoring group must make to effectively arrange the concert and publicize it will be given, primarily in written materials. The music group will make clear its readiness to advise in the preparations, and its own specific needs during the ministry period.

5. The music group also achieves some objectives in this first meeting—establishment of rapport with the sponsors, some orientation to the area and cultural setting, and beginning to understand the people's needs, preferences in musical styles, and their value system as it relates to proclaiming the Gospel.

Before the next meeting, the sponsoring group will have much to do in preparation for the concert—publicity, housing, concert location, ticket sales, prayer support. Much of this depends on involvement of interpersonal networks and will give many opportunities for witnessing. The music group will correspond with the sponsoring group during this time, showing their interest in the coming concert, and sharing the results of concerts in other areas.

6. The second meeting between the music group and the sponsors should be more formal, covering preparation for the concerts and the follow-up program. This should begin a period of steady interaction between the two groups of at least 2 or 3 days prior to a concert, and longer if a series of concerts is possible. Other meetings follow, both for informal interaction and prayer as well as for necessary business.

The sponsoring group needs encouragement in the completion of its tasks. The close contact now will give excellent input through interpersonal networks for inviting and bringing people to the concert. The great majority of the concert audience will decide to come "at the last minute," as a result of personal invitations to something already publicized in the media.

The music group needs, at this point, deepening knowledge of the area and the interests of its people. Being there well before the concert helps greatly in tailoring the program to the expected audience in terms of music styles, sequence of numbers, and comments given. Technical reasons also require members to be there in advance, to ensure that all is adequately prepared. Physical and psychological rest is also necessary, and clear time for spiritual preparation before the actual concert.

Toward the end of the concert, after presentation of the Gospel message and an invitation to personally receive Christ, comment cards will be available for the audience. The sponsoring group will use these for follow-up. They will look for professions of faith in Christ, those desiring more information or wanting to be involved in a bible study. The music group will greatly benefit from the audience feedback concerning both the message and the music.

Immediately following the final song of the concert comes a very significant time for interpersonal interaction. Members of the music group come offstage and mingle with the audience that wish to talk. Where possible, a nearby place is announced where there is an informal setting conducive to informal interaction—light refreshments, chairs, space to move about, etc. During this time as conversations develop, individual invitations are given to some type of follow-up meeting.

This after-meeting helps build a bridge between the media oriented concert and the interpersonal networks of the sponsoring group. In the days following the concert, the music group will stay in the area to be available for help in follow-up, beginning of Bible studies, or preparation for personal witnessing. Music group members may go one-on-one with members of the sponsoring group to follow up on contacts developing from the concert.

Follow-up concerts primarily for Christians can be scheduled in the future to reinforce commitments made earlier. Music workshops may be planned, led by the music group, to help local people develop their own music groups or enhance the music side of their group worship.

—From an unpublished paper by
John Bowers, Western Seminary

Careful thought has yielded a plan that links the media with the interpersonal approach. The plan demonstrates an effective approach that links the two essential parts of effective Christian communication.

SUMMARY

Making the decision to change begins with a sense of need. It is a six- stage process:

1. **Awareness** *of an alternative to the present behavior or beliefs*

2. **Interest** *in one or more of the alternatives*

3. **Consideration** *of the alternatives to see whether one is sufficiently attractive to make a change worthwhile*

*4. **Choice** of which alternative to follow, or a choice to reject all of the available alternatives*

*5. **Action** to implement the choice that is already made, thereby making an internal choice visible*

*6. **Readjustment** of behavior patterns, friends, and even lifestyle as a result of the decision that has been made.*

The process of change is best seen as a series of circular movements in which there is an apparent moving back and forth between the various stages of decision-making change. One innovation frequently leads to another, and then another. Change is a continuous process growing out of discontent with the present and a new awareness of possibilities.

Communication can stimulate change, in different ways at different points in the process of change. Massive effort may be wasted if it is directed at accomplishing the right thing at the wrong stage in the process. The kind of communication most influential at each stage can be outlined as follows:

• Awareness and interest: Use of public media—meetings, rallies, and parades as well as radio, television and the press—is highly effective for arousing the desire for change.

• Consideration and choice: Interpersonal networks are most influential at this point in change. Thought and discussion among friends weigh new benefits against the loss of familiarity and existing advantages.

• Action and readjustment: After the choice to change is made, both the media and interpersonal networks are useful in guiding implementation and helping the readjustment that is necessary as a result of the change.

Adequate Christian communication strategy must use both interpersonal and media methods, supplementing each other.

▼ BIBLIOGRAPHY

Berger, Charles R., and Steven H. Chaffee, eds. *Handbook of Communication Science*. Newbury Park, Calif.: Sage, 1987.

Engel, James F. *Contemporary Christian Communication*. Nashville: Nelson, 1979.

Goodenough, Ward Hunt. *Cooperation in Change.* New York: Russell Sage Foundation, 1963.

Hovland, Carl I., Irving L. Janis, and Harold H. Kelley. *Communication and Persuasion: Psychological Studies of Opinion Change.* New Haven: Yale University Press, 1953.

James, Ross W., ed. *Case Studies in Christian Communication in an Asian Context.* Manila: OMF Literature, 1989.

Kincaid, D. Lawrence, ed. *Communication Theory: Eastern and Western Perspectives.* Human Communication Research Series. New York: Harcourt Brace Jovanovich, 1987.

Klapper, Joseph. *The Effects of Mass Communication.* New York: Free Press, 1960.

23

➤ Feedback is a critical concept, maybe *the* critical one. (Robert Cramer)

➤ When you become aware of what is happening, you can know how to make the right things happen.

REACTING TO RESPONSE

PROPOSITION 23: Perceived and actual feedback shapes the message.

Once there was a young fellow who was given an old car. Having his own car had been his dream, so he washed, polished, changed the oil—doing everything he knew how to do. He purchased a mechanic's manual to learn how to tune up the engine. Then he decided to make some changes. He installed new fenders and bumpers and added a thin stripe that ran from the front to the back. The car really looked great.

Finally he decided to take it for a short drive. As the car began moving, there was a peculiar noise, "Whooom—thump—rrrreeee," then again, "Whooom—thump—rrrreeee." He stopped, got out, and looked all around the car. Then he found the trouble: a flat tire and a wheel that was flat on one side. The car could barely move because that one wheel was so flat, but of course it was flat only on one side. What could the young fellow do now?

He could make the engine more powerful so the car would go—even with one flat wheel. Or he could make all the wheels flat so the car would not shake as much: It would be symmetrical. He could simply forget about the flat wheel, now that he knew what was causing the noise, and try to drive as if the wheel were a normal round one.

337

Or he could take off the flat wheel and replace it with one that was perfectly round and complete.

There is little question what he would do (unless he is a very unusual and very stupid young fellow): Change the wheel. You can't go anywhere in a car whose wheels aren't round.

For most of us it seems easier to understand wheels and cars than to create understanding. But there is an important similarity. Just as a car needs complete round wheels to make progress, so the circle of communication must be complete for understanding to make progress. It is *feedback* that completes the circle.

Rather than completing the circle, some zealous workers try to get a more powerful engine. It seems easiest to "speak louder": building a bigger church building with a more polished program, memorizing a smoother presentation of spiritual truth, or trying in some other way to be more emphatic and overwhelm the audience. Completing the circle by listening to what the audience is saying, what the audience is needing and wanting, is a better way than shuffling them to one side while we proclaim.

By comparing our work with what others are doing, we can ignore the fact that the circle is not complete. That is similar to saying that one wheel isn't so bad because all the others are just as flat-sided. Our ministry may not be going well, but never mind, nobody else's is either! Or perhaps we admit that results are not what might be expected, but then we defend the lack by criticizing our critic's own shortcomings. "When they measure themselves

338

"OK, now do it again with a little more enthusiasm!"

by themselves and compare themselves with themselves, they are not wise" (2 Cor. 10:12).

Perhaps expecting things to go smoothly is expecting too much. We are in the world, and the world hates the things of God, so we can anticipate trouble, opposition, and attempts to stop Christian work. It is best merely to keep on doing what we are doing, showing our faithfulness and courage in the face of adversity. We know what is needed, they don't, so let's keep on keeping on. Whooom—thump—rrrreeee. Whooom—thump—rrrr-eeee.

The sensible course is to find out which wheel is flat and replace it. When our communication is one-sided, it simply is not complete, and the vehicle of understanding can make poor progress at best. How do we replace one-sided wheels—that is, how do we alter one-sided communication? By seeking feedback and paying attention to it.

339

Now, in human intercommunication, we often ask for feedback but it's doubtful just how often we really want it or intend to let it affect us. I don't know if that is the essential human condition or just a property of many groups whose communication I've been privileged to monitor and participate in. But I bravely assert it.

Feedback is a critical concept, maybe *the* critical one. There is something psychologically satisfying about venturing a response and seeing it have the effect of actually modifying the originator of the communication. . . .

One of the best definitions of communication known to me is interchange, where both or all participants are fully open to others' persuasiveness and their own change.

—Robert Cramer, "Many Groups, One World"

Progress toward understanding is stopped when communication efforts are only one-way. The vital, and missing, element is usually feedback—inviting our intended audience to participate with us in the process.

We constantly respond to other people. What they say and do shapes how we act, what we think about, even what we become. That is feedback. Without it there is hesitancy and uncertainty: Is this really what I should do? Am I doing this right? What now? As discussed often in earlier chapters, we are social creatures and depend on other people for stimulation, guidance, and approval. Much of their response is informal feedback of which we are not consciously aware. When we become aware of feedback, we can raise its value for our personal live and our ministries.

The pastor of a small suburban church was puzzled and hurt by the steady drop in attendance at services. Some members left formally, others simply disappeared. He prayed; he thought. He tried to organize things better, giving careful instructions to ushers, deacons, and elders, telling them exactly what to do so that everything would function smoothly. That did not seem to help.

Some sympathetic members saw that the pastor was not succeeding in his ministry. So they came to him with comments they had heard: "We're not getting anything out of the sermons." "What the pastor says does not relate to my life." "He does not seem to care what I think."

Of course the pastor was hurt. He defended his actions: "That's their problem; it's not mine." He did not change. People stopped trying to talk about how they felt and "voted with their feet" by leaving the church. Just before the church died, the pastor resigned and left, too.

The pastor was trying to run the ministry of the church with an incomplete wheel; he did not solicit and did not want honest feedback, so the circle of communication remained incomplete.

In a study involving more than two hundred interviews with Christian workers from approximately twenty-five nations of Africa, Asia, Europe, and North America, remarkably similar answers were given to the question, "Why do some church services seem ineffective in causing significant change in Christian conduct?"

The answer given most frequently (87.5 percent) was a variation of these:

> The speaker may not know his audience, their problems, life situations, or their needs in general. The message will not touch them in any way. . . .
>
> Preachers do not try to relate their sermons to the needs of the people.
>
> The speaker may not be actively involved in the daily lives of the congregation. Because he is not involved, his mental image of the audience may be incorrect bringing him to the wrong conclusion as to kind of messages needed and how to present them.
>
> The speaker may be more interested in the message and its presentation than in the audience.
>
> As a result of his lack of exposure to the audience, he has an improper attitude toward the audience, thinking they are not interested in spiritual matters or are not capable of understanding "the deep things of God."

Frequent comments (55 percent) were made about a lack of listening to the congregation:

> The situation is made worse if some feedback mechanism is neither used nor encouraged. This means there is no live relationship between the two parties involved in communication—thus, no communication.
>
> The process of communication is not understood and feedback is minimal.

The study findings were well summed up by one participant, "The people fulfill their perceived function of 'coming to church' without expectation of change—and thus, no change occurs."

Deliberately seeking feedback and proper use of feedback to modify the form and presentation of the message are the missing element in the Christian ministries referred to by these widely scattered ministers and missionaries.

When a person is strongly convinced of the correctness of the message, it is all too easy to slip over the line that separates message from method. The method becomes as absolutely right as the message itself. Arrogance and closed-mindedness, qualities of a faulty messenger,

It is often emotionally difficult to accept negative feedback. But failure to try leads to deterioration in communication. More than a flat-sided wheel may result; the circle may break completely, destroying any possibility of understanding.

Disturbed by seemingly arrogant memos from a co-worker, a teacher sent a reply that stated exactly what the memos seemed to be saying and the attitude they projected. The co-worker's response did nothing to correct the circle; it did not give the message "I'm sorry you did not understand what I was saying." Instead, all the blame was put on the other person. No attempt was made to find ways through feedback for clarification of the issues or improvement of style.

Feedback is such a common part of activities that we do not always realize we are using feedback to change our behavior. The challenge in improving communication is to make conscious use of signals that we continually receive.

seem to become qualities of the message. Listening to feedback is a way to avoid this.

Feedback is everywhere. It completes the circle, turning monologue into dialogue. But all feedback is not of equal value. How can we distinguish between what is worthwhile and what is best discarded?

Informal feedback is normally part of all social interaction, whether in conversations, parties, classrooms, meetings, or business transactions. We simply need to learn how to recognize and interpret it. The twelve signal systems show in how many different ways that feedback can come.

In our home culture we can "read" the signals easily, but in new cultural settings it is very possible to misinterpret those signals. Have the guests left food on the plate because they did not like it, to show that the portion was so generous that they could not eat it all? Is the workman refusing to look me in the eye because he is dishonest, or to show respect? Learning how to understand the signals given is the first step to making good use of informal feedback.

Learning comes through listening and observing. Silent awareness is often the best way to gain valuable feedback. It also shows clearly that you want feedback, that you are trying to learn, and that other people are important to you. It is the listener who is most likely to minister to others. "The missionaries who learned most from the

Lotuho, were also the ones who contributed most to the Lotuho understanding of their message." Karl-Johan Lundstrom's summary statement rests on a thorough analysis of more than forty years of missionary work among the Lotuho of southern Sudan ("The Lotuho and the Verona Fathers").

Giving feedback to others is clearly an important responsibility, one that must be handled with great care. As you are listening, you can usually determine what response will be accepted. Sometimes the feedback you want to give is not the feedback sought: At best, what you offer will not be heard; at worst, it can lead to argument and broken relationships.

A Christian living in a Mediterranean Muslim culture was troubled by the undisciplined behavior of friends' children. The wife, Fatima, especially was constantly complaining about how unruly and how "bad" their children were.

> We asked them if they would like to study what the Bible said about disciplining children, to which they gave a polite yes. However, the study and my talking fell on deaf ears. There was no feedback. But their complaints about their own children continued, and no reference was ever made to our study.
>
> Watching other families of that culture, I began to see that this complaining was merely a favorite theme for casual conversation among friends and neighbors. It was

Frankly, listening is hard work. Research shows that when a person truly listens, the heart beats faster, more blood circulates, and body temperature rises slightly.

Listening is hard work because most people think about four times faster than a person can talk. Most people speak from 150 to 300 words per minute. But we can hear from 400 to 1,000 words per minute. So, it's easy to let our minds wander while others are talking.
—*Oregon Prison Fellowship Newsletter*, Summer 1988

YIKES! NO! ARRG!

"So . . . if there are no more comments, we'll change the order of worship on Sunday."

343

just something to talk about, and actually a way of asking for a compliment from the listener. The parent wanted to hear in response to his complaint, "Oh no! He's not bad, he's a good boy!" My talking was irrelevant since they had no felt need in that area. I had formed my message (that the Bible is relevant to life) around a misperception of my audience.

At other times, attempted feedback will be rejected because the person is openly defensive. Even implied criticism arouses resentment. It can be made more palatable by stating your praise for the person first (but the commendation must be honest, not merely sugar water!) and then raising questions in troublesome areas, rather than embarking on a direct confrontation. Feedback is so valuable that it is worth risking friends' temporary upset in order to help them gain a more accurate picture of what they are doing. Even so, there are cultures in which any kind of negative feedback is never overtly given. The praise you receive for your work must be tempered by the small clues that will show true response to your efforts.

When you are the target of critical feedback, it is hard not to be defensive—but it is well worth the effort. Listen! While others talk out their disagreement or dislike of your work, listen closely. Ask questions that help to bring out the whole picture as they see it. Paraphrase what they have said, and ask whether that is what is meant. When they have finished, thank them for their opinions. Then take your notes and privately try to evaluate what has been said, so that you can learn from it. Do not try to fight back—it takes two for an argument. Arguments rarely give valuable feedback.

Not all informal feedback has equal value. It takes the right people to give you the right feedback on each subject. There is no point in asking someone who does not speak Spanish how your Spanish fluency and pronunciation are developing. Your Scottish friend probably cannot tell you whether the East Indian curry you are cooking is well done, but he could tell you about kilts and heather. For opinions of value, ask those with knowledge about the subject.

▼ THE IMPACT OF "GHOST" FEEDBACK

There is another kind of informal feedback that has massive influence on most of our communication efforts. It is *perceived feedback*. Perceived feedback is what we think is there, but actually is not. It is "ghost" feedback, existing in the imagination. We react to it *as we think it is.* For example, we expect someone to be critical of the way we speak or even the fact that we are speaking. So we begin by apologizing for "daring to say something about this matter." We act afraid of negative comment before anyone has said anything—or even had time to think anything! There has been no feedback, but our message is shaped by our expectation of feedback.

Perceived feedback can be as powerful as real feedback in affecting the message; at times it is even more powerful. When our expectation is correct, there is no problem. But if we expect feedback different from the response that actually comes, our message will not have been "on target." We prepared it with a wrong view of the audience in mind. In effect, we talked with someone who was not there and ignored those who were there. We have already seen (proposition 8) how the communicator's image of the audience governs the timing, presentation, and content of the message. Anticipating a particular kind of feedback shapes the message as strongly as actually receiving that feedback.

It is very important to have a correct idea of the audience, to anticipate correctly what the feedback will be.

© 1979 Rob Portlock

"Of course, feel free anytime to let me know what you think of the job I'm doing as your pastor."

345

It is also critical to get accurate feedback—responses that are representative of the true reaction. Too often we hear from a few who claim to represent the whole and then base our response on the view of only those few. How can we be sure that the feedback we receive is truly representative of the whole group we wish to reach?

▼ THE NEED FOR FORMAL, SYSTEMATIC FEEDBACK

So far, we have talked about informal feedback, which is essentially unsystematic. Systematic feedback, usually called evaluation or research, is an essential part of any significant effort. It is recognized as an integral part of effort in education. No student earns certificates and degrees without evaluation. Often the evaluation, through examinations, reports, papers, and seminars, results in the student's redoing some work or even changing the achievements being attempted. Individuals, teachers, whole school systems, and teaching methods are routinely evaluated. But that is not always considered enough. "The lack of a strong evaluation component in most nonformal, or for that matter formal, education projects has hindered the development of learning systems with the result that errors are repeated and difficulties recur in education programs around the world." So concluded a review of educational innovations.

If researchers consider that education is not evaluated often and thoroughly enough, how do we stand in Christian ministry? Evaluation is essential if we are serious about winning the world, or any part of it, to Jesus Christ. Failing to seek systematic feedback through evaluation is failing to use our opportunities in a Spirit-guided manner. It can too easily result in blind and rigid adherence to irrelevant methods. Instead of our sensitivity to the Holy Spirit's leadership being increased, an unchallenged satisfaction (perhaps even smugness) dulls our sense of need for his direction.

Evaluation can happen at two levels, which will be labeled "unstructured" and "structured."

Unstructured evaluation is much like informal feedback. Seldom deliberate, it is nevertheless part of the normal give-and-take of communication. It is not systematic and not subject to the demands of research methodology. Information is collected as possible, in conjunction with other duties. This information can be very useful, particularly when it is noted and periodically reviewed.

Unstructured feedback on ministry can be increased in value if some guiding questions are kept in mind:

• Has the program effort brought renewal and revitalization to the existing churches?

• Is the continued ministry of the local churches enhanced as a result of the special effort? In other words, did the campaign or program open up new areas and new groups, demonstrating the effort's strategic value?

• Has the effort added *new converts* to the local churches?

• Are new churches resulting from the efforts? What percentage of the efforts are successful? What modifications does this indicate in methods? targets? personnel?

• Has the effort resulted in an ongoing movement, or has it remained one solitary event in the community?

Structured evaluation, by contrast, is a *deliberate* effort to get specific information about what is happening and how this outcome stacks up against objectives. It includes clearly identifying the audience and describing them, identifying the attitudes and responses of people involved, and collecting specific information that can guide ministry development. Structured feedback is formal and systematic, guided by methods of social research.

"Let's go over my sermon again. Surely I must have said something."

The Christian communicator who plans for feedback has many devices available—if the media are locally oriented. He can go to the city gathering places and to the villages, to seek interviews on the current goals and problems of the people. Opinions of the ordinary citizen must be sought and used. Forums can be made up of typical audience members. Local speakers can be used for broadcasts or articles. Encouragement, possibly even rewards, can be given for letters to the editor. Discussion groups centering in specific programs or article content have been used with great success. The possibilities for feedback are limited only by too little involvement with the target audience.

With any sizable program, structured evaluation should be planned as an integral part of the effort. Without accurate feedback, almost any program or organization can become a self-perpetuating machine with little regard to effectiveness and without even a clear recognition of what the goals are or ought to be. We need to know how much people understand of the message we bring, as well as how much and what they *mis*understand of that message. It is necessary to know what is accepted and practiced, and what is rejected. With which of our intended audiences have we failed to establish good communication? Beware of answering such weighty questions with guesses, supported by a few testimonies, some examples, and a letter or two.

One gentleman asked, "What is the value of research? I read a report, and it tells me nothing I did not already know." He is indeed a fortunate man! But even if he already thought a thing was true, now he *knows* it is true. After proper research is completed, guessing and indecision are no longer necessary. Good evaluative research removes the sting and division resulting from a thousand unresolved arguments over what is succeeding and what is best. Good evaluative research moves beyond the collection of illustrations that prove a point. It may be a thorough case study or a careful statistical study. Each of these kinds of formal feedback fills a particular need.

What makes good evaluative research—research that will provide critically needed systematic feedback? Six segments are present in good research design:

1. Defining the audience
2. Identifying program goals and objectives
3. Establishing criteria for measuring achievement
4. Determining what measurements will be used
5. Selecting sampling procedures
6. Interpretation of the findings

Defining the Audience

When there is no clear idea of who is involved in the communication process, there is no way to measure what is happening. Christians desire to tell the whole world of Christ, so the audience is everybody. Directors of an American Christian radio station listed among its objectives "to present instruction and challenge for the Christian of every age; to provide balanced Christian music, leaning to the conservative side; and to confront non-Christians with Christ's claim on their lives." That statement of intended audience is so broad that it includes anyone and everyone. While more sweeping than some, this view of a desired audience is common.

In fact, however, the audience will be much more sharply and narrowly defined. Where the initiator of communication does not have a clear view of the audience, the audience selects itself. Those who like what is offered will listen and have some reaction; those who dislike it will simply ignore the effort at communicating. A beginning step in formal feedback is to find out who the audience really is, separating desire from actuality.

Identifying Program Goals

What is it that the communication effort is trying to do? Certain types of objectives are obviously helpful and needed, such as to publish a magazine every month reaching a circulation of X thousand, or to produce five fifteen-minute programs each week teaching basic Gospel truths. This type of objective tells us exactly what we need to accomplish and helps us plan our work.

But it is possible to do a considerable amount of work and still accomplish little or nothing. What are the broad goals of a ministry? Can those goals be reduced to smaller goals that could be accomplished in a given period of time? Are the overall goals consistent with Scripture? Without a clear understanding of overall goals and repeated statement of them, specific objectives may be reached that merely keep us busy without going anywhere.

The overall goals guide evaluation; progress toward those goals is what must be seen. Checking for achievement of lesser objectives may not tell us anything about the effectiveness of our ministry.

Establishing Criteria

How will you know whether goals are being reached? One person may be satisfied with frequent mention of the ministry in Christian magazines, while another wants a large flow of letters from non-Christians. Often it is thought to be enough proof of God's blessing if an organization functions without major internal quarrels and the daily routine goes smoothly. Still another worker says that the final evidence is that all bills are paid and there is at least a small amount of money remaining. Which standard will be accepted for evaluating the work?

Standards acceptable to all interested parties must be fixed before any evaluation begins. Those standards must be met before it is possible to say that objectives or overall goals are being met. These standards, or criteria, must be considered both appropriate and acceptable as evidence by all who are concerned with the evaluation. Criteria must be observable—not a feeling or mood; measurable—objective in nature and independent of impressions, so that "how much" is something that can be expressed in numbers; and free of personal bias—the satisfaction of criteria being independent of personal wishes.

After the evaluative research has started, the criteria cannot be changed. That would be like changing the rules of a game after it has begun.

Choosing Measurement Methods

After criteria are decided, a method to measure those criteria must be selected. Often, direct measurements of spiritual ministries are impossible, yet indicators can be found that show what is happening. The indicators that can be measured can be used as criteria, if they are indeed relevant to the program goals.

Attendance at Christian meetings may be an indicator, both in totals and in regularity of specific members. Another indicator may be measurement of people's attitudes, using contemporary social research skills. Unsolic-

feedback

ited statements can also be an indicator of what is being accomplished.

Postal response is one of the most commonly used indicators of effectiveness for ministries. But caution must be exercised: Many studies indicate that people who write letters are not typical of the total audience. Two statistically valid studies of radio audiences in an African nation were compared with the results of a direct mail survey. The studies were done at the same time, to determine favorite radio stations. Ninety-three percent of the direct mail respondents indicated station A as their favorite. Among the general population measured in the statistical study, only 32 percent cited station A as their favorite. The comparison concluded, "If the direct mail data were all that Station A programmers had, they would be led to believe that they had captured the majority of the radio audience and that religion is one of the two most preferred program types. But the more valid data from the statistical study indicated just the opposite. Mail response and mailing list surveys are not valid indicators of effectiveness." Mail response does have value, but it must be cautiously interpreted lest misleading measures of effectiveness are obtained.

Survey questionnaires are the most popular form of audience measurement. But a great deal of good research can be done without ever using a survey questionnaire. Of the many types of social measurement tools available, which one is best? Which one is appropriate? Such questions are best answered by seeking guidance from a trained researcher.

After you have chosen the best tool, how is it used in a particular situation? Is there any way to be sure that the tool is working as expected? Supervised practice is often necessary before these various tools can be adequately used. It may be wisest not to attempt using professional tools in an amateur way. Undetected inaccuracies may so distort the findings that it might have been better not to have undertaken such research.

Sampling: Who Will Be Measured?

Who is to be measured? Will the entire audience be measured, or just the people who are readily available? or a special segment of the total audience? Measuring even a large number of people in no way guarantees that the results will be accurate for the total population. In fact, it will be more accurate to measure a small sample representatively drawn from the total population than to attempt to measure everyone in the population and fail. Accuracy is related to the number of people measured only if very strict conditions for sampling are followed.

Different results will be found when different segments of the population are measured. Measurement of a group that accurately represents your target audience, then, is fundamental to valid evaluative research. Quoting large numbers is often a way to sidestep the requirements of accurate sampling. The procedure used at this point determines the validity of the total study.

Interpretation: What Has Been Learned?

All the measurements have been taken, and there is a pile of dumb papers, sprinkled with mute numbers. How can these papers be made to speak and give the answers required? Simply coding the answers and processing numbers with a computer does not guarantee a meaningful result. Analysis of the responses requires several different skills—an understanding of the problems for which solutions are being sought, awareness of the cultural patterns of the group studied, and enough knowledge of statistics to handle the data correctly.

Fresh questions must be asked of the data. For example, is radio listenership related to age in this study? Do we find a relationship between income and church membership? What link does there appear to be between church membership and reading habits? Are there different patterns in use of television among different language groups? different economic groups? different educational levels? Some knowledge of communication theory is necessary in order to ask these questions and to be sure that important areas are not omitted.

The analysis must clearly show whether the criteria that were agreed upon as the marks of effective ministry have been met. A good analysis will indicate where further research is needed to clarify important points.

Parts of the evaluative research process can be done by any concerned person, but other parts require qualified personnel. This kind of research is a cooperative task. It cannot be adequately accomplished by an agency alone, nor can it be accomplished by the researcher alone. With cooperation, each party contributes strengths. The resulting research will be worth the time and effort involved.

▼ UTILIZING THE FEEDBACK

Having obtained a good, valid piece of evaluative research, what do we do with it? There is a useful three-step sequence (introduced in proposition 5) to guide the use of the report.

First, has activity in the program been relevant and as previously agreed? Frequently we set our objectives but fail to plan activities that would lead us toward those objectives. The evaluation report will tell us only whether we are reaching the objectives. It will not tell us whether we have followed the plan. It is not uncommon to find that a program is agreed upon, objectives are accepted, but then the program is not followed. Perhaps there are not enough finances or staff, or perhaps we have become so accustomed to doing things in a particular way that a new program is ignored. If the report says that we are not achieving our goals, but we realize that we have not even followed the program, the program should not necessarily be abandoned. We have not given it a chance.

Second, what alternative actions are possible? If we have failed to reach our objectives, though we have confirmed that our actions have been relevant to the objectives and as previously agreed, we must now consider changing the program. There may be difficulties in this: Once a program is under way it can be hard to stop. Workers become emotionally involved and do not like to consider their work a possible failure. But when evaluation shows that something is not working, change is imperative.

Third, is the goal realistic? Perhaps the work has been relevant to the objective, the program has been conducted as agreed, and there is the conviction that what is being done is correct. But still the goal is not being achieved. In such a situation, it may be right to reconsider the objectives. They may not be realistic; they may overlook problems later discovered or fail to take into account changed conditions. Goals should be changed only with great care. We run the risk of masking ineffectiveness by changing what we say we should do to conform with what has actually happened.

Why go to all this trouble for feedback? Why not just do what feels right and hope for the best? Formal feedback can help avoid six common dangers to straight thinking and good communication.

First, *premature conclusions.* Anxious to get ahead with the work, we receive the beginning of feedback and conclude that is the whole story. If we looked a little more deeply, we might have a completely different picture. Early returns in American elections seldom give a true picture of the final results. The early returns come from urban areas, which often vote differently from rural areas. Representative returns are needed if we are to gain a correct picture.

If a conclusion is reached prematurely, it can cause misperception of later feedback. What is negative is made to seem positive (or vice versa) if we have already made up our minds about the nature of the feedback. Generalizing too quickly from too little evidence is a serious danger.

Second, *ignoring adverse evidence.* This again is a problem of perception; we may not functionally perceive what feedback is really saying. We have decided on a certain course of action. Any evidence that says it should be otherwise is ignored. It is a case of the common jocular saying, "My mind is made up; don't confuse me with the facts."

Third, *thinking within fixed limits.* When Thomas Edison employed a highly trained mathematician, one of the first assignments was to calculate the spatial capacity of one of Edison's electric light globes. The mathematician spent three or four days using calculus and a number of sophisticated techniques, and finally he produced an answer. Edison looked at the pages of calculations, looked at the light globe, and said, "Looks good. I'll check it." He filled the globe with water, poured the water into a measuring cylinder, and told the mathematician, "You were almost right!" Water and a measuring cylinder were much easier to use than mathematical calculations. But the mathematician was trained to use mathematics, not to think creatively. He set limits on his thinking—and the best solution lay outside those limits.

Fourth, *the inability or failure to collect all the facts.* We may get some facts and think that we have them all. When we lack adequate awareness of the size of a task or the complexities involved, a few facts seem like a wealth of information. Without some knowledge of the overall task (in other words, theoretical knowledge) it is not possible to know how to gather required information or to know when enough has been gathered.

Fifth, *inaccuracy of our observations.* All of us see what we want to see in a particular situation—again, it is a problem of functional perception. Even trained observers will be influenced by personal bias, especially when they care about what they are observing. In the proclamation of God's Word, which of us does not care intensely about what is happening? Consequently, our observations about ministry are seldom completely accurate. Only the application of careful controls can help us toward more accurate observations.

Sixth, *mistaking coincidence for cause and effect.* Two things happen near each other in time, and we easily conclude that they are related. We change the music in church services and have an increased attendance. The color of a book jacket is changed, and sales increase. But has one thing *caused* the other? Or was the increased response due to some other unsuspected cause? Perhaps the increased attendance results from the fact that a new Christian began to visit more people and invite them to church. Perhaps the book is selling well because current events have suddenly made the topic important to people.

Without careful checking—careful further research in many cases—false understandings may develop. It is exactly in this way that superstitions begin—a black cat crossed my path last night and today I fell and hurt my leg; therefore, black cats produce bad luck. The rainmaker performs his ceremonies with precise dancing and words. Rain comes. But did it come because of the ceremony, or did the rainmaker hold his ceremony when he discerned that the rains were coming?

Proclaiming the Gospel on the basis of near-superstitions may result when we fail to distinguish between coincidence and cause-and-effect.

It is to avoid these mistakes in Christian ministry that we are compelled to seek formal feedback. It is not a substitute for the Spirit's leading, but a way to see his leading more clearly. Our humanness limits our ability to see clearly. But God has given us the means to see his best more clearly amid many lesser alternatives.

▼ A BIBLICAL PERSPECTIVE

There are practical reasons that we should attempt to measure effectiveness in ministry, but is it biblical for us to do so? No passage directly commands, "Measure effectiveness," but many suggest that that is what should be done. For example, Matthew 25:14-30 gives us Christ's parable of use of resources. Differing amounts of money were allotted to different servants, and they were expected to use the money effectively. The two who did were praised and given reward, while the one who did not was condemned. Christ used the story to teach, "For everyone who has will be given more, and he will have an abundance. Whoever does not have, even what he has will be taken from him." Clearly the servants were evaluated, and they received direct feedback: "And throw that worthless servant outside" (Matt. 25:29–30). With such serious warning, it would indeed be folly to ignore consideration of effectiveness in our service.

Adam and Eve received feedback from their actions. So did Abraham, Joseph, and Moses. Perhaps the easiest example to grasp is Gideon, who sought to know God's leading by putting a fleece outside on successive nights. He agreed on criteria, and God worked within those human conditions so that Gideon could clearly know what he was to do. Paul received feedback, some that encouraged him and some that nearly killed him—stoning at Lystra, a riot in Ephesus, imprisonment in Jerusalem. The letters to the seven churches of Asia Minor at the beginning of Revelation are incisively penetrating feedback on the state of the churches as Christ viewed them.

Repeatedly, feedback is modeled and given through Scripture. And it promises a Day when the whole world will have devastatingly accurate feedback from God him-

self. "And I saw the dead, great and small, standing before the throne, and books were opened. Another book was opened, which is the book of life. The dead were judged according to what they had done as recorded in the books. . . . Behold, I am coming soon! My reward is with me, and I will give to everyone according to what he has done" (Rev. 20:12; 22:12).

Feedback completes the circle of communication in human affairs, and in God's eternal purposes.

SUMMARY

The communication process is not complete until the intended receiver has reacted to the transmitted message. Since communication is an act of creating understanding that involves two or more parties, communication is incomplete until understanding has developed.

In interpersonal communication, the response is prompt and has immediate effect on the shaping and reshaping of the message. Feedback is slower and more difficult to obtain in mass media, but should nevertheless have an important effect on shaping the message. Accurate feedback is critically important for all kinds of communication.

Informal feedback is pervasive and often not directly recognized. Formal feedback is a deliberate effort to determine response—an effort that is particularly important when the communicating parties are removed from each other by space, time, or social structure. Methods of evaluative research provide basic approaches to obtain accurate feedback in such cases.

▼ BIBLIOGRAPHY

Bernard, H. Russell. *Research Methods in Cultural Anthropology.* Newbury Park, Calif.: Sage, 1988.

Cramer, Robert. "Many Groups, One World." *Media Development* 28, no. 2 (1981).

Engel, James. *How Can I Get Them to Listen? A Handbook on Communication Strategy and Research.* Grand Rapids: Zondervan, 1977.

Fowler, Floyd J., Jr. *Survey Research Methods.* Applied Social Research Methods Series. Vol. 1. Newbury Park, Calif.: Sage, 1984.

Lowry, Dennis T. *A General outline for Conducting Program Evaluation Studies*. Daystar Occasional Paper. Nairobi: Daystar Communications, 1975.

Lundstrom, Karl-Johan. *The Lotuho and The Verona Fathers: A Case Study of Communication in Development*. Doctoral diss., Uppsala University, Sweden, 1990.

Miller, Donald E. "Evaluating the Effectiveness of Christian Mass Media Output." *Spectrum* (Fall–Winter 1975). Wheaton College Graduate School.

Morris, Lynn Lyons, and Carol Taylor Fitz-Gibbon. *Evaluator's Handbook*. Beverly Hills, Calif.: Sage, 1978.

Smith, Donald K. *How Do We Know Who Is Listening?* Daystar Occasional Paper. Nairobi: Daystar Communications, 1970.

Treece, Eleanor Walters, and James William Treece, Jr. *Elements of Research in Nursing*. St. Louis: Mosby, 1982.

Yin, Robert K. *Case Study Research*. Applied Social Research Methods Series. Vol. 5. Beverly Hills, Calif.: Sage, 1989.

General Bibliography

Adler, Ron, and Neil Towne. *Looking Out/Looking In: Interpersonal Communication.* San Francisco: Rinehart, 1975.

Aldrich, Joseph C. *Life-Style Evangelism.* Portland, Oreg.: Multnomah Press, 1981.

Alexander, John. *The Other Side* (January 1978).

Allen, Roland. *The Compulsion of the Spirit: A Roland Allen Reader.* Edited by David Paton and Charles H. Long. Grand Rapids: Eerdmans, 1983.

Anderson, Alpha E. *Pelendo.* Minneapolis: Free Church Publications, 1967.

Anderson, James A., and Timothy P. Meyer. *Mediated Communication: A Social Action Perspective.* Beverly Hills, Calif.: Sage, 1988.

Arthur H. *The Grieving Indian.* Winnipeg: Intertribal Christian Communications, 1988.

Augsburger, David. *Caring Enough to Hear.* Ventura, Calif.: Regal, 1982.

_____. "Communication Is Co-Response." *Spectrum* 4 no. 1. Wheaton College Graduate School.

_____. "Writing Is Translating," *Festival Quarterly* (Summer 1975).

Augustine. *On Christian Doctrine.* Translated by D. W. Robertson, Jr. New York: Macmillan, 1986.

Backman, Carl W., and Paul F. Secord. *A Social Psychological View of Education.* New York: Harcourt, Brace, 1968.

Baehr, Theo. *Getting the Word Out: How to Communicate the Gospel in Today's World.* San Francisco: Harper & Row, 1986.

Bailey, Faith C. *Adoniram Judson: Missionary to Burma.* Chicago: Moody Press, 1980.

Bales, Robert F. "How People Interact in Conferences." *Scientific American* 192 (1955), 31–55.

Banasik, Sandra. "A Living Language." *Wherever* (Spring 1982).

Barbara, Dominick A. *How to Make People Listen to You.* Springfield, Ill.: Charles C. Thomas, 1971.

Barnlund, Dean C. "A Transactional Model of Communication." In *Foundation of Communication Theory.* Edited by Kenneth Soreno and C. David Mortenson. New York: Harper & Row, 1970.

Barnouw, Victor. *Culture and Personality.* Homewood, Ill.: Dorsey Press, 1973.

Bauer, Raymond A. "The Audience." In *Handbook of Communication.* Edited by Ithiel de Sola Pool et al. Chicago: Rand McNally, 1973.

_____. "The Communicator and the Audience." *Journal of Conflict Resolutions* 2, no. 1 (March 1958), 66–77.

Bavinck, J. H. *An Introduction to the Science of Missions.* Part 2. (Inleiding in de Zendingswetenschap.) Translated by David Hugh Freeman. Philadelphia: Presbyterian and Reformed, 1960.

Bayly, Joseph T. *Psalms of My Life.* Wheaton, Ill.: Tyndale House, 1969.

Berger, Charles R., and Steven H. Chaffee, eds. *Handbook of Communication Science.* Newbury Park, Calif.: Sage, 1987.

Bernard, H. Russell. *Research Methods in Cultural Anthropology.* Newbury Park, Calif.: Sage, 1988.

Bernstein, Theodore. *Watch Your Language!* New York: Great Neck Press, 1958.

Booth-Butterfield, Melanie, and Steve Booth-Butterfield. "Conceptualizing Affect as Information in Communication Production." *Human Communication Research* 16, no. 4 (1990), 451–76.

Botts, Timothy. "God Is for Me!" In *Doorposts.* Wheaton, Ill.: Tyndale House, 1986.

Bready, J. Russell. *England: Before and After Wesley.* New York: Russell and Russell, 1938.

Brewster, E. Thomas, and Elizabeth S. Brewster. "Bonding and the Missionary Task." In *Perspectives on the World Christian Movement.* Pasadena, Calif.: William Carey Library, 1981.

Brislin, Richard W. *Cross-Cultural Encounters: Face-to-Face Interaction.* New York: Pergamon, 1981.

Brislin, Richard W., et al. *Intercultural Interactions: A Practical Guide.* Cross-Cultural Research Methodology Series 9. Beverly Hills, Calif.: Sage, 1986.

Browne, Benjamin P. *Interlit.* Elgin, Ill.: David C. Cook Foundation, 1972.

Burke, James. *The Day the Universe Changed.* Denver: Little Books, 1987.

Burt, Ronald S., and Michael J. Minor. *Applied Network Analysis: A Methodological Introduction.* Beverly Hills, Calif.: Sage, 1983.

Carpenter, Ted. *They Became What They Beheld.* New York: Outerbridge & Diestfrey, 1970.

Carroll, John B., ed. *Language, Thought, and Reality: Selected Writings of Benjamin Lee Whorf.* Cambridge, Mass.: MIT Press, 1956.

Cartwright, Dorwin. "Achieving Change in People." *Human Relations Journal* 4, no. 4 (1951), 381–92.

Chaffee, Steven H., and Charles R. Berger. "What Communication Scientists Do." In *Handbook of Communication Science.* Edited by Charles R. Berger and Steven H. Chaffee. Newbury Park, Calif.: Sage, 1987.

Chu, Godwin C., Syed A. Rahim, and D. Lawrence Kincaid. *Communication for Group Transformation in Development.* Communication Monographs 2. Honolulu: East-West Communication Institute, 1976.

Cicero de Oratore. Translated by E. W. Sutton. Vol. 1, book 1. Cambridge: Harvard University Press, 1942.

Claus, Tom, and Dale W. Kietzman, eds. *Christian Leadership in Indian America.* Chicago: Moody Press, 1976.

Common Ground (April 1987). Lutherville, Md.: Search Ministries.

Cramer, Robert. "Many Groups, One World." *Media Development* 28, no. 2 (1981).

Crouch, Paul, and Win Arn. "Is TV Appropriate for Mass Evangelism?" *Christianity Today* (16 October 1987).

Davidman, Joy. *Smoke on the Mountain.* Philadelphia: Westminster, 1954.

Davis, R. J. *Africa Now* 45 (8 July 1969). Sudan Interior Mission.

Deats, Richard. "Discovering the Enemy." *The Other Side.*

Delia, Jesse G. "Communication Research: A History." In *Handbook of Communication Science.* Edited by Charles R. Berger and Steven H. Chaffee. Newbury Park, Calif.: Sage, 1987.

De Sola Pool, Ithiel. "Mass Media and Their Interpersonal Social Functions." In *People, Society and Mass Communication.* Edited by Lewis A. Dexter and David Manning White. New York: Free Press, 1964.

De Sola Pool, Ithiel, et al., eds. *Handbook of Communication.* Chicago: Rand McNally, 1973.

Dexter, Lewis A., and David Manning White, eds. *People, Society and Mass Communications.* New York: Free Press, 1964.

Doob, Leonard W. *Communication in Africa: A Search for Boundaries.* New Haven: Yale University Press, 1961.

Dougherty, Janet W. D., ed. *Directions in Cognitive Anthropology.* Urbana: University of Illinois Press, 1985.

DuBois, Cora. "The Dominant Value Profile of American Culture." *American Anthropologist* 57 (1955).

Ellis, Jane. "Broadcasting to Russia: How Much Is Getting Through?" *Spectrum* (Winter 1977–1978). Wheaton College Graduate School.

Engel, James F. *Contemporary Christian Communications.* Nashville: Nelson, 1979.

_____. *How Can I Get Them to Listen? A Handbook on Communication Strategy and Research.* Grand Rapids: Zondervan, 1977.

_____. "Whom Do We Serve—the Sheep or the Shepherd?" *Spectrum* (Winter 1977–1978). Wheaton College Graduate School.

Engel, James F., Roger D. Blackwell, and David T. Kollat. *Consumer Behavior.* 3d ed. Hinsdale, Ill.: Dryden, 1978.

Engel, James F., and H. Wilbert Norton. *What's Gone Wrong with the Harvest?* Grand Rapids: Zondervan, 1975.

Ericksen, Kenneth. *The Power of Communication.* St. Louis: Concordia, 1986.

Fabun, Don. *Communications: The Transfer of Meaning.* San Francisco: International Society for General Semantics, 1988. Copyright 1968 by Kaiser Aluminum & Chemical Corp.

Festinger, Leon. *A Theory of Cognitive Dissonance.* New York: Harper & Row, 1957.

Fischer, Louis. *The Life of Mahatma Gandhi.* New York: Harper & Row, 1950.

Fowler, Floyd J., Jr. *Survey Research Methods.* Applied Social Research Methods Series. Vol. 1. Newbury Park, Calif: Sage, 1984.

Fuglesang, Andreas. *Applied Communication in Developing Countries: Ideas and Observations.* Stockholm: Dag Hammarsjköld Foundation, 1973.

Gans, H. J. "The Creator-Audience Relationship in the Mass Media: An Analysis of Movie-Making." In *Mass Culture.* Edited by B. Rosenberg and David Manning White. New York: Free Press, 1957.

Gerbner, George, director. Study by Annenberg School of Communications, University of Pennsylvania and the Gallup Organization. Quoted in *The Good Newspaper* 2, no.15 (23 May 1984).

Gibbons, Boyd. "The Intimate Sense of Smell." *National Geographic* 170, no. 3 (September 1986).

Gibney, Frank. *Five Gentlemen of Japan: The Portrait of a Nation's Character.* New York: Farrar, Strauss and Young, 1953.

_____. *Japan: The Fragile Superpower.* New York: Norton, 1979.

Gilbert, Avery N., and Charles J. Wysocki. "The Smell Survey: Its Results." *National Geographic* 172, no. 4 (October 1987).

Giles, Ray. *Impact* 31, no. 3 (n.d.). Christian Missionary Fellowship.

Ginsburg, Herbert, and Sylvia Opper. *Piaget's Theory of Intellectual Development.* Englewood Cliffs, N.J.: Prentice-Hall, 1969.

Goodenough, Ward Hunt. *Cooperation in Change.* New York: Russell Sage Foundation, 1963.

_____. "Multiculturalism as the Normal Human Experience." *Anthropology and Education Quarterly* 7, no. 4 (November 1976).

Gottlieb, Benjamin H., ed. *Social Networks and Social Support.* Sage Studies in Community Mental Health 4. Beverly Hills, Calif.: Sage, 1981.

Griffin, Em. *The Mind Changers.* Wheaton, Ill.: Tyndale House, 1976.

Guerry, Vincent. *Life with the Baoulé.* Translated by Nora Hodges. Washington, D.C.: Three Continents, 1975.

Guinness, Os. *The Gravedigger File.* Downers Grove, Ill.: InterVarsity Press, 1983.

Hayford, Jack W. "Character Before Communication." *Religious Broadcasting* (February 1985).

Hesselgrave, David J. *Communicating Christ Cross-Culturally.* 2d ed. Grand Rapids: Zondervan, 1990.

Hickson, Mark L., III, and Don W. Stacks. *Nonverbal Communication.* Dubuque, Iowa: Wm. C. Brown, 1985.

Hiebert, Paul G. *Anthropological Insights for Missionaries.* Grand Rapids: Baker, 1986.

Hinkle, L. E., Jr., and H. G. Wolff, "Ecologic Investigations of the Relations Between Illness, Life Experiences and the Social Environment." *Annals of Internal Medicine* 49 (1958), 1373–88.

Hirokawa, Randy Y., and Marshall Scott Poole, eds. *Communication and Group Decision Making.* Beverly Hills, Calif.: Sage, 1986.

Hirsch, E. D. *Validity in Interpretation.* New Haven: Yale University Press, 1967.

Hirschfield, Robert. "Rebuilding the City." *The Other Side* (December 1987).

Hoover, Stewart M. *Mass Media Religion: The Social Sources of the Electronic Church.* Newbury Park, Calif.: Sage, 1988.

Hopler, Thom. *A World of Difference: Following Christ Beyond Your Cultural Walls.* Downers Grove, Ill.: InterVarsity Press, 1981.

Horsfield, Peter G. *Religious Television: The American Experience.* White Plains, N.Y.: Longman, 1984.

Horton, Susan R. *Thinking Is Writing.* Baltimore: Johns Hopkins University Press, 1982.

Hovland, Carl, Irving Janis, and Harold Kelley. *Communication and Persuasion.* New Haven: Yale University Press, 1953.

Hunt, Gladys. *Listen to Me!* Downers Grove, Ill.: InterVarsity Press, 1969.

Ifrah, Georges. *From One to Zero: A Universal History of Numbers.* New York: Penguin, 1988.

Issues Management Letter (10 September 1987).

Jackson, K. D., and Johannes Moeliono. *Communication and National Integration in Sudanese Villages: Implications for Communication Strategy.* Honolulu: East-West Communication Institute, 1972.

James, Ross W., ed. *Case Studies in Christian Communication in an Asian Context.* Manila: OMF Literature, 1989.

Jayaweera, Neville D. "Christian Communication in the Third World." *Occasional Essays.* (December 1978). Latin American Evangelical Center for Pastoral Studies, CELEP.

Jews for Jesus Newsletter 6 (1981), 5741.

Johnson, David W., and Frank P. Johnson. *Joining Together: Group Theory and Group Skills.* Englewood Cliffs, N.J.: Prentice-Hall, 1987.

Johnson, James L. "The Shadow That Hangs Over the Communicator." *Spectrum* (N.d.). Wheaton College Graduate School.

Katz, Elihu, and Paul F. Lazarsfeld. *Personal Influence: The Part Played by People in the Flow of Mass Communications.* New York: Free Press, 1955.

Keesing, Felix M., and Marie M. Keesing. "Opinion Formation and Decision Making." In *Communication and Culture: Readings in the Codes of Human Interaction.* Edited by Alfred E. Smith. New York: Holt Rinehart, 1966.

Kerwin, Frank. "The Right Answer." *Guideposts* (June 1988).

Khalaf, Samir. "The Americanization of George." *Christian Science Monitor,* 22 September 1987.

Kincaid, D. Lawrence, ed. *Communication Theory: Eastern and Western Perspectives.* Human Communication Research Series. San Diego: Academic Press, 1987.

King, Martin Luther. "I Have A Dream." Public address, 28 August 1963.

Klapper, Joseph T. *The Effects of Mass Communication.* New York: Free Press, 1960.

_____. "What We Know About the Effects of Mass Communication: The Brink of Hope." *Public Opinion Quarterly* (1957–1958).

Klem, Herbert J. *Oral Communication of the Scripture: Insights from African Oral Art.* Pasadena, Calif.: William Carey Library, 1981.

Knapp, Mark L., Michael J. Cody, and Kathleen Kelley Reardon. "Nonverbal Signals." In *Handbook of Communication Science.* Edited by Charles R. Berger and Steven H. Chaffee. Newbury Park, Calif.: Sage, 1987.

Kuethe, James L. *The Teaching-Learning Process.* Glenview, Ill.: Scott, Foresman, 1968.

Kuhn, Isabel. *In the Arena.* Robesonia, Pa.: OMF Books, 1960.

Lamb, Roger. "Reading Facial Expressions." In *Eye to Eye: How People Interact.* Edited by Peter Marsh. Topsfield, Mass.: Salem House, 1988.

Lau, Alfred. "The Dauntless Eagles." *Impact* (September 1978). Singapore.

Laye, Camara. *A Dream of Africa.* London: Collins, 1968.

Lerbinger, Otto. *Designs for Persuasive Communication.* Englewood Cliffs, N.J.: Prentice-Hall, 1972.

Lingenfelter, Sherwood G., and Marvin K. Mayers. *Ministering Cross-Culturally: An Incarnational Model for Personal Relationships.* Grand Rapids: Baker, 1986.

Lippman, Walter. "The World Outside: The Pictures in Our Heads." In *The Process and Effects of Mass Communication.* Edited by Wilbur Schramm and Donald Roberts. Urbana: University of Illinois Press, 1971.

Littlejohn, Stephen W. *Theories of Human Communication.* 3d ed. Belmont, Calif.: Wadsworth, 1989.

Loewen, Jacob. *Culture and Human Values: Christian Intervention in Anthropological Perspective.* Pasadena, Calif.: William Carey Library, 1975.

Logan, Robert K. *The Alphabet Effect*. New York: Morrow, 1986.

Lomnitz, Larissa Adler. *Networks and Marginality: Life in a Mexican Shantytown*. New York: Academic Press, 1977.

Lowry, Dennis T. *A General Outline for Conducting Program Evaluation Studies*. Daystar Occasional Paper. Nairobi: Daystar Communications, 1975.

Lum, Ada. "What Does It Take to Be a Missionary?" *His* 37 (November 1976).

Lundstrom, Karl-Johan. *The Lotuho and the Verona Fathers: A Case Study of Communication in Development*. Doctoral diss., Uppsala University, Sweden, 1990.

Lundstrom, Karl-Johan, Donald K. Smith, and Samuel Kenyi. *Communicating for Development: A Practical Guide*. Geneva: Lutheran World Federation, 1990.

Luzbetak, Louis J. *The Church and Cultures*. Maryknoll, N.Y.: Orbis, 1988.

Mander, Jerry. *Four Arguments for the Elimination of Television*. New York: Morrow, 1978.

Marsh, Peter, ed. *Eye to Eye: How People Interact*. Topsfield, Mass.: Salem House, 1988. Esp. chaps. 3, 4, and 8.

Mason, Richard. *The World of Suzie Wong*. London: Collins, 1957.

Massey, Craig. "Communication Is Not the Key to Marriage." *Moody Monthly* 89, no. 3 (November 1988).

Mayers, Marvin K. *A Look at Filipino Lifestyles*. Dallas: Summer Institute of Linguistics, 1980.

_____. *Christianity Confronts Culture: A Strategy for Crosscultural Evangelism*. Grand Rapids: Zondervan, 1987.

McLuhan, Marshall. *Counterblast*. New York: Harcourt, Brace, 1969.

_____. *The Medium Is the Message*. New York: Bantam, 1967.

_____. *Understanding Media: The Extensions of Man*. New York: McGraw-Hill, 1964.

McQuail, Denis. *Mass Communication Theory: An Introduction*. Beverly Hills, Calif.: Sage, 1983.

Mehrabian, Albert. *Silent Messages*. Belmont, Calif.: Wadsworth, 1971.

Meltzoff, Andrew. "Imitation of TV Models by Infants," *Child Development* 59 (1988).

Melvin, James. *A Testament of Hope: The Essential Writings of Martin Luther King, Jr.* San Francisco: Harper & Row, 1986.

Michener, James. "Farm of Bitterness." Excerpt from *Hawaii*. Readers' Digest Condensed Books 11, no. 1 (Winter 1960).

Miller, Donald E. "Evaluating the Effectiveness of Christian Mass Media Output." *Spectrum* (Fall–Winter 1975). Wheaton College Graduate School.

Miller, Gerald R. "Persuasion." In *Handbook of Communication Science*. Edited by Charles R. Berger and Steven H. Chaffee. Newbury Park, Calif.: Sage, 1987.

Milne, A. A. "The House at Pooh Corner." In *The World of Pooh*. New York: E. P. Dutton, 1957.

Morris, Lynn Lyons, and Carol Taylor Fitz-Gibbon. *Evaluator's Handbook*. Beverly Hills, Calif.: Sage, 1978.

Muggeridge, Malcolm. *Christ and the Media*. Grand Rapids: Eerdmans, 1977.

Myrdal, Jan. *Report from a Chinese Village*. New York: Pantheon, 1965.

Narula, Uma, and W. Barnett Pearce. *Development as Communication: A Perspective on India*. Carbondale, Ill.: Southern Illinois University Press, 1986.

Nelson, Ron. "How the Christian Message Came to the Fulani." *WACC Journal* (1981–1982).

Newby, Eric. *A Book of Traveller's Tales*. New York: Viking Penguin, 1985.

New Educational Media in Action: Case Studies for Planners. Vols. 1–3. Paris: United Nations Educational and Scientific Organization, 1967.

Nicholls, Kathleen. "Tell the Story Powerfully in Local Cultural Forms." *Evangelical Missions Quarterly* 19, no. 4 (n.d.).

Nichols, Sue. *Words on Target: For Better Christian Communication*. Richmond: John Knox, 1970.

Nida, Eugene. "The Word Is Winning." *Decision* (December 1987).

Oliver, Robert T. *Culture and Communication: The Problem of Penetrating National and Cultural Boundaries*. Springfield, Ill.: Charles C. Thomas, 1962.

Olsen, Bruce. *Bruchko*. Carol Stream, Ill.: Creation House, 1973.

Open Doors (May–June 1978).

Orwell, George. "Politics and the English Language." *New Republic* (17 June 1946).

Otte, Ralph G. "Are We Worshiping or Watching?" *Eternity* 22, no. 9 (April 1971).

Packard, Vance. *The Hidden Persuaders*. New York: McKay, 1957.

Padilla, C. René. *Missions Between the Times: Essays by C. René Padilla*. Grand Rapids: Eerdmans, 1985.

Parlato, R., et al. *Breaking the Communications Barrier*. New Delhi, India: CARE, 1973.

Paton, Alan. *Cry, the Beloved Country*. New York: Scribner, 1948.

Perse, Elizabeth M. "Involvement with Local Television News." *Human Communication Research* 16, no.4 (n.d.), 556–81.

Petersen, Jim. *Evangelism as Lifestyle*. Colorado Springs, Colo.: NavPress, 1980.

Pickthall, Muhammad Marmaduke. *The Glorious Qur'an*. London: Muslim World League, 1977.

Rao, Y. V. Lakshmana. *Communication and Development: A Study of Two Indian Villages*. Minneapolis: University of Minnesota Press, 1966.

Rheingold, Howard. *They Have a Word for It.* Los Angeles: Tarcher, 1988.

Richardson, Don. *Peace Child.* Glendale, Calif.: Regal, 1974.

Riley, John, and Matilda Riley. "Mass Communication and the Social System." In *Sociology Today.* Edited by Robert K. Merton. (New York: Harper & Row, 1965).

Rokeach, Milton. *Beliefs, Attitudes and Values: A Theory of Organization and Change.* San Francisco: Jossey-Bass, 1968.

_____. *The Nature of Human Values.* New York: Free Press, 1973.

Rokeach, Milton, ed. *Understanding Human Values.* New York: Free Press, 1979.

Roloff, Michael E., et al. "Acquiring Resources from Intimates." *Human Communication Research* 14, no. 3 (Spring 1988), 364–96.

Ruesch, Jurgen, and Weldon Kees. *Nonverbal Communication: Notes on the Visual Perception of Human Relations.* Rev. ed. Berkeley: University of California Press, 1972.

Samovar, Larry A., and Richard E. Porter. *Intercultural Communication: A Reader.* 4th ed. Belmont, Calif.: Wadsworth, 1985.

Saunders, Denys J. *Visual Aids for Village Workers.* Mysore, India: Christian Association for Radio and Audio-Visual Service, 1960.

Schaller, Lyle E. *The Change Agent.* Nashville: Abingdon, 1972.

Schramm, Wilbur. *Big Media, Little Media: Tools and Technologies for Instruction.* Beverly Hills, Calif.: Sage, 1977.

_____. *Mass Media and National Development: The Role of Information in the Developing Countries.* Stanford, Calif.: Stanford University Press and the United Nations Educational, Scientific and Cultural Organization, 1964.

_____. *Men, Messages and Media.* New York: Harper & Row, 1973.

Schramm, Wilbur, and W. Danielson. "Anticipated Audiences as Determinants of Recall." *Journal of Abnormal and Social Psychology* 56 (1958).

Schramm, Wilbur, and Donald F. Roberts. *The Process and Effects of Mass Communication.* Urbana: University of Illinois Press, 1971.

Scovel, Myra. *Richer by India.* New York: Harper & Row, 1964.

Seamands, David. *The Healing of Memories.* Wheaton, Ill.: Victor, 1985.

Sellard, Dan. "Teaching Listening." Eugene (Oreg.) *Register–Guard,* 1 June 1980, 5D.

Sherif, Muzafer. "Group Influences upon the Formation of Norms and Attitudes." In *Social Psychology.* Edited by E. Maccoby et al. 3d ed. New York: Holt, Rinehart, 1958, 219–32.

Sinha, Durganand. *Psychology in a Third World Country: The Indian Experience.* Beverly Hills, Calif.: Sage, 1986.

Smalley, William A., ed. *Readings in Missionary Anthropology.* Vol. 2. Enlarged ed. Pasadena, Calif.: William Carey Library, 1978.

Smedes, Lewis. "Preaching to Ordinary People." *Leadership* (Fall 1983).

Smith, D. Vance, with Aloisio Ojetuk. *The Way of Fire and Water.* Geneva: Lutheran World Federation, 1984.

Smith, Donald K. *How Do We Know Who Is Listening?* Daystar Occasional Paper. Nairobi: Daystar Communications, 1970.

Sogaard, Viggo. *Everything You Need to Know for a Cassette Ministry.* Minneapolis: Bethany House, 1975.

Sorenson, Robert C. "Media Research and Psychological Warfare." In *People, Society and Mass Communication.* Edited by Lewis A. Dexter and David Manning White. New York: Free Press, 1964.

Speer, David C. *Nonverbal Communication.* Sage Contemporary Social Science Issues 10. Newbury Park, Calif.: Sage, 1972.

Spradley, James P., ed. *Culture and Cognition: Rules, Maps and Plans.* New York: Chandler, 1972.

Spurgeon, Charles. *Morning and Evening.* Reprint, Grand Rapids: Zondervan, 1990.

Stack, Carol B. *All Our Kin: Strategies for Survival in a Black Community.* New York: Harper & Row, 1974.

Stark, Dame Freya. *The Journey's Echo.* London: John Murray, 1963.

Stendal, Russell. *Rescue the Captors.* Burnsville, Minn.: Ransom Press, 1984.

Taylor, Howard, and Mary G. Taylor. *Hudson Taylor's Spiritual Secret.* Chicago: Moody Press, n.d.

Thayer, Stephen. "The Language of Touch." In *Eye to Eye: How People Interact.* Edited by Peter Marsh. Topsfield, Mass.: Salem House, 1988.

The Way 18, no. 9 (September 1974).

Tournier, Paul. *A Listening Ear.* Minneapolis: Augsburg, 1987.

Trans, Carol. "Anger Defused." *Psychology Today* (July 1973).

Treece, Eleanor Walters, and James William Treece, Jr. *Elements of Research in Nursing.* St. Louis: Mosby, 1982.

Tuan, Yi-Fu. *Topophilia: A Study of Environmental Perception, Attitudes, and Values.* Englewood Cliffs, N.J.: Prentice-Hall, 1974.

Tucker, Ruth. *Sacred Stories.* Grand Rapids: Zondervan, 1989.

Tuggy, Arthur. *The Philippine Church.* Grand Rapids: Eerdmans, 1971.

Ugboajah, Frank Okwu. "Cultural Factors in Communication for Rural Third World Development: The African Case." *Communicatio Socialis Yearbook* 6 (1987).

Valli, Eric, and Diane Summers. "Honey Hunters of Nepal." *National Geographic* 174, no. 5 (November 1988).

Vaughan, John N. *The World's Twenty Largest Churches: Church Growth Principles in Action*. Grand Rapids: Baker, 1984.

Vespey, Godfrey. *Communication and Understanding*. Hassocks, Sussex, England: Harvester Press, 1977.

Vigeveno, H. S. *The Listener*. Glendale, Calif.: Regal, 1971.

Villanueva, Maribel. "Pop Music and Celebrities: An Evangelistic Strategy?" *ASIACOM* (January–March 1989). Asian Institute of Christian Communication Newsletter.

Wall, Muriel. "Cultural Factors Cause Insight to Affect Eyesight." *Mosaic* 3 (November 1976). Rutgers University, Intercultural Relations and Ethnic Studies Institute.

Weaver, Carl H., *Human Listening*. Indianapolis: Bobbs-Merrill, 1972.

Webber, Robert E. *God Still Speaks: A Biblical View of Christian Communication*. Nashville: Nelson, 1979.

Wenburg, John R., and William W. Wilmot. *The Personal Communication Process*. New York: Wiley, 1973.

Westley, Bruce H. "The Relevance of Group Research to Development." In *Communication for Group Transmission in Development*. Edited by Godwin Chu, Syed A. Rahim, and D. Lawrence Kincaid. Honolulu: East-West Communication Institute, 1976.

Wilson, Ron. *Multimedia Handbook for the Church*. Elgin, Ill.: David C. Cook, 1975.

Winter, Ralph, and Steve Hamilton. *Perspectives on the World Christian Movement*. Pasadena, Calif.: William Carey Library, 1981.

Yin, Robert K. *Case Study Research: Design and Methods*. Applied Social Research Methods Series 5. Beverly Hills, Calif.: Sage, 1989.

Index of Persons

Subject Index

Absolute Meaning, God as, 61–63
Academic shell, 187
Academic study, 44, 107
"Academish" language, 107–8
Acceptance, 86, 309
Action, 42, 94, 118, 131, 134–35, 137–39, 141–42, 184, 199, 214, 226, 244, 279, 288, 314–15, 321, 323–25, 327, 329, 331, 335, 354
Adaptability, 103
Afghanistan, 181–83
Africa(ns), 33–35, 45–47, 73, 89, 102, 105, 108, 112–13, 130, 145, 148–49, 152, 154–55, 157, 161–62, 170, 192–93, 206, 223, 238–41, 246, 248, 256, 262–64, 268, 274, 311, 341, 351
Afro-Americans, 193, 231, 248
Album cover cartoon, 292
Alcoholics Anonymous, 311
Alphabet writing, 150
Alternatives, 22, 86, 91, 138, 172, 191, 208–9, 229, 326, 329, 334–35, 355
America(ns), 37, 57, 106, 162, 168, 228, 246, 321, 341; core of, 263. *See also* United States
"Andy Capp" cartoon, 72, 93
Anger cartoon, 292
Architecture, 102, 152
Argentina, 46
Armenians, 255
Artifacts, cultural, 237, 252
Artifactual system, 146, 150, 152, 162–63, 168
Asia Minor, 255, 356
Attitudes, 19, 26, 74, 101, 133, 135–36, 139–41, 176, 177, 191, 215, 258, 276, 295, 303, 311, 347; and behavior, 141–42; changing, 76, 137–38, 140, 142, 171, 186, 313; group, 214, 304, 308, 315
Attitude shift, 137
Audience(s), 16, 17, 26, 31, 53, 55, 58, 66, 92–93, 98, 101, 105, 106, 134, 136, 140, 160, 173–75, 186, 188–89, 191,

194, 199–200, 242, 243, 273, 299, 306–8, 338, 340–41, 344–45, 347–49, 351–52; active, 176, 178; and folk media, 192–93; as fundamental, 18–19; biblical examples of, 247–48; church and, 194–95; contextual factors, 206–9; defining, 347–49; extended, 166–71, 184, 187; image of, 116–23, 344–46; individual factors, 201–4; knowing, 27–30, 74, 100, 122–23, 284; listening, 69, 74–75, 78–79; "mass," 167–68, 214–15; multiple, 69, 125–31, 166, 183; potential, 166, 182, 183, 185; primary, 126–31, 232; relationship to, 194, 260; response, 25, 94, 198, 340–41; secondary, 126, 129–31; size, 181–85
Audio cassettes, 189–90
Audio system, 152–53, 162, 163
Awareness, 49, 63, 74, 322–24, 334

Baoulé people, 42–43, 315
Barter, 231
Basic assumptions, 31, 261, 266
Behavior, 141–42; patterns, 237, 252–53, 266, 335
Beliefs, 19, 34–36, 251–65
Believability of message, 163
Bengali people, 46
Bennington College, 309
"Better or Worse" cartoon, 155
Bible, the, 53, 69, 76, 98, 108, 117, 128, 147, 149, 154, 177, 226, 252, 255, 264, 268, 281, 344. *See also* Scripture
Bible class, 305–6
Bible schools, 37, 86–88, 130
Bible stories, 243
Bible study, 29, 45, 65, 76, 85, 224, 311, 334, 343
Biblical examples, 247–48, 314–15, 355–57
Biblical perspective: on communication process, 48; on hearing, 76–79; on

Pictographs, 150
Pictorial styles, 148–50
Pictorial system, 148–50, 161–63
Pictures, 150, 234–44
Pinball analogy, 199
Poland, 319
Political experiences, 108–11
Possessiveness, 29
Prayer, 274; cartoon, 239
Preaching, 20, 23, 26–27, 37, 71,
 83–84, 91, 142, 238, 241, 247,
 251, 277, 289
Preacher, 27, 63, 69, 79, 83, 88,
 91, 106, 114, 119, 121, 138,
 161, 168, 193, 320
Predispositions, 200
"Pre-owned" as euphemism, 75
Priest anecdote, 290
Primary audience, 126–31, 232
Primary network, 223
Process, communication as
 process, 41–49
Proclamation, 26, 76–77, 79, 135,
 144, 145, 170, 207, 247, 252,
 298–99, 333, 355
Program goals, 349
Programming, 84, 167, 172,
 177–78, 188–89, 205, 208, 246
Propositions, list of, 16–19
Proximity in perception, 280–84
Psychological differences, 105,
 107–8
Psychotherapy, 313
Public media, 318, 320, 326–32
Purpose, 17

Question-and-answer technique,
 193
Questionnaires, 351
Qur'an, the, 101–2, 255, 266

Racial prejudice, 112, 139
Radio, 26, 58, 60, 71, 99, 129,
 131, 152, 161, 166, 168–70,
 172, 174, 177–78, 181, 183,
 185, 187–91, 194–95, 199,
 204, 207–8, 227, 246–47, 250,
 289, 305, 307, 314, 318, 320,
 326, 329, 332–33, 335, 338,
 348, 351–52
Radio listening clubs, 194, 247
Rational dimension of
 communication, 286–90
Readers' clubs, 194
Reading, 29, 71, 138, 165,
 188–89, 241–43, 275, 277,
 313–14, 352

Readjustment, 324–25, 327–29,
 335
Reality, 15, 21, 26–27, 108,
 170–71, 176, 187, 209,
 257–58, 260, 263, 272, 278,
 293, 296, 304, 307–8, 310,
 324; vs. image 116–19, 123
Recall, 99, 132, 161, 174
Receiver, 29, 46, 53, 56–57,
 63–64, 68, 174, 296, 200, 231,
 269, 271, 273–74, 282–83, 357
Reciprocity, 29–30, 40
Reference groups, 306–8
Referents, 52, 54, 55, 93, 106
Reinforcement, 134–35, 161,
 179, 199, 209; of opinion,
 171–72
Reinterpretation, 201–2, 269–70
Rejection, 15, 20–21, 36, 48, 79,
 201–2, 206, 246, 254, 256,
 258–59, 265, 273–74, 309, 322
Relationships, 34–35, 44, 69, 76,
 86–87, 102, 109, 143, 147,
 162, 177, 179, 194–95, 206,
 216–18, 222–24, 226, 228,
 231, 252, 255, 257, 267, 275,
 295, 297, 305, 311–12,
 314–15, 321–22, 325, 328,
 343; in cultures, 263;
 perceptual, 280–84; personal,
 330–32
Religious beliefs, 181–82
Research, 27, 71, 80, 187, 195,
 208, 214, 224, 229, 233, 243,
 267, 281, 284, 294, 301–2,
 317–18, 336, 343, 346–48,
 350–53, 355, 357–58
Respondent, 29, 67–68, 291
Response, 55, 303, 337; criteria
 for, 349–50. See also Feedback
Revolution, 224–25
Ritual, 237
Ritual extension, 229
Rocket analogy, 91
Role-playing, 140–41, 143, 161,
 299
Roman Catholic faith, 328
Romania, 319
Russia, 157, 185, 308, 319–20

Salesmanship, 323
Salvation, 66, 76, 78–79, 88, 134,
 169–70, 202, 309
Sampling for feedback, 348,
 351–52
Satellite, 170

Scripture Index

CREATING UNDERSTANDING